Stabilizing World Commodity Markets

Stabilizing World Commodity Markets

Analysis, Practice, and Policy

Edited by
F. Gerard Adams
University of Pennsylvania
Sonia A. Klein
Wharton Econometric
Forecasting Associates

Lexington Books
D.C. Heath and Company
Lexington, Massachusetts
Toronto

Library of Congress Cataloging in Publication Data
Main entry under title:

Stabilizing world commodity markets.

Representative selection of papers presented at a conference held at Airlie, Va., Mar. 17–20, 1977, and sponsored by the Ford Foundation.
1. Commodity control—Congresses. 2. Price regulation—Congresses. I. Adams, Francis Gerard, 1929– II. Klein, Sonia. III. Ford Foundation.
HF1428.S7 382.1 77-7805
ISBN 0-669-01622-5

Published simultaneously in Canada

Printed in the United States of America

International Standard Book Number: 0-669-01622-5

Library of Congress Catalog Card Number: 77-7805

Contents

	Preface	vii
	Introduction: An Overview of Stabilizing World Commodity Markets *F. Gerard Adams*	ix
Part I	*Modeling World Commodity Markets*	1
Chapter 1	**Commodity Markets and Models: The Range of Experience** *Walter C. Labys*	3
Chapter 2	**Commodity Market Modeling and the Simulation of Market Intervention: The Case of Coffee** *Derek J. Ford*	35
Chapter 3	**International Rice Buffer Stock Operations: A Simulation Study** *Olarn Chaipravat*	63
Chapter 4	**Primary Commodity Markets in a World Model System** *F. Gerard Adams*	83
Chapter 5	**Potentials of Econometrics for Commodity Stabilization Policy Analysis** *Lawrence R. Klein*	105
Part II	*Theoretical Considerations of Commodity Market Stabilization*	117
Chapter 6	**The Distribution of Welfare Gains from Price Stabilization: A Survey of Some Theoretical Issues** *Stephen J. Turnovsky*	119
Chapter 7	**Buffer Stock Analysis for Agricultural Products: Theoretical Murk or Empirical Resolution?** *Alexander H. Sarris* and *Lance Taylor*	149
Chapter 8	**Commodity Instability and Market Failure: A Survey of Issues** *Gordon W. Smith*	161
Chapter 9	**Is Price Stabilization Theoretically Desirable?** *Edwin Burmeister*	189

Part III	*Economic, Political, and Institutional Considerations in Commodity Policy*	193
Chapter 10	**Political Economy of an Integrated Commodity Program** *David L. McNicol*	195
Chapter 11	**Producers' Associations and Commodity Markets: The Case of CIPEC** *Stephen A. Zorn*	215
Chapter 12	**A European View of Commodity Problems: Stabilization of Prices and Stabilization of Receipts** *Alexandre Stakhovitch*	235
Part IV	*Integrated Commodity Stabilization Programs*	241
Chapter 13	**Commodity Trade Policy Initiatives and Issues** *Constantine Michalopoulos* and *Lorenzo L. Perez*	243
Chapter 14	**A Hard Look at Prospects for Commodity Agreements** *Helen Junz* and *Paul MacAvoy*	271
Chapter 15	**An Alternative Common Fund Proposal** *Richard W. Fisher* and *Robert V. Roosa*	287
Chapter 16	**International Commodity Agreements: An Evaluation of the UNCTAD Integrated Programme for Commodities** *Jere R. Behrman*	295
	Index	323
	List of Contributors	337
	About the Editors	339

Preface

This book contains a representative selection of papers presented at a conference on Stabilizing World Commodity Markets: Analysis, Practice, and Policy held at Airlie, Virginia, March 17-20, 1977. The conference was sponsored by the Ford Foundation and organized by F. Gerard Adams under the general direction of a committee consisting of C. Fred Bergsten, William H. Branson, Charles Frank, Hendrik Houthakker, Lawrence R. Klein, L. Solis, Wouter Tims, and Peter Ruof. The conference also served as a vehicle for presenting work on commodity market modeling and policy simulation being carried on by a team at the University of Pennsylvania under sponsorship of the Rockefeller Foundation. Papers based on research by the World Bank, Project LINK, and UNCTAD were also included. Participants in the conference, numbering 76, included representatives from international organizations, academic institutions, national governments, commodity organizations, and commodities businesses.

We would like to thank the Ford Foundation, the conference committee, the authors of the papers, and other participants for contributing to a stimulating and instructive conference.

F. Gerard Adams and Sonia A. Klein

Introduction: An Overview of Stabilizing World Commodity Markets

F. Gerard Adams

The issues of commodity market stabilization have become central not only to the North-South dialogue and the new international economic order sought by the developing world but also to the summit negotiations among the industrial countries. What was, for many years, an occasional effort to limit price fluctuations on a commodity-by-commodity basis has recently become an effort to develop coordinated international commodity policies targeted on mixed objectives of price stabilization, income support, international aid transfer, and protection against inflationary price swings. The urgency and importance of these issues is greater now even than it was a year or two ago. In the intervening period, a number of important new policy initiatives have been floated. These are being considered at the level of international negotiating conferences, within the international organizations and commercial institutions, and at the level of national governments.

Commodity policy strategy is being handled on a practical basis by specialists in the international organizations, commodity exchanges, business firms, and government agencies. Their work involves day-by-day confrontation with the commercial and technological realities of commodity markets. Quite separately, often with little practical experience of the real world, academic economists have been developing the theoretical underpinnings for stabilization. Also out of the academic world has come econometric modeling of commodity markets, a tool with great potential for testing the implications of alternative policies and for simulating markets under stabilization programs. It was our hope that a conference would serve as a meeting place, to bring together the people from these two worlds—the practical world of policy making and the world of economic theory and econometric modeling. The theorists and econometricians would become more aware of the real problems and issues. The policy makers would get a perception of the potential of more formal schemes of theory and modeling.

The issues to be considered in this overview can be seen to fall into two broad classes: first, the problems faced by policy planners, and second, the methodological research problems as they are seen in the academic world. We need to "marry" these two approaches to establish some notions of what research activity can contribute to help resolve some of the practical questions faced by the policy makers.

A Diversity of Markets

Turning first to the real world, the most striking facts are the inconsistencies between the basic distinctions we are accustomed to use—industrial countries and developing countries, producers and consumers, market economies and socialist planned economies, etc. The distinctions between these categories are far from clear, nor are they mutually exclusive. And this is a reason for the diversity of interests among the participants in efforts to stabilize commodity markets. The real situation is quite mixed. The industrial countries are also producers of primary materials, copper and wheat for example. Developing countries are frequently consumers rather than producers of primary commodities, and in many cases they lose rather than benefit from high commodity prices. Petroleum is, of course, the most striking example. The distribution between market economies and planned economies does not correspond to the distribution between producers and consumers—while the planned economies have tended toward self-sufficiency as a broad group, they are increasingly purchasers of commodities on world markets. Countries that are, on balance, producers of one commodity are frequently consumers of another. The preceding classification looks very different if it is seen from the perspective of the market for wheat as compared to the market for coffee. A critical point here is the diversity between the commodities themselves, with respect to their production and/or consumption and the organization of the markets, and with respect to the potentials for stabilization policy.

The primary commodities have in common only the fact that they represent bulk production at an early stage of the productive process. They differ greatly in the conditions of production and consumption. This is an important consideration in determining price instability and the appropriate policy responses. The industrial raw materials, nonferrous metals in particular, are significantly affected by fluctuations in both demand and inventory building related to the business cycle. Supply shortages, sometimes resulting from political instability in the producer countries, have also been known to contribute to the price fluctuations of these commodities. In the case of agricultural products, however, the principal source of instability represents the impact of natural forces—drought, disease, frost, or excessively wet field conditions. The slowness of the supply response, particularly in the case of tree crops, and the inelasticity and slowness of demand responses add to the instability of some markets.

With respect to market organization, an important measure is the degree of concentration in production. This is an issue of particular concern at this time because of the rise in the last four or five years of blocks of producer countries who are exercising their power over markets, their ability to control supplies, and their ability to raise prices. OPEC and IBA are, of course, the most striking examples. Markets differ greatly in the extent to which they offer opportunities for cartelization. In addition, the influence of large dominant producers or consumers—the Canadian producers in the case of nickel, Brazil in the case of coffee, Zaire in the case of cobalt, and possibly a consumer monopsony in the case of tea—indicate that many markets are far from the idealized conditions of competition frequently assumed in economic theory. Governments and multinational firms greatly influence market operations.

The diversity of the commodities and of market organization greatly affect the possibilities for commodity market stabilization. The possibilities for stabilization and the alternative stabilization mechanisms are almost as varied as the commodity markets themselves. Thus buffer stock policy can apply only to the limited list of commodities that are storable, are of high value relative to bulk, and are traded in open commodity exchanges. Production or export limitations are more suited to bulk products, particularly those produced and distributed in integrated commercial channels. These approaches require the cooperation of the consumer countries for their effective implementation. The recent exhaustion of the tin buffer stock is but one illustration of a checkered history of commodity price stabilization schemes. Buffer stocks as well as consumer and producer organizations have come and gone—the best that can be said is that some of them have succeeded in stabilizing prices some of the time. The current emphasis on integrated commodity stabilization schemes, a turn toward comprehensive and coordinated stabilization of many commodities, represents a new challenge. Not only are we turning toward commodity stabilization from a base of broad international cooperation, but we are also considering stabilization from a broad cross-commodity basis, recognizing, I hope, the difficulties of the task and the diversity of approaches that will be required.

Diversity of Objectives

The direct gains from price stabilization—a question considered in depth by economic theorists—may well be overshadowed by other considerations. Commodity market stabilization policy is likely to be aimed at multiple objectives. One approach is in terms of price instability only. The objective of policy would simply be to stabilize price around some long-term trend, smoothing out excessive fluctuations that hinder development objectives in the producer countries and that cause inflationary pressures among the consumers. But an alternate view is to seek stability at a "high" price, using the price mechanism as a means of resource transfer from the consumer countries, presumed to be high-income, to the producers, assumed to be developing countries.

An altogether different view is to see market stabilization as a question of income maintenance. Here we are not talking so much about instability of prices as about providing a stable flow of income to the producer countries. The question of stable income, which calls for income supports at times when the value of exports falls below some desired trend level, is closely intermingled with the broader question of international distribution of income, income transfers for economic development, and the terms of trade between developed and developing countries.

Finally, there is still another view that suggests that economic issues are secondary to the underlying political questions related to the fading of the age of colonialism in the postwar years. One view of stabilizing commodity markets is to gain a larger measure of control for the producer countries over their product output, prices, earnings, and, possibly, refining, transport, and commercialization. This can be seen as a political issue, to be pursued even at economic costs. Control over scarce resources and what is done with them may well be part of the ethos of many countries who have recently escaped from colonial dominance.

The approach to these issues differs greatly depending on the country. Some are seeking finance for development and an increase in their per capita income. Others, on the consumer side, are concerned with questions of price instability and inflation. Indeed, one of the distinguishing marks of the present period is the growing concern with stabilization not only among developing countries but among the developed industrial countries as well. For the first time in many years, the European Community and the United States have expressed support for some form of coordinated commodity market stabilization program.[1] While the outcome of negotiations is unclear, and the schemes being considered range widely both with respect to mechanisms and objectives, the next few years will see important steps in the direction of market stabilization. We turn now to the principal questions that call for study.

Methodological Issues

Methodological investigations should not be limited to an academic view. Theoretical and econometric research promise to open vast new vistas. But it must also be directed toward the real-life problems of commodity market management and stabilization. If, as is often the case, research cannot provide unequivocal answers to real-life problems, it must seek to provide strategies or priorities for optimal policy action. This represents a vast scope, much of it as yet unrealized, for theoretical and econometric research.

What are the problems that need to be considered with regard to modeling of commodity markets? First, there are serious questions of model structure. A fairly standard pattern of commodity model structure is being used in many econometric commodity models.[2] While the general outlines of market behavior have been captured by this structural framework, practicing commodity market modelers are aware of its considerable shortcomings that affect all sides of the market. With regard to demand, substitution between alternative primary materials (for example, copper and aluminum) and the role of technology in this process are imperfectly understood and measured. On the supply side, the determinants of increased agricultural yields (the Green Revolution), the long-run supply potential of mineral resources, and the impact of new technologies (such as the recovery of nonferrous metal nodules from the ocean floor) are not well integrated into models. Significant problems also exist with regard to the price mechanism. The failure of most commodity market models to capture the upsurge of commodity prices that occurred in 1973-1974 is only one illustration of the problems. Behind that failure lies a fragile treatment of anticipations—if anticipations are considered at all—and perhaps also a broader question that has not been addressed concerning the possibility of a "flight out of money" into commodities. Important new work is being done on the questions of how to build into the models the operation of producer country cartels. There is another aspect that is particularly important for work on market stabilization: that is the question of how to take account of stabilization policies.[3] If we assume a known model structure with coefficients estimated on the basis of historical data, the conventional approach has been simply to add the actions of a buffer stock or export restrictions to the model program. But the questions are "Does the structure of the model change? Do the parameters change?" If we impose on the system a price stabilization scheme, one that is announced and that has hope of being successful, do the incentives for production or for inventory holding change? This troublesome question has not been adequately examined, and it raises questions about much of the policy-simulation work being carried on.

A second aspect of modeling that needs to be discussed is the application of optimal control. Optimal control simulations that can accommodate a number of policy targets are at the forefront of model applications.[4] They appear to have great potential. But we do not yet know what optimal control simulations can contribute to commodity policy making and to practical buffer stockpile management.

A third area is the question of the linkage between the market and the economies of producer and consumer countries. In terms of modeling, this leads to a linked system of commodity and country models, ultimately a world model system.[5] Such a framework, although greatly simplified, offers the possibility of examining the feedback effects between producer and consumer countries. There are many unanswered questions here. We cannot really be sure of the ultimate impact of commodity price stabilization. Do developing countries grow more rapidly in a world of stable or fluctuating prices? Do the industrial countries gain enough from the increase in manufactured goods exports to the developing world to justify the higher average raw material prices that a price stabilization program is likely to entail? One way to examine these total feedbacks is in a combined world modeling system.

There is also important new work being done in the theory area. Much new activity concerns questions of efficient markets, rational expectations, and the possibility of market failures.[6] This work promises to make a contribution not only to optimal policy management but also to the more technical issues of how to properly structure market models.

The other major concern of theory has been in establishing a theoretical framework for a cost-benefit calculation for price stabilization. As the simplifying assumptions underlying the theory have been loosened, the complexity of a priori specifying, whether there are gains and to whom, has become apparent. While a general broad conclusion is not within reach, progress has been made on the implications of specific situations on the magnitude and the allocation of gains from price stabilization.[7] Yet a serious shortcoming of this work remains—the fact that commodity stabilization schemes are likely to have many targets. Direct gains from price stabilization, as measured, for example, in the profits or losses of a buffer stockpile authority, are likely to be less consequential than the indirect impact of price stabilization on the development path of the producer countries or on inflation in the consumer countries.

Political and Economic Realities: The Issues of Policy

Concern with political and economic realities can have a two-way focus in the context, i.e., first, on the way in which theory and modeling can take into account the real world and, second, on the way in which policy making can take into account the contribution of modeling and theory. Analysis and policy planning for the commodity markets requires simplifying assumptions, but the policy maker cannot escape the fact that he operates in the real world. This involves recognition of the mechanism of the market, the forces operating in it, and the constituencies that it affects. What are the technologies and economics of supply and consumption? What is the nature of market clearing processes? Does the product travel through integrated channels, or do free markets operate at various stages of production? What is the relation between spot prices, contract prices, producer prices, and grower prices? What is the role of speculation? What is the influence of transportation, processing, and marketing? What is the role of producer associations, multinational enterprises, governments, and, last and sometimes least, the consumer?[8] What has been the history of past efforts to stabilize the market?[9] What is the effect of fluctuations of quantity and price on revenues? This must be seen not only from the standpoint of the major producers, but also from the view of the smaller countries who may have little, if any, influence on the world market.

Hopefully, some generalizations may be possible; but, as we have already noted, market characteristics are diverse. Policy studies will need to be market specific. The ultimate choice of the modalities of market stabilization, its targets, and its management depends on political as well as economic considerations. Even the 10 commodities chosen as the core group in UNCTAD's Integrated Commodity Programme call for strikingly different approaches.[10] Compare, for example, the problems of jute, produced in large part in one of the poorest countries and competing with synthetic substitutes, with those of coffee, which has recently been enriching its producers.

It is clear that the diversity of commodity markets must be recognized in the integrated view of commodity market policy that represents the significant turn of policy recently. The Integrated Commodity Programme (ICP) being promoted by the Group of 77 is most controversial.[11] Much needs to be done to distinguish fact from rhetoric. What would ICP really mean, and how would it operate? Is it simply an effort to smooth out excessive price fluctuations in primary commodity markets? Or does it imply, as many would suggest, an attempt to systematically raise primary commodity prices and provide additional resources for development? Is its basis economic, or does it represent primarily a political response by the developing world to their perceived view of the industrial (ex-colonial) countries?

There are, in addition, severe practical issues on the implementation and effectiveness of such a scheme. Is it a realistic objective to stabilize prices, perhaps using buffer stocks, for the many diverse commodities included in the proposal? Are there gains from treating the commodities as part of an integrated program? Will the swings in one market offset those in others? Or, as is also plausible, will the failures to stabilize one market make more difficult the stabilization of the others? What are the resources necessary to support the "common fund," and where will they come from?

Other integrated approaches to stabilization are also being given an international forum. A recent proposal calls for an international bank to fund producer country stockpiling.[12] Coordinated national stockpiles would be a means for stabilization, if national governments can work together effectively. Such approaches would avoid the central stabilization agency that would be required for the implementation of an integrated buffer stock and stabilization scheme like ICP. While integrated programs are only in the negotiating stage, specific commodity stabilization organizations have had a renaissance, and negotiations to reestablish a number of international commodity agreements are under way.

Commodity market stabilization must not be seen entirely in terms of stabilization of commodity prices, as was noted earlier. Income stabilization may well be a preferred objective, although, perhaps surprisingly, the developing countries have preferred to focus on stabilizing prices. Income stabilization is particularly important, since price stabilization alone may not go far toward helping the very poor, the countries of the "*n*th world," where annual per capita income falls below $100. Two organizations targeted toward stabilizing revenue streams rather than price already exist, the IMF compensatory facility and the European Community's Stabex scheme.[13] The IMF facility has sharply increased its lending activities. Stabex, which operates on a much smaller scale, provides export income on a soft loan and grant basis and has proved particularly valuable to some of the small poor countries. Expansion of such income-support agencies is planned.

To meet the social objectives of development policy, to benefit large and small countries and particularly low per capita income countries, commodity price stabilization is surely not enough. Commodity market stabilization will include significant elements of income transfer. If so, the transfers must be from the "have" countries to the "have nots." Income stabilization and development aid will be an integral part, perhaps explicit but more likely implicit, of any overall international commodity compact.

Integrated schemes for stabilizing price and income offer new promise for international agreement at this time. The broader and more comprehensive the scheme, the harder it is to reach agreement. However, the more the scheme can recognize the diversity of interests of producer and consumer countries, the greater the possibility of reconciling these diverse aims. We are at a crossroads in decision making on international commodity market stabilization. More than ever before, there is hope for enacting and implementing a comprehensive program. If it is to work, it must reflect the thinking of the best minds—researchers from the academic world, government administrators, and commodity market practitioners. At this time we must establish a measure of what we know and what we need to know to stabilize world commodity markets.

Notes

1. Indeed, while the Airlie Conference was in session, President Carter announced in his address to the United Nations that "the United States is willing to consider, with a positive and open attitude, the negotiation on agreements to stabilize commodity prices, including the establishment of a common funding arrangement for financing buffer stocks where they are a part of an individual negotiated agreement." (Carter's speech at the U.N., March 17, 1977).

2. An overview of alternative approaches to commodity market modeling is provided by Walter Labys in Chapter 1. Derek Ford presents an example of a specific commodity model (coffee) in Chapter 2.

3. Chapter 3, Olarn Chaipravat's discussion of stockpile policy for rice, is an illustration.

4. Optimal control is discussed by Lawrence Klein in Chapter 5.

5. Such a system is discussed by F. Gerard Adams and Lawrence Klein in Chapters 4 and 5.

6. These subjects are treated by Alexander Sarris and Lance Taylor and by Gordon Smith in Chapters 7 and 8.

7. This is the conclusion of Stephen Turnovsky in Chapter 6.

8. Some of these questions are addressed by Stephen Zorn in Chapter 11.

9. For a consideration, see the analysis by David McNicol in Chapter 10.

10. See a discussion by Alexandre Stakhovitch in Chapter 12.

11. The Integrated Programme for Commodities is the subject of extensive consideration by Constantine Michalopoulos and Lorenzo Perez, Helen Junz and Paul MacAvoy, and Jere Behrman in Chapters 13, 14, and 16.

12. This proposal is discussed by Richard Fisher and Robert Roosa in Chapter 15.

13. Stabex is discussed by Alexandre Stakhovitch in Chapter 12.

Part I
Modeling World Commodity Markets

1 Commodity Markets and Models: The Range of Experience

Walter C. Labys

In recent years, interest in analyzing, modeling, and forecasting international commodity markets has increased notably, particularly in the wake of worldwide inflation and shortages. This chapter attempts to provide an overview of commodity markets, commodity modeling approaches, and the present state of the art. The nature, location, and structure of these markets are considered first. Commodity modeling is then explained, and the major modeling methodologies are described, including possibilities for integrated model development. To provide a basis for future model application, the final section discusses needs and directions for model improvement.

Commodity Markets Described

Primary commodity markets embody foods and raw materials in an unprocessed and partially processed state. These commodities can be extracted from the land (fuel and nonfuel minerals), grown on the land (annual and perennial crops, including timber), raised on the land (cattle and poultry), or harvested from the water (fish or plants). Since it is sometimes not clear where processing ends and manufacture begins, Table 1-1 provides a list of goods commonly termed *primary commodities.*

Of the many facets of commodity market structure important for consideration, I have focused on market organization, spatial distribution, market behavior, technical characteristics, and international stockpiles.

Market Organization

Markets for commodities tend to be located near the major geographical nodes of production and consumption. Deviations from this pattern normally result from historical circumstances, such as that of previously important trading routes or communication centers. An attempt to pinpoint the major commodity

Table 1-1
Primary Commodities Traded Internationally[a]

Agricultural-Food	*Fuel Minerals*	*Husbandry*
Apples	Coal	Cattle
Bananas	Gas	Hogs
Cocoa	Petroleum	Poultry
Coconuts	Uranium	Sheep
Coffee		
Corn		
Dates	*Nonfuel Minerals*	*Marine*
Flaxseed		
Grapefruit	Aluminum	Fresh Water Fish
Grapes	Asbestos	Salt Water Fish
Groundnuts	Bismuth	Shell Fish
Lemons	Cadmium	
Melons	Chromite	
Olives	Cobalt	*Partially Processed*
Oranges	Columbium	
Pepper	Copper	Beef
Potatoes	Diamonds	Cotton Oil/Meal
Rapeseeds	Gold	Fertilizers
Rice	Iron	Fish Oil/Meal
Sorghums	Lead	Groundnut Oil/Meal
Soybeans	Magnesium	Hides
Sugar	Mercury	Lauric Oil/Meal
Tea	Molybdenum	Linseed Oil/Meal
Tomatoes	Nickel	Lumber
Wheat	Phosphate	Olive Oil
	Platinum	Palm Oil/Meal
	Propane	Pork
Agricultural-Materials	Salt	Scrap Metals
	Shellac	Soybean Oil/Meal
Abaca	Silver	Steel
Cotton	Sulfur	Tallow
Jute	Tin	Textiles
Timber	Titanium	Tung Oil
Tobacco	Tungsten	Whale Oil
Rubber	Vanadium	Wine
Wool	Zinc	

[a]This list is intended to be representative rather than exhaustive

markets has been made in Table 1-2, which specifies centers of major price making activity. For the industrialized countries, Chicago, London, New York, and Hamburg are the most important. For the developing countries, Calcutta, Manila, and Buenos Aires are significant.

Markets can also be characterized according to the nature of the underlying contractual arrangements. Markets can be identified as *spot markets* when they feature physical exchange of the commodity and contracts specifying delivery on the spot. They are termed *futures markets* when they involve the exchange of paper contracts that specify forward delivery accompanied by terms permitting easy transfer of liability. These markets are popularly known for the hedging and speculative needs they accommodate. Forward markets are more difficult to identify, since forward contracts that specify delivery at some time forward are most often negotiated privately. Spot markets tend to be located at points of production, such as in the developing countries. Futures markets are located in major financial centers, such as Chicago, London, and New York.

A final aspect of market organization is the degree of competition present. Commodity markets can be highly competitive, involving a number of producers and consumers, such as for wheat. Markets can also feature administered and quasi-administered pricing, such as that of the OPEC cartel, or they can contain a single monopoly or dominant producing firm that influences prices and quantities to ensure profit maximization, such as for cobalt.

Spatial Distribution

Knowing the geographic location of commodity producers and consumers or exporters and importers is essential for understanding market organization and behavior. Such information also indicates the extent to which commodity arrangements or stabilization mechanisms will affect different nations. Table 1-3 identifies some of the more important exporting and importing nations for a number of commodities. Reflected in that table are some of the spatial difficulties encountered in specifying the incidence of benefits derived from international commodity arrangements. Many of the commodities are typical in that they are produced in developing countries and consumed largely in industrialized countries; here stabilization relief and income maintenance are implied principally for the developing producing countires. However, some important commodities, such as wheat, copper, or beef, show origin from both developing and developed countries and incidence would have to be spread accordingly.

Market Behavior

The market behavior of different commodities is concerned with the magnitude of price and quantity fluctuations, as well as with the underlying factors responsible for those fluctuations. Table 1-4 provides a classification of commodities into groups according to the relative degree of price fluctuations. Coffee, sugar, zinc, and tungsten exhibit the widest price variability ranging from 50 to 68 percent. Next in magnitude are wheat, linseed oil, wool, and sisal, with variability ranging between 42 and 49 percent.

Identifying the factors responsible for fluctuations in these and other com-

Table 1-2
Locations of Major Commodity Markets

Markets[a]	*Bananas*	*Barley*	*Beef*	*Boneless Beef*	*Broilers*	*Cattle*	*Cocoa*	*Coconut Oil*	*Coffee*	*Copper*	*Copra*	*Cottonseed*	*Citrus*	*Corn*	*Cotton*	*Eggs*[b]	*Feeder Cattle*	*Fishmeal*	*Flaxseed*	*Grain Sorghums*	*Gold*	*Hogs*	*Iron Ore*
London		SF	S				SF	S	SF	F	S			SF	S								
New York				F			SF		SF	SF		SF	F	S	SF			F					
Hamburg	S		S				S		S	S			S										
Calcutta																							
Chicago					F	F								SF		F	F			F		F	
Rotterdam											S			S									S
Manila								S			S												
Marseilles											S		S										
Winnipeg		SF																	F		F		
Buenos Aires																				S			
Colombo								S															
Singapore											S												
Minneapolis		S																					
Bangkok																							
Chittagong																							
Djakarta																							
Istanbul		S																					
Montevideo			S																				
Sao Paulo														S	S								
Amsterdam							S																
Kansas City														F					F	S			
Le Havre							S		S														
Liverpool													S										
Melbourne																							
Sydney																							
Paris							F																
West Coast						F		F		F						F							

[a]S = Spot market, F = Futures market
[b]Frozen and Fresh
[c]And platinum

modity markets requires an analysis of the particular characteristics of individual markets; for examples, see Labys (1973); and Labys and Granger (1970). In brief, market fluctuations can arise on the demand side or on the supply side. World demand is dependent on prices, economic activity, prices of one or more substitutes, and possible technical influences. World supply varies with prices as well as with ecological factors, such as climate for agricultural commodities or richness of deposits for mineral commodities. Inventories normally found on the demand as well as the supply side of the market are held for precautionary, transactions, and speculative motives.

Jute	Lead	Lumber	Lumber (Stud)	Linseed	Groundnuts	Mercury	Oats	Palladium[c]	Palm Oil	Pepper	Plywood	Pork Bellies	Potatoes	Propane	Rapeseed	Rice	Rubber	Rye	Sheep/Lambs	Silver	Soybeans	Soybean Meal	Soybean Oil	Sugar	Tea	Tin	Wheat	Wool	Zinc
S	F								S							S	S			F			F	SF	S	F	SF	SF	F
S				S		F		F			F		F	F						F	S			SF	S	S	S	SF	
																	S								S		S		
S										S					S	S									S				
		F					F				F	F	F					F	S	F	SF	F	F		S		SF		
								S													S								
																S								S					
					S			S																					
				S			F								SF			F									S		
																			S								S		
																	S								S				
										S							S												
				S																							SF		
																S	S												
S																									S				
																S								S					
																											S		
																			S										
									S																				
																											SF		
																												S	
																			S										
																												SF	
																						F		F					
																				F				F					

The price adjustments needed to bring demand and supply into equilibrium are rather substantial where demand and supply are relatively inelastic. This situation arises on the demand side where raw materials represent only a small portion of a product's value and on the supply side where rigidities or capacity limits constrain production. Under such conditions, inventory adjustments play a substantial role in dampening or amplifying the price fluctuations generated. Where demand and supply are more price elastic, inventory adjustments become less important.

Table 1-3
Geographic Distribution of Major Commodity Exporters and Importers

Wheat	*Bananas*	*Maize*	*Rice*	*Coffee*	*Cocoa*
Major Exporters					
United States	Ecuador	United States	United States	Colombia	Ghana
Canada	Costa Rica	Argentina	Thailand	Brazil	Nigeria
Australia	Honduras	France	China	Ivory Coast	Brazil
France	Panama	S. Africa	Burma	Angola	Cameroon
USSR	Guatemala	Thailand	Italy	Uganda	Ivory Coast
Major Importers					
USSR	United States	Japan	India	United States	FR Germany
China	Japan	Italy	Indonesia	FR Germany	USSR
Japan	FR Germany	FR Germany	Bangladesh	France	Netherlands
United Kingdom	France	United Kingdom	Vietnam	Italy	United States
FR Germany	Italy	Netherlands	Korea	Netherlands	United Kingdom

Rubber	*Lumber*	*Bauxite*	*Copper*	*Iron Ore*	*Tin*
Major Exporters					
Malaysia	Canada	Australia	Belgium	Australia	Malaysia
Indonesia	Finland	Jamaica	Canada	USSR	Bolivia
Sarawak	Sweden	Surinam	Chile	Canada	Indonesia
Sri Lanka	FR Germany	Guinea	Zambia	Brazil	Thailand
Thailand	Philippines	Guyana	Zaire	Sweden	China
Major Importers					
United States	Japan	United States	Japan	Japan	United States
Singapore	France	USSR	FR Germany	FR Germany	Japan
Japan	FR Germany	Japan	United Kingdom	United States	United Kingdom
FR Germany	United States	Canada	Belgium	Belgium-Lux.	France
United Kingdom	Netherlands	FR Germany	France	France	FR Germany

Tea	*Sugar*	*Soybeans*	*Palm Oil*	*Coconut Oil*	*Cotton*	*Wool*
Major Exporters						
India	Brazil	United States	Malaysia	Philippines	United States	Australia
Sri Lanka	Cuba	China	Indonesia	Indonesia	USSR	New Zealand
Japan	Australia	Brazil	Zaire	Sri Lanka	Egypt	S. Africa
USSR	Philippines	Canada	Nigeria	Malaysia	Turkey	Argentina
Kenya	Dom. Rep.		Sabah		Brazil	Uruguay
Major Importers						
United Kingdom	United States	FR Germany	United Kingdom	United States	Japan	Japan
United States	Japan	Japan	Germany	FR Germany	FR Germany	United Kingdom
Egypt	E.E.C.	Netherlands	Netherlands	United Kingdom	France	France
USSR	USSR	Spain	Iraq	Japan	China	Italy
Netherlands		Italy	United States	Canada	Italy	FR Germany

Zinc	*Lead*	*Jute*	*Tungsten*	*Beef*	*Petroleum*	*Coal*
Major Exporters						
Canada	USSR	Bangladesh	USSR	Australia	Saudi Arabia	USSR
Belgium-Lux.	Australia	India	China	Argentina	Iran	United States
Australia	Canada	Thailand	Bolivia	New Zealand	Kuwait	FR Germany
Japan	United Kingdom	Brazil	Australia	Ireland	Libya	Poland
Zambia	Mexico	Zaire	Portugal	France	Venezuela	United Kingdom
Major Importers						
United States	United States	China	United States	United States	Japan	Japan
FR Germany	Australia	United States	Japan	Italy	United States	France
United Kingdom	FR Germany	United Kingdom	United Kingdom	United Kingdom	United Kingdom	Belgium-Lux.
India	United Kingdom	E.E.C.	FR Germany	FR Germany	Italy	Italy
Italy	FR Germany	Japan	Sweden	France	FR Germany	Canada

Table 1-4
Commodities by Degree of Price Fluctuation

Groups 1 and 2		*Group 3*		*Group 4*	
Coffee	68%	Copper	36%	Abaca	25%
Sugar	63%	Beef	35%	Palm Oil	24%
Zinc	61%	Cocoa	35%	Groundnut Oil	24%
Tungsten	54%	Sunflower Oil	31%	Tin	22%
Wheat	49%	Corn	31%	Pepper	20%
Linseed Oil	46%	Lead	29%	Jute	20%
Wool	45%	Cotton	29%	Rice	19%
Sisal	42%	Rubber	28%	Tea	15%
		Coconut Oil	27%	Manganese	14%
		Soybean Oil	27%	Iron	14%
		Palm Kernel Oil	26%	Bananas	13%
				Aluminum	8%

Source: Underlying data from *Commodity Price Bulletin,* UNCTAD, Geneva, various issues, 1954-1973.

Note: Fluctuations are measured by the coefficient of variation expressed as a percent using monthly prices.

Technical Characteristics

Technical characteristics of a commodity are important for determining the degree of interchangeability it possesses with other commodities or with synthetic substitutes. These characteristics, in fact, determine the boundary of commodities when they are defined in terms of properties such as conductivity, energy, or protein content.

Technical characteristics, together with economic and quality or taste considerations, determine the relative substitutability of commodities on the demand side. Where synthetic substitutes exist, there is the danger that a commodity's market share will be eroded by a synthetic with lower and more stable prices. Where a number of substitutes with similar characteristics exist, changes in market share occur with only small changes in relative prices. This is particularly true for mineral commodities that compete closely in product composition at the intermediate demand level.

On the supply side, substitution relates more to the return obtained from investing productive capital in one commodity as compared to another. When the price of soybeans increases, for example, land planted in cotton will now be taken over for soybeans. One can also think of investments shifting from mining operations in one mineral to another.

International Stockpiles

A final characteristic of market structure is the quantity of inventories existing for different commodities. Variations in this quantity can be wide, as shown in

Table 1-5. These stocks are held for purposes of commercial transactions (lead), food reserves (wheat), security reasons (copper), or price stabilization (tin). Whether or not they are sufficient to stabilize prices in the context of international commodity agreements depends on their size relative to that estimated as being necessary for buffer stock operation.

Commodity Modeling Approaches

The methodologies applied to modeling commodity markets are almost as diverse as the markets. There is no all-purpose model, and the different methodologies concentrate on different aspects of explaining history, policy analysis, and forecasting. Generally speaking, a *commodity model* is a quantitative representation of a commodity market or industry; the behavioral relationships included reflect demand and supply aspects of price determination as well as other related economic, political, and social phenomena. Here we examine the basic mechanisms of commodity market adjustments as well as the related modeling methodologies.

Modeling the Market Mechanism

The most common type of mechanism from which commodity modeling methodologies have developed reflects the microeconomics of competitive market behavior. Focusing on the price adjustment that serves to clear the market, a rudimentary commodity model can be expressed in four equations, although much more complex structures are used in practice.

$$D = d(D_{-1}, P, P^c, A, T)$$

$$Q = q(Q_{-1}, P_{-\theta}, N, Z)$$

$$P = p(P_{-1}, D, \Delta I)$$

$$I = I_{-1} + Q - D$$

Table 1-5
End-of-Year Stocks in Terms of Month's Supply, 1972

1.0 to 1.9 mo.	*2.0 to 3.9 mo.*	*4.0 to 5.9 mo.*	*6 mo. or more*
Wheat	Cocoa	Sugar	Coffee
Grains	Wool	Tobacco	Rubber
Tea	Copper	Cotton	
Jute	Tin		
Zinc			
Lead			

where D = commodity demand
Q = commodity supply
P = commodity prices
P^c = prices of substitute commodities
$P_{-\theta}$ = prices with lag distribution
I = commodity inventories
A = income or activity level
T = technical factors
N = natural factors
Z = policy variable influencing supply

Demand is explained as being dependent on prices, economic activity, prices of one or more substitute commodities, and possible technical influences, such as the growth of synthetic substitutes. Other possible influencing factors and the customary stochastic disturbance term are omitted here and elsewhere to simplify presentation. Accordingly, supply would depend on prices as well as natural factors such as weather, geological conditions, or a possible policy variable. A lagged price variable is included since the supply process is normally described using some form of the general class of distributed lag functions.

Prices are explained by demand and inventories, although this equation is sometimes inverted to explain inventory demand. The model is closed using an identity that equates inventories with lagged inventories plus supply minus demand. Where the price equation is inverted to represent inventory demand, the identity can be recognized as the equivalent supply of inventories equation.

This model can more appropriately be described as a general system of first- or higher-order difference equations solvable within a simulation framework. This requires that its variables be classified as endogenous variables or targets D, Q, I, and P; lagged endogenous variables D_{-i}, Q_{-i}, I_{-i}, and P_{-i}; and exogenous variables P^c, A, T and Z. Of the latter group, Z is also known as an instrument or policy controllable variable. We normally refer to the above equation system in its matrix form:

$$\Gamma Y + B_1 Y_{-i} + B_2 X = U$$

where Y equals a $G \times n$ matrix of current endogenous variables; Y_{-i} equals a $G \times n$ matrix of lagged endogenous variables; X equals a $M \times n$ matrix of exogenous and policy controllable variables; U equals a $G \times n$ matrix of current disturbance terms; Γ and B_1 equal $G \times G$ matrices of coefficients on the current and lagged endogenous variables respectively; and B_2 equals a $G \times M$ matrix of coefficients on the exogenous and policy variables. The equivalent reduced form is given by:

$$Y = \Pi_1 Y_{-i} + \Pi_2 X = V$$

where Π_1 equals a $G \times G$ matrix of reduced-form coefficients on the lagged endogenous variables, and Π_2 equals a $G \times M$ matrix of reduced-form coefficients on the exogenous and policy variables X.

A more complete representation of this model is given by its final form:

$$Y = \Pi_1^{s+1} Y_{-s-1} + \sum_{j=0}^{s} \Pi_1^j \Pi_2 X_{-j} + \sum_{j=0}^{s} \Pi_1^j V_{-j}$$

If Π_1 is such that Π_1^{s+1} approaches a null matrix as s approaches infinity, then we obtain for the deterministic part:

$$Y = \sum_{j=0}^{s} \Pi_1^j \Pi_2 X_{t-j}$$

The Π_2 represents the impact multipliers, and the product $(1 - \Pi_1)^{-1}\Pi_2$ defines the stationary multipliers. Partial sums of the form

$$\sum_{j=0}^{s} \Pi_1^j \Pi_2$$

provide the dynamic multipliers that can be of a cumulative nature.

Utilizing the model for historical explanation, policy analysis, decision making, or prediction normally takes place by simulating its structural or reduced form, where the stochastic disturbance terms can be suppressed or generated. For models that are dynamic, nonlinear, and simultaneous, a numerical solution is typically imposed. Interpreting the model as a set of n equations $(j = 1, 2, \ldots, n)$ that can be written as:

$$Y_j = f_j(Y_1, \ldots, Y_n; Y_{1,-i}, \ldots, Y_{n,-i}; X_1, \ldots, X_m)$$

Iteration is performed using the Gauss-Seidel algorithm

$$Y_j^r = f_j(Y_1^{r-1}, \ldots, Y_n^{r-1}; Y_{1,-i}, \ldots, Y_{n,-1}; X_1, \ldots, X_m)$$

which converges when

$$\left| \frac{Y_j^r - Y_j^{r-1}}{Y_j^{r-1}} \right| < K$$

for some preassigned K. A complete set of values for the endogenous variables can be obtained by forming successive solutions through time. Note that since the model is dynamic, the solution is evolutionary and generates its own values for the endogenous variables with only the exogenous variables given. Naylor (1971) and Epps (1975) have shown how to extend commodity simulation analysis by conducting stochastic simulation that involves a series of replications, each spanning multiple observation intervals.

Simulation can also facilitate the investigation of the stability and cyclical properties of commodity models. Investigation of these properties normally has been based on the linear nonstochastic representation of the model. This follows from examining the characteristic roots λ of the determinant

$$|\Pi_1 - \lambda I| = 0$$

Stability occurs when the real roots lie within the unit circle. If the roots are imaginary, or $\lambda = a + b_i$, stability requires that the modulus $|M| = \sqrt{a^2 + b^2} < 1$. Interpretation of the cyclical properties stems from the periodicity of oscillations $T = 1/f$, where $R = 2\Pi f$ is the angle generated by the modulus with respect to the real axis, $R - \tan^{-1}(b/a)$. Simulation now enters when the investigation is extended to the linear stochastic representation. Here stochastic behavior normally arises from random variation in the equation disturbances and/or the exogenous variables. Thus random "shocks" can be added to these model components, and through successive simulations the cyclical behavior of the model can be observed.

Finally, simulation can be extended to include optimization by using optimal control theory to steer the endogenous or state variables Y close to some target A through the appropriate choice of some policy or control variables Z.

Table 1-6
Commodity Modeling Methodologies Compared[a]

Quantitative Approach	*Solution Process*	
	Descriptive	*Optimizing*
Econometric	Market Models Process Models Systems Models	Programming Models i. Spatial Equilibrium ii. Recursive Programming Market Models involving feedback control
Engineering	Input-Output Models Industrial Dynamics Models Systems Models Resource Base Models	Programming Models i. Linear Programming ii. Quadratic Programming Systems Models

[a]A modeling methodology may appear in more than one category, depending on its particular emphasis with regard to quantitative approach and solution process.

The above model, now referred to as the system of motion or transformation equations, is rewritten to distinguish the exogenous variables X not subject to control from the variables Z subject to control.

$$Y = B_1 Y_{-1} + B_2 Z + B_3 X + U$$

Performance of the system will be measured by deviations of Y from the target vector A, as embodied in some objective or welfare function W. For the simplest case of a finite horizon, discrete interval, deterministic control problem, one searches for the optimal sequence of controls Z^* from the set of admissible sequences C that will transform the commodity system Y from its initial conditions $Y(0)$ through the control region R in such a way that the welfare function W is optimized. In this case, minimize

$$W = w(Y_1 - A_1, Z_1; \ldots ; Y_T - A_T, Z_T)$$

subject to

$$Y = f(Y_{-i}, Z, X)$$

$$Y(0) = Y_0$$

$$Y \epsilon R;\ Z \epsilon C$$

where T is the length of the horizon. This basic methodology has been applied most frequently in commodity modeling. Further description can be found in Labys (1973, 1975) as well as in Adams and Behrman (1976). A recent, major application of interest has been in the work of Burrows (1976), which analyzes the impact of supply restrictions and buffer-stock schemes on the nonferrous metals markets.

Alternative Modeling Methodologies

While the preceding approach relates to what is known as a *market model,* there are other approaches or methodologies that serve different modeling purposes. While a detailed description of each modeling approach would be useful, we are limited here to focusing on their essential characteristics.[1]

In Table 1-6 these features have been delineated according to the quantitative approach and the solution process adopted. The quantitative approach refers to the underlying mathematical orientation of the models. In this case they can be econometric models whose parameters are statistically estimated or engineering-type models whose parameters are based on experimentation or extraneous information. Models of a descriptive type that embody the econometric approach typically describe market history, although the market description can be extended into the future for purposes of policy analysis or forecasting. Econometrically estimated parameters and their accompanying structural equations are also employed in a related class of programming models whose goal is optimizing some aspect of commodity behavior, such as spatial transfers. Alternatively, optimization can be achieved by operating a market model with a control-theoretic algorithm, as described earlier.

Models embodying an engineering approach are more difficult to differentiate, and the characterization is somewhat more fuzzy. Most of these models, such as composite input-output, industrial dynamics, systems, and resource base models, are restricted to being descriptive in nature. Systems models, however, can also achieve optimization, where they embody programming techniques or some other maximization framework. Programming models lacking econometric components would fall into this latter category.

To provide a more precise definition of each of these approaches, their essential characteristics have been summarized in Table 1-7. These include the purpose of the methodology, the underlying quantitative framework, the economic behavior that is typically described, and examples of commodity application. *Commodity process models,* although econometric models, have been designed to supplant market models in several respects. Process models deal with supply and demand within an industry rather than across a market; they thus focus on the transformation of commodity inputs into finished products. Whereas market models balance supply and demand to provide an equilibrium price, prices in a process model are normally a function of production and material costs. The emphasis is also different; process models concentrate on the industrial production process, requirements for raw materials, and labor and plant capacity.

The development of the process model has been mainly through the efforts of Adams (1973). Adams and Griffin (1969) have shown it to be effective in modeling the petroleum industry, and Higgins (1969) has applied it to the steel industry. More recent experiments have involved improving the structural representations of these models. On the supply side, Adams and Griffin (1972) have shown how engineering data can be introduced by utilizing a linear programming model to explain the transformation from product output to the demand for inputs. On the demand side, Tsurumi (1976) criticizes the use of industrial activity variables to explain demand in process modeling of the Japanese steel industry. Instead, he hypothesizes that activity variables follow some form of distributed lag pattern and that the related lag structure can be determined from the future production planning behavior of steel consumers. To accomplish the latter, he introduces a suboptimization model of steel demand based on the discrete maximum control principle.

Programming models typically deal with spatial or interregional efficiency in commodity production, distribution, and utilization. The most common of these, termed *spatial equilibrium models,* normally embodies the following components: (1) a system of equations describing the aggregate demand for one or more commodities of interest in each of the included markets as well as the aggregate supply of the commodities in each of the markets, (2) the distribution activities over space, and (3) the equilibrium conditions. While the demand and supply equations imply a structure similar to that of a market model, the equilibrium process is more adequately represented through the identification of the profits to be realized from the flow of commodities, i.e., the excess of a price differential between two points minus transportation costs. Profit maximization is assured through the use of an algorithm that allows commodities to transfer until demand equals supply in every spatially separated market. So that policy decisions can be evaluated more realistically, the equilibrium conditions and other definitional equations can be used to impose constraints on the model parameters.

The theoretical and empirical background to the spatial equilibrium approach can be found in the study by Takayama and Judge (1971), while recent advances and examples of commodity models appear in the papers edited by Judge and Takayama (1973).

Recursive programming models can be considered a special case of adaptive intertemporal spatial equilibrium models. Applications to commodity markets thus far have not been extensive, since this approach requires data disaggregated below the market level. A recursive program has been described by Day (1973) as "a sequence of constrained optimization problems in which one or more objective functions, constraint or limitation coefficients of a given problem depend functionally on the optimal primal and/or dual solution vectors of one or more problems earlier in the sequence." To obtain this recursive dependence of the coefficients on preceding solutions, a set of feedback functions is used. The rationale behind this approach is that it emulates a decision maker who proceeds according to a succession of behaviorially conditioned, suboptimizing decisions. The decision maker, in protecting himself from errors of estimation and forecasting, reviews his maximization plans each period based on current information. The sequence of decisions as a whole must then converge to some desired optimum.

So far the commodity-related applications based on recursive programming have attempted to explain substitution patterns during agricultural transition as well as to describe the role of technological change in commodity extractive industries; for examples, see studies by Day and Tabb (1972); Nelson (1971); Singh and Ahn (1972); and Abe (1973).

Of the models embodying the engineering approach, *industrial dynamics models* utilize behavioral relationships similar to econometric models. However, they emphasize the attributes of commodity systems that lend themselves to engineering or systems analysis: amplification and time delays, feedback and control, and stability and damping. Meadows (1970) further developed this

Table 1–7
Commodity Modeling Methodologies and the Modeling Process

	Modeling Process			
Methodologies	*What is the purpose of the methodology?*	*What quantitative method is used?*	*What economic behavior is specified?*	*Examples of Commodity Applications*
Market Model	Demand, supply, inventories interact to produce an equilibrium price in competitive or noncompetitive markets	Dynamic microeconometric system composed of difference or differential equations	Interaction between decision makers in reaching market equilibrium based on demand, supply inventories, prices, trade, etc.	Beef Maize Cocoa Coffee Sugar Copper Tin
Process Model	Demand and production determined within an industry, focusing on transformation from product demand to input requirements	Dynamic microeconomic difference equation system suitable for integrating linear programming on production side	Interaction between decision makers in industries, markets, national economies based on demand, inventories, production, investment, capacity utilization, commodity inputs, prices, etc.	Petroleum Steel
Input-Output Model	System regarded as process that converts raw materials into intermediate and final products via intermediate processes. Investment strategies evaluated in terms of raw materials supply and demand	Input-output model combined with macroeconomic framework or disaggregated raw materials balance framework	Interactions between nonfuel and fuel commodities and macro markets in reaching materials and energy balance including supply-demand determination	Substitutions: Glass Polyvinyl Chloride Polyethylene Substitutions: Coal Gas Oil

Optimization and Programming Models 1. Linear and Quadratic Programming Spatial Equilibrium	Spatial flows of demand and supply and equilibrium conditions assigned optimally in equilibrium depending on configuration of transportation network	Activity analysis of a spatial and/or temporal form. Degree of complexity depends on endogeneity and method of incorporation of demand and supply functions	Interaction between decision makers in allocating shipments (exports) and consumption (imports) optimized through maximizing sectoral revenues or minimizing sectoral costs	Wheat Sugar Livestock Petroleum Beef Cocoa
2. Recursive Programming	Production conditions and input revenue determined through primal/dual of linear program. Recursivity introduced through feedback component which includes profit, capital and demand	Activity analysis involving a sequence of constrained maximization problems in which objective function, limitation coefficients depend on optimal primal/dual solutions attained earlier in the sequence	Interaction between decision makers in reaching market equilibrium involves adaptive intertemporal processes related to production, investment and technological change	Coal Iron and Steel Wheat, Corn, and Soybeans
Industrial Dynamics Dynamic Commodity Cycle Model	Demand, supply, inventories interact to produce an equilibrium price emphasizing role of amplifications and feedback delays	Dynamic microeconometric differential equation system that features lagged feedback relations and variables in rates of change	Interaction between decision makers in adjusting rate of production to maintain a desired level of inventory in relationship to rate of consumption	Aluminum Broilers Cattle Copper Hogs Orange Juice
Systems Model	Demand, supply and other major variables and objectives considered as a complete system rather than a single market	Dynamic microeconometric equation system which when formed into a simulation framework is coupled with activity analysis and/or decision rules	Interaction between decision makers belonging to the system environment based on performance variables such as revenues, costs as well as market variables such as demand, supply, prices, etc.	Beef Energy Fish Livestock Multicommodity Rice
Resource Base Model	Geological descriptions of deposits linked to economic concepts of mineral exploration, mining and production costs, investment, and transportation.	Geostatistical analysis of mineral deposits including probabilistic analysis of resource base linked to supply-demand in a system framework	Interactions between resource base, known reserves, depletion exploration, and supply-demand based on probabilistic description of resource base and investment and production costs.	Uranium Nonferrous Metals

approach, based on Forrester (1965), with his *dynamic commodity cycle model,* which concentrates on the inventory formation aspect of market models. Two coupled negative feedback loops–consumption and production–each act to adjust inventory coverage to desired levels. Another feature of the model is that producers and consumers may employ any function of current and past prices to form expectations about future prices. In addition, functional relationships are expressed in continuous time with "period" analysis being replaced by "rate of change" analysis. Production and consumption are assumed to adjust continuously to price changes, rather than discontinuously between equilibrium points.

To apply industrial dynamics, it is preferable to select those commodities which display some form of cyclical behavior in production and prices. In the original Meadows (1970) study, models were constructed for hog, cattle, and broiler markets. Further extensions of the hog model have been made by Naill et al. (1973), and Raulerson and Langham (1970) found the approach useful in analyzing the frozen concentrated orange juice industry. More recently, Strongman et al. (1976) have applied it in a systems dynamics context to the international copper market.

Systems models can embody any of the methodologies discussed so far. Their advantages rest in their affording study of a commodity system when data are inadequate, when an objective function is difficult to specify, or when the system is too complex to be optimized using conventional methods. However, this approach can suffer from "data fitting," with important behavioral elements being neglected. Formulating commodity models with a systems approach usually entails structuring the major objectives and variables to be considered as a complete system rather than constituting a single market or industry; it then incorporates one or more analytical or quantitative methods to produce a model emulating that system.

Examples of systems models describing industry behavior are those often referred to as computer simulation models: (1) Cohen's (1960) model of the shoe, leather, and hide sequence; (2) the Naylor, Wallace, and Sasser (1967) model of the textile industry; and (3) the Baughman (1974) model of the U.S. energy system. The common properties of these models include the selection of variables that describe the basic flow characteristics of the industry rather than conventional market behavior, as well as the adoption of a fully recursive structure that permits an evolutionary description of the industry variables extending over a large number of future periods.

Systems models explaining agricultural behavior tend to combine econometric as well as engineering information. Examples of such models developed within the USDA are described in the *Systems Workshop Proceedings* (1970) and in a study by Crom (1970). More recently, Haidacher, Kite, and Matthews (1975) have constructed a multicommodity systems model that emulates the decision-making process involved in the administration of the U.S. surplus commodity removal program.

Not much has been reported on the development of systems models falling into the optimization category. Of possible interest is the systems model of the U.S. rice industry designed by Holder et al. (1971), which employs linear and nonlinear programming methods to determine optimal locations and quantity flows. Linear programming studies that relate to energy systems also exist, one example being the energy system planning framework of Hoffman (1974).

To include models embodying an input-output framework stretches the definition of commodity modeling, but it does help with an understanding of the special problems associated with modeling the minerals markets. *Composite input-output models* integrate the supply and demand patterns for particular commodities with the industrial structure and aggregate income determinants of the national economy. Such a combined modeling approach has proven useful for describing the minerals industry, where a single mineral is used in a number of different industries and final end-uses. Although possibilities for constructing such models had been considered earlier by Wang and Kokat (1967), only recently has development increased.

Of the three extensions of interest, the first is the *minerals demand model* recently discussed by Krueger (1976), as developed by the Federal Preparedness Agency of the GSA to explain how the future consumption of ferrous and non-ferrous metals can be forecast by combining projections of raw material consumption ratios, which relate materials consumption to industrial output. Components of the modeling structure thus include an estimate of GNP derived from a macroforecasting model, computed ratios reflecting materials consumption per unit of industrial output for individual industries, and an input-output table that converts the economic estimates to production estimates and subsequently to minerals consumption.

The second is the *materials process product model* devised by Saxton and Ayres (1976), based on Ayres and Kneese (1970), which replaces the dollar valuation of transactions flow of input-output analysis with the material flows of commodities and energy. This changes technology from a fixed factor to one that can be analyzed within the model. Primary and residual outputs are derived directly from a description of a specific materials conversion procedure. The latter begins with primary commodities and transfers them into final products (and wastes) by going through various process stages, e.g., beginning with separation and purification and ending with packaging and distribution. As such, it deals with (1) commodities characterized by their elemental composition and physical state, (2) processes defined in terms of energy and commodity inputs and outputs as well as value added, and (3) final products. At present, the model has been applied to analyze policies relating to options for international industrial development as well as to linkages between technology, economy, environment, and commodity flows.

The final variant or *macrointerindustry model* integrates the determinants of demand and supply embodied in conventional macroeconometric models with the determinants of industry or commodity demand and supply as reflected in the input-output model. A model of this type has been built by Hudson and Jorgenson (1974), who relate U.S. growth to the demand and supply of energy and other commodities reflected in an interindustry structure. The overall quantitative structure of the model can be explained in terms of two components. The first is an econometric model of interindustry transaction for nine domestic industries, where five of these relate to energy commodities—coal, crude petroleum and natural gas, refined petroleum, electricity, and gas. The second component is the macroeconometric growth model, which has been modified to integrate demand and supply conditions for consumption, investment, capital, and labor. Submodels generate the components of final demand based on expenditures obtained from the macro model. Now included in detail via the interindustry coupling is the often neglected supply side.

In contrast to energy balance models, the present framework views energy as one of the many interacting parts of the economy, linking energy developments to variables such as employment, income, and consumption, which are the ultimate ends of energy use. Simulation analysis carried out so far has evaluated the long-run impact of energy policy changes on energy demand and supply, on energy imports, and on U.S. economic growth.

As recently described in Vogely (1975), *resource base models* concentrate on utilizing geostatistical methodologies to interrelate the reserve and supply aspects of mineral commodity markets. While they sometimes feature economic relationships or variables describing costs and prices, they are hardly commodity models as presently defined. They fail to integrate geological-economic relationships explaining reserves and supply with those describing intermediate and final demand, including market equilibrium conditions. Rather they involve consideration of known and unknown mineral occurrences whose existence in the earth's crust can be defined as either economically or subeconomically exploitable. Combining economic relationships on the reserve and supply side and including the demand side would relate reserves and supply to factors such as consumption changes, reflecting trends in conservation, scrap generation and recovery, and changing technology in the production of intermediate goods; for example, see Price and Thillainathan (1976).

The future potential of these models can be found in a recent survey by Harris (1975). Applications consist of the Harris (1975) uranium supply study in New Mexico and the Harris et al. (1970) study of mineral supply in the Canadian Northwest. Similar in character is the Torries (1975) probability model of the availability of domestically produced uranium in the United States and the Singer (1975) application of geostatistical techniques to develop a mineral resource assessment for Alaska.

Combined Modeling Methodologies

A final area of commodity modeling to be considered pertains to the development of multicommodity models as well as the integration of them with models describing national economic behavior. There appear to be three main directions in these linkage efforts. The first would involve composite input-output models, as previously described, where commodity demand and supply behavior is interrelated with an input-output framework describing the national economy.

The second direction begins with the realization that common technical properties make certain groups of commodities highly competitive in substitution as product inputs. Rather than consider each commodity in a partial equilibrium context, groups of commodity markets are combined in a general equilibrium framework. Recent attempts in this direction have involved either multicommodity spatial equilibrium models or combinations of commodity market models.

Of the former, considerable work has taken place to interrelate feed-grain markets, as viewed in the Guedry (1973) model of the U.S. feed-grain economy and the Kost (1975) model of the E.E.C. grain-livestock economy. Spatial models of international trade in food commodities have also been constructed, such as that by Blakeslee et al. (1973), and USDA (1974) world food model, and the Japanese (1974) agricultural model. More recently, Takayama (1975) has integrated both food and energy commodity behavior within a single spatial model.

Regarding multicommodity market models of an econometric type, Adams (1975) has constructed a tightly integrated model of the world oils and fats market. Methods for linking minerals models by iterating over price and product input variables have been described by Perlman and Allingham (1975). Actual solutions of such systems have been obtained by Adams (1975) in his ocean floor nodule study involving aluminum, copper, nickel, cobalt, and manganese models.

The last major direction of linkage relates to the integration of commodity market models with macro models of the national economy. Once again, differentiation exists. Beginning with the agricultural commodities, we find the very wide area of agricultural sector modeling. King (1975) has presented an overview of this area, and recent advances can be seen in the work of Byerlee and Halter (1974), Roop and Zeitner (1976), and Heien (1976). Both Wharton E.F.A. and Data Resources Inc. offer computer-linked modeling systems for these areas. Mineral commodity models integrated with macro models are also available in this form, as described by Tinsley (1976). Finally, an attempt has been made to integrate individual commodity models with macro models onto the existing LINK structure, as indicated by Adams (1973), or alternatively by integrating simple income determination relationships with a substantial number of commodity models, as accomplished in SIMLINK by Hicks (1975).

Needs and Directions for Improvement

To discuss the deficiencies and needs of commodity models as well as possibilities for improvement is difficult without referring to specific commodity models and their properties. At this point, we can only summarize some of the more critical of these problems and possibilities for solution.

Supply

The most pressing need in modeling commodity supply is to integrate technical, geological, and biological information and parameters into appropriate economic relationships. To date, most research has centered on producer formulation of price expectations and risk. Nerlove (1956) was the first to formulate supply relations dynamically, based on the partial adjustment mechanism. The included price-expectations variable subsequently was expanded beyond naive expectations to include extrapolative, adaptive, and rational expectations. Behrman (1968) modified the supply-response mechanism to include expectations on yields as well as on prices. And French and Matthews (1971) review applications to perennial crops that include specification regarding profit expectations for new acreage planted, acreage removed, and yields.

Essential to the expectations formulation is the nature of the reduced form of the dynamic relationships that normally include various distributed lag structures. Nerlove's (1956) work begins with a geometric lag scheme, but more complex structures can easily be adopted. Chen et al. (1972) illustrate the use of polynomial lags in explaining milk-production response, while a similar work by Mielke et al. (1974) centers on hog supply. In contrast, Burrows (1971) has utilized the inverted V lag in explaining demand as well as supply response in nonferrous metal markets.

Finally, Just (1974) extends the adaptive-expectations geometric lag model to include quadratic lag terms indicative of risk. Concepts of expected prices and yields are thus extended to include not only subjective evaluation of mean values of gross returns but also the variance of these returns. His results proved effective for crops where risk is a major factor.

Demand

In addition to dynamic relationships of the preceding type, Houthakker and Taylor (1966) have extended the specification of commodity demand relations to include a dynamic differential formulation. Demand analysis is now considered in continuous time, and the concept of demand adjustment is replaced by stock adjustment. Other efforts have related to systems of demand equations where simultaneity and substitution patterns are important. Stemming from the work of Brandow (1961), Court (1967), and Byron (1970), Labys (1977) has estimated a demand system model for the oils and fats market. A more sophisticated approach is that of Christensen and Manser (1974), who use "indirect translog utility functions" for explaining meat consumption patterns.

However, the more pressing needs involve the description of substitution patterns between commodities serving as intermediate inputs at the derived demand level as well as measuring corresponding elasticities of substitution. One attempt to solve the latter problem based on the translog approach is that of Kraft and Kraft (1975), who analyze interfuel substitution patterns. Others, such as Newcomb (1972), advise that an activity analysis framework is a better way of handling the problem. And a paper by Fisher and Pry (1972) suggests that substitution patterns, particularly those involving synthetics, can be interpreted using a technological or logistic methodology. Here also the need to introduce relationships linking the theory of intermediate demand to production technology is particularly strong.

Prices

Specification of price relationships in models has received the least attention in commodity modeling. Labys and Granger (1970) have indicated how spectral analysis can decipher cycles found in commodity prices and thus improve the formulation of price relationships. Some of their attention was directed to construction of time series of unobservable component equations such as in the ARIMA model; Leuthold et al. (1970) has also made a comparison of forecasts by these methods. With respect to price relationships embedded in models, Labys (1973) has stressed the importance of recognizing stock as compared to flow specifications as well as of emulating the behavior of monopolists and other noncompetitive price setters. Finally, commodity prices need to be adjusted for inflation, and this should involve more explanation in a model than the use of simple price deflators.

Markets

A major problem in assembling these components into a market structure relates to this very need for a noncompetitive market description. Price relationships as well as the simulation framework have to be modified, as shown in the works of Burrows (1971) and of Epps (1975). Another perhaps more serious problem is that the general equilibrium framework normally adopted does not explain how prices and quantities are actually determined in commodity markets. In short, the explicit disequilibrium characteristics of these markets have been neglected. Our models have been "dynamized" in the sense of yielding the dynamic paths of the endogenous variables that correspond to some short-run equilibrium position, but these positions are not necessarily in agreement with the associated steady-state path. *Tâtonnement* is implied where trading takes place only at an equilibrium price. To explore price determination outside of equilibrium, Wymer (1975) has suggested that continuous adjustment systems provide a suitable alternative.

Estimation

There now exist a number of estimation procedures based on maximum likelihood and fixed-point algorithms that permit us to handle previously difficult needs, such as dealing with simultaneous equation systems with autocorrelated disturbances or equation systems structured in differential equations; for examples, see Kuh (1974) and Wymer (1975). To this must be added the current work on RIDGE regression; for example, see Vinod (1974). These are further embodied in computer software that enables the estimated model to be solved and verified using stochastic or nonstochastic simulation. Although these developments satisfy a number of requirements of commodity modelers, many difficult estimation and data problems remain.

One such problem is that of estimating price and income elasticities of demand and price elasticities of supply. Some recent work suggests that incorporation of prior information obtained from sources outside the sample period can improve elasticity measurement notably. For example, means and variances as well as probability distributions of price elasticities for various commodities can be obtained from existing studies. Labys and Hunkeler (1974) have shown that fairly complete information of this type is available for the more important commodities, while for others it can be obtained by aggregating commodities into groups with similar behavior, such as beverages or nonferrous metals. Taking a Bayesian viewpoint, one can combine these prior probabilities with sample information to obtain posterior probabilities relating to parameters of interest. In this respect, Drèze (1971) has devised a Bayesian limited-information estimation procedure and has incorporated prior information to measure elasticities embedded in a commodity market model.

A final problem of importance is that structural change in commodity markets can have as its immediate impact the obsolescence of certain estimated parameters in a model system. Recent attention to this situation by Cooley and Prescott (1973) has involved applications of the theory of time-varying parameters. That such an approach should be taken follows from the realization that the "true" parameters can be viewed as an outcome of a stochastic or some other time-series process with given mean. Among the estimation methods proposed are random coefficient models, systematic variation models, and Kalman-filter models.

Commodity Speculation

Speculation normally is associated with those price effects related to speculative stockholding, forward trading, and futures market activity. Until recently, the impact of these effects on commodity futures markets was thought to be small. But as shown by Labys and Thomas (1975), futures speculation has been rather closely related to the recent price movements on commodity spot markets. Since speculation and futures market activity normally increase during periods of change and uncertainty, these factors should be incorporated to improve the adjustment process of short-term commodity models. By including them, there is also the possibility of introducing economic and monetary information also known to influence speculative activity. Thus the resulting commodity model becomes more finely tuned to macro influences responsible for economic upheavels.

Climatic Effects

The inclusion of climatic effects into commodity models is an often-stated panacea for coping with poor forecasting performance. But national and international stocks of agricultural commodities might be low, with no buffers available to help to mitigate wide price fluctuations caused by changes in climate. Econometric developments that can serve as a basis for introducing climatic effects into commodity models are few. While recent studies of patterns of water supply and consumption deal with long-run analysis, the performance of short-run models depends more on the use of weighted precipitation and temperature indices. In this regard, a major difficulty in relating weather and commodity activity is that discrepancies exist between weather data tabulated for places and economic data aggregated by regions.

But some notable progress has been made. For example, Maunder (1970) has provided a broad outline for incorporating climatic variations in modeling techniques, such as linear programming and input-output. He also suggests how weather forecasts can be improved for updating model predictions. In reference to econometric analysis, Oury (1965) explains how these effects could be included in production and price behavioral relationships. And Maunder (1972) presents a number of weighting methods used to integrate rainfall, mean temperature, and days with water deficit into relationships explaining the production of butterfat in the New Zealand dairy industry. While such models might improve forecasting during abnormal weather periods, one might also want to experiment with effects of episodic events such as typhoons, tornados, or droughts based on probabilistic functions that represent the likelihood of their occurrence.

Government Policy

A final yet obvious factor that influenced the performance of commodity models during the recent period was political or government intervention.[2]

Commodity markets involving some degree of government intervention normally are modeled by including policy variables or instruments through which policy is implemented. Such variables normally are specified as exogenous and relate to policies such as duties, subsidies, and price support or acreage allotments. Examples of the impact of trade policies on long-term forecasts can be found in the spatial equilibrium trade model of Schmitz and Bawden (1973) related to wheat. With respect to support price and acreage restriction policies, Houck et al. (1972) have shown how to combine these policies into an "effective support price" variable. The impact of these policies as related to soybean support prices as well as to crops competing with soybeans is evaluated in their soybean model.

A more recent approach would consider government intervention that has continued for a sufficiently long time that it exhibits certain regularities. This behavior can be described analytically and integrated into a commodity model, the government or policy variables becoming endogenous. Among the theories available for explaining this behavior, the political regularities can be regarded as manifestations of optimizing behavior on the part of policy makers. Simulation studies that attempt to maximize some social welfare function normally stem from this theory. However, an approach advocated by Zusman (1974, p. 2) as being more realistic would view "political behavior as a process of accommodation among conflicting interests, where the attained political-economic equilibrium represents a simultaneous solution to the economic system and the associated political conflict." To illustrate this view, he further presents a sugar model embodying the political relationships according to the theory of cooperative games, with implications given for Israel's sugar import policy.

Obviously, there are other aspects of commodity modeling to be dealt with and a host of additional problems to be solved. Commodity modeling is indeed a much larger field than I envisioned when I began this survey two years ago. But I have attempted to review essentials, and I hope that this leads to further awareness of the potentials and limitations of this area of modeling.

Notes

1. A more complete survey of the approaches, including their more formal mathematical representation, is available from the author.

2. Portions of this discussion appear in W.C. Labys, "The Problems and Challenges for International Commodity Models and Model Builders," *Am. J. Ag. Econ.* 57 (1975):877.

References

Abe, M.A. "Dynamic Microeconomic Models of Production, Investment and Technological Change of the U.S. and Japanese Iron and Steel Industries."

In G. Judge and T. Takayama (eds.), *Studies in Economic Planning over Space and Time.* Amsterdam: North-Holland, 1973.

Adams, F.G. "From Econometric Models of the Nation to Models of Industries and Firms." *Wharton Quarterly Business Review* (1973).

——. "The Integration of World Primary Commodity Markets into Project Link: The Example of Copper." Paper prepared for the annual meeting of Project LINK, Stockholm, September 3-8, 1973.

——. "Applied Econometric Models of the Non-Ferrous Metal Markets: The Case of the Ocean Floor Nodules." In W. Vogely (ed.), *Mineral Materials Modeling.* Baltimore: Johns Hopkins Univ. Press, 1975.

——. "An Interrelated Econometric Modeling System for Fats and Oils Commodities." A study prepared for the United Nations Conference on Trade and Development, Wharton School, Univ. of Pennsylvania, 1975.

——, and J. Behrman. *Seven Models of Agricultural Commodity Markets.* Cambridge: Ballinger, 1976.

——, and J.M. Griffin. "An Econometric Model of the U.S. Petroleum Refining Industry." In L.R. Klein (ed.), *Essays in Industrial Econometrics,* vol. I. Philadelphia: Economics Research Unit, Univ. of Pennsylvania, 1969.

——, and J.M. Griffin. "An Econometric Linear Programming Model of the U.S. Petroleum Industry." *Journal of the American Statistical Association* 67 (1972):542-551.

Ayres, R.U., and A.V. Kneese. "Production, Consumption and Externalities." In A. Kneese et al., *Economics and the Environment: A Materials Balance Approach.* Washington, D.C.: Resources for the Future, 1970.

Baughman, M.L. "A Model for Energy-Environment Systems Analysis." In *Energy Modeling.* London: IPC Science and Technology Press, 1974.

Behrman, J. *Supply Response in Underdeveloped Agriculture.* Amsterdam: North-Holland, 1968.

Blakeslee, L.L., E.O. Heady, and D.F. Framingham. *World Food Production, Demand and Trade.* Ames, Iowa: Iowa State Univ. Press, 1973.

Brandow, G.E. *Interrelationships Among Demands for Farm Products and Implications for Control of Market Supply.* Pa. Agric. Exp. Sta. Bull. 680, Penn State Univ., University Park, 1961.

Burrows, J.C. *Cobalt: An Industry Analysis.* Lexington, Mass.: Lexington Books, D.C. Heath, 1971.

——. *Tungsten: An Industry Analysis.* Lexington, Mass.: Lexington Books, D.C. Heath, 1971.

——. "A Framework for Analyzing Commodity Supply Restrictions." Charles River Associates Study prepared for the Experimental Technology Incentives Program. National Bureau of Standards, Gaithersburg, Md., 1976.

Byerlee, D., and A.N. Halter. "A Macro-Economic Model for Agricultural Sector Analysis." *Am. J. Agr. Econ.* 56 (1974):520-533.

Byron, R.P. "Restricted Aitken Estimation of Sets of Demand Relations." *Econometrica* 38 (1970):816-830.

Chen, D., R. Courtney, and A. Schmitz. "A Polynomial Lag Formulation of Milk Production Response." *Am. J. Agr. Econ.* 54 (1972):77-83.

Christensen, L.R., and M. Manser. "Estimating U.S. Consumer Preferences for Meat, 1947-1971." Workshop Series 7403, Social Systems Research Institute, University of Wisconsin, Madison, 1974.

Cohen, K. *A Computer Model of the Shoe, Leather and Hide Sequence.* Englewood Cliffs: Prentice-Hall, 1960.

Cooley, T.F., and E.C. Prescott. "Systematic (Non-Random) Variation Models Varying Parameter Regression: A Theory and Some Applications." *Annals of Economic and Social Measurement* 2 (1973):463-474.

Court, R.H. "Utility Maximization and the Demand for New Zealand Meats." *Econometrica* 35 (1967):424-446.

Crom, R. "A Dynamic Price-Output Model of the Beef and Pork Sectors." Technical Bulletin No. 1426, Economic Research Service, USDA, Washington, D.C., 1970.

Day, R.H. "Recursive Programming Models: A Brief Introduction." In G. Judge and T. Takayama (eds.), *Studies in Economic Planning Over Space and Time.* Amsterdam: North-Holland, 1973.

——, and W.K. Tabb, "A Dynamic, Microeconomic Model of the U.S. Coal Mining Industry." SSRI Research Paper, Univ. of Wisconsin, Madison, 1972.

Drèze, J.H. "Bayesian Limited Information Analysis of the Simultaneous Equation Model." CORE Discussion Paper No. 7111, Center for Operations Research and Econometrics, Catholic University of Louvain, 1971.

Epps, M.L. "A Simulation of the World Coffee Economy." In W.C. Labys (ed.), *Quantitative Models of Commodity Markets.* Cambridge: Ballinger, 1975.

Fisher, J.C., and R.H. Pry. "A Simple Substitution Model of Technological Change." In M.J. Certon (ed.), *Practical Applications of Technological Forecasting for Industries.* New York: Wiley, 1972.

Forrester, J.W. *Industrial Dynamics.* Cambridge: M.I.T. Press, 1965.

French, B.C., and J.L. Matthews. "A Supply Response Model for Perennial Crops." *Am. J. Agr. Econ.* 53 (1971):478-490.

Guedry, L.J. "An Application of a Multi-Commodity Transportation Model to the U.S. Food Grain Economy." In G. Judge and T. Takayama (eds.), *Studies in Economic Planning Over Time and Space.* Amsterdam: North-Holland, 1973.

Haidacher, R.C., R.C. Kite, and J.L. Matthews. "Application of a Planning Decision Model for Surplus Commodity Removal Programs." In W. Labys (ed.) *Quantitative Models of Commodity Markets.* Cambridge: Ballinger, 1975.

Harris, D.P. "Geostatistics in the Appraisal of Mineral Resources." In W.A. Vogely (ed.), *Mineral Materials Modeling,* RFF Working Paper EN-5. Baltimore: John Hopkins Univ. Press, 1975.

——, G. Barry, and A. Freeman. "The Methodology Employed to Estimate Potential Mineral Supply of the Canadian Northwest–An Analysis Based on Geologic Opinion and Systems Simulation." *Proceedings of the Ninth International Symposium on Decision Making.* June 1970.

Heien, D. "Price Determination Processes for Agricultural Sector Models." Paper presented at the annual meetings of the American Economic Association, Atlantic City, 1976.

Hicks, N.L. "The SIMLINK Model of Trade and Growth for the Developing World," Bank Staff Working Paper No. 220, World Bank, Washington, D.C., 1975.

Higgins, C.I. "An Econometric Description of the U.S. Steel Industry." In L.R. Klein (ed.), *Essays in Industrial Econometrics,* vol. II. Philadelphia: Economics Research Unit, Univ. of Pennsylvania, 1969.

Hoffman, K.C. "A Unified Framework for Energy System Planning." In *Energy Modeling.* London: IPC Science and Technology Press, 1974.

Holder, Jr., S.H., D.L. Shaw, and J.C. Snyder. "A Systems Model of the U.S. Rice Industry." Technical Bulletin No. 1453, Economic Research Service, USDA, Washington, D.C., 1971.

Houck, J.P., M.E. Ryan, and A. Subotnik. *Soybeans and Their Products: Markets, Models and Policy.* Minneapolis: Univ. of Minnesota Press, 1972.

Houthakker, H.S., and L.D. Taylor. *Consumer Demand in the United States: 1929-1970.* Cambridge: Harvard Univ. Press, 1966.

Hudson, E.A., and D.W. Jorgenson. "U.S. Energy Policy and Economic Growth, 1975-2000." Discussion Paper No. 372, Harvard Institute of Economic Research, 1974.

Japan, Ministry of Agriculture and Forestry. *The World Food Supply and Demand and Projections of Agricultural Products for 1980 and 1985.* Tokyo: Association of Agricultural and Forestry Statistics, 1974.

Judge, G.G., and T. Takayama, eds. *Studies in Economic Planning Over Space and Time.* Amsterdam: North-Holland, 1973.

Just, R.E. "An Investigation of the Importance of Risk in Farmers' Decisions." *Am. J. Agr. Econ.* 56 (1974):14-25.

King, G.A. "Econometric Models of the Agricultural Sector." *Am. J. Agr. Econ.* 57 (1975):164-171.

Kost, W.E. "Trade Flows in the Grain-Livestock Economy of the E.E.C." In W. Labys (ed.), *Quantitative Models of Commodity Markets.* Cambridge: Ballinger, 1975.

Kraft, J., and A. Kraft. "Interfuel Substitution and Energy Consumption in the Industrial Sector." Working Paper, Federal Energy Administration, Washington, D.C., 1975.

Krueger, P.K. "Modeling Future Requirements for Metals and Minerals." *Proceedings of the XIV Symposium of the Council for the Application of Computers and Mathematics in the Minerals Industries.* State College, Pa., October 1976.

Kuh, E. "Introduction to Special Issues on Estimation of Equation Systems." *Annals of Economic and Social Measurement* 3 (1974):i–iii.

Labys, W.C. *Dynamic Commodity Models: Specification, Estimation and Simulation,* Lexington, Mass.: Lexington Books, D.C. Heath, 1973.

——, ed. *Quantitative Models of Commodity Markets.* Cambridge: Ballinger, 1975.

——. "Commodity Models Bibliography." College of Mineral and Energy Resources, West Virginia University, 1976. Mimeographed.

——. "Multicommodity Substitution Patterns in the International Fats and Oils Market." *European Review of Agricultural Economics* 4 (1977):69-78.

——, and C.W.J. Granger. *Speculation, Hedging and Commodity Price Forecasts.* Lexington, Mass.: Lexington Books, D.C. Heath, 1970.

——, and J. Hunkeler. "Survey of Commodity Demand and Supply Elasticities." Res. Memo. No. 48, Research Division, UNCTAD, Geneva, 1974.

——, and H. Thomas. "Speculation, Hedging and Commodity Price Behavior: An International Comparison." *Applied Economics* 7(1975): 287-301.

Leuthold, R.M., A.J. MacCormick. A. Schmitz, and D.G. Watts. "Forecasting Daily Hog Prices and Quantities: A Study of Alternative Forecasting Techniques." *Journal of the American Statistical Association* 65 (1970): 90-107.

Maunder, W.J. *The Value of the Weather.* London: Methuen, 1970.

——. "National Econoclimatic Models: Problems and Applications." Technical Note No. 208, New Zealand Meteorological Service, Wellington, 1972.

Meadows, D.L. *Dynamics of Commodity Production Cycles.* Cambridge: Wright-Allen, 1970.

Mielke, K.D., A.C. Zwart, and L.J. Martin. "North American Hog Supply: A Comparison of Geometric and Polynomial Distributed Lag Models." *Canadian Journal of Agricultural Economics* 24 (1974):15-29.

Naill, R.F., N.J. Mass, J. Randers, and M.K. Simpson. "Dynamic Modeling as a Tool for Managerial Planning: A Case Study of the U.S. Hog Industry." Thayer School of Engineering, Dartmouth College, Hanover, 1973. Mimeographed.

Naylor, T.H. *Computer Simulation Experiments with Models of Economic Systems.* New York: Wiley, 1971.

——. W. Wallace, and W. Sasser. "A Computer Simulation Model of the Textile Industry." *Journal of the American Statistical Association* 62 (1967): 1338-1364.

Nelson, J.P. "An Interregional Recursive Programs Model of Production, Investment, and Technological Change." *Journal of Regional Science* 11 (1971): 33-47.

Nerlove, M. "Estimates of the Elasticities of Supply of Selected Agricultural Commodities." *Journal of Farm Economics* 37 (1956): 286-301.

Newcomb, R.T. "Towards a Dynamic Theory of Substitution and Technological

Change in the Materials Market." Paper No. 68-47, College of Earth and Mineral Sciences, Pennsylvania State Univ., 1972.

Oury, B. "Allowing for Weather in Crop Production Model Building." *Journal of Farm Economics* 47 (1965):270-283.

Perlman, L., and M. Allingham. "Econometric Supply-Demand Models." In W. Vogely (ed.), *Mineral Materials Modeling.* Baltimore: Johns Hopkins Univ. Press, 1975.

Price, D.H., and V. Thillainathan. "A Systems Study of Natural Resource Usage." *Proceedings of the XIV Symposium of the Council for the Application of Computers and Mathematics in the Mineral Industry.* State College, Pa., 1976.

Raulerson, R.C., and M.R. Langham. "Evaluating Supply Control Policies for Frozen Concentrated Orange Juice with an Industrial Dynamics Model." *Am. J. of Agr. Econ.* 52 (1970):197-208.

Roop, J.M., and R.H. Zeitner. "Agricultural Activity and the General Economy: Some Macro Model Experiments." Paper presented at the annual meetings of the American Economic Association, Atlantic City, 1976.

Saxton, J.C., and R.U. Ayres. "The Materials Process Product Model: Theory and Applications." *Proceedings of the XIV Symposium of the Council on the Application of Computers and Mathematics in the Minerals Industry."* State College, Pa., October 1976.

Schmitz A., and D. Bawden. *World Wheat Economy: An Empirical Analysis.* Giannini Foundation Monograph No. 32. Univ. of California at Berkeley, 1973.

Singer, D.A. "Mineral Resource Models and the Alaskan Mineral Resource Assessment Program." In W.A. Vogely (ed.), *Mineral Materials Modeling,* RFF Working Paper EN-5. Baltimore: Johns Hopkins Univ. Press, 1975.

Singh, I.J., and C.Y. Ahn. *A Dynamic Model of Agricultural Development in Southern Brazil: Some Retrospective Policy Simulations (1960-70).* Occasional Paper No. 113. Department of Agricultural Economics and Rural Sociology, Ohio State University, Columbus, 1972.

Strongman, J.E., W.R. Killingsworth, and W.E. Cummings. "The Dynamics of the International Copper System." *Proceedings of the XIV Symposium of the Council for the Application of Computers and Mathematics in the Mineral Industry.* State College, Pa., 1976.

Takayama, T. "World Food and Energy Model: A Market Oriented Approach." Department of Economics, Univ. of Illinois, Urbana, 1975. Mimeographed.

——, and G.G. Judge. *Spatial and Temporal Price and Equilibrium Models.* Amsterdam: North-Holland, 1971.

Tinsley, C.R. "Computer Application of Non-Ferrous Econometric Models from the Raw Materials Consumer Perspective." *Proceedings of the XIV Symposium of the Council for the Application of Computers and Mathematics in the Mineral Industries.* State College, Pa., 1976.

Torries, T.F. "A Probabilistic Model of the Availability of Domestically Produced Uranium in the United States," In W.A. Vogely (ed.) *Mineral Materials Modeling,* RFF Working Paper EN-5. Baltimore: Johns Hopkins Univ. Press, 1975.

Tsurumi, H. "Demand for Steel Products in Japan: A Suboptimization Approach." Department of Economics, Rutgers University, 1976. Mimeographed.

U.S. Department of Agriculture. *Proceedings of a Workshop on Systems Research in the Livestock Industries.* Economic Research Service, Washington, D.C., 1970.

——. *The World Food Situation and Prospects to 1985.* Foreign Agricultural Economic Report No. 98, Economic Research Service, Washington, D.C., 1974.

Vinod, H.D. "RIDGE Estimation of a Trans-Log Production Function." *Proceedings of the American Statistical Association,* Business Economics Section, 69 (1974):596-601.

Vogely, W.A., ed. *Mineral Materials Modeling,* RFF Working Paper En-5. Baltimore: Johns Hopkins Univ. Press, 1975.

Wang, K.L., and R.G. Kokat. *An Inter-Industry Structure of the U.S. Mining Industries.* IC 8338, United States Bureau of Mines, Washington, D.C., 1967.

Wymer, C.R. "Estimation of Continuous Time Models with an Application to the World Sugar Market." In W.C. Labys (ed.), *Quantitative Models of Commodity Markets.* Cambridge: Ballinger, 1975.

Zusman, P. "The Incorporation of Social Power in Economic Models." Department of Economics, Hebrew University, 1974. Mimeographed.

2 Commodity Market Modeling and the Simulation of Market Intervention: The Case of Coffee

Derek J. Ford

Introduction

This chapter explores aspects of modeling and simulating intervention in a world commodity market, with particular attention to the case of coffee. Important institutional and structural aspects of the production of coffee, the demand for it, and its international trade are outlined. On the basis of this foundation, a simple model of the world coffee market is developed. This simple model is designed to indicate the basic structure of the more detailed model then constructed. The detailed model takes account of more aspects of the market and is a more useful tool for discussing the simulation of market intervention. A brief account is given of historical intervention in the world coffee economy. Alternative ways of intervening in the world coffee market are discussed on an analytical basis, and the simulation of these alternatives is considered in detail in the context of the model that has been developed.

Institutional and Structural Aspects of the World Coffee Market

There are several important institutional and structural elements of the world coffee market that must be taken into account in the development of an adequate model of this market. Most of these are not unique to coffee but are applicable also in one way or another to the modeling of the markets for other agricultural crops. The details that are discussed here are those which are directly relevant to the modeling of the world coffee market, but the essential features are characteristic of other commodity markets as well.

On the supply side of the market, several factors are important in the development of a model of coffee. The first is the biological lag between the time that coffee trees are planted and the time that first harvests occur. The second is the asymmetric relationship between coffee prices and the stock of coffee trees. The third is the small proportion of total costs that are variable in the short run, and the implications this has on harvesting decisions. The fourth is the determinants of the yield of coffee per unit area of trees. The fifth is the distinction between the two different types of coffee trees; and the last is the different methods of processing ripe coffee cherries that are used in different coffee-producing areas.

Coffee trees are an important component of the capital stock involved in the production of coffee. For many agricultural crops, harvesting of output occurs within 12 months of the planting of the crop. For these crops, planting and harvesting decisions effectively occur within the same time period in the context of annual time intervals. In such cases, the modeling of the production of these commodities does not have to take into account the existence of a capital stock such as trees. The production of many other perennial agricultural commodities, though, is dependent on the stock of a resource such as trees or bushes. Examples of these commodities are as diverse as coffee, cocoa, tea, rubber, citrus and temperate tree fruits, nuts, and asparagus. In all these cases, decisions to expand the capital stock are made in response to the price and profit expectations held by producers in one period of time, but the expansions in output as a result of these decisions do not occur until several periods later. This lagged response of output to price changes that is an essential aspect of the production of these commodities has to be taken into account when they are modeled. In the case of coffee, the time lag between the planting of new trees and the first output ranges from two years in the case of the robusta variety to four years in the case of the arabica species. Mature yields are not obtained until a year later than this, though. So for coffee production there is an observed relationship between expansions in output and the increases in price that occurred three to six years earlier, depending upon the type of coffee trees that are predominant in different coffee producing areas of the world.

In contrast, though, if producers have pessimistic expectations about the long-term future course of coffee prices and costs of production, the tree stock can be reduced in a relatively short period of time. This implies that rapid declines in coffee prices can trigger reductions in the tree stock almost immediately. This observation, coupled with the necessary biological lag between planting and output expansion, implies that an asymmetric relationship between the stock of mature trees and the real price of coffee may be an essential element of the modeling of coffee production. Increases and decreases in real coffee prices of the same absolute size are expected to lead to impacts on the level of output after different lengths of time.

The importance of the tree stock in the production of coffee raises another aspect of the modeling of its production. The most important element of the overall cost of coffee production is the cost of the tree stock, which is fixed in the short run. Once an area of coffee trees is in existence, the variable costs of obtaining output are primarily associated with harvesting and plantation care. In many producing areas, relatively little attention is devoted to the tree stock, so that in the short run the major variable cost is the cost of harvesting.

Short-run output decisions are therefore based largely on the relationship between output prices received by producers for coffee and the labor costs associated with obtaining output from the existing stock of trees. Coffee prices have frequently been substantially greater than marginal harvesting costs.[1] This implies that for a given stock of coffee trees and a particular crop on those trees just prior to harvesting, the optimal response is to harvest the available crop. The upper bound on the yield of output is the physical crop on the stock of trees. It is rarely profitable to harvest at less than this rate, given the usual wide surplus of the marginal return to producers over the marginal cost of harvesting per unit of output. This has two implications for the modeling of the short-run yield of output. Implicitly, the price to producers may be taken as the primary determinant of the short-run response of output. Following the preceding analysis, though, it is expected that only a weak empirical relationship is likely to be found between current producers prices and the yield of coffee. For a given stock of trees, physical yield is determined by the two-year cycle and meteorological influences, and the optimal economic yield is the available physical yield itself.

The physical yield from a stock of mature trees is determined by four factors. The first of these is the age structure of the tree stock itself. Although some authors assert that the yield per tree declines substantially after about 10 years,[2] other evidence indicates that under appropriate conditions coffee trees can continue to bear economically fruitful yields for as long as 80 or even 100 years.[3] With such a life expectancy for coffee trees, it is expected that the age structure of the tree stock in a given area will change only slowly over time, and therefore the average yield per unit area of trees will change slowly in response to changes in the age structure of the tree stock. This implies that although the level of the average yield per unit area of trees is determined in part by the age structure of the tree stock, this is a slowly changing influence that, in the short run at least, is not an important element in determining variations in average yields.

Of much more importance is the biological two-year bearing cycle that affects arabica trees in particular, although it is relatively unimportant for robusta trees. It has been observed that arabica trees have a tendency to bear heavy and light crops in alternate years, which has given rise to the concept of "off" years and "on" years in the coffee-producing countries of Latin America.[4] The two-year cycle is not inevitably deterministic, though. Unusual weather can reduce output in what would have been an "on" year; unusually large yields might be obtained in the following year; and the aggregate effect over time would be an observed phase shift in the two-year cycle. Similarly, during periods in which new trees are reaching maturity, it is possible for these trees to come into production with a different phase from those already in production. Again there may be observed changes in the phasing of the aggregate two-year cycle. Whatever the exact reason for the alternately light and heavy crops, and for the occasional phase shifts that are observed in these cycles, they are sufficiently well-defined and empirically observed in arabica-producing areas that they must be taken into account when coffee production is explained.

The third set of factors that affect the physical yields of coffee trees are the meteorological influences. Excessive rain during the flowering of coffee trees reduces their productivity. Inadequate rainfall prior to the blossoming of arabica trees reduces their yields, and similar drought conditions between flowering and harvesting reduces the yields of all kinds of coffee trees. High winds, hurricanes, and hail storms also have an adverse effect on output. In frost-prone coffee-producing areas in southern Brazil, mild frosts can affect current productivity, and severe frosts can damage trees sufficiently that their future productivity is reduced almost to zero. In addition, inclement weather at the time that coffee cherries should be harvested can affect the picked yield from a given physical yield. This is not very important for the species of coffee trees that hold their cherries on the trees because harvesting can be done whenever the weather is appropriate. However, it is important in areas in which arabicas are the predominant type of trees, because arabicas drop their cherries shortly after they become ripe. Therefore, harvesting is limited to the relatively brief period between the ripening of the cherries and their falling off the trees. In this situation, bad weather can delay harvesting sufficiently that there are losses of the actual physical yield.

The fourth influence on the yield of coffee is the negative effect of the many organisms and insects that damage coffee trees and coffee cherries. Some of these can have a substantially deleterious effect on yields. The severity of the attacks of these various pests and the responses of producers in attempting to control their effects are important variable influences on coffee yields.

Although botanists recognize between 50 and 100 different species of coffee trees, two different kinds of trees account for over 99 percent of world production of coffee. The arabica species of trees is the predominant one planted in the Western Hemisphere. On the other hand, the robusta variety of the *Coffea canephora* species produces about 75 percent of output in Africa, Asia, and Oceania. There are many physical differences between arabica and robusta trees, such as their size; age to maturity; physical yields; responses to soil types, elevation, shade, and meteorological factors; and resistance to pests. Although these factors are important in accounting for differences in yields between different coffee-producing areas, the distinction between the two kinds of trees is more important on the consumption side of the world coffee market. Arabica coffee is processed and produces a desirable beverage. However, robusta coffee has an unpleasant taste when roasted, ground, and brewed. Consequently, arabica coffees have traditionally commanded higher prices than robustas because of this important taste difference when processed as ground coffee. Nevertheless, soluble coffee processors have been able to use robusta coffee just as well as arabica coffee to produce acceptable beverages; so the increasing acceptance of soluble coffee since the late 1940s has led to a relative expansion in the demand for robusta coffee.

In addition to the consumption distinction between the arabica and robusta coffees, there is one further important distinction in production. In Brazil, in particular, ripe coffee cherries are initially processed by spreading them in the sun so that the outer flesh is dried to a crisp husk. This husk is then hulled from the dried cherries to leave the coffee beans. In a few areas of Brazil, and in most of the remainder of Latin America, the picked cherries are pulped, fermented in vats of water, and the bulk of the outer flesh is removed before the beans are spread in the sun to dry. These two alternative methods of processing the cherries have given rise to the terms *unwashed arabicas* and *washed arabicas* respectively. Even though coffee may be grown on the same kinds of trees in different parts of Latin America, these two methods of processing the ripe cherries result in dried coffee beans that ultimately may produce coffee beverages of different qualities. Traditionally, therefore, Brazilian coffee has been lower priced than coffee from other parts of Latin America in recognition of this quality difference. In recent years, though, apparent improvements in quality control during processing in Brazil have led to a reduction in the share of unpleasant tasting coffee produced by the dry processing method, with a consequent disappearance of some of the traditional price differentials between Brazilian and other Latin American coffee.

All these elements are important institutional and structural factors on the supply side of the world coffee economy that have to be taken into account when this market is modeled. In addition, there are also factors on the demand side of the market that have to be taken into account. These affect both the demand for coffee and the structure of its international trade.

On the demand side of the market, the most important element to be recognized is the two ways in which coffee beverages can be made. Traditionally, the dried coffee beans have been roasted, and then the different kinds of roasted beans have been ground to varying degrees of fineness and blended. This ground coffee has then been used in a variety of ways to make coffee beverages. However, since the late 1940s, coffee processors have developed end-products of coffee that are instantly soluble in water. When this distinction between the two kinds of coffee end-products is combined with the fact that robusta coffee does not produce a desirable beverage in ground form but does in soluble form, the expansion in the demand for soluble coffee becomes an important element in the derived demand for different kinds of green coffee. In particular, this has led to an expansion in the relative demand for robusta coffee, which has led, in turn, to increases in its price relative to arabica coffee, and hence to later increases in its supply. The distinction in end-use between ground and soluble coffee is an important factor on the demand side of the world coffee market and must be incorporated in a model of this market.

The structure of the international trade of coffee has also been affected by the development and increasing acceptance of soluble coffee. Arabica coffee is grown in most of Latin America, whereas robusta coffee predominates in coffee-producing countries outside Latin America. The expansion in the demand for robusta coffee has led to expansions in output outside Latin America, primarily in Africa, and to increased shares of imports into consuming countries from the robusta-producing ones. In the past 30 years, Latin America has become a relatively less important supplier of coffee on the world market, and Africa has become increasingly more important.

Another aspect of structural importance is the breakdown on a world basis of the distribution of the production and consumption of coffee. Production is confined almost entirely to tropical countries in Latin America, Africa, Asia, and, to a minor degree, in Oceania. About 20 percent of world coffee production is consumed within the producing countries themselves. The remaining 80 percent enters international trade, and almost 90 percent of that is imported into the nonproducing countries in North America and Europe. The distinction between countries that are primarily coffee producers and those which are primarily coffee consumers also corresponds approximately to a distinction between developing and developed countries. Coffee is produced in tropical developing countries, and for some of these is of significant importance as a source of foreign exchange earnings. Coffee consumption, however, occurs largely in the developed countries. This geographical distinction between coffee-producing and coffee-consuming countries means that it is easier to identify the potential costs and benefits from market intervention in the world coffee market than in the markets for many other commodities. Briefly, these are the important structural aspects of the world coffee market that need to be recognized when considering the ways in which this market may be modeled.

An Aggregate Model of the World Coffee Market

A very simple model of the world coffee market is outlined in this section in order to clarify the theoretical basis of the more detailed relationships specified in the following section. The simple model is then restructured to take into account more institutional and structural detail of the world coffee market, to construct a more realistic model, and to incorporate the elements necessary to allow for the simulation of market intervention.

The logic of an aggregated model of the world coffee market is as follows. The world demand for coffee (C) is a function of the price of coffee (P), as well as other influences such as income (Y), population (N), and the prices of alternative commodities (PA). This demand function is

$$C = f(P; Y, N, PA, \ldots) \tag{2.1}$$

Two functions jointly determine the current level of coffee production (X). The productive area of coffee trees (A) depends on the area of trees in the previous period [$L(A)$] and also on a lag distribution of past real prices [$\phi(P/PA)$] to allow for both the impact of prices on new planting and the gestation period of several years between the time new trees are planted and the time they reach economic maturity. This area function depends only on predetermined variables and is

$$A = f[L(A), \phi(P/PA)] \tag{2.2a}$$

The yield of coffee per unit area of productive coffee trees (X/A) depends on the two-year botanical cycle ($D2$), meteorological influences, and possibly on prices just before harvest [$L(P)$]. Trends in productivity, the age and variety structure of the tree stock, agronomic practices, and so on are represented by a time trend (T). The yield function is then

$$X/A = f[D2, \text{weather}, L(P), T] \tag{2.2b}$$

Equations (2.2a) and (2.2b) taken together imply that current production is a function both of short-run and long-run influences, all of which are predetermined with respect to a current period of time. Thus:

$$X = f[L(P), \phi(P/PA), D2, \text{weather}, T] \tag{2.2}$$

The current supply of inventories (S_s) is determined through an identity by taking inventories in the previous period [$L(S)$], adding current production, and subtracting current demand. This is

$$S_s = L(S) + X - C \tag{2.3a}$$

The demand for inventories (S_d) is assumed to contain an activity component and a speculative component. The activity component is the result of the need to hold inventories in order to satisfy demand, and the level of demand for inventories for this purpose depends directly on the level of final demand for coffee. The speculative component is the result of attempts to minimize the impact of expected future price changes and depends on the relationship between future expected prices and current actual prices. The use of an adaptive adjustment mechanism for price expectations translates this causal influence into the relationship between current and past prices. Therefore, the inventory demand function is

$$S_d = f[C, P; L(P)] \tag{2.4a}$$

Setting the demand for inventories equal to the supply of inventories as an equilibrium condition and then renormalizing equation (2.4a) so that price is the dependent variable gives the following two equations.

$$S = L(S) + X - C \tag{2.3}$$

$$P = f[C, S; L(P)] \tag{2.4}$$

Equations (2.1) to (2.4) form a four-equation system with four endogenous variables C, X, S, and P. In principle, this simple system could be estimated and then solved for these four variables in terms of the predetermined variables it contains, which are the exogenous influences on both demand and supply, and the lagged endogenous variables contained in the system. However, this simple set of relationships cannot adequately capture enough detail of the world coffee market and is too simplistic to be useful for the purpose of policy simulations.

Further Disaggregation of the Structural Model

This simple model is less than adequate for the purpose of simulating intervention in the world coffee market. A model is needed with increased detail in two directions. A substantial degree of disaggregation is essential to capture adequately the responses of production, international trade, and demand to relevant influences. In addition, sufficient policy variables have to be included in the structure of the model to allow for the simulation of market intervention. These are the two considerations that are dominant in the specification developed in this section.

On the production side of the model, several fairly obvious reasons exist for disaggregating world coffee-producing areas. The first is the distinction between robusta and arabica coffee, which corresponds approximately to coffee production in Latin America and to that in other producing countries outside Latin America. The distinction between unwashed and washed arabicas corresponds to the production of coffee in Brazil and to that in other countries in Latin America. So any disaggregation on the production side of the model is first into three regions—Brazil, other Latin American countries, and non-Latin American countries. Further disaggregation is made by selecting important states within Brazil; treating Colombia, the second most important coffee-producing country, separately; and perhaps treating several of the other relatively important countries separately also.

The basic approach of explaining the production of coffee in two parts—in terms of the area of the tree stock and the yield per unit area—is regarded as the most satisfactory. In this way, the long-run influence of coffee prices on the level of output is captured through the influence on the stock of trees, and the short-run determinants of output are captured through their influence on the yield of coffee from the existing tree stock. The area of trees (A) is a function of the real farmers prices of coffee (PF/PA), lagged to allow for the botanical fact that there is a time lag between the planting of new coffee trees and the first economically significant harvest. Also, these functions would be specified in a nonlinear form that appropriately allows for asymmetric responses to changes in real producer prices of coffee and contains a partial adjustment mechanism to allow for the fact that the response of the actual area of trees to the desired area will not be instantaneous. In addition, appropriate variables (DU) can be included in the functions to allow for the deliberate intervention of administrative authorities in the stock of coffee trees. Therefore, a general functional relationship for explaining the area of coffee trees is

$$A = f[PF/PA \text{ lagged}, DU, L(A)] \tag{2.5}$$

The yield of coffee per unit area (X/A) is hypothesized to be a function of the two-year botanical cycle ($D2$); meteorological influences such as rainfall (WR), frosts (WF), and winds (WW); and possibly the economic influence of real farmers prices at the time of the coffee harvest. These are usually in the period preceding that in which the harvest reaches the world market. Some of these influences are captured using real variables; and others, by the inclusion of appropriate dummy variables. Slow changes in yields as a result of slow changes in the variety composition of the tree stock, the age structure of the tree stock, and agronomic practices may be captured by the inclusion of a time trend (T). Such yield functions are represented generally as

$$(X/A) = f[D2, WR, WF, L(PF/PA), T] \tag{2.6}$$

If the area of trees and the yield per unit area in a coffee-producing region are explained by equations (2.5) and (2.6), then the level of coffee production in any period is determined from the identity

$$X = (X/A) \cdot A \tag{2.7}$$

Since reliable time series data on the area of coffee trees are not available for many producing regions, the level of output in these cases must be specified to depend directly upon both the long-term influences on the tree stock and the short-term influences on the yield of coffee from the existing stock of trees. The output equations are then of the form

$$X = f[(PF/PA) \text{ lagged short and long}, DU, D2, WR, WF, WW, T] \tag{2.8}$$

The consumption of coffee (C) within a producing region may be treated either as an exogenous variable or as a function of the real domestic price of coffee (*PC/PG*), real income (*Y/PG*), population (*N*), and perhaps a time trend to capture slow shifts in consumption habits. In the latter case, the hypothesized relationship is of the form

$$C = f[(PC/PG); (Y/PG), N, T] \tag{2.9}$$

Exportable production (*XEX*) is then defined as the amount of coffee available for export out of current production. This is simply the difference between production and consumption and is determined through the identity

$$XEX = X - C \tag{2.10}$$

The change in the level of inventories of green coffee within a production region (ΔS) is the level of current exportable production less the quantity of coffee exported (*QEX*), less the quantity of coffee actually destroyed or otherwise removed from coffee inventories for nonusual reasons (*SD*), where appropriate. Thus:

$$\Delta S = XEX - QEX - SD \tag{2.11}$$

On the demand side of the model, there are several ways in which the coffee-consuming areas of the world can be disaggregated. The United States absorbs over one-third of world coffee imports and should be treated separately as the most important coffee-importing country. No other individual country imports more than 10 percent of world coffee imports, so regional aggregations of countries are most appropriate for the remainder of world demand. Europe absorbs approximately one-half of world imports and is a second consuming region. The remainder of the world importing countries together form a third consuming region. There are some empirical studies that have used a finer disaggregation scheme on the demand side of the world coffee market, but these have usually required reaggregation for the purpose of explaining international trade in coffee. Excessive disaggregation on the demand side of the overall model produces relatively little further information, since it has been shown that coffee demand in most countries is very inelastic with respect to price and income changes. So the most reasonable level of disaggregation on the demand side of the model is: the United States, Europe as a whole, and other coffee importing countries.

The following set of disaggregated relationships is appropriate for explaining the components of the demand for coffee in the United States. A more simplified set of relationships that relate directly to import demand have to be specified for other consuming regions for which adequate data are not available and for which aggregations of countries introduce such problems as the measurement of average price levels.

The consumer demand for coffee (strictly internal disappearance, as no data are available for levels of consumer inventories) is divided into the demand for regular coffee and the demand for soluble coffee. The consumer demand for regular coffee (*CR*) is hypothesized to depend on the usual influences that are postulated in conventional economic theory. These are: its own real price (*PCR/PG*), the real price of soluble coffee (*PCS/PG*), the real price of alternative beverages (*PCB/PG*), real income (*YPD/PG*), and population (*N*). This demand function is therefore written generally as

$$CR = f[(PCR/PG), (PCS/PG); (PCB/PG), (YPD/PG), N] \tag{2.12}$$

The demand for soluble coffee is explained in a slightly different manner. During the period from the late 1940s until the late 1960s, soluble coffee had a pattern of demand characteristic of that of a new commodity. Initially, soluble coffee was only a very small proportion of all coffee consumed. Its share of the market expanded rapidly during the 1950s, but the expansion slowed during the 1960s as per capita consumption in many countries trended toward apparent asymptotic ceilings. This typical diffusion of a new commodity is allowed for by specifying the demand for soluble coffee (*CS*) as a function of an appropriate S-shaped learning curve $[\theta(T)]$. Deviations of the observed consumption of soluble coffee from this fitted trend are hypothesized to be the effect of the usual economic influences. The demand function for soluble coffee is therefore

$$CS = f[\theta(T); (PCS/PG), (PCR/PG); (PCB/PG), (YPD/PG), N] \tag{2.13}$$

The demand for the two end-products is converted to the green-bean equivalent by multiplying regular coffee demand by the inverse of its estimated extraction rate from green beans (1.19 = 1/0.84) and by multiplying soluble coffee by the inverse of its corresponding variable extraction rate ($1/r$). The subtraction of the green-bean equivalent of the small quantities of net imports of the end-products (*QRIM, QSIM*) from the sum of the green-bean equivalent demand for soluble and regular coffee gives the total demand for the quantity of green beans for roasting (*R*) through the identity

$$R = 1.19 * CR + (1/r) * CS - QRIM - QSIM \tag{2.14}$$

The demand for inventories of green beans (*S*) in a consuming region is assumed to be price affected but not to have an impact on the world level of coffee prices. This is because, in most periods, the level of inventories held in consuming countries is a relatively small share of overall world inventories, most of which are held in producing countries. Also, the inventories in the consuming countries vary much less over time than do the inventories held in the producing countries. For these reasons, then, the demand for inventories in a consuming region is hypothesized to have a primary activity component, and perhaps a secondary speculative component. The activity demand for green-bean inventories depends on the demand for roasting. The speculative demand is represented by the ratio of current import prices to those in the preceding period [*PIM*/*L*(*PIM*)]. Since it is not expected that the actual level of inventories adjusts immediately to the desired level of inventories, the actual change in the level of inventories of green beans (ΔS) will be a function of the level of inventories held at the end of the preceding period [*L*(*S*)]. The complete function for the demand for inventories in a consuming region is therefore

$$\Delta S = f\,[R, PIM/L(PIM); L(S)] \tag{2.15}$$

The demand for imports of green beans (*QIM*) is the sum of the demand for roasting and the demand for inventories plus the small quantity of green beans exported without processing (*QGEX*). This identity is

$$QIM = R + \Delta S + QGEX \tag{2.16}$$

Effectively, then, the demand for coffee imports depends on coffee prices, with other variables providing additional explanation of demand. For those consumption regions for which data are available in appropriate detail, the model is three behavioral equations and two identities. For other consumption regions, the total demand for imports would be specified directly as a function of appropriate variables that enter the more detailed functions already outlined.

The shares of imports into a consuming region from each of the producing regions are hypothesized to depend on two sets of influences: the relative prices of coffee from each of the producing regions, and the share of consumer demand for coffee that is satisfied by soluble coffee. The relative prices of different types of coffee affect their import demand, since there is some substitution between types in response to relative price changes. In particular, washed and unwashed arabicas are at least partial substitutes for each other in regular coffee blends, and robustas and unwashed arabicas are substitutes in the production of soluble coffee. Similarly, increased demand for soluble coffee relative to that for regular coffee is expected to increase the import demand for robustas, decrease that of washed arabicas, and leave relatively unchanged that for unwashed arabicas. In addition, it is not expected that import shares adjust instantaneously, so current import shares depend on those in the previous period. Since these influences are hypothesized to affect the demand for imports into a consuming region from each producing region, it follows that the demand for exports from a particular producing region (*QEX*) depends on the relative prices of different types of coffee, the relative importance of soluble coffee, and world import demand for coffee (*QIMW*). These export demand functions for each producing region are then of the form

$$QEX = f(\text{relative prices, soluble coffee share, } QIMW;\ QEX \text{ lagged}) \quad (2.17)$$

The major remaining component of a model of the world coffee market is a price sector. All coffee prices tend to move very similarly over time, with some minor variations as a result of fluctuations in the flows to which particular prices refer. Two other important factors in the determination of coffee prices are the dominance of Brazil on the supply side of the world coffee economy and the price-affecting export quotas operated under the International Coffee Agreements during the period from 1963 to 1972.

The dominance of Brazil on the supply side of the world coffee market, coupled with the observation that all spot market prices move similarly over time, implies that attention should be focused on the price-affecting actions of administrative authorities in Brazil. The fact that the Brazilian authorities have intervened both internally and externally in the world coffee market suggests that Brazil should be treated as a dominant oligopolist. Many different policy tools have been used by the Brazilian authorities in attempts to affect coffee prices. Direct measures have included: buying coffee on the world market; export quotas; minimum export prices; sacrifice quotas; internal purchases of coffee; direct reduction of the physical supply of coffee by the destruction of a part of the domestic inventories of coffee; and taxation, both implicit, through the manipulation of exchange rates, and direct, levied on coffee itself. Indirect measures have included restrictions on the planting of coffee trees and, possibly, the manipulation of information. However, the goal of these policies has not been merely to allocate the current supply between demand and inventories so as to maximize the foreign exchange earnings from coffee exports. Other goals have included the provision of government revenue, the satisfaction of internal political pressures from coffee producers, and the orderly distribution of coffee from farms to export. The relative importance of these goals is likely to have varied over time.

In the face of a multiplicity of goals, as well as policy measures for which adequate information is not available, a simple hypothesis is made. It is hypothesized that the available supply of coffee in Brazil is a determining influence on the policies followed by Brazilian authorities and that these decisions in turn affect the market price of coffee in Brazil (*PBR*). It is expected that higher levels of exportable production (*XEX*) and larger existing inventories [$L(S)$] both lead to policy changes that have the effect of reducing coffee prices. The policy changes of Brazilian authorities in response to changes in the available supply of coffee are not necessarily expected to bring about an immediate response in prices. Therefore, the current market price of coffee in Brazil will also depend on its lagged price. These hypotheses give the following function:

$$PBR = f[XEX; L(S), L(PBR)] \tag{2.18}$$

It is hypothesized that, after a very short period of time, changes in the market price of coffee within Brazil are reflected in changes in the spot market price of Brazilian coffee in New York (*PMBR*). Other Brazilian influences in this price are the exchange rate between the Brazilian cruzeiro and the U.S. dollar (*ERBR*) and the Brazilian export tax rate (*TXEBR*). This key market price for coffee also depends on the available supply of coffee on the world market relative to the demand for it. The available supply is disaggregated into existing inventories of green beans in producing regions at the end of the previous period [*L*(*SW*)] and the current level of exportable production (*XEXW*), since there is substantial empirical evidence that equivalent increases in existing inventories and current exportable production do not have identical effects on coffee prices. The world demand for coffee is represented by the level of world imports (*QIMW*). In addition, the impact of the existence of the International Coffee Organization (ICO) can be allowed for by the use of a dummy variable (*DICA*), and the effect of the ICO export quotas (*QUW*) on prices also can be incorporated in the function. The relationship for the spot market price of Brazilian coffee is therefore

$$PMBR = f[PBR, XEXW, QIMW; ERBR, TXEBR, L(SW), DICA, QUW] \tag{2.19}$$

The spot market prices of coffee from the other producing regions are then determined by movements of *PMBR;* they are also affected by changes in the availability of coffee from that particular producing region, as represented by both current exportable production and the accumulated inventories of green beans at the beginning of the period. In addition, the selective adjustment of particular quotas by the ICO will also affect the price of coffee from that region. Therefore, the function for the spot market price of coffee from a non-Brazilian producing region (*PM*) is

$$PM = f[PMBR, XEX; L(S), QU] \tag{2.20}$$

A world spot market price for coffee (*PMW*) is defined by using the ICO formula currently used to calculate an overall indicator price. In this formula, the prices for coffee from Colombia (*PMCOL*) and other Latin American countries apart from Brazil and Colombia (*PMOLA*) are averaged. This average is then averaged together with prices for coffee from Brazil (*PMBR*) and non-Latin American countries (*PMNLA*). The resulting definitional identity is

$$PMW = [(PMCOL + PMOLA)/2 + PMBR + PMNLA]/3 \qquad (2.21)$$

The average price of coffee imported into a consuming region (*PIM*) is a simple function of the world market price:

$$PIM = f(PMW) \qquad (2.22)$$

The average price of coffee exported from a production zone (*PEX*), however, is specified as a function of the spot market price for coffee from that zone:

$$PEX = f(PM) \qquad (2.23)$$

Consumer coffee prices are hypothesized to depend on the market prices of the relevant types of coffee used in each of the end-products and on internal processing costs, which are represented by a general price index (*PG*). Then:

$$PR = f(PM \text{ washed and unwashed arabicas}; PG) \qquad (2.24)$$

$$PS = f(PM \text{ robusta and unwashed arabica}; PG) \qquad (2.25)$$

The price received by farmers (*PF*) in a producing region varies closely with the average export price of coffee, although in some cases allowance might have to be made for the fact that at times the manipulations of administrative authorities have caused internal prices received by producers to move differently from export and world market prices. In general, though,

$$PF = f(PEX) \qquad (2.26)$$

The supply, demand, and price relationships outlined include all the necessary stochastic functions for a model of the world coffee market. However, a few other identities are needed to close the structure of the model or as useful indicator variables or for policy simulation purposes.

World aggregates for exportable production, exports, imports, and inventories are derived through identities by summing appropriate variables across producing regions or consuming regions. The total revenue from coffee exports (*TRE*) from each producing region is the product of the quantity of coffee exported and the price per unit exported. Thus:

$$TRE = QEX * PEX \qquad (2.27)$$

Similarly, the total expenditure on coffee imported into each consuming region

(TRI) is given by the product of the quantity of coffee imported and the price per unit imported. Thus:

$$TRI = QIM * PIM \tag{2.28}$$

The world aggregate value of all coffee exported and the corresponding world aggregate value of all coffee imported are found by summing the respective individual values.

Historical Intervention in the World Coffee Market

Five important phases of intervention in the world coffee market have taken place prior to the present. These are the interventions by the Brazilian state of Sao Paulo from 1902 to 1930; the intervention by the Brazilian federal government from 1931 to 1937; the period of operation of the Inter-American Coffee Agreement from 1941 to 1945 during World War II; the informal arrangements between groups of coffee-producing countries from 1955 to 1961; and the operation of the International Coffee Agreements from 1962 until 1972. In each of these cases, the world coffee market was affected in some way either by the operations of the most important coffee-producing country, Brazil, or by arrangements effected by groups of countries.

At the turn of the century, almost three-quarters of world coffee production originated in Brazil, a large proportion of this in the state of Sao Paulo alone. Rapid expansion of the area of coffee trees led to a prohibition on planting in 1902 that lasted for 10 years. Forecasts of an exceptionally large crop for the 1906-1907 crop year led to coffee purchases on the world market in an attempt to forestall an anticipated serious decline in coffee prices. The intervention inventories so acquired were gradually released in succeeding years as coffee prices rose again. This first attempt at intervention by Sao Paulo affected the world coffee market in two ways. The expansion in output was effectively dampened by the prohibition on the planting of new coffee trees. The purchase of coffee on the world market and its storage for later disposal was the first large-scale attempt at removing existing coffee from the available supply on the world market. This was apparently at least a partially successful attempt at intervention that restrained a price decline that would have been even greater than that which did occur. The Sao Paulo authorities were apparently convinced of the success of this intervention and intervened on two more occasions in a similar manner. Purchase and storage of coffee were repeated when an exceptionally large crop was forecast for the 1917-1918 crop year, and again in 1920 when coffee prices fell rapidly during the postwar depression. In both cases, the intervention inventories were held within Brazil and were liquidated at later dates when coffee prices were rising again. In the early 1920s a new method of intervention was introduced, the control of the flow of coffee from the Brazilian interior to the ports of export. A substantial system of warehouses was constructed, and entries into these warehouses provided the basis for further control of the flow of the existing supply onto the world market. This system was expanded and broadened during the mid-1920s and provided the basis for withholding coffee from the world market during the bumper crop years of 1927-1928 and 1929-1930. Maintenance of price levels in the face of exceptionally large harvests created a situation that could not be continued indefinitely. The high prices on the world market were reflected in the high prices received by Brazilian producers; and, without any controls on production, the area of the tree stock continued to expand as a result of the optimistic expectations held by the Brazilian producers. The withholding of output from two bumper crops left the Sao Paulo authorities with exceptionally large inventories, with very little surplus warehouse capacity, and with large debts accumulated from the borrowing that financed the intervention schemes. All these factors, combined with the general fall in prices during the Great Depression, led to the inability of the Sao Paulo government to continue intervention policies beyond 1930. These were then taken over by the Brazilian federal government.

The second phase of major intervention in the world coffee market lasted from 1931 until 1937. The Brazilian federal government continued to regulate the supply of coffee available in Brazil for the world market; the planting of new coffee trees was again prohibited; and a third new feature was added to the existing controls: a part of the existing inventories of coffee was burned or otherwise removed from the existing supply. This last program was carried out on such a scale that from the time of its inception in mid-1931 until it apparently ended in 1944 the equivalent of approximately three years' worth of world consumption of coffee was deliberately destroyed. However, in the depression years these policies had only a marginal impact on coffee prices, since the size of the extremely large Brazilian inventories was widely known at that time. Several abortive attempts to obtain the cooperation of the other coffee-producing countries were made during the 1930s. In addition, other internal policy measures were introduced, such as sacrifice quotas based on the distribution of coffee to the ports of export, export taxes, and internal taxes on the movement of coffee.

By the late 1930s, two lessons had been learned from this phase of Brazilian market intervention. The first was that while the real costs of intervention were being borne within Brazil, other coffee-producing countries were benefiting from the Brazilian policies without having to bear any of the costs of those policies. The other lesson was that the Brazilian policies themselves were not particularly effective, and that any really effective policies of intervention would require international cooperation. The perception of these realities and the failure to obtain international cooperation led Brazil to abandon unilateral intervention programs in 1937, although the destruction of a part of the existing inventories was continued on a small scale for several more years.

The third phase of intervention in the world coffee market occurred during World War II. The wartime loss of the European markets to Latin American exporters in 1940 and apprehensions about the stability of the coffee market in North America led to a situation of cooperation among the Latin American producing countries. The Inter-American Coffee Agreement that went into effect early in 1941 provided for a system of export quotas into the U.S. market. This system was operative until the end of the war in 1945. Although the agreement was essentially an orderly marketing device that contained no provisions that affected prices, and was partly dependent on U.S. wartime benevolence in any case, it is important for two reasons. It was the first international agreement that had been achieved among coffee-producing countries. It was also innovative in that it included an important consuming country within the parties to the agreement.

A decline in the area of trees in Brazil, a series of poor harvests during the 1940s, the start of the recovery of European demand for coffee after World II, and the general postwar and Korean War inflation combined to produce a situation of relative undersupply of coffee and rising coffee prices. The pressures for market intervention disappeared and did not surface again until prices began to decline from an all-time high in mid-1954. A rapid expansion in the area of coffee trees in the early 1950s during the period of relatively high prices led to fears of a rapid expansion in output and a large fall in coffee prices in the late 1950s. This led to renewed attempts to reach international cooperation to forestall the decline in prices.

The fourth phase of market intervention lasted from 1955 until 1961 and consisted of relatively informal and ineffective marketing arrangements between various groups of coffee-producing countries. However, these agreements suffered from two deficiencies. They did not include all important coffee-producing countries or any coffee-importing countries, and the export quotas that were set proved to be too large to have any impact on the world market. In any case there were no provisions for the enforcement of the export quotas if some countries had chosen to ignore them. The quotas would only have been effective to the extent that individual producing countries chose to follow procedures to limit their own exports.

The fifth phase of intervention in the world coffee market lasted from 1962 until 1972. This was preceded by continuing declines in coffee prices after 1960, a new U.S. administration in 1960 that was more sympathetic to international commodity agreements than the previous one had been, and increasing interest on the part of more-developed coffee-importing countries in the problems of the less-developed countries. These factors all combined to produce a climate in which a broad-based agreement could be made that involved both coffee-producing countries and coffee-consuming countries. The International Coffee Agreement of 1962, and its successor of 1968, were joined by countries that produced about 99 percent of world coffee and consuming countries that absorbed about 96 percent of world imports of coffee. The agreement was therefore almost as broadly based as is conceivably possible. The most important aspect of these agreements was the formation and enforcement of a system of coffee export quotas. Signatory producing countries agreed to accept coffee shipped from signatory exporting countries only if accompanied by the appropriate certificates of origin or, later, the proper coffee export stamps, and to report levels of coffee imports to the International Coffee Organization that was created by the first agreement. Exports to certain importing countries designated "new markets" were exempt from the system, as were exports from producing countries to nonsignatory importing countries, and imports into consuming countries from nonsignatory producing countries. These exemptions from the import quota system were initially designed to accommodate the realities of the world market, although they allowed the development of what came to be known as "tourist coffee." This was coffee shipped from signatory producing countries to either new markets or to nonsignatory consuming countries and then reshipped to signatory importing countries without the original certificates of origin or export stamps. Along with the development of an export quota system came the development of a system of indicator prices. These were computed on a daily basis on the New York market for several broad classes of coffee. The export quotas were set in advance for each coffee year on the basis of negotiation and agreement. Within each coffee year the indicator prices were used in various ways to lead to adjustment of quotas on the basis of current market situations. Predetermined price floors and ceilings were agreed upon for each coffee year. If indicator prices remained below price floors for more than a given number of days continuously, the export quotas were reduced. However, whenever prices moved above the price ceilings for more than a certain length of time, the export quotas were increased. Thus the system was made responsive to market conditions in a way that had not been accomplished with the more restricted agreements prior to 1962. As the loophole provisions were worked out, the problems relating to international trade in soluble coffee were settled, and both the indicator price and export quota systems were continually refined, the agreement began to work reasonably well by the end of the 1960s. Coffee prices were relatively stable, at least by historical standards; there was a slow decumulation of inventories as a result of declines in production, particularly in Brazil; and there was a steady expansion in world demand for coffee. By the early 1970s, all these factors were producing a movement away from a situation of excessive supply toward one of relative equilibrium between production and consumption. This movement toward equilibrium was sharply disrupted by a series of frosts, droughts, and excessive rainfall in coffee-producing areas in

Brazil. Sharply reduced output in that country in both 1970-1971 and 1971-1972 led to upward pressure on coffee prices. With rapidly increasing coffee prices during 1971, some coffee-producing countries felt that they had more to gain by following independent policies than by belonging to the international agreement. This attitude was manifested in the disagreements over the quotas that were to be set for the 1972-1973 coffee year. Quotas were not agreed upon, and the economic provisions of the International Coffee Agreement effectively lapsed. At the same time, negotiations for a new agreement foundered on disagreements over basic quotas and policies to be followed. The 1968 agreement was extended in modified form without its economic provisions for two years in October 1973, and a new International Coffee Agreement signed in 1976 continues today. At the present time, the International Coffee Organization is basically a data gathering and disseminating agency, and there are no restrictions on the export of coffee. Indicator prices are still computed on a daily basis, and there is provision for the restriction of exports if prices fall below the average levels of 1975. However, with the decline in production in Brazil in recent years as a result of damaging frosts in several consecutive winters, a deficiency of production relative to consumption, and the near exhaustion of worldwide coffee inventories, it will be several years before this provision is implemented, if it ever is.

In a sense, the interventions in the world coffee market have moved full cycle during the past 60 years. Beginning with intervention by Sao Paulo from 1902 to 1930, followed by Brazilian federal intervention from 1931 to 1937, Latin American and U.S. cooperation during World War II, informal but increasingly more broadly based agreements among coffee-producing countries from 1955 to 1961, and a full-scale international export control scheme involving both producing and consuming countries from 1962 until 1972, the world coffee market has now moved back into an unregulated state, at least on an international level. Intervention presently is strictly unilateral, done according to the goals of particular national governments.

There are several methods of market intervention that stand out in this review of the historical experience of the world coffee market. Serious attempts to substantially affect the course of future output by restraining expansion of, or actually reducing, the stock of coffee trees have been made only in Brazil from 1902 to 1912, during the 1930s, and for five years in the mid-1960s. To the extent that in these periods Brazil produced a substantial share of world output, these programs were successful in dampening future output increases that would otherwise have occurred. However, they did not occur in the framework of international cooperation: in each case they left Brazil with a smaller share of world markets than at their inception, and they imposed both short-run and long-run real costs on Brazil while providing benefits to other coffee-producing countries as well as to Brazil. At the present time, with Brazilian production representing less than 30 percent of world output, such unilateral measures would be much less successful in stabilizing the future level of output and the course of coffee prices. Export restraint was a feature both of Brazilian programs prior to World War II and of the operation of the export quotas system under the International Coffee Agreements from 1962 until 1972. Historical experience has shown that controls on the available supply of coffee on the world market through controls on exports can have at least some impact on prices at a world level. However, this experience has shown, as might be expected from the general theory of cartels, that international cooperation in market intervention will last only as long as the cooperating parties expect to gain more from such cooperation than they would by acting independently. This means, in effect, that international cooperation in the world coffee market will succeed during times of relatively pessimistic expectations about the future course of prices but can be expected to be relatively weak during times in which optimistic expectations are held about the future. The final relevant aspect of the historical experience is that the accumulation of inventories by a particular producing country is not a long-run solution to the problems of output and price instability, but that the widespread accumulation of inventories in many producing countries is a feasible possibility if there is sufficient intent and cooperation to affect the world market.

There are other intervention methods used on a unilateral basis by less-important coffee-producing countries that have at least had impacts within those countries, even though their effects on the world coffee market have been negligible. Other countries in addition to Brazil have at times imposed restrictions on the expansion of the area of coffee trees. Export taxes and other internal taxes have been used not only to raise government revenue but also to restrict the flow of coffee exports. In many countries, government agencies have effectively held monopolistic powers at some level between the production of coffee at the farm level and its export. In such cases, it has usually been required that all production be sold to the government authority, which in turn has then regulated the outflows of coffee toward export. In these situations, the prices received by farmers have been effectively controlled, although it is unlikely that prices would move divergently from world levels for long periods of time. The reason for this assertion is that in times of rising world prices, internal political pressures from producers on the government authority are likely to lead to upward pressure on the prices farmers receive. In times of declining world prices for coffee, there will eventually be decisions made by these authorities to reduce prices paid to farmers, since the funds in the hands of such authorities are usually derived from sales of coffee, and continuous financial deficits are usually not an available option. All these methods of internal intervention are, at least in principle, possible on a cooperative basis if producing countries are convinced that the individual gains from such cooperation will at least be as great as the costs imposed by their application. For this reason, it is worthwhile to consider these policies, even though they have not been used on a widespread basis as part of international intervention in the world coffee market.

Simulating Market Intervention

The structure of the model as it is outlined allows for simulation experiments to analyze the effect of various forms of intervention in the world coffee market. Both national and international methods of intervention can be simulated, although there are some policies that cannot be dealt with using the model as described. Methods of national intervention that affect the world coffee market are first discussed, followed by those of an international nature.

The effects of some national policy measures on the whole world coffee market can be simulated with this model, although the lack of substantial historical experience with some of these procedures in the recent past makes the estimation of the sizes of their impacts rather difficult.

Perhaps the most easily simulated national control policy is restriction on the expansion of the area of coffee trees. This is a policy that has been used in some countries with apparent success, at least for moderately short periods of time. In the context of the model, a restriction on the expansion of the tree stock is easily simulated by treating the area of trees as an exogenous variable and keeping it fixed at a particular level during simulations. In this way, the influence of changes in coffee prices cannot affect the size of the tree stock. Simulated variations in output are the result only of the short-run influences on yields, without long-run changes taking place as a result of the impact of price variations on the tree stock.

Deliberate diversification programs that reduce the stock of coffee trees can also be simulated in the same way. The area of the tree stock is exogenized and divorced from the level of coffee prices. In this way, the stock of coffee trees can be reduced during simulation to observe the impact of diversification programs of various magnitudes, and also to observe the effect of this policy in combination with other market stabilization policies that might have the effect of increasing prices. This would be a particularly useful policy combination to simulate, since market stabilizing policies that also increase price levels tend, in the absence of controls on the expansion of the tree stock, to lead to expansions in the areas of trees, and in output, and hence increase the pressure and costs of the control programs.

Manipulations by national authorities of the internal prices received by coffee producers are also relatively easy to deal with. In some situations, producers prices have been controlled such that their movements over time have been dissimilar to world coffee price movements. Such price insulation is simulated by treating the appropriate farmers prices as exogenous variables that do not depend on world market prices. In this way it would be possible to investigate whether, during times of rising prices on the world market, national suppression of price increases at the farm level would be a satisfactory method of preventing expansions of the tree stock and hence future expansions of output that would then depress prices on the world market. Clearly this is a policy measure that is likely to be difficult to carry through in many countries for internal political reasons but that might in fact have long-term benefits if both internal political pressures could be resisted and if sufficient international cooperation between coffee-producing countries could be obtained to get coordination of national internal coffee policies.

Internal and export taxation of coffee is another national policy measure that is relatively easy to deal with in the context of this model. These taxes can be set to reduce producers prices below what they would otherwise be, while still allowing variations in export prices to have an impact on the farmers prices. Thus it would be possible to stabilize farmers prices by varying the rate of taxation on coffee, even in the face of fluctuating world market prices, and without having farmers prices necessarily divorced completely from world coffee price movements. At one extreme, simulations of this policy measure would be equivalent to the one already described, but other intermediate impacts on farmers prices could also be simulated.

There are several national control policies that are difficult to model. The minimum export prices set by Brazil have probably had the effect of restricting the outflow of coffee, although it is not clear that such price floors have had any substantial impact on world market prices, particularly in the context of annual time intervals. The other national policy tool that cannot be dealt with easily in the context of this model is internal restrictions on the flow of coffee from farms to export, and actual quantitative restrictions on exports. One way of dealing with these policies would be to adjust the level of exportable production to reflect divergences between the physically available supply of coffee in producing regions and the supply actually available to the world market. This would then have an impact on world coffee prices, and therefore on the demand for coffee, and the demand for exports from the producing regions in particular. An alternative way of incorporating export restrictions would be to exogenize the levels of exports and force total world imports to be equal to total world exports in an identity. In this way the usual iterative solution of the model would pick up the impact of export restrictions on world trade and on coffee inventories held in producing regions, although the short-run impact of such policies on prices would not be adequately captured.

The two major international methods of intervention in the world coffee market can be simulated in the context of the structure of this model, although neither simulation captures all the possible effects of these policies. An international system of export quotas can be simulated, at least indirectly, since historical experience with the operation of such a system under the aegis of the International Coffee Agreements allows this to be built into the specification of the model, as well as allowing estimates of its impact. Buffer stock manipulations can also be simulated, although the lack of historical experience in the world coffee market with this form of control requires that some assumptions be made that may not be entirely valid.

The influence of export quotas on market prices, such as in the period from 1963 until 1972 when the International Coffee Organization export quotas system was effectively in operation, is directly built into the specification of the model. Simulated changes in these quotas would have an impact on prices, which in turn affect the demand for coffee and, hence, the demand for coffee exports from producing regions. A slightly more complicated but superior method of simulating the impact of an international export quota system would be to introduce two changes into the system for comparison with the control solutions. On the one hand, the impact of the quotas on prices would operate as already outlined. In addition, coffee exports would be set at quota levels, and world imports of coffee would be forced to equal world exports of coffee. During simulation, this constraint on coffee imports would have a reverse feedback impact on prices, so in iterations toward model solution the export quotas would have a direct effect on prices through the key price relationships and a more indirect effect on prices through the restraint placed on coffee demand.

Two aspects of the ICO export quotas system are not built into the model. The indicator prices were allowed to move freely within prescribed ranges; but when they passed above ceilings or below floors for more than a given number of days, the export quotas were either reduced or increased respectively. This aspect of the system is not built into the model because both the price floors and ceilings were revised intermittently by a process of negotiation between participant countries. The quota adjustments were the result of ICO executive decisions; the quota changes are almost imperceptible in the context of annual time intervals; and the details of the length of the trigger periods were changed from year to year during the operation of the system. Even so, the simulation of the impact of quota changes is possible by directly changing the exogenous quota variables, although the actual operation of the quota system had a rather complicated method for determining quota adjustments. The other aspect of the ICO export quotas system that is not modeled is the direct effect of the export quotas on the level of exports. Here the modeling was not done because there is only weak evidence that, at an annual level at least, the export quotas affected the levels of coffee that were actually exported, although the movements of exports from non-Brazilian coffee-producing countries did follow the export quotas somewhat more closely than did those from Brazil. Unilateral Brazilian policies may, in fact, have had a substantially greater impact on the course of prices during this period than did the operation of the ICO export quotas system.

With two qualifications that are discussed below, buffer stock manipulation can be easily simulated. Entries into buffer stocks can be treated as equivalent to reductions in exportable production, and vice versa. These movements would directly affect the world market price of coffee and, hence, all components of the model. For example, a decision to increase the size of the buffer stock would be simulated by removing the amount of the increase from exportable production. This would increase the key market prices, which in turn would increase other prices within the system, reduce the demand for coffee, and reduce the demand for exports from producing zones. Increases in prices would also occur at the farm level, so output in future periods would be increased unless other policy measures were incorporated within the simulation to prevent it. One addition that would have to be made to the model would be a function for the cost of holding coffee in the buffer stocks. Since this method of market intervention has not been used on an international level in the world coffee market, such a function would be hypothetical and could not be estimated on the basis of past information. There is yet another complication with buffer stocks that would be difficult to deal with. The size of the buffer stock would be known to those who operate in the market. As the size of the buffer stock increases to very high levels, there would likely be speculative downward pressure on prices, since there would be some upper limit to the size of the buffer stock that the controlling authorities would be willing to carry. Similarly, a decline in the size of the buffer stock to very low levels would likely induce additional speculative upward movements in prices if it were widely believed that the buffer stock would soon be depleted. Therefore, both extremely small and extremely large buffer stock sizes might trigger price movements beyond those likely to occur during periods of "normal" buffer stocks. These changes would be more difficult to capture during simulation than the impact of buffer stock movements at what are more normal buffer stock levels.

The impact of market intervention in the world coffee economy on both the less-developed countries (LDCs) and the developed countries (DCs) is relatively easy to determine, at least in an approximate way. World coffee production takes place almost entirely in the LDCs. However, approximately 95 percent of coffee consumption outside these producing countries occurs in the DCs. The division of the world into coffee-producing and coffee-consuming countries very closely approximates LDC and DC interests respectively in the world coffee economy. Changes in the revenues generated by coffee exports will give an indication of the impact of policy changes on the LDCs. Similarly, changes in the import expenditures on coffee will give a measure of part of the impact of market intervention on the DCs. For producing regions that are modeled in finer detail, a further measure of impacts can be derived by observing the changes in revenue obtained by coffee farmers, the main group within these economies that will be directly affected by market intervention. For consuming regions that are modeled with relatively more detail, the corresponding impacts can be obtained by observing the changes that occur in consumer expenditures on coffee. Hence the natural division of the world into producing and consuming regions and the amount of detail built into the structure of the model together allow for direct measurement of the impact of market intervention on both the LDCs and the DCs.

A final comment on the use of simulation in the context of this model to investigate intervention in the world coffee market: stochastic simulation can be used in the determination of whether or not market intervention schemes can provide a stabilizing influence on the world coffee market. In these cases the pertinent comparisons would be those between the cyclic behavior of the system under the assumption of no intervention compared with the behavior in situations in which market intervention is simulated. It would be hoped that such a comparison would show that it is likely that market intervention can have a positive effect of stabilizing the fluctuations in the world coffee market. Otherwise, at least a part of the rationale for intervention will not be supported on the basis of the empirical evidence provided by the model.

Notes

1. This assertion is borne out by several empirical studies of the relationship between short-run costs and returns for coffee producers. An early study by Rowe (1932:41–45, 88–89), based on data obtained in Sao Paulo, Brazil, showed that for a normal crop year plantation costs that were fixed in the short run were estimated to make up 75 percent of the total costs of production. Variable costs comprised only 25 percent of the total cost of production, which included allowances for the capital funds invested in plantations. These estimates were based on the 1926–1927 crop year, in which producers received a return that covered approximately the full cost of production including implicit returns to capital. However, with only one-quarter of these costs being variable in the short run, it is not surprising that the comparison of returns to short-run costs led producers to feel that they were very well off at the time.

2. See Wellman (1961:345–351), for example, for a summary of several of these studies.

3. See Rowe (1932:77, 88); and Wellman (1961:337).

4. Wellman (1961:357–360) rationalizes the two-year cycle in terms of relative exhaustion of the tree stock during years of heavy yields, followed by light crops in the following years when the trees recover and revive after the previous heavy crops.

References

Rowe, J.W.F. (1932) *Brazilian Coffee.* Royal Economic Society Memorandum No. 34, Studies in the Artificial Control of Raw Material Supplies No. 3. London, Royal Economic Society.

Wellman, F.L. (1961) *Coffee: Botany, Cultivation, and Utilization.* London: Leonard Hill.

3 International Rice Buffer Stock Operations: A Simulation Study

Olarn Chaipravat

Introduction

The objectives of this study are: (1) to make stochastic simulations of the world rice markets and resulting world prices of rice during a 20-year period from 1978 to 1997, (2) to estimate possible sizes and resource requirements of the international rice buffer stock operations in order to stabilize the world price within given ranges around its long-term, normal trend, and (3) to assess profitability of the international buffer stock operations at various rates of interest and other charges.

Analytical Framework

Annual World Rice Price Formation

An econometric model of the world rice market was constructed and used by the Bank of Thailand for its forecasting and policy simulation purposes. The conceptual scheme and empirical results of this model were described in two previous reports–*Aggregate Structures of Production and Domestic Demand for Rice in Thailand, A Time Series Analysis, 1951-1973*[1] and "An Econometric Model of World Rice Markets."[2] The annual model is a straightforward demand-supply interaction with the world price of rice as the equilibrating factor.[3] The domestic demand (*DD*) for rice in each country is divided into the consumption demand (*DU*) that is used up in any one year and the stock building demand (ΔST) by private traders during the year. The total domestic demand equation, therefore, depends on a common set of variables for each country: population (*N*), real income (*RY*), domestic price of rice relative to the cost of living index (*PR*/*CPI*), carryover stock at beginning of the year (ST_{-1}), differ-

The author is grateful to various staff members of the Department of Economic Research, Bank of Thailand for their statistical and computer programming assistance, especially to Mr. Sayan Pariwat and Mrs. Sunet Ratanawanit.

ence between expected future price (EPR) and current price (PR) of rice, and a disturbance term:

$$DD_t^i = DU_t^i + \Delta ST_t^i = f(N_t^i, RY_t^i, PR_t^i/CPI_t^i, ST_{t-1}^i, EPR_{t/t+1}^i - PR_t^i, \mu_t^i)$$
$$i = 1, 2, 3, \ldots, n \tag{3.1}$$

(The superscript i represents each country; the subscript t represents each year; and μ is the disturbance term.)

Rice outputs in individual countries and, collectively, world production are exogenously determined for the most part by weather conditions during the production period and subsequently marketed in the following calendar year. It is assumed, therefore, that the current market price of rice has no influence on the amount of output being marketed during the current year.[4]

The world rice markets are in equilibrium when total world output or supply ($\sum_i Q_{t-1/t}^i$) is equal to total world domestic demand:

$$WQ_{t-1/t} = \sum_{i=1}^{n} Q_{t-1/t}^i = \sum_{i=1}^{n} DD_t^i = WDD_t \tag{3.2}$$

With a further assumption that speculators form their opinions regarding future prices on the basis of the "adaptive expectations" hypothesis, the expected price of rice can be expressed as a function of current and past prices. Substituting all domestic demand equations from (3.1) in (3.2) yields one global equilibrium condition that is in terms of rice outputs, populations, real incomes, cost of living indices, carryover stocks, past years' prices, and current domestic prices of rice of all countries. All these variables except current prices can be treated as exogenous. Only current domestic prices are to be solved as endogenous variables.

Since there are n domestic prices (PR_t^i) to be solved, we must add n additional equations of domestic price relationships with the "world price" (XPR_t^{TH}).

$$PR_t^i = \rho_t^i(XPR_t^{TH} + MM_t^i)$$
$$i = 1, 2, \ldots, n \tag{3.3}$$

XPR_t^{TH} is the world price as measured by the export price of Thai rice in U.S. dollars per ton. Gross markups (MM_t^i) can be taken as exogenous, representing transportation costs, trade margins, and export or import taxes, while exchange rates (ρ_t^i) expressed in terms of domestic currencies per U.S. dollar are policy instruments of individual countries.

Substituting n equations of PR_t^i from (3.3) into the global equilibrium condition yields a single equation of the following form (omitting random disturbances):

$$XPR_t^{TH} = f(N_t^i, RY_t^i, CPI_t^i, ST_{t-1}^i, PR_{t-j}^i, Q_{t-1/t}^i, \rho_t^i, MM_t^i)$$
$$j = 1, 2, \ldots, m$$
$$i = 1, 2, \ldots, n \tag{3.4}$$

Since all righthand side variables of (3.4) are exogenous or policy instruments, the world price of rice (XPR_t^{TH}) can be determined. Substituting the solved value of XPR_t^{TH} into each of the n equations from (3.3) yields equilibrium values of n domestic rice prices in individual countries (PR_t^i). Substituting each value of PR_t^i in the domestic demand equation (3.1) for each country yields the value of domestic demand (DD_t^i) of that country. Once the value of DD_t^i is determined, together with the known value of domestic output ($Q_{t-1/t}^i$), X_t^i, which represents the volume of net exports (+) or net imports (-) of each country, can be solved from the following identity:

$$X_t^i = Q_{t-1/t}^i - DD_t^i \tag{3.5}$$

The values of world price, domestic prices, and export or import volumes of rice for all countries are therefore solved simultaneously from this model, once the values of such exogenous and policy variables as populations, incomes, cost of living indices, past years' prices, carryover stocks, outputs, exchange rates, transportation costs, and export or import taxes of individual countries are specified.

Long-Term Price Simulation

Under the assumption that, except for the annual weather-induced disturbance term (ν), world rice output (WQ) tends to grow exponentially at a constant rate (g), future values of world rice output can be deterministically or stochastically generated from the following equation:

$$WQ_{t-1/t} = Ae^{g(t-1)} \cdot \nu_{t-1} \tag{3.6}$$

or

$$\ln WQ_{t-1/t} = \ln A + g(t-1) + \ln \nu_{t-1}$$

The deterministic simulation is made when the disturbance term ν_{t-1} is assumed to be unit ($\ln \nu_{t-1}$ being zero); while in the stochastic simulation, ν_{t-1} or $\ln \nu_{t-1}$ is allowed to take on different values of randomly selected numbers. In this study the random numbers for future periods will be selected from in-sample residual values of the least squares estimate of equation (3.6).

If world rice output grows smoothly at rate g in the future, a long-term trend of the "normal" world price of rice can be generated for any set of assumptions regarding changes in exogenous variables: population, income, cost of living index, carryover stock, exchange rate, transportation cost, trade margin, export or import taxes, etc. If, on the other hand, world output is allowed to fluctuate around its long-term trend by using randomly selected values for the disturbance term $\ln \nu_{t-1}$, then different intertemporal patterns of world price can be generated for the same set of exogenous variables. These stochastically generated patterns of world price movements will be used in order to determine resource requirements and profitability of the international rice buffer stock operations.

International Buffer Stock Operations

An international rice buffer stock authority can be created with a given amount of financial and other resources. The primary function of this buffer stock authority would be to stabilize future world prices of rice within a given range. If the *free market price* threatens to dip lower or rise higher than the *target price range,* the authority would intervene in the free markets by purchasing or selling a sufficient amount of rice into or from its own stock to keep the market price (so-called intervention price) within the target range. If the free market price is within the target range, no intervention is required.

It is obvious that unless the target price range is set around the "normal" or "natural" price line generated deterministically from equation (3.6), the buffer stock operations will not be neutral in the sense that the authority will eventually run out of its rice stock or accumulate an ever-increasing surplus depending on whether or not the price target is set at lower or higher than the normal level. It is assumed in this chapter that the buffer stock authority always sets its price target at the normal world price.

The authority can vary the size of its target price range, e.g., ±5 percent of the normal price. In this way minimum and maximum price targets will be adopted by the authority in its operations. The narrower the target price range, the higher are resource requirements for the buffer stock authority.

Minimum Beginning Stock and Financial Requirement. It is necessary for the authority to start with a minimum stock of its own rice in order to ensure that if a drought should occur in the very first years of its operations that threatens to push free market price above the maximum price target, it will have some rice to sell in order to force the intervention price to be within the target range. I shall attempt to estimate minimum sizes of this beginning stock and the implied financial requirement (or debt) of the authority under different degrees of confidence that the buffer stock authority does not run out of its rice stock during the simulated period.

Maximum Credit Need. For a given size of initial buffer stock, the authority will subsequently buy or sell rice on its own account in order to stabilize the world price. The year-end stock and outstanding debt to finance this stock will fluctuate from year to year. It will be useful to estimate the highest value of such a debt in order to negotiate for a maximum credit line that will be adequate to carry the necessary stock when an extremely large purchase must be made.

Profitability of Buffer Stock Operations. The buffer stock operations are judged to be profitable if, after having paid all interest, storage, and other charges, the market values of carryover stocks generally exceed the outstanding values of total debt obligations. If it so desires, the buffer stock authority can actually try to realize this profit by selling an extra amount of its stock for cash. Such a sale will depress the market price until the new value of remaining stock is equal to the amount of existing debt. This profit-taking activity will interfere with the price-stabilization function of the authority and should not be done until after it has been decided that the buffer stock operations will be discontinued. If the interest and other charges are relatively high, it is possible that market values of existing stocks are always lower than outstanding debts. In this case, the international buffer stock operations are said to be not profitable and cannot be maintained indefinitely. This critical rate of interest and other charges can be ascertained from the stochastic buffer stock simulations.

Formal Relationships of Buffer Stock Simulations

Let the time horizon of the buffer stock operations be T years and the initial stock at the beginning of the first year be BST_0. The normal world rice output in each year ($NWQ_{t-1/t}$) is generated from the following equation:

$$NWQ_{t-1/t} = Ae^{g(t-1)}$$

$$t = 1, 2, \ldots, T$$

or

$$\ln NWQ_{t-1/t} = \ln A + g(t-1) \tag{3.7}$$

For each $NWQ_{t-1/t}$, the normal world price of rice ($NXPR_t^{TH}$) is generated using equations (3.1), (3.2), and (3.3), together with assumed values of the exogenous variables. The target price range is defined by the lower ($LXPR_t^{TH}$) and upper ($UXPR_t^{TH}$) target prices:

$$LXPR_t^{TH} - UXPR_t^{TH} = NXPR_t^{TH} \pm m \cdot NXPR_t^{TH} = (1 \pm m)NXPR_t^{TH}$$
$$t = 1, 2, \ldots, T \qquad (3.8)$$

where m is the desirable price margin.

Actual world rice output in each year is generated from the following equation:

$$WQ_{t-1/t} = Ae^{g(t-1)} \cdot v_{t-1}$$

or

$$\ln WQ_{t-1/t} = \ln A + g(t-1) + \ln v_{t-1} \qquad (3.9)$$

Values of $\ln v_{t-1}$ are drawn randomly from a set of historically estimated residuals of the least squares regression equation (3.9). For each $WQ_{t-1/t}$ a free market world price of rice ($FXPR_t^{TH}$) is generated in the same way as the normal world price. This free market price is then compared with the target price range in order to determine the amount of buffer stock operation ($BSTO_t$) during the year.[5]

$$\begin{array}{llr} \text{If } FXPR_t^{TH} < LXPR_t^{TH} \text{ then} & BSTO_t > 0 & \\ \text{If } LXPR_t^{TH} \leqslant FXPR_t^{TH} \leqslant UXPR_t^{TH} \text{ then} & BSTO_t = 0 & (3.10) \\ \text{If } FXPR_t^{TH} > UXPR_t^{TH} \text{ then} & BSTO_t < 0 & \end{array}$$

The buffer stock operation ($BSTO_t$) is equivalent to an extra increase or reduction in total world demand for rice by the international buffer stock agency. The global demand-supply equilibrium condition will be changed from (3.2) into the following equation:

$$WQ_{t-1/t} = \sum_{i=1}^{n} DD_t^i + BSTO_t = WDD_t \qquad (3.11)$$

For this new equilibrium equation the value of the intervention world price ($IXPR_t^{TH}$) can be solved by using equations (3.1), (3.11) and (3.3), and the same values of exogenous variables. The intervention world price will be within the target price range ($LXPR_t^{TH} - UXPR_t^{TH}$):

$$\begin{array}{llr} \text{If } BSTO_t > 0 \text{ then} & IXPR_t^{TH} = LXPR_t^{TH} & \\ \text{If } BSTO_t = 0 \text{ then} & LXPR_t^{TH} \leqslant IXPR_t^{TH} = FXPR_t^{TH} \leqslant UXPR_t^{TH} & (3.12) \\ \text{If } BSTO_t < 0 \text{ then} & IXPR_t^{TH} = UXPR_t^{TH} & \end{array}$$

Starting with the initial stock of BST_0, carryover stock at the end of year t is

$$BST_t = BST_{t-1} + BSTO_t \qquad t = 1, 2, \ldots, T \tag{3.13}$$

If the initial stock BST_0 is purchased at a special price of $SXPR^{TH}$, the initial debt of the buffer stock authority ($DEBT_0$) is

$$DEBT_0 = SXPR^{TH} \cdot BST_0 \tag{3.14}$$

If annual interest and other charges amount to a proportion r of existing debt, total interest and other charges during the year ($INTC_t$) are equal to:

$$INTC_t = r \cdot DEBT_{t-1} \tag{3.15}$$

Since the buffer stock purchase or sale is carried out at the intervention price, current value of such operation ($BSTP_t$) is

$$BSTP_t = IXPR_t^{TH} \cdot BSTO_t \tag{3.16}$$

Total expenditure by the buffer stock authority during year t ($BSTX_t$) is

$$BSTX_t = BSTP_t + INTC_t \tag{3.17}$$

Outstanding debt at the end of each year ($DEBT_t$) is equal to the value of carry-over debt plus total expenditure during the year:

$$DEBT_t = DEBT_{t-1} + BSTX_t \qquad t = 1, 2, \ldots, T \tag{3.18}$$

If the year-end buffer stock is evaluated at the current intervention price, the value of such a stock ($VBST_t$) is

$$VBST_t = BST_t \cdot IXPR_t^{TH} \tag{3.19}$$

Imputed profit at the end of each year ($PBST_t$) is

$$PBST_t = VBST_t - DEBT_t \tag{3.20}$$

The minimum values of the initial buffer stock ($\min BST_0$) and the initial debt

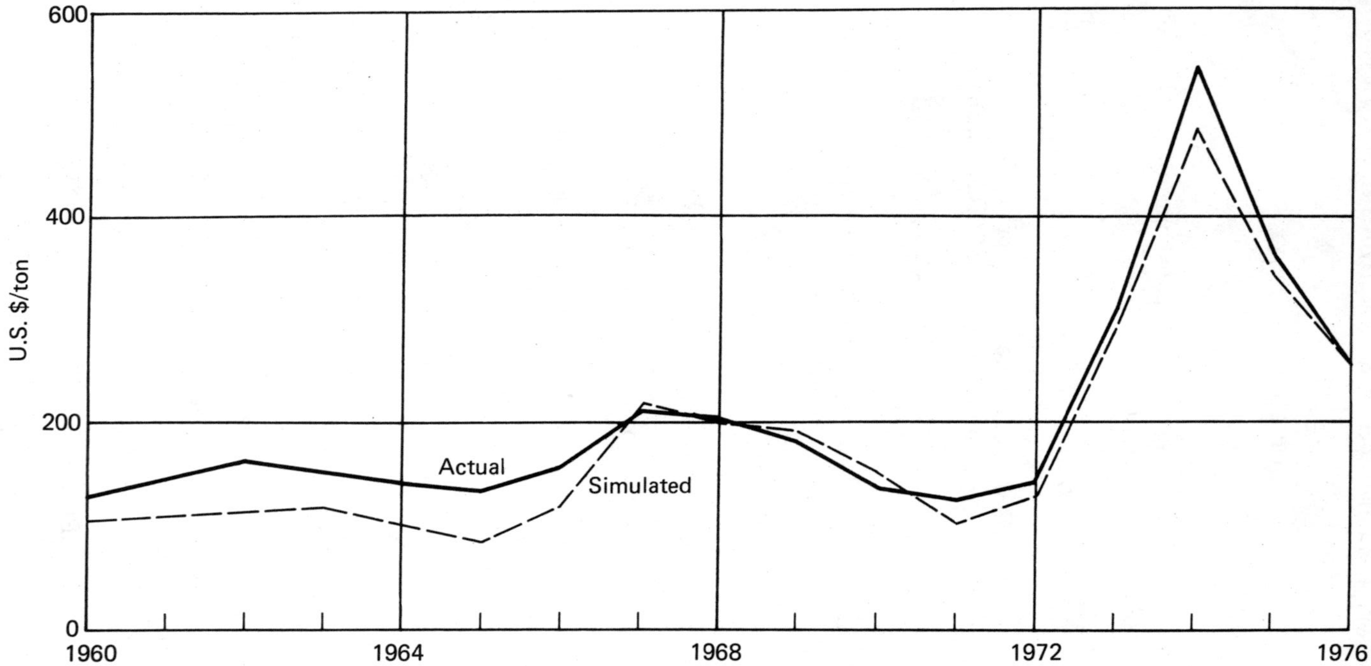

Figure 3-1. Simulated and Actual Values of World Rice Price, 1960–1976 (5 Percent Thai White Rice, F.O.B. Bangkok).

($\min DEBT_0$) required to ensure that the authority will not run out of its own stock during the T years of its lifetime can be estimated by using stochastically generated simulation results. The maximum credit need ($\max DEBT_t$) and profitability ($PBST_t$) of the buffer stock operations can be similarly ascertained from the same set of simulation results.

Historical Simulations

Using actual values of world rice output[6] and other exogenous variables, simulated values of the world price are obtained for the 17-year period from 1960-1976.[7] The simulated values are plotted together with their actual values in Figure 3-1. In view of the extremely volatile nature of world price fluctuations, the model seems to track actual movements of the export price of 5 percent Thai white rice, f.o.b. Bangkok, reasonably well. Major turning points during the 1966-1971 and 1972-1976 cycles are adequately captured by the model even though the percentage difference between the actual and simulated values in the sample period is still large. The mean absolute percentage error (MAPE) of the world rice price simulation for the 1960-1976 period is about 12.7 percent.

It should be noted that sudden jumps in the world price occurred in 1967 and 1973, the marketing periods following the drought-stricken years of 1966 and 1972, when world rice output was lower than its normal trend by about 5.9 and 5.4 percent respectively. Except for 1974, when the oil shock and resulting worldwide inflation generated an extremely strong demand-pull tendency on the world price of rice, intertemporal movements in the world price seem to have been caused mainly by weather-induced shifts in the world rice output. This conclusion is further supported by the fact that the total world demand for rice is very price inelastic. The magnitude of this elasticity was estimated to be about -0.1 in 1976.[8] Since the supply curve is perfectly inelastic and the demand curve is very price inelastic, a small shift of the supply curve will result in a relatively large change in the equilibrium world price. I will therefore attempt to generate future fluctuations in the world price by stochastically inducing shifts in the future world rice output.

The world rice output fluctuated around its trend value during the past 20 years. Using data from 1956-1975, the following ordinary least squares equation was estimated:

$$\ln WQ_{t-1/t} = 10.94836 + 0.02364\,(t-1) \qquad (3.21)$$
$$(21.813)$$

$$R^2 = .9615 \qquad SE = .0279 \qquad DW = 2.0515$$

The two largest negative residuals occurred in the most severe drought years of 1966 and 1972. The values of these 20-year historical residuals are used as the shock numbers to be randomly selected without replacement for future 20-year-period (1977–1978 through 1996–1997) stochastic simulations of world rice output and price. Unless there is a widespread and fast adoption of high-yielding technology and modern cultivation practices by traditional rice farmers in most developing countries, the future world rice output is likely to grow in the long run at the rate of about 2.364 percent a year. Year-to-year variations in output around this trend line will be generated by the randomly selected weather disturbances.

Simulation Results

All simulations are performed under the same set of assumptions regarding changes in values of the exogenous and policy variables.

1. Population (N_t) in each country grows at the same annual rate as that observed during the years 1970–1973. Collectively, total population in about 83 countries covered in our study grows at the average annual rate of about 2.1 percent.

2. Real income (RY_t) in most countries is assumed to grow at constant annual rates of 6 to 7 percent, except for Malaysia, in which the real annual growth rate is 8.5 percent.

3. The domestic inflation rate as measured by the change in the cost of living index (CPI_t) is assumed to be 5 percent a year for most countries, except Japan, South Korea, the United Kingdom, Portugal, Spain, and Yugoslavia, in which past records suggest that the annual inflation rate should be somewhat higher than the assumed worldwide rate of 5 percent. The inflation rate in Argentina is assumed to be 30 percent a year, while that of relatively stable Malaysia is 3 percent.

4. For countries with a 5 percent inflation rate, it is assumed that their exchange rates (ρ_t) in terms of the U.S. dollar will remain the same as in 1976. For countries with higher rates of inflation, their currencies are assumed to be devalued relative to the U.S. dollar by the same percentage as the excess of their inflation rates over the 5 percent benchmark. No revaluation is assumed for the Malaysian currency, however.

5. Gross markups (MM_t) are assumed to remain the same as those actually observed in 1976, except for Japan, in which this markup is allowed to increase at the annual rate of 3 percent to reflect the Japanese government's policy of continuously raising its domestic price of paddy to preserve the real income of farmers.

6. Once the international buffer stock is created, it is reasonable to assume that individual countries' carryover stocks in the hands of private traders are

always at their normal working levels. For Japan, this normal carryover stock is assumed to grow at the annual rate of 3 percent.

7. For countries in which none of the independent variables can explain the domestic demand for rice, this demand is assumed to grow at the annual rate of 2.5 percent from its most recently observed actual value.

8. The United States will try to reduce its excessive carryover stock of 1 million tons of milled rice by exporting half this amount in 1977 and the other half in 1978 in addition to the amount of regular exportable surplus resulting from its annual production and domestic consumption.

9. The annual domestic demand for all residual countries is assumed to be equal to the 1971-1975 average of 4.4 million tons of paddy equivalents during the entire simulation period.

10. The world price of rice is estimated to be U.S.$297.50 a ton in 1977.

Normal World Rice Output and Price

Deterministically simulated values of normal world rice output over the period 1977-1978 through 1996-1997 show an increase at the annual rate of 2.364 percent from 351.506 million tons of paddy in 1977-1978 to 550.070 million tons in 1996-1997. The resulting world price also increases from $375.50 in 1978 to $1006.60 a ton in 1997. The annual rate of price increase is relatively fast in early years but tends to slow down in later periods. Taking the initial and terminal years of 1978 and 1997, the average annual rate of price increase amounts to only 5.35 percent. With the assumed worldwide annual inflation rate of 5 percent, the long-term real price of rice hardly changes at all during the future 20-year period.

Controlled Simulation of World Output and Price

In order to give a preliminary picture of year-to-year world price fluctuations around the normal trend line, a controlled simulation is made under the assumption that the intertemporal pattern of weather-induced random shocks on world output during the future 20-year period will be identical with the observed pattern during the past 20 years.[9] The same 20-year sequence of historically estimated residuals ($\ln \nu_{t-1}$) is imposed on the future world rice output projection. Figures 3-2 and 3-3 show simulated annual fluctuations of world rice output and price around their normal trend values during 1977-1978 through 1996-1997. It should be noted that the degree of variation in output is less than that in price. For 1987-1988, in which the shocked output is about 5.85 percent lower than its trend value, the simulated price is about 18.0 percent higher than its normal value.

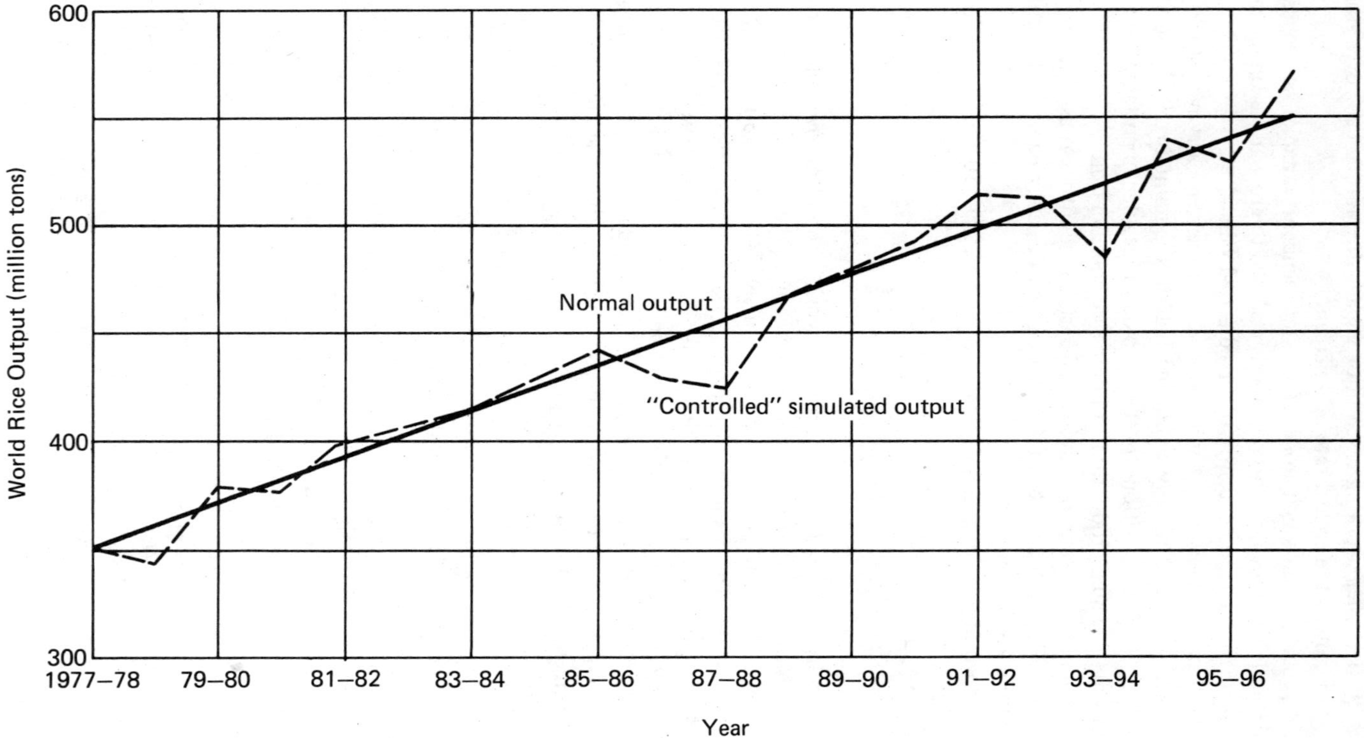

Figure 3-2. Controlled Simulation of World Rice Output Fluctuations around Its Normal Value, 1977-1978 through 1996-1997.

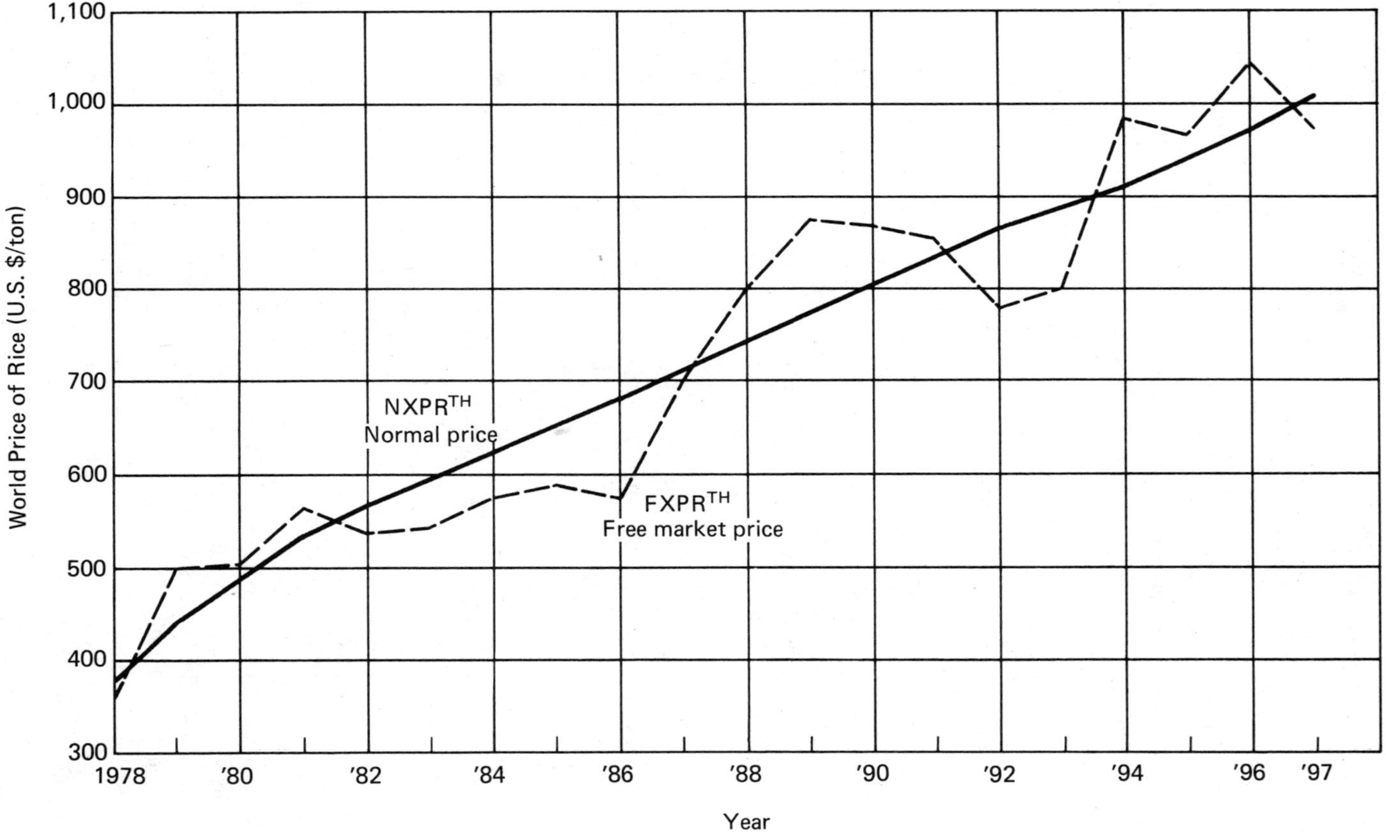

Figure 3–3. Controlled Simulation of World Rice Price Fluctuations around Its Normal Value, 1978–1997.

Stochastic Simulations of Output and Price

Thirty different sets of stochastic simulations were generated for the 1977–1978 through 1996–1997 period. Twenty values of historical residuals ($\ln v_{t-1}$) from the 1956–1957 through 1975–1976 sample period were drawn randomly without replacement to represent annual weather disturbances on world rice output during the future 20-year period. The average values of stochastically simulated output and price for each year are relatively close to their simulated normal values.

Minimum Initial Buffer Stock and Financial Requirement

Based on the 30 sets of stochastic simulations and a further assumption that the desired price margin and annual interest rate are 7.5 percent (m and r equal to 0.075), nonnegative values of minimum beginning stocks (min BST_{1977}) were calculated in such a way that for each simulation none of the year-end stocks during the 20-year period was negative (i.e., the buffer stock authority is not allowed to experience a shortage of its own rice when a relatively large sale is required; see Figure 3-4).[10] The sample mean of these minimum stocks is 27.73 million tons, and the standard deviation is 28.48 million tons of paddy equivalents. Under the assumption that the required minimum sizes of this beginning stock are normally distributed with the calculated mean and standard deviation, confidence levels can be attached to different values of the proposed initial stock. For example, if the beginning stock is at least 3.81 million tons of paddy equivalents, we are 20 percent confident that the authority will not run out of its stock in any one year of the 20-year period. In order to gain higher degrees of confidence, a larger size of beginning stock is required.

In order to estimate the minimum financial resources needed to start the buffer stock operations, it is assumed that the authority will negotiate to "transfer" parts of the existing stocks from individual countries and use them as the beginning international buffer stock. In order not to disturb the free markets, a fair price must be multilaterally negotiated. In our simulations we assume that the normal price of rice for 1978 ($373.50 a ton) is used to transfer the required stocks.[11] To be 20 percent confident that the authority will not run out of its own stock during the 20-year period, at least $938.7 million are needed to finance the initial stock of 3.81 million tons of paddy equivalents, or 2.51 million tons of milled rice. If we want to be at least 50 percent certain, the required initial financial resource increases to about $6.837 billion in order to finance 27.73 million tons of paddy equivalents, or about 18.30 million tons of milled rice.

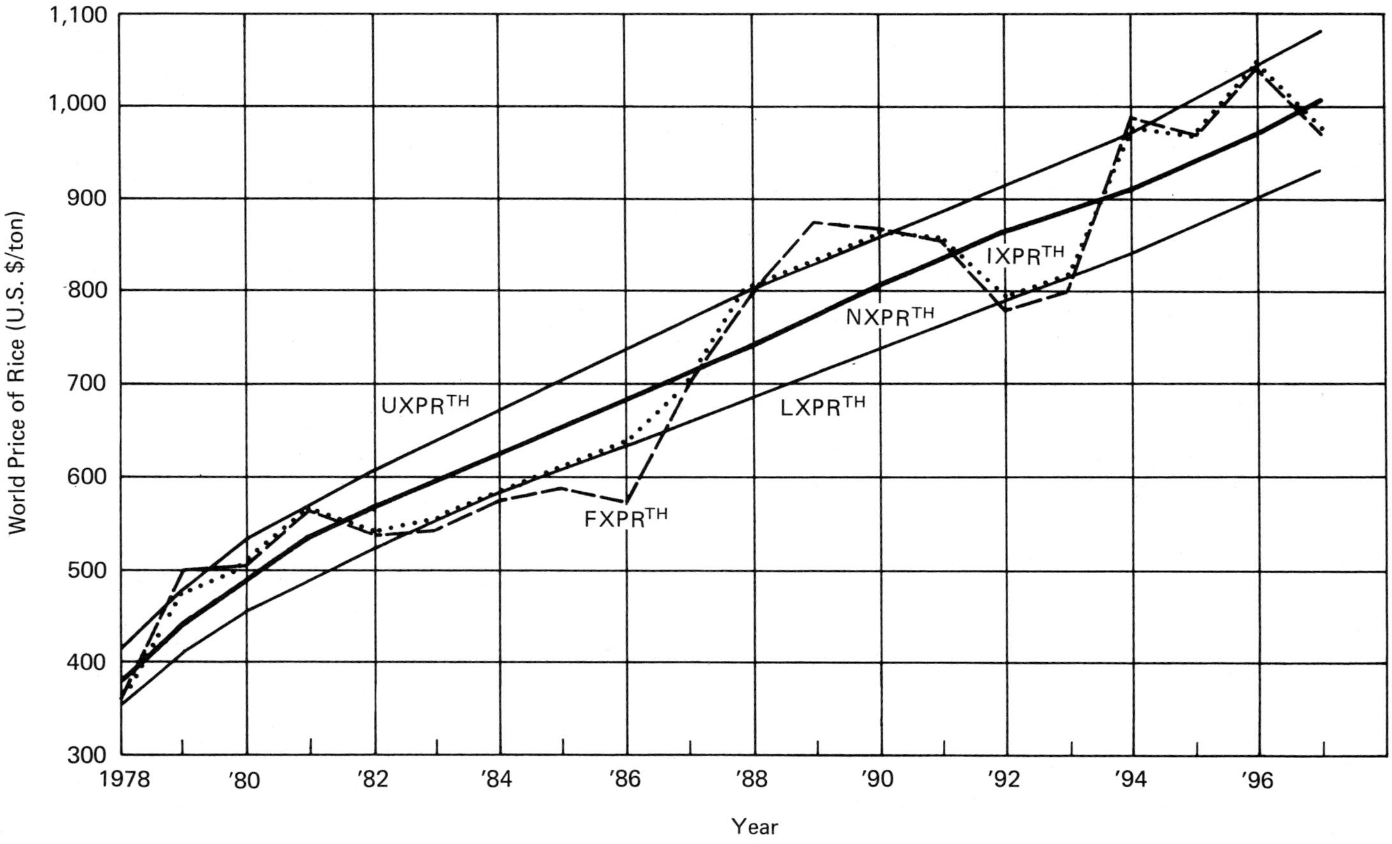

Figure 3–4. Controlled Simulation of International Buffer Stock Operations to Stabilize World Price of Rice within 7.5 Percent Margin around Its Normal Value, 1978–1997.

Maximum Credit Need

For any year in which the authority has to purchase a large amount of rice in order to stabilize the world price within a given range, a large amount of accumulated surplus must be maintained at the end of that year. It is necessary for the authority to negotiate for a maximum credit line in order to have adequate resources to finance this large carryover stock. This maximum credit requirement can occur in any one year depending on particular intertemporal patterns of weather-induced disturbances on output. If a credit ceiling of $20.07 billion can be negotiated by the authority, we are 20 percent confident that this amount of credit will be enough to finance the largest accumulated stock that might be required in at least one of the future 20 years. If the credit ceiling is raised, the chance will be higher that the buffer stock operations will not be interrupted for lack of financial resources. In order to be at least 90 percent confident that the authority will have enough money to cover unusually large purchases, a maximum credit line of $51.68 billion is required.

Combining the minimum initial debt and the maximum credit line, which together will ensure success of the buffer stock operations, it can be concluded that at least $10.49 billion to $40.42 billion must be actually used or committed to assure a 70 percent probability of success for the 20-year buffer stock program. If only $0.94 billion to $20.07 billion are authorized, the probability of success will be reduced to about 20 percent. It is clear that even with a relatively wide price margin of 7.5 percent around its normal value and a reasonably low interest rate of 7.5 percent a year, the size of financial requirements for successful operations of the buffer stock authority is quite substantial compared with the volume and value of world rice trade.[12]

Profitability of Buffer Stock Operations

If profitability is assessed at the end of the 20-year period, an imputed market value of the remaining stock is compared with the amount of oustanding debt at the end of 1997. If the imputed value is higher than the outstanding debt, the buffer stock operations are said to be profitable. With the 7.5 percent annual interest rate, the buffer stock program does not seem to be profitable. There is a 70 percent chance that the buffer stock authority will suffer a loss after its 20-year operations. The probability of making some positive profit is only 30 percent. This is to be expected in view of the fact that without any random shock on world rice output, the long-term normal price of rice tends to increase at the average annual rate of only 5.35 percent, while the annual interest charge is assumed to be 7.5 percent during 1978-1997.

Sensitivity Analysis of Profitability and Resource Requirement

If the annual interest rate is reduced to 5 percent and all other assumptions are kept unchanged, the maximum credit need is reduced for a given confidence level that the operations are successful. The chance of making some positive profit at the end of the 20-year period is also increased from about 30 percent in the first case to about 95 percent in this case. It is fairly reasonable to state, therefore, that if adequate resources can be provided at a 5 percent annual interest rate,[13] the international buffer stock operations will not only be successful but also profitable, in the sense that the authority will be able to pay for all interest and other costs and have some imputed profit left at the end of the 20-year period.

Conclusion

The world rice model is used to generate stochastic international buffer stock simulations under the assumption that the relative magnitude of weather-induced random disturbances on future world rice output will be roughly the same as that of the past 20 years, even though exact intertemporal sequences of these shocks are allowed to vary. Without the buffer stock arrangement, the world price of rice will fluctuate rather wildly around its long-term normal value depending on the particular sequences of the random shocks. The international buffer stock authority can be established with a minimum initial stock of its own rice in order to make sure that it will not run out of accumulated stock in the early years of its operations. With an adequate amount of beginning stock and the implied financial resource requirement, the authority must be provided with a maximum credit facility in order to assure that it will not run out of funds when unusually large purchases of rice are necessary. Once adequate volumes of minimum initial fund and maximum credit line are provided or committed, the buffer stock authority will be assured of success in its stabilization activities. Although the operations are successful, the authority may suffer a loss at the end of its stipulated lifetime if the rate of interest on borrowed funds, storage, and other charges are too high compared with the "natural" or normal rate of world price increase. Adequate financial resources at relatively low interest rates are therefore necessary to implement successful and profitable international buffer stock operations.

Based on a reasonable set of assumptions regarding changes in values of the determinants of worldwide demand for rice, e.g., 5 percent world annual inflation rate, 2.1 percent world population growth rate, 6 to 7 percent annual growth in real income, together with the stated assumption regarding weather-induced shocks on world rice output, it is estimated that at least $12.75 billion to $46.36 billion of financial resources at 5 percent annual interest rate are needed to assure a 70 percent chance of successful and profitable operations of the international buffer stock authority in its efforts to stabilize the world price of rice within a 5 percent margin around its normal value during the 20-year period 1978–1997.

The size of required financial resources is relatively large compared with the value of annual international rice trade, which in 1976 amounted to about $2.5 billion. These resource requirements are not, however, prohibitively large compared with the total volume and value of world rice output. This is because a relatively small share of world rice output is traded internationally. In 1976 the total volume of the world trade in rice accounted for only 4.0 to 4.5 percent of the annual world production of this crop. Other factors, such as world food security, welfare of a large segment of the world population who produce and/or consume rice, balance of payments instability of both exporting and importing countries, and so on, must be taken into consideration in trying to assess the desirability and feasibility of the international rice buffer stock arrangement. In any case, a reasonable rate of increase in the normal world price of rice (i.e., about 5.35 percent per year) will also assure that if the required financial resources, however large, can be provided at about a 5 percent annual rate of interest and other charges, the buffer stock operations will be successful in achieving the stabilization objective and at the same time profitable enough to pay for the interest and other costs.

Notes

1. Olarn Chaipravat, Bank of Thailand Paper No. 4, Bangkok, April 1975.

2. Olarn Chaipravat and Sayan Pariwat, in *Proceedings of the Second Pacific Basin Central Bank Conference on Econometric Modeling,* Bank of Korea, Seoul, June 8-11, 1976, forthcoming.

3. The export price of 5 percent Thai white rice, f.o.b. Bangkok, is used as the world price, since it is the most widely quoted price in the world rice markets.

4. This assumption is justifiable when the objective is to make a forecast of the current market price of rice. Once the multiperiod simulation is attempted, the effects of lagged price variables on production responses should be taken into consideration. However, some studies, including my own, indicate that in the case of Thailand the rice planted area response to lagged price changes is quite inelastic and the price elasticity is much lower than those of other cash crops. See Jere R. Behrman, *Supply Response in Underdeveloped Agriculture, A Case Study of Four Major Annual Crops in Thailand, 1937–1963,* Amsterdam: North-Holland, 1968; and Olarn Chaipravat, *Aggregate Structures of Production and Domestic Demand for Rice in Thailand,* p. 2.

Subsequent results of our long-term simulations should therefore be viewed within the context of this restrictive assumption. The supply block will be improved when the necessary data become available.

5. If a purchase is made, $BSTO_t$ is positive; if a sale, $BSTO_t$ is negative; if there is no intervention, $BSTO_t$ is zero.

6. By January of year t in which we want to make the price forecast, the world rice output ($WQ_{t-1/t}$) can be estimated with a reasonable degree of accuracy.

7. For 1976, estimated values of most exogenous variables are still preliminary.

8. Olarn Chaipravat and Sayan Pariwat, "An Econometric Model of World Rice Markets."

9. This is often referred to as the "sunspot" assumption because there seem to be relatively regular cycles of weather disturbances with severe droughts occurring overy 4-6 years, e.g., 1966-1967 and 1972-1973.

10. Figure 3-4 shows, as an example, simulated and calculated values of normal ($NXPR^{TH}$), lower ($LXPR^{TH}$), upper ($UXPR^{TH}$), free market ($FXPR^{TH}$), and intervention ($IXPR^{TH}$) world prices for the "controlled" or "sunspot" simulation with the assumed target of 7.5 percent price margin around its normal value. Other simulations are generated in the same fashion.

11. The conversion ratio of 0.66 ton of milled rice for 1 ton of paddy is used in our calculations. For simplicity, all milled rice is evaluated at the world price (5 percent white rice, f.o.b. Bangkok), where in fact there are many grades of rice with different prices.

12. The annual world trade in 1976 is estimated to be about 9-10 million tons of milled rice or about \$2.25 billion to \$2.50 billion.

13. This 5 percent rate includes storage and other charges as well.

4 Primary Commodity Markets in a World Model System

F. Gerard Adams

The phenomena of inflation, recession, burgeoning foreign exchange earnings in some countries, and extraordinary foreign debt burdens in others evidence the spectrum of the impact of primary commodity price movements on the world economies in recent years. Current proposals for market stabilization cannot be fully evaluated without considering the direct and indirect impacts of commodity market conditions. Yet we lack an integrated empirical framework in which commodity policy alternatives can be examined and their worldwide impact traced. Since markets for primary commodities are transnational, their behavior and their effects are unlikely to be captured either in individual country models or even in a system of country models like Project LINK.[1] This represents a serious omission.

The purpose of the work described in this chapter is to integrate the process of price determination in primary commodity markets into a world model system. Econometric models of the principal commodities in international trade (excluding, for the present, petroleum) are tied into the LINK system to make commodity prices endogenous and to feed them to producer-country export prices, to consumer-country import prices, and into the domestic economies of developed and developing countries. This work represents the first experiments with full feedback integration of commodity models into LINK, creating a merged system of commodity and country models that will be referred to as COMLINK.

The Mechanism of COMLINK

In principle, international trade in primary commodities may be considered simply as another way to classify trade flows—in place of broad aggregates by Standard International Trade Classification (SITC) category measured in dollars, we may consider trade of particular commodities, like coffee, in terms of bags

P. Tinakorn, J. Gana, C. Weinberg, J. Gajda, F. Sterbenz, B. Sellekaerts and others assisted in this research. Lawrence Klein, V.K. Sastry, J. Gomez, K. Ruffing, and other members of LINK greatly influenced this project.

or of another appropriate physical measure. If trade statistics and commodity shipment numbers can be reconciled, one approach to integration of commodity models with models of world trade would be to build up the import and export flows from the commodity trade flows as projected by the commodity statistics, particularly for broad categories like SITC 0 + 1 and 2 + 4, which are made up of a variety of commodities.[2] Moreover, commodity trade information is not typically generated by commodity models; they are concerned with overall production and consumption rather than with imports and exports. For these reasons the focus of COMLINK is on commodity prices, providing an endogenous explanation for these prices and introducing them into a linked system of country models.

The components of the system are:

1. The LINK country models and their trade flow interrelations.
2. The commodity models.
3. The linkages between country models and commodity models and between commodity models and country models.

The LINK Country Model System

The LINK system consists of 13 country models plus models for the developing regions and for the socialist bloc.[3] The models vary greatly in size from the United States model, which contains more than 200 endogenous variables, to the model for France, which has less than 20 endogenous variables. Most of the models for the developed countries fall into the traditional Keynesian mold. Each of them includes the typical final demand-output-employment-income mechanism. There is an endogenous explanation of imports in relation to domestic demand and domestic prices relative to foreign prices; and in some models, there is also an endogenous explanation for exports as a function of world trade and export prices relative to world prices.

With regard to commodity prices, the problem is the price determination mechanism. Most of the country models explain prices, frequently including export prices, in relation to domestic costs and market conditions. For products for domestic markets, and perhaps also for exports of manufactures, this may be a reasonably accurate treatment. But in the case of primary commodities, where worldwide markets frequently exist for homogeneous products, such an approach would miss the essentials of the price determination process. For these commodities, price setting is related to demand and supply on the entire world market.[4] Both exporters and importers must accept the world market price, although through monopoly, monopsony, or national or international price stabilization agencies they may have substantial influence over its determination. We must recognize, moreover, that there are numerous instances of intervention, so that prices actually received by producers or paid by consumers may not correspond to those prevailing on free world markets. In any case, it is necessary in COMLINK to override the export price determination mechanism in the country models.

The important developing countries bloc is treated in LINK with a model of the regions of the developing world, DEVE, prepared by UNCTAD.[5] The DEVE model treats eight regions of the world separately, providing a geographic breakdown by continent as well as a breakdown between oil-producing regions and those which are not oil producers. Income determination in the DEVE model is supply constrained, with emphasis on the available capital stock, investment, and imports. Finally, imports are determined by export earnings, net capital transfers, and reserves. This model has been constructed to provide maximum linkage to world primary commodity prices—38 individual commodity prices. In all cases the respective UN commodity export price indexes are used. These are translated by regression equations into unit value indexes for SITC categories. These price indexes enter into the determination of each region's export unit values and into the value of the regions' export earnings.

The country models are linked together through trade flows for four categories of trade: SITC 0 + 1, food and raw materials; SITC 2 + 4, industrial and intermediate materials; SITC 3, fuel; and the broad category of SITC 5-9, comprising manufactures. The linkage between the different country models is through the import and export flows and through import and export prices.

Imports are determined in the individual country models, but in LINK the country export equations are overruled. Exports are determined by an empirical mechanism that translates import demand into exports at the country level.[6] Similarly, export prices are determined in the country models and are then translated in LINK as appropriately weighted averages into import prices for the importing countries. In addition, a number of direct country-to-country relationships appear in some of the country models, but such ties are not central to the LINK mechanism.

The LINK solution procedure involves an initial so-called pre-LINK solution of each of the country models individually. Beginning at this point, the linkage mechanism replaces the country model explanations of exports and of import prices, and solutions proceed iteratively. Each country model is solved in turn, new figures for exports and for import prices are computed, and a new round of solutions is carried out. A consistent solution for all the models is reached when the total of world imports is reconciled with world exports, and when each of the country models has reached convergence.[7]

The COMLINK Commodity Models

Altogether 23 commodity models for 30 commodities have been integrated into COMLINK. A list of these models and their sources is presented in Table

Table 4–1
Commodity Models Integrated into the LINK System

Commodity	*Source of the Model*	*Type of Model*[a]	*Size of Model: Number of Endogenous Variables*
Coffee	Adams-Behrman[c]	C,I	6
Cocoa	Adams-Behrman[c]	C,I	6
Tea	Adams-Behrman[c]	C,I	6
Cotton	Adams-Behrman[c]	C,I	8
Wool	Adams-Behrman[c]	C,I	8
Wheat	Adams-Behrman[c]	C,I	9
Rice	Adams-Behrman[c]	C,I	8
Sugar	Adams-Behrman[c]	C,I	8
Fats and Oils[b]	Adams[d]	C,NI	27
Copper	Adams[e]	C,I	30
Nickel	Adams[f]	M,NI	23
Iron Ore	Klein[g]	C,I	35
Rubber	Behrman[h]	C,NI	3
Tin	Behrman[h]	C,NI	2
Leather	Behrman[h]	C,NI	2
Tobacco	Behrman[h]	C,NI	2
Maize	Behrman[h]	C,NI	2
Bauxite	Behrman[h]	C,NI	2
Hides	Behrman[h]	C,NI	2
Jute	Behrman[h]	C,NI	2
Sisal	Behrman[h]	C,NI	2
Bananas	Behrman[h]	C,NI	2
Beef	Behrman[h]	C,NI	2

[a]Type of model: C = competitive market; M = monopolistic market; I = including inventory stocks; NI = not including inventories.

[b]Including separate values for coconut oil, palm kernel oil, palm oil, groundnut oil, soybean oil, animal fats and oils, and linseed oil.

[c]Adams-Behrman (1976).

[d]Adams (1975).

[e]Adams (1973).

[f]Adams (1974).

[g]Klein (1975).

[h]Behrman (1975).

4–1. While the models vary considerably with regard to size and complexity, they fall into the common pattern of many recent econometric models of commodity markets.[8] In terms of structure, the models are differentiated principally by whether or not inventories have been considered. In one case, there is concern also for monopoly structure of the market, but in general the models assume competitive markets. They differ in terms of aggregation largely by whether they show detail on a country-by-country basis or whether they aggregate consumption and/or production on a regional or world basis. The majority of these models have been specially constructed for integration into

LINK, call for simple input variables drawn from the LINK country models, and produce estimates directly of the United Nations commodity export price indexes.[9]

The lag structures built into the models give them rich dynamic response characteristics. A shock on the supply side, such as a sharp reduction of output as a result of a drought, will affect inventories and price. The response of demand and of supply will be spread over time, so that a readjustment may take several years affecting all sides of the market. Changes in demand, such as those associated with the business cycle or with stockpile purchases, will also set off a series of adjustments. While most of the models display dynamic characteristics, there are considerable differences among them in the process of adjustment, the degree of price response, and the length of time required for readjustment.[10] In most cases, however, the models describe well the historical movement of supply, demand, and price.

The COMLINK Linkages

Country Models to Commodity Models

In principle, the linkage from country models to commodity models is quite simple. The demand equations of the typical commodity models already embody linkages to economic conditions in the consuming countries, in the form of industrial activity, consumption or income, and domestic prices. On the supply side, the commodity market models depend on the country models only for a general price index.

In practice, the reconciliation of input variables specified by the commodity models and those available from the country models in LINK poses some difficulties. In some instances, particularly in the case of the Adams/Behrman and the Behrman commodity models that were designed for use in the LINK system, only aggregation is required.[11] These models use GDP for developed, developing, and socialist countries and OECD deflators as inputs drawn from the country models. In other cases it has been necessary to construct a series of linkage equations that translate "country" variables into the specific input variables called for by the commodity models, e.g., the industrial production indexes that enter the copper and nickel models.

This is strictly a one-way linkage. Since there is no feedback in this part of the system, the commodity models simply project forecasts for commodities in line with the LINK country forecasts. A solution of the LINK country model system permits solution of the commodity models as a sort of "postrecursive" block.

From Commodity Prices to Export Prices

In order to accomplish the feedbacks of commodity prices into the country models, we first translate commodity prices into export prices. The issue arises since the commodity market models compute prices for individual commodities—either prevailing world market prices or, in the case of the models designed for LINK, the United Nations world export price indexes for primary materials. The LINK country models for developed economies, however, deal only with broader categories—the unit value indexes for SITC 0 + 1, SITC 2 + 4, and SITC 3.

Drawing on the commodity prices, we override the mechanism that determines export prices for these categories in the developed-country models. In some of these, the export prices are simply exogenous. In others, there are export price equations, not all of them, perhaps, solidly based on economic logic. For primary commodities in agriculture, energy, and metals, there is generally a prevailing world market price. While export sales are not all at this price, movements over time of the prices of different varieties are likely to follow this common pattern. Consequently, we assume that the movement of the world price is dominant. What is required at this point is a linkage between the commodity prices and the country export unit value indexes, for example,

$$PX_{ij} = f(\Sigma w_{ijk} P_k)$$

where PX_{ij} is the export unit value index for SITC i in country j, and w_{ijk} is the weight of commodity k in country j's exports of SITC i, and P_k is the UN commodity export price index for commodity k.

A series of linkage equations of this type for each developed country have been constructed. These equations for PX_{0+1} and PX_{2+4}, summarized in Table 4-2, provide a means of translation of world commodity prices into export prices for the developed countries.[12]

Even though these equations relate two types of export price measures, the fits are not always good, and the elasticities deviate from unity in many cases. There is also evidence of time lags. On average, a 1 percent increase in commodity prices translates into a less than 1 percent increase in export prices. This phenomenon is disturbing since it tends to attenuate the impact of commodity inflation; but it may have some real basis. Export unit value indexes are a mixture of spot and contract prices and may be less volatile than commodity prices, which are largely based on spot transactions. Moreover, since they are unit value indexes, they are aggregated with current weights, whereas commodity prices are combined with fixed weights. However, the problem may be related to the fact that the commodities for which we have endogenous price data represent the various SITC categories only very imprecisely.[13] The correspondence between SITC two-digit categories and commodity prices used in the present version of COMLINK is shown in Table 4-3.

Table 4-2
Price Linkage Equations

Country	*Equations*	$\bar{R}^2$	*DW*	*E***
Australia	$PX_{01} = .7437 + .2943\hat{P}_{01AUSTL}$ $\quad\quad(6.48)\quad(2.70)$	.478	1.34	.292
	$\hat{P}_{01AUSTL} = (41PBEEF + 40PWH + 10PSU)/10000$			
	$PX_{24} = .2819 + .8173\hat{P}_{24AUSTL}$ $\quad\quad(2.45)\quad(6.74)$	.850	.834	.732
	$\hat{P}_{24AUSTL} = (6PHIDS + 40PWOOL + 50PIOR + 4PFTO)/10000$			
Austria	$PX_{01} = .7311 + .2769\hat{P}_{01AUSTR}$ $\quad\quad(9.85)\quad(4.23)$	.666	.899	.295
	$\hat{P}_{01AUSTR} = (70PBEEF + 10PSU + 8PTBC)/10000$			
	$PX_{24} = .3082 + .7068\hat{P}_{24AUSTR}$ $\quad\quad(3.91)\quad(7.97)$	.876	2.87	.669
	$\hat{P}_{24AUSTR} = (70PLUMB + 8PIOR)/10000$			
Belgium	$PX_{01} = .3326 + .1478\hat{P}_{01B} + .4828PX_{01_{-1}}$ $\quad\quad(1.30)\quad(1.01)\quad\quad(1.28)$	.583	1.701	.153
	$\hat{P}_{01B} = (47.5PBEEF + 19PWH + 3PSU + 7PCF + 3PTBC)/10000$			
	$PX_{24} = .2796 + 1.44\hat{P}_{24B}$ $\quad\quad(2.77)\quad(7.20)$	.807	.263	.715
	$\hat{P}_{24B} = (27PWOOL + 15PIOR + 7PFTO)/10000$			
Canada	$PX_{01} = .4181 + .2708\hat{P}_{01C} + .3447PX_{01_{-1}}$ $\quad\quad(1.33)\quad(3.45)\quad\quad(1.10)$	.685	1.751	.249
	$\hat{P}_{01C} = (25PBEEF + 60PWH)/10000$			
	$PX_{24} = .1249 + 1.1353\hat{P}_{24C}$ $\quad\quad(0.98)\quad(6.16)$	.826	.986	.861
	$\hat{PX}_{24C} = (6PFTO + 2PRUB + 49PLUMB + 3PIOR)/10000$			
Finland	$PX_{01} = .6786 + .2272\hat{P}_{01FI}$ $\quad\quad(12.86)\quad(5.18)$	.771	2.43	2.83
	$\hat{P}_{01FI} = (72PBEEF + 11PWH + 7PSU)/10000$			

Table 4–2 Continued

Country	*Equations*	$\bar{R}^2$	*DW*	*E***
Finland (continued)	$PX_{24} = .3799 + .5061\hat{P}_{24FI}$ (3.63) (5.59)	.796	1.743	.604
	$\hat{P}_{24FI} = (7PHIDS + 9PLUMB)/10000$			
France	$PX_{01} = .2550 + .9248\hat{P}_{01FR}$ (4.62) (13.6)	.959	1.771	.745
	$\hat{P}_{01FR} = (28PBEEF + 36(.3PMAIZ + .7PWH) + 7PSU)/10000$			
	$PX_{24} = .5769 + .5314\hat{P}_{24FR}$ (4.98) (3.51)	.607	2.076	.413
	$\hat{P}_{24FR} = (5PHIDS + 8PRUB + 11PLUMB + 25PWOOL + 24PIOR + 6PFTO)/10000$			
Germany	$PX_{01} = -.1186 + .2561\hat{P}_{01G} + .9031PX_{01_{-1}}$ (0.58) (2.12) (3.15)	.920	1.793	.217
	$\hat{P}_{01G} = (43PBEEF + 21PWH)/10000$			
	$PX_{24} = .1868 + 1.5825\hat{P}_{24G}$ (0.81) (3.69)	.631	1.171	.818
	$\hat{P}_{24G} = (5PLUMB + 16PIOR + 8PFTO + 28PWOOL)/10000$			
Italy	$PX_{01} = .3912 + .4.5314\hat{P}_{01I}$ (2.07) (3.15)	.553	1.160	.602
	$\hat{P}_{01I} = (3PBEEF + 9PWH)/10000$			
	PX_{24} No equation*			
Japan	PX_{01} No equation*			
	PX_{24} No equation*			
Netherlands	$PX_{01} = .2447 + .2991\hat{P}_{01N} + .4572PX_{01_{-1}}$ (1.97) (4.21) (2.28)	.975	1.625	.302
	$\hat{P}_{01N} = [52PBEEF + 8PWH + 2PSU + 2(PCF + 3PCO) + 4PTBC]/10000$			
	$PX_{24} = .0420 + 2.1018\hat{P}_{24N}$ (0.23) (5.22)	.773	.932	.957
	$\hat{P}_{24N} = (4PHIDS + 8PRUB + 12PIOR + 10PFTO + 10PCT)/10000$			

Table 4-2 Continued

Country	Equations	$\bar{R}^2$	DW	E**
Sweden	$PX_{01} = .0779 + 1.0500\hat{P}_{01S}$ (0.60) (6.47)	.840	1.451	.914
	$\hat{P}_{01S} = (26PBEEF + 43PWH)/10000$			
	$PX_{24} = .1904 + .6784\hat{P}_{24S}$ (1.59) (6.55)	.843	1.225	.803
	$\hat{P}_{24S} = (2PHIDS + 76PLUMB + 23PIOR)/10000$			
United Kingdom	$PX_{01} = .5704 + .9820\hat{P}_{01UK}$ (6.28) (5.14)	.768	.963	.448
	$\hat{P}_{01UK} = (15PBEEF + 7PWH + 6PSU + 8PTE + 7PTBC)/10000$			
	$PX_{24} = .6666 + .4888\hat{P}_{24UK}$ (5.49) (3.06)	.540	1.175	.356
	$\hat{P}_{24UK} = (22PHIDS + 10PRUB + 34PWOOL + 11PIOR)/10000$			
United States	$PX_{01} = .0849 + .4119\hat{P}_{01US} + .5841PX_{01_{-1}}$ (0.50) (2.52) (2.45)	.904	1.965	.338
	$\hat{P}_{01US} = [12PBEEF + 60(.4PWH + .1PRI + .3PMAIZ) + 14PTBC]/10000$			
	$PX_{24} = -.0929 + .6677\hat{P}_{24US} + .3640PX_{24_{-1}}$ (0.78) (4.95) (1.73)	.944	1.479	.739
	$\hat{P}_{24US} = (5PHIDS + 48PFTO + 3PRUB + 20PLUMB + 12\,PCT + 1PIOR)/10000$			

PX_{01}, PX_{24} = export unit value indexes for SITC 0 + 1 and 2 + 4.
P_{ij} = trade weighted commodity price index for SITC i and country j.

Commodity prices—UN export price indexes:

PBEEF = beef
PWH = wheat
PSU = sugar
PHIDS = hides and skins
PWOOL = wool
PCO = cocoa
PCT = cotton
PIOR = iron ore
PFTO = fats and oils
PTBC = tobacco
PLUMB = lumber
PCF = coffee
PRUB = rubber
PRICE = rice
PCP = copper

*Exports are negligible for these categories.
**Elasticity

Table 4-3
Correspondence between SITC Categories and Commodity Prices Used in Bridge Equations

Export Unit Value for SITC Categories			*Export Price UN Index from Commodity Models*
SITC 0 + 1	00	Live animals	Beef
	01	Meat	
	02	Milk and eggs	
	03	Fish	
	04	Cereals	Wheat, rice, maize[a]
	08	Fodder	
	06	Sugar	Sugar
	07	Coffee and cocoa	Coffee, tea, cocoa[a]
	12	Tobacco	Tobacco
	09	Other	None
	05	Fruits	
SITC 2 + 4	21	Hides and skins	Hides and skins
	22	Nuts and seeds	Fats and oils (UN fats and oils)
	23	Rubber	Rubber
	24	Lumber	Lumber
	25	Paper and pulp	
	26	Fibers	Wool, cotton, jute, sisal[a]
	28	Minerals (metals)	Iron ore, copper[b]
	41	Fish oils	
	42	Vegetable fats and oils	Fats and oils (UN fats and oils)
	43	Animal oils	
	27	Minerals (nonmetals)	None
	29	Shells	

[a]Weighted average, using world trade weights, supplemented by information about special countries.

[b]Weighted 50 percent iron ore and 50 percent copper; the latter to represent movement of all nonferrous metal prices.

For the developing countries the problem of export prices is handled somewhat differently. For these countries the DEVE model developed by UNCTAD calls directly for particular commodity prices—the United Nations export price indexes for numerous commodities. These are also the prices used in many of our commodity models. Thus the linkage is straightforward. Within DEVE, the commodity prices are converted to larger price aggregates on the basis of regression relationships:

$$PX = f(P_1, \ldots, P_n)$$

where PX is the broader aggregate price index and $P_1, \ldots, P_n$ are commodity prices.

From Export Prices to Import Prices

The next step in the backward linkages is the question of import prices. One approach would have been to establish import prices in a way similar to that used for the computation of export prices. Here, however, the methodology of LINK is helpful. The job has already been done. The standard LINK computation is to compute import prices as a weighted average of export prices; for example,

$$PM_{ij} = \sum_k a_{ijk} PX_{ik}$$

where the a_{ijk} equal $(X\$_{ijk}/M\$_{ij})_0$, and PM_{ij} stands for the import unit value index for SITC category i into country j, and the weights represent the share (for SITC category i) of country k's shipments in the value of country j's imports. This translation methodology assures that the import prices correspond to the appropriate export prices in the LINK system, and that world import prices match world export prices. Thus if commodity prices are properly converted into export unit values for SITC categories, the mechanism will also translate them into import unit value indexes to the importing countries.

From Import Prices to Domestic Prices and Export Prices of Manufactures

The final link in the chain is the feedthrough of import prices to the domestic price level and to export prices of manufactures. This connection is internal to the country models. Despite the fact that this is likely to be a "weak link" in many cases, we have been obliged to accept the existing structure of the country models.[14] Many of the country models are quite imperfect in this regard. For example, in the Wharton model of the United States economy, sector prices are insensitive to import prices; and in turn, final demand prices, including manufactures export prices, show no movement when there is a change in import prices. There is, moreover, another linkage between world commodity prices and domestic prices. Even when a country is not an importer, world commodity prices may influence domestic commodity prices, for example, the relation between the world wheat price and agricultural prices in the United States.[15] In this case, the causation is from the world price to the domestic price rather than the other way.

Summary of the Linkage Procedure

The mechanism that has been added to LINK serves to provide a simultaneous solution of the country models and the commodity models. To operate the combined model system, a linked country model solution is obtained first. Then the commodity models are added, yielding first a one-way linked solution corresponding only to the linkage described in the section entitled Country Models to Commodity Models. Finally, the feedback linkages are added and a simultaneous solution of the entire system is obtained. This solution includes the feedback from commodity models to the country models and back again.[16]

An important question is whether this mechanism catches all the price effects from world commodity markets. Unfortunately, the answer to this query must be in the negative. There is a high probability that parts of the potential impact of commodity prices are not captured. We note, for example the elasticities of export prices with respect to commodity prices that are less than unity. We are aware that some of the country models do not fully integrate import prices into domestic price determination, so that domestic prices and export prices do not fully reflect the impact of world commodity prices. The country models may also miss some direct impacts of world market prices in the determination of domestic prices. Finally, there may also be reason to suspect that in some respects the effect of commodity prices may be overstated. Government intervention may serve to isolate domestic prices from world market prices—the U.S. farm price supports and similar arrangements that apply elsewhere, for example. Movements in exchange rates, not presently considered in LINK, may serve to offset the effect of some commodity price changes. And, finally, we have made no allowance for policy responses on the part of commodity organizations or national stockpiles, which may limit price fluctuations in commodity markets. Realistic forecasting of the COMLINK system will require appraisal of the results on a country-by-country and commodity-by-commodity basis. Responses of international and domestic policy agencies will ultimately need to be considered in forecast simulations.

The COMLINK Linkage Computation

The experimental linkage computations described in this chapter are only the first of a series of experiments planned with the entire COMLINK system.

Alternative Computations

The following computations are intended to illustrate the potentials of the system and the kind of response it produces. Two types of computations are presented covering the period 1976-1978.

A Control Solution

The exogenous inputs into this calculation for the country models correspond to the inputs of the LINK country model solution of December 1976. For the commodity models, the principal inputs are drawn from this country model solution.

Disturbed Simulations

These solutions introduce the impact of disturbances on the supply or demand side. Except for the specific adjustments in the models related to the "disturbance," all exogenous variables for country and commodity models remain as in the control solution. Only two disturbed simulation alternatives are considered in this chapter.

World Drought Simulation. The first alternative evaluates the effect on the world economy of a serious shortfall on the supply side. We have assumed that for one year only (1976) agricultural crops fall some 20 percent short of what they would have been otherwise.[17] The effect is obtained simply by adjusting downward the constants of the agricultural supply functions by appropriate magnitudes in 1976. In the subsequent years, the constants of the functions are adjusted back to their normal levels, and the high prices provide incentives for a substantial additional expansion of agricultural production. The commodity markets differ greatly in their response to prices, but in the aggregate we will see that the drought episode sets off important swings in agricultural prices.

Stockpiling Simulation. The second alternative shows much smaller effects. We have introduced a substantial copper stockpiling program, purchases amounting to about 10 percent of the supply each year from 1976 to 1978. This has an impact on copper price of about 20 percent; but copper accounts for a relatively small weight in total trade, and the elasticity linking the unit value index for SITC 2 + 4 to the copper price is relatively low. Consequently, the impact on the export unit value index for SITC 2 + 4 is very modest. Very small passthrough effects can be seen in the price measures for manufactures trade as well. The impact on OECD gross domestic product is very small, perhaps nonsignificant.

Computational Results of the World Drought Simulation

The results of the computations conform generally with our prior expectations. The comparisons shown in Table 4-4 and 4-5 are between a control simulation and the alternative simulations. The critical issue in this case would be whether

Table 4-4
COMLINK Results: World Variables

A. Commodity Prices (1975 = 1.0)

SITC 0 + 1 *Year*	*Cocoa*	*Coffee*	*Beef*	*Sugar*	*Wheat*
COMLINK Control					
1976	1.95	1.73	0.75	0.78	0.96
1977	1.15	1.49	1.12	0.97	0.93
1978	0.74	1.55	1.60	1.25	0.93
COMLINK World Drought[a]					
1976	2.58	2.79	1.18	1.54	0.97
1977	1.17	1.21	0.90	0.86	0.98
1978	0.74	1.80	1.69	0.91	0.98

SITC 2 + 4 *Year*	*FTOL*	*IORE*	*COPPR*
COMLINK Control			
1976	1.09	1.03	0.62
1977	1.19	1.05	1.71
1978	1.35	1.08	2.30
COMLINK World Drought			
1976	1.21	1.03	0.63
1977	1.65	1.05	1.71
1978	1.33	1.08	2.30

B. World Prices (1970 = 1.0)

Year	*PX0 + 1*	*PX2 + 4*	*PX3*	*PX5 - 9*	*PX0 - 9*	*POECD*
1975	1.734	1.904	5.235	1.837	2.145	1.516
COMLINK Control						
1976	1.762	1.831	5.675	1.827	2.126	1.654
1977	1.757	2.112	6.105	1.879	2.207	1.761
1978	1.973	2.299	6.519	1.965	2.324	1.900
COMLINK World Drought						
1976	2.187	2.163	5.706	1.850	2.218	1.668
1977	1.452	2.094	6.104	1.856	2.154	1.756
1978	2.138	2.365	6.532	1.969	2.350	1.902

C. Trade Values (billions of 1970 US$)

Year	*VX0 + 1*	*VX2 + 4*	*VX3*	*VX5 – 9*	*VX0 – 9*
1975	77.387	63.480	192.804	523.021	856.629
COMLINK Control					
1976	85.515	66.030	198.280	584.757	934.582
1977	89.931	74.269	220.868	655.365	1040.433
1978	108.681	86.589	247.746	762.658	1205.674
COMLINK World Drought					
1976	102.042	73.835	199.493	595.219	970.589
1977	76.783	73.797	220.958	647.545	1019.083
1978	115.246	87.430	246.601	760.840	1210.117

Table 4–4 Continued

D. OECD GDP (billions of 1970 US$)	
COMLINK Control	
1976	2309.300
1977	2427.492
1978	2553.281
COMLINK World Drought	
1976	2315.753
1977	2422.631
1978	2549.592

[a]20 percent reduction in supply of agricultural SITC 0 + 1, 2 + 4 categories except for cocoa, coffee, and beef (10 percent reduction).

the addition of the commodity model feedbacks affects real output and price in the country models and the flow of world trade. There are indications that the feedbacks do make a significant difference in the country models. We have not presented comparisons along these lines here since it was not possible to provide strictly comparable runs with and without commodity model feedback links.[18]

In Table 4–4 we present the aggregate or world variables produced by the COMLINK system: the prices of the principal commodities, the world trade price indexes by SITC category,[19] the values of world trade by SITC category, OECD gross domestic product, and OECD domestic price deflator. Table 4–5 shows country-specific results for some major countries in the COMLINK system. The figures for 1975 are common to all solution alternatives.

The COMLINK control simulation is roughly in line with the path projected by the December 1976 LINK control forecast. As noted earlier, no detailed comparisons are attempted, and we have not shown the figures for that forecast since there are some other minor conceptual differences between the solutions.[20] The COMLINK control solution shows a path of economic recovery from the recession low for economic activity and trade (OECD gross domestic product increases at 5 to 6 percent and world trade increases at 7 to 10 percent per year). There is great diversity and movement among the prices of the primary commodities in this control solution.[21] While prices of tropical beverages rise very sharply in 1976 and swing thereafter, prices of beef, sugar, wheat, and copper decline in 1976 and rise after that. The trade unit value indexes reflect the movements of the underlying commodity prices in terms of broad averaging. For SITC 0 + 1, trade unit values are fairly flat until 1977 and increase sharply to 1978. For SITC 2 + 4, the trade unit value index declines from 1975 to 1976 and rises fairly sharply thereafter.

At this point we will turn to a comparison of the world drought simulation with the control solution. The purpose of this comparison, primarily for the

Table 4–5
COMLINK Results: Major Countries

	PX					PM							
1976	*0 + 1*	*2 + 4*	*3*	*5 - 9*	*0 - 9*	*0 + 1*	*2 + 4*	*3*	*5 - 9*	*0 - 9*	*PGDP*	*GDP*	*VX - VM*
COMLINK Control													
France	1.39	1.62	5.61	2.31	2.11	1.76	1.79	5.77	1.87	2.29	1.88	158.77	-11.53
Germany	1.90	1.40	3.60	1.81	1.84	1.56	1.83	5.92	1.95	2.16	2.14	223.43	+14.85
Japan	1.91	2.22	4.79	1.77	1.78	1.96	1.92	5.69	1.77	2.76	1.65	268.27	+ 7.61
United States	2.15	2.49	2.71	1.54	1.70	1.81	1.69	5.31	1.80	2.19	1.47	1154.02	- 3.25
DEVE	1.84	1.76	6.60	1.98	3.31	1.84	1.94	6.13	1.80	2.08			+43.18
COMLINK World Drought													
France	1.81	1.79	5.87	2.40	2.29	2.17	2.12	5.81	1.89	2.39	1.91	156.75	-10.65
Germany	2.03	1.61	3.63	1.82	1.86	1.93	2.16	6.03	1.99	2.30	2.14	223.16	+14.75
Japan	1.92	2.60	4.63	1.77	1.78	2.35	2.26	5.67	1.79	2.93	1.74	272.35	+ 6.80
United States	2.25	2.78	2.72	1.56	1.75	2.41	2.08	5.32	1.81	2.30	1.47	1158.81	+ 0.57
DEVE	2.80	2.12	6.60	2.01	3.59	2.21	2.27	6.14	1.82	2.14			+43.90
COMLINK Stockpiling													
France	1.39	1.65	5.61	2.31	2.12	1.76	1.82	5.77	1.87	2.30	1.88	158.70	-11.54
Germany	1.90	1.44	3.60	1.81	1.84	1.56	1.87	5.92	1.95	2.16	2.14	223.40	+14.85
Japan	1.91	2.25	4.79	1.77	1.78	1.96	1.94	5.69	1.77	2.77	1.65	268.49	+ 7.60
United States	2.15	2.49	2.71	1.54	1.70	1.81	1.70	5.31	1.80	2.19	1.47	1154.20	- 3.12
DEVE	1.84	1.77	6.60	1.98	3.31	1.84	1.96	6.13	1.80	2.08			+43.25
1977													
COMLINK Control													
France	1.66	1.93	5.73	2.13	2.08	1.73	2.09	6.24	1.93	2.39	1.93	167.28	-10.14
Germany	2.13	1.72	3.76	1.87	1.92	1.64	2.12	6.63	1.98	2.20	2.23	242.62	+18.81
Japan	1.99	2.07	5.22	1.87	1.88	1.89	2.22	6.05	1.82	3.02	1.89	290.04	+ 5.79
United States	2.17	2.62	2.86	1.60	1.77	1.71	1.99	5.68	1.86	2.29	1.56	1203.56	-10.47
DEVE	1.58	2.04	7.26	2.05	3.43	1.84	2.18	6.64	1.86	2.16			+42.73

COMLINK World Drought													
France	1.53	1.98	5.34	1.91	1.90	1.42	2.05	6.24	1.93	2.34	1.91	169.68	-11.24
Germany	2.07	1.75	3.76	1.87	1.90	1.42	2.11	6.68	1.95	2.13	2.22	242.53	+18.44
Japan	1.99	2.40	5.34	1.87	1.89	1.55	2.19	6.07	1.81	2.96	1.86	288.70	+ 5.67
United States	2.14	2.89	2.87	1.61	1.78	1.26	1.91	5.68	1.85	2.22	1.56	1200.51	-12.34
DEVE	1.01	1.90	7.26	2.02	3.14	1.56	2.18	6.64	1.84	2.11			+42.16
COMLINK Stockpiling													
France	1.66	1.99	5.73	2.13	2.08	1.73	2.12	6.24	1.93	2.39	1.93	167.20	-10.16
Germany	2.13	1.81	3.76	1.87	1.92	1.64	2.15	6.63	1.98	2.21	2.23	242.56	+18.86
Japan	1.99	2.12	5.22	1.87	1.88	1.89	2.24	6.05	1.82	3.03	1.89	290.30	+ 5.82
United States	2.17	2.63	2.86	1.60	1.77	1.71	1.97	5.68	1.86	2.29	1.56	1203.76	-10.20
DEVE	1.58	2.04	7.26	2.05	3.43	1.84	2.19	6.64	1.86	2.16			+42.38
1978													
COMLINK Control													
France	2.02	2.10	5.58	1.95	2.00	1.93	2.27	6.59	2.08	2.57	2.04	179.10	-15.55
Germany	2.33	1.93	3.93	1.98	2.03	1.87	2.30	7.39	2.10	2.37	2.41	255.40	+22.20
Japan	2.00	1.93	5.36	1.89	1.90	2.08	2.42	6.41	1.93	3.30	2.13	302.83	+ 9.70
United States	2.31	2.85	3.23	1.74	1.92	1.93	2.21	6.02	1.93	2.41	1.65	1272.99	- 0.55
DEVE	1.79	2.15	7.77	2.15	3.60	2.04	2.34	7.09	1.93	2.23			+25.59
COMLINK World Drought													
France	2.07	2.21	5.64	1.98	2.04	2.11	2.33	6.61	2.08	2.60	2.05	178.24	-15.63
Germany	2.36	1.91	3.94	1.98	2.03	2.00	2.39	7.42	2.11	2.41	2.41	254.57	+20.76
Japan	1.99	2.24	5.30	1.89	1.90	2.25	2.47	6.41	1.93	3.35	2.16	302.56	+ 9.21
United States	2.33	2.91	3.25	1.74	1.93	2.18	2.27	6.02	1.93	2.44	1.65	1272.34	- 1.01
DEVE	2.18	2.21	7.77	2.16	3.73	2.18	2.41	7.09	1.93	2.25			+31.43
COMLINK Stockpiling													
France	2.02	2.21	5.58	1.95	2.00	1.93	2.32	6.59	2.08	2.58	2.04	179.02	-15.67
Germany	2.33	2.07	3.94	1.98	2.04	1.88	2.34	7.40	2.10	2.38	2.41	255.23	+22.22
Japan	2.00	2.02	5.35	1.89	1.90	2.08	2.46	6.41	1.93	3.32	2.14	303.12	+ 9.63
United States	2.31	2.86	3.24	1.74	1.92	1.93	2.24	6.02	1.93	2.41	1.65	1273.29	- 0.31
DEVE	1.79	2.16	7.77	2.15	3.60	2.04	2.37	7.09	1.93	2.23			+29.58

year 1976, is to show the feedthrough from commodity prices to the unit value index of the corresponding export and import categories and, finally, the impact on domestic prices and on export prices of manufactures. In the world drought simulation, commodity prices average significantly higher in 1976 than under the more favorable crop production conditions assumed in the control solution. This is particularly true of cocoa, coffee, and sugar, which, even in the control solution, occupy a low inventory position and consequently show a great deal of price volatility. As we would expect, higher commodity prices show up in higher trade unit value indexes for SITC 0 + 1 and SITC 2 + 4 (see Table 4-4). We would anticipate that the increase in primary commodity import prices would filter through to raise the export unit values for manufactures. Indeed the system shows a modest increase in the SITC 5-9 unit values. There is also an increase, albeit a very much smaller one, for the OECD domestic price deflator. A somewhat surprising result, which requires further study, is that the gross domestic product of the OECD countries shows some increase as a result of the world drought.[22] We examine this phenomenon further below.

It is also interesting to observe the passthrough of prices to some of the industrial countries and to the developing world, as shown in Table 4-5. Here import and export unit values are identified separately. Again, a comparison between the control solution and the world drought simulation for 1976 indicates that the export unit values for SITC 0 + 1 and SITC 2 + 4 for the DEVE countries rise very sharply. Export unit values for primary commodities also rise for the industrial countries, although this is of somewhat lesser interest since these commodities represent a relatively small share of their trade. In response to higher world export unit values, the import unit values for SITC categories 0 + 1 and SITC 2 + 4 are sharply higher.[23] It is of interest, then, to observe whether there is a passthrough of these higher import prices for raw material inputs to the export prices for manufactures in SITC categories 5-9. This is an imperfect part of many of the country models. Even so, in many cases a modest impact is observed.

The effects on domestic prices, incomes, and balance of payments vary greatly between countries. This aspect of model performance requires additional study, focusing on the structural characteristics of each of the country models, as well as on their linkage to world commodity markets. We note, in particular, that the trade balance of the DEVE countries improves by relatively little, $0.7 billion in the world drought simulation as compared to the control solution. Not shown on the table is the fact that DEVE exports increase by approximately $8 billion, with most of the increased earnings channeled into greater imports. On the side of primary commodities, the principal impact of the world drought has been on prices; real trade has actually declined. With respect to trade in manufactures, the price increases have been much smaller and purchases by the DEVE countries are significantly larger in real terms. In the industrial countries, the combination of lower real imports and larger real exports appears to stimulate economic activity despite higher commodity prices. This feedback effect is a good illustration of the potentials of the complete COMLINK system.

Turning now to the later years of the world drought simulation, the resumption of normal production conditions and the incentives associated with the high prices in 1976 result in a sharp downswing of commodity prices in 1977.[24] It is difficult to interpret clearly the aggregate consequences of the price swings produced by the commodity models since there are lags at various levels of the entire system. The sharp price decline in 1977, particularly in SITC 0 + 1, filters through to the unit value index for manufactures and even to the OECD deflator. The gross domestic product of the OECD countries is a little lower than in the control simulation, but we cannot be sure whether that is the result of the change in commodity prices or whether it reflects the lagged effects of the previous year's price movement. The problem of allowing for lagged effects is also apparent when the price surge resumes in 1978, an endogenous result of the dynamics of the models rather than a new drought. There is a corresponding movement of the price indexes, but in this instance the OECD gross domestic product comes out somewhat lower than in the control simulation.

Concluding Remarks

It is apparent that substantial work still remains to be done. The mechanism for the integration of commodity market models into LINK needs further elaboration. Nevertheless, the structure of the price linkage mechanism is operational, and we can see how commodity prices filter through trade into the economies of the individual countries. We can also see that the earnings of developing-country commodity producers flow back to the developed world in the form of additional exports. The impacts of commodity market behavior on the world economy are highly complex and may well have counterintuitive results once all the feedback channels are considered. For this reason, despite its difficulty, a system like COMLINK is worth building and exercising. We have barely scratched the surface of its possible use. In the coming weeks we expect to carry out numerous additional simulations. This work will attempt to evaluate the impact of commodity markets on the developed and developing world. For example, what is the effect of droughts or other supply constraints? What is the effect of additional stimulus to world economic activity on commodity prices and back to the world economy? What would be the impacts on the entire world economy of stockpiling or supply management policy designed to stabilize commodity prices?

Notes

1. For a description of LINK, see R.J. Ball (1973).
2. A reconciliation of commodity flows and trade flows may be possible, but only at a five-digit SITC level.
3. Detailed equations for the country models in LINK are contained in J. Waelbroeck (1976).
4. In some areas, domestic markets are "closed," and only the net balance of imports and exports from such areas will affect the world price.
5. A discussion of DEVE is contained in UNCTAD (1975). Additional information on the most recent version of the model can be obtained from the UNCTAD Secretariat.
6. For an explanation, see R.J. Ball (1973).
7. This is, of course, a somewhat heuristic explanation of the solution procedure of LINK. For a more detailed discussion, see K.N. Johnson and A. van Peeterssen, "Solving and Simulating the LINK System," in J. Waelbroeck (1976).
8. For a discussion of this pattern and a comprehensive listing of commodity models, see Labys (1973); and Labys (1975).
9. For an explanation of these indexes, see United Nations (1970).
10. For discussion of the dynamic properties of such models, see Adams and Behrman (1976); and Behrman (1975).
11. Even in these cases data discrepancies prevent the use of the LINK variables directly. We assume that the commodity model variable moves by the same percentage changes over time as the aggregated variable coming from the country models.
12. For fuel prices, SITC 3, we do not have any models at this point. Consequently, the export price for the category as a unit is treated as exogenous.
13. Another curious phenomenon is the large share of primary commodity exports that appear in the data as originating in countries where they clearly do not originate—cocoa in the Netherlands, for example. These are goods being processed or in entrepôt trade. Presumably they also appear in the import statistics for these countries. If so, there is no harm done.
14. Other studies of the international transmission of inflationary impulses in the framework of Project LINK also suggest that the effects are relatively weak. See, for example, Hickman and Lima (1976); and Hickman (1974).
15. Such a relationship is embodied in the DEVE model of the developing world, but it is not a feature of most models of industrial countries.
16. Typically, six iterations between country models and commodity models are required to obtain a reasonably stable solution.
17. For coffee, cocoa, and beef, the cutback was only 10 percent. These markets are already so short of supplies and inventories that the models would not operate when a further cutback of output as large as 20 percent was assumed.

18. In order to make the price feedbacks effective in the country models, we were forced to remove some of the constraining equations of the LINK system. As a result, the comparisons would confuse the impact of the commodity models with the effect of lifting the constraints.

19. For the world as a whole, import prices, of course, equal export prices.

20. The addition of the commodity models to the LINK system has the potential for altering real activity, trade, and prices in the country model system. The feedbacks from country models to commodity models also mean that the outcome of the commodity models can be affected by a simultaneous solution of the entire system.

21. For purposes of this demonstration, we have not attempted to update the commodity price forecasts of the control solution. Some of them may no longer seem realistic in the light of recent developments.

22. No downward adjustments of GDP at the country level to allow for the poor crops have been made. Moreover, counterinflationary policies at the level of the industrial countries, which would serve to depress their real output, have not been introduced in this simulation.

23. Small changes in the unit values for SITC 3, fuels, are the result of the balancing constraints of the LINK system.

24. Some downswing is already apparent in the control solution. The responses differ greatly between the commodity markets. In the case of coffee, for example, it is the reduction in consumption in 1977 associated with the high price in 1976 that causes the price decline in 1977; while in the case of beef or sugar, it is the upsurge of supply in 1977 responding to the high price in 1976.

Bibliography

Adams, F.G. 1973. "The Impact of Copper Production from the Ocean Floor: Application of an Econometric Model." Paper prepared for UNCTAD, Philadelphia, December 1973.

——. 1974. "The Impact of Nickel Production from the Ocean Floor: An Econometric Appraisal." Paper prepared for UNCTAD, Philadelphia, March 1974.

——.1975. "An Interrelated Econometric Modeling System for Fats and Oils Commodities." A Study prepared for UNCTAD, Philadelphia, 1975.

——, and J.R. Behrman. 1976. *Econometric Models of World Agricultural Commodity Markets.* Cambridge, Mass.: Ballinger, 1976.

Ball, R.J., ed. 1973. *The International Linkage of National Economic Models.* Amsterdam: North-Holland, 1973.

Behrman, J.R. 1975. "Mini Models for Eleven International Commodity Markets." Paper prepared for UNCTAD, processed, 1975.

Hickman, B. 1974. "International Transmission of Economic Fluctuation and

Inflation. In A. Ando et al. eds., *International Aspects of Stabilization Policies.* Boston: Federal Reserve Bank of Boston, 1974.

——, and A. Lima. 1976. "Price Determination and Transmission of Inflation in the LINK System." Paper prepared for the meeting of Project LINK, Venice, September 1976.

Klein, L.R. 1975. *Commodity Market Studies–Progress Report.* A paper prepared for Project LINK, Philadelphia, 1975.

Labys, W.C. 1973. *Dynamic Commodity Models: Specification, Estimation and Simulation.* Lexington, Mass.: Lexington Books, D.C. Heath, 1973.

——, ed. 1975. *Quantitative Models of Commodity Markets.* Cambridge, Mass.: Ballinger, 1975.

United Nations. 1970. *Methods Used in Compiling the UN Price Indexes for Basic Commodities in International Trade.* Stat. Papers Series M, No. 29, Rev. 1, New York, 1976.

UNCTAD. 1975. "Regional Models of Developing Countries." New York, December 12, 1974. Rev. Jan. 1975.

Waelbroeck, J.L. 1976. *The Models of Project LINK.* Amsterdam: North-Holland, 1976.

5 Potentials of Econometrics for Commodity Stabilization Policy Analysis

Lawrence R. Klein

The Modeling Approach

Joseph, the original agricultural forecaster, used common sense (labeled ad hoc reasoning by today's academic economist) mixed with subjective powers of inference, OPEC used brute market force; but both went far in commodity market policy making without the use of models. OPEC, however, is now firmly in the modeling business, and that suggests that the approach does have a great deal of merit.

In a sense, econometrics received its motivated start from commodity model building in agriculture, encompassing both food and nonfood crops. Given the hunch that demand for agricultural products is price inelastic, models to predict farm prices became a subject of analytic inquiry in order to stabilize farm incomes. The empirical studies of the early econometricians found, indeed, that demand was price inelastic in this sector; and the quantitative magnitude of that elasticity became an important statistic or parameter estimate for policy implementation.

Early intuition also suggested, in agriculture, that supply is highly variable to the point of being unstable through time, and that the focus of attention should be on demand. The general workings of the cobweb became evident, however, and that simple dynamic model has withstood a great deal of criticism, showing through even today in many of the models—even beyond agricultural models.

To continue this line of historical thought, we can now see the confluent progress of macro model building for national economies, which also began at an early stage with the work of Tinbergen, together with commodity model building. Today we recognize not only the need for stabilization of agricultural income but also of balance of trade, balance of payments, and inflation policies intimately tied with commodity movements. Therefore, highly specific commodity models are being integrated with national macro models. This is a development that will not be turned back; but it is worthwhile to pause at the present time and try to judge where it might take us, how much to expect, and what would be the best econometric practice.

Models for What?

As at the beginning of any exercise, there is a natural desire among economists to want to be able to predict price movements. This might be advantageous to the speculator, the commodity processor, the shipper, or to public officials in a ministry of agriculture, mines, interior, national resources, or a similar commodity-related bureau. A greater challenge occurs in the design of buffer stock operations. With that objective, the model builder should be trying to answer such questions as the size of stock needed for satisfactory operation, the periodic buy/sell decisions, the revenue implications of alternative price levels, and the adequacy of stocks for national security purposes. To some extent, the buffer stock operator, working through a model, is gaming against nature and general market tendencies. Random shocks and significant exogenous disturbances are among the destabilizing influences that are meant to be buffered.

Mainly, but not entirely, commodity modeling for buffer stock operations involves short-run analysis. In a longer-term perspective, commodity modeling, together with national economy modeling, is a tool for use in analysis of North-South relationships. The fundamental UNCTAD study, *Trade Prospects and Capital Needs of Developing Countries,* of the middle 1960s was an ambitious attempt to model the capital transfer problem with a great deal of commodity analysis embedded in the vast array of national models for the developing world. In a sense, one can say that OPEC implemented, through control over a strategic commodity, a lopsided variant of a policy recommendation of the UNCTAD study. Capital needs for growth in the developing world, estimated at that time at roughly $20 billion per annum (also figured roughly as 1 or 2 percent of the developed-world GNP) through UNCTAD model analysis, were never carried out in practice until OPEC forced the issue.

Commodity models are practically always open systems, i.e., they depend on certain economic variables that are determined outside the market mechanism of the particular commodities being analyzed. Typical among such variables are activity levels, the general price level, and closely related prices. By integrating commodity models with national models, some of these external variables can be generated within the integrated system, but most commodities are consumed and produced in several different countries simultaneously. In nearly all cases, a commodity is produced in a few countries, at least, and consumed worldwide. There will of course be some dominant or major consumers; but as the world economy grows, there is bound to be more and more dispersion of consumption. To make a proper integration of commodity models with macro models of the economy as a whole, it is literally necessary to go to the whole-world scale. The technique of integration has been achieved in the successful simultaneous solution of commodity models with Project LINK in full feedback mode, as reported by F.G. Adams in this book. The procedure has been seriously discussed for some four or five years and is now a reality. The process is, very roughly, something like this:

1. With given assumptions about commodity supply conditions, the LINK model can be solved for world trade and production (in total and by country).
2. With LINK generated demand levels, the commodity models can be solved on a world basis.
3. The commodity model solutions determine price and therefore export earnings of producing countries. These change the LINK solution.
4. Iterate, restarting with step 1, etc.

Symbolically, we have:

$$p_j = f_j(\sum_i X_i)$$

where $j = 1, \ldots, m$ commodity models with jth commodity price dependent on world GDP totals $(\sum_i X_i)$ and other variables.

$$X_i = g_i(E_i)$$

where $i = 1, 2, \ldots, n$ country models with ith country's GDP dependent on its exports.

$$E_i = h_i(p_1, \ldots, p_m)$$

where $i = 1, 2, \ldots, n$ export determination with the ith country's exports dependent on its range of commodity prices that are determined in the world market. Export earnings are determined by volume and price.

If we start with assumptions about all the p_j, we can estimate exports and export earnings from h_i functions. These determine country output levels from g_i—as part of the LINK system, in a consistent way. World totals of demand determine prices of commodities from f_j functions. The new estimates of commodity prices reactivate the LINK solutions from h_i, and we continue iterating until convergence is attained.

An idea has become a reality, and the joint application of commodity macro model systems is now a real possibility for analysis that is likely to remain with us.

There is great flexibility in this approach because it is modular in concept. We are able, in fact, to work on the national econometric models and world trade system in LINK apart from the commodity models. We are also able to work on individual commodity models, improving them or adding new ones to the system. These two areas of research are then brought together in joint simulation, each time trying to improve the approximation to the world economy. In this way, we operate the commodity models in *satellite* mode. Either they can be studied as open systems by themselves, or they can be attached in a consistent way to the whole LINK system.

Matters of Accuracy

There are great policy hopes being pinned on modeling success. Therefore, the needs for particular uses must be set against the levels of precision that can be attained in the near future. Whatever numerical precision is ultimately achieved, it should be stressed that there are definite gains to be realized from understanding, alone. By the very process of trying to model the steps in commodity supply, demand, and price determination, we learn much, by way of understanding, about how the market works. In this way, qualitative results can be stated. This is all to the good, but quantitative results are needed if intervention is contemplated in the interest of stabilization.

In this quantitative sense, there are real limits to accuracy. It remains to be proved that commodity models can be applied in the full sense that we have in mind for sophisticated stabilization schemes or for prediction. The limitations can be set out under the following heads: (1) data problems, (2) degrees of freedom (sample size), and (3) inherent stochastic nature of behavior (noise).

Data

The typical data base that lies behind a commodity model consists of statistics on production, shipments, exports, imports, prices, stocks, consumption, and scrap (in some markets only). These are almost always wanted on a country-specific basis. Many of these are regularly reported for most major markets, but there are notable stumbling blocks. The most elusive data are for stocks. In building many specific commodity models over the years, I have noticed that stock data are often available for the United States, but not for anywhere else. In the case of the United States, private stock holdings may be less available than public holdings. In some instances, producer association data are available on stocks, but generally a data gap exists in this most important area. This is of the utmost importance because the key to price formation is stock size in relation to normal needs and stock variation. Stocks are especially deficient in those commodity markets where centrally planned economies play an important role. The centrally planned economy is usually secretive about a broad range of data, but especially so in the case of stocks.

This is most likely to be a stumbling block in the modeling of metal markets. Also in metal markets, scrap can play an important role as a supplementary material source. Scrap that is a byproduct of the manufacturing process can be more readily estimated by a simple standardized formula; but for other kinds of scrap, there are many small dealers, and their collective record keeping leaves much to be desired.

Historical data on stocks and scrap may be effectively lost to researchers for an indefinite period of time. Therefore, researchers should try to adapt to working with the latest sample and forget about nostalgic times. Their efforts will have to be a progressive analysis of the recent past and the future.

Degrees of Freedom

Not only are some data hard to get (stocks and scrap), but the bulk of commodity data are for fairly short time periods—say since the 1960s or possibly back to the mid-1950s. Some commodity statistics may be recoverable for 50 or so more years, but complete data files covering all the model variables will not be able to be carried back en masse in a way that permits comprehensive model building. We therefore face a not uncommon degrees-of-freedom shortage. Reliability of sample estimates of model parameters will be shaky in reflection of this degrees-of-freedom shortage.

Contrary to what some investigators may think, focusing on narrowly defined markets for specific commodities does not mean that the appropriate models will turn out to be small, i.e., consisting only of a few equations explaining supply, demand, and price determination (market clearing). If a careful analysis is attempted for a microcosmic entity, the resulting system is probably going to have to be large. Many special factors are at work in a detailed market; and by attempting to explain them all, we are led to micro market equation systems that are fully as large as macro model equation systems. For example, the Wharton agricultural model, covering just U.S. grains, livestock, and nonfood crops has as many equations as the typical national macro model. Going in a micro direction for model building does not save equations or system size. If a number of countries are involved both as producers and consumers for some commodity, there must be equation detail for each significant or major participant. There will then be a proliferation of equations to generate the country-specific variables needed and badly wanted by participating sponsors.

Error

Apart from the identities of a system, error is always present in econometric equations. Models exhibit errors when simulated—both in historical mode, over the same period, and in forward projections (including ex post as well as ex

Table 5-1
Mean Absolute Percentage Errors, Copper (1955-1971)

U.S. Producers' Price	4.90%
U.S. Dealers' No. 2 Scrap Buying Price	9.55%
London Metal Exchange Price	8.04%
U.S. Consumption	4.44%
Foreign Consumption	2.20%
U.S. Production, Old Scrap	3.84%
U.S. Production, New Scrap	6.49%
U.S. Mine Production	3.16%
Scrap Recovery by Noncommunist World (excl. U.S.)	3.61%
Refined Production by Noncommunist World (excl. U.S.)	3.67%
Mine Production by Noncommunist World (excl. U.S.)	3.55%

ante extrapolations). To get an idea of the order of magnitude of error to be expected. Table 5-1 presents a typical case of simulation errors of a copper model over its historical period, 1955-1971. This is not the whole sample period for the model, but the earlier years of the Korean War are deleted from this exercise. Also, the copper model is open with respect to general economic activity. Many exogenous inputs are assigned observed values.

The scrap price, the London Metal Exchange price, and U.S. production (new scrap) are estimated with fairly large errors. The other variables in the table all show moderate accuracy—5 percent would be a pretty good target level of adequate performance. On this, as an average basis, we can say that the copper model being analyzed here meets overall accuracy standards. If all errors were less than 5 percent, or better, less than 1 percent, we could attach a great deal of confidence to the use of this model. There will be better and worse models, but this indicates that a standard model for an often-studied important market can reasonably well be used to good advantage, and is not hopelessly dominated by unexplained noise.

Scope of the Effort

As I have noted on many occasions, the world's commodity markets are dominated by some 30 to 40 commodities. The main commodities—all in this group—will account for more than three-fourths of all world trade in commodities. The effective study of commodities for interrelated stabilization policy must include this whole range, or the bulk of it, in order to work well. Results to date suggest that this is possible. Not only were exemplary cases integrated with the LINK model, but a substantial number were. If we can carry commodity research to the point of estimating models for a considerable number of cases and solving them together with the LINK system, there is no reason why we cannot go all the way and include the whole range of 30 to 40 cases.

Main classes of commodities are ordered by type. There are grains, fibers, other field crops, tree crops, nonferrous metals, ferrous metals, fuels, and other industrial materials. They each have their particular characteristics, many of which are in important institutional settings that must be taken into account fully.

Grains: Both developed and developing countries are primary producers. Since farmers and food are both strategic in politics and in general life, grains are usually given some special price supports. In addition, the United States has PL480 (for aid shipments), and Canada operates under the Wheat Marketing Board. Grains are particularly subject to the vagaries of weather.

Fibers: Like grains, fibers are produced in developed as well as developing countries in large volume. Their prices are supported in some major countries.

Other Field Crops: A notable case is sugar. It is an important cash crop, vital to the welfare of whole nations. Natural forces have made supply variable, but this does not seem to have happened with the frequency observed for grains. World sugar agreements have acted as important industrial constraints. Developed nations are important on both the producing and consuming side of the market.

Tree Crops: These are produced almost entirely in developing countries. Japan is an exception as far as tea production is concerned. The Coffee Agreement is not as effective as it was intended to be, but it is sufficiently important that its provisions should be built right into the model. The long lead time for tree maturity is important in determining the appropriate time shape of lagged response.

Nonferrous Metals: These can be stockpiled–almost indefinitely if the market and financing are appropriate. Production is not concentrated exclusively in the developing countries–both the Soviet Union and the United States are important producers and have large stakes in this sector of modeling. Australia, Canada, and other industrial countries are also primary suppliers. Some of the commodities in this group are organized under producer associations–CIPEC, the International Tin Council–and might be distributed under a marketing agreement. Environmental restrictions impact significantly in this area of model building.

Ferrous Metals: These materials are closely tied to developments in the steel industry. The same thing could be said about some of the nonferrous metals that are used in specialty steels. As in the case of nonferrous metals, a great deal of producer activity is in the developed as well as in the developing countries.

The technology of the use of iron ore may bring about some extensive specification changes. This metal is mined in both developed and developing countries.

Fuels: These commodities have had such great publicity and created such public awareness that it is hard to be innovative. The treatments of oil, natural gas, and coal should be kept separate from one another. OPEC is tightly organized, but the publicly released aspects should be included in the model in the most detail possible. Coal is not as important in the world community as is oil, but it (coal) merits a great deal of attention. It is found (for export) in both developing and developed countries.

Other Industrial Materials: These make up a (strong) residual group. Rubber should be treated like agricultural commodities for modeling, but synthetic rubber may come to dominate an ever-increasing share of the market. New technology for natural rubber must be taken into account in future scenarios.

It was remarked that some of the commodities traded on world markets are supplied in large quantity by the Soviet Union and also by her partner countries in Europe's East Bloc. This poses a real question about our ability to model the whole world as we should. It is going to prove to be impossible for the time being—and probably indefinitely—to get reliable data on stocks, production, consumption, trading price, and other key pieces of information, statistical or otherwise. Markets in some model exercises are closed, through the use of estimated data for related variables. Stocks and prices, however, are likely to continue to prove to be elusive. An assumption can be made that prices follow world markets, but that is not accurate for internal prices in CMEA trade or for bilateral agreements. It is not only a matter of those goods which are supplied by the Soviet Union or its partners; it is also a matter of their bulk acquisitions. Two notable cases are Cuban sugar and Egyptian cotton. Commodities like these are not always traded with the Soviet Union on the basis of bilateral agreements, but they have been often enough in the past to affect some statistical sample estimates in model building.

To model comprehensively the world of commodities is not without its obstacles, but it is not a pure dream. It is within the limits of a reasonable research effort to do most of the world for most of the main commodities. A great deal is already under way or already accomplished; so it is largely a matter of time until we bring it to a satisfactory conclusion.

Applications of Control Theory Methods to Commodity Markets

Economic policy, generally, and commodity stabilization, particularly, offer opportunities for use of optimization methods under the heading of optimal control. It is possible to model commodity markets, as indicated in this chapter and this whole book, but one might try to go further than simply to simulate examples of desired time paths of prices, supplies, shipments, and stocks that give us either predicted or improved values of the variables involved. One might seek optimal values.

Optimal values may be defined as follows. Let the model of a commodity market be written as

$$F(y_t', \ldots, y_{t-p}'; x_t', \ldots, x_{t-p}'; z_t', \ldots, z_{t-q}'; w_t', \ldots, w_{t-q}', \theta') = e_t$$

and define the criterion or loss function as

$$L = L[(y_1 - y_1^*)', \ldots, (y_h - y_h^*)'; (z_1 - z_1^*)', \ldots, (z_h - z_h^*)']$$

The optimal control problem is the solution to the minimization process

$$L = \min \qquad \text{s.t. } F = e_t \qquad t = 1, \ldots, h$$

The meaning of the symbols is explained by the definitions: F is a column vector of functional relationships with as many elements as there are endogenous variables (y_t, x_t) in the system; y_t is a column vector of target endogenous variables with y_t^* as target values; x_t is a column vector of nontarget endogenous variables; z_t is a column vector of instrumental exogenous variables, with z_t^* as instrument values; w_t is a column vector of noninstrument exogenous variables; θ is a column vector of parameters (economic reaction coefficients); e_t is a column of random errors; L is a (scalar) loss function; and h is the horizon over which the optimal policy is to be executed.

The optimal control problem is therefore one of choosing policy instruments so as to minimize loss over the horizon $t = 1, 2, \ldots, h$. By minimizing loss, we mean to bring the values of y_t as close as possible to prearranged *target* values by proper choice of instrument values. The loss function is made to depend on instrument values, as well as target values, so that the policy maker does not choose extreme values of instruments in order to achieve policy aims. In other words, we impose a cost of instrumentation.

The policy maker is not free to seek an optimum, even taking account of the cost of instrumentation, but must observe the limits of what is economically feasible. The descriptive model of the economy

$$F = e_t$$

serves as a set of constraints. The constraints system is generally a nonlinear, dynamic, stochastic model of the economy.

Having built a (dynamic, stochastic, nonlinear) commodity model ($F = e_t$), we then use its empirical estimate, at first in nonstochastic mode ($\hat{F} = 0$), to serve as a constraint system for achieving a policy maker's goals. The policy maker—stockpile authority in this case—sets his targets for stock volume, for its distribution (geographically or by commodity variety), for price, and for consumption. He next selects a criterion function, dependent on departure of variables from their targets, and finally computes the optimal values. A simple loss function will probably be chosen—quadratic or exponential are customary cases.

The optimality of this result depends on how good the constraint system is as a description of reality, on taking account of the stochastic nature of the system, and on the time horizon. It is optimal in a limited sense and should not be taken to mean that one cannot find a better solution. Perhaps by modifying the constraint system (by statute or otherwise), it may be possible to reach a far superior position on the surface of the loss function. Random numbers can be generated from appropriate distribution functions to relax the assumption that $e_t = 0$. Stochastically generated optimal control can be implemented.

These suggestions, including the simplest case, may seem to pose formidable computational problems, but recent advances have enabled econometricians to overcome the obstacles of numerical analysis. Many fine programs exist for finding optimal solutions, and these can be brought into use without much trouble or cost (per simulation). Actually, individual commodity models tend to be of only moderate size, and their evaluation in optimal mode is likely to be much easier than is the case with the large economywide econometric models of some 500 to 1000 equations.

Given our present technical capabilities in dealing with the methods of optimal control, it would seem that commodity market studies offer fruitful opportunities for making some tentative and experimental applications. A large amount of effort has been expended at both the methodological and substantive level in studying the performance of the macro economy with the techniques of optimal control. There are probably more caveats and more difficulties in making these kinds of applications than in the *partial* analyses of individual market models. The most successful engineering applications of control methods are in running individual plants or within-plant operations. By analogy, we would be well advised in econometrics to take a more limited area of application to investigate the use of such methods in the control of sociopolitico-economic processes. A well-defined commodity market model in which a fair amount of experience has been generated from construction and operation through simulation search techniques would be a good starting point. Models of copper, tin, cocoa, or similar commodities have been subjects for stochastic simulation, buffer stock operation, and stabilization rules. It would be rewarding, at least from an operational viewpoint, to examine carefully the functioning of automatic control mechanisms for one of these commodities or others that have already been strongly researched. The steps would be:

1. Careful construction of a model in one of those fields, with great attention paid to the parametric specification in the light of control applications—care in specifying F and estimating θ from data samples. The model should be worldwide, covering the whole geographical market.
2. Attention paid to stochastic specification, estimation of the covariance matrix, $Ee_te_t' = \Sigma_e$.
3. Exploration of alternative loss functions L, targets y_t^*, and instruments z_t.
4. Computation of the optimal policies from $L = \min$, s.t. $\hat{F} = 0$ (deterministic case), or $\hat{F} = \hat{e}_t$ (stochastic case).
5. Careful study of the results of (4) to examine plausibility of the optimal paths; i.e., are requirements for values of z_t attainable? Calculation of error bands to show ranges within which the controls must operate and ranges of final results.

If the control theory applications are approached in the proper investigative light, it may be possible to develop some promising stabilization methods. A careful study should focus on one commodity market and see how far that case may be taken with present data and methodological capabilities.

Hopes

Even if it were decided that active stabilization policies were to be seriously pursued, it could not be said from the econometric side that we are ready to step in and provide the kind of accuracy needed to do a good economic policy job. The approach through formal econometric modeling for commodity market stabilization is still experimental.

Several trial cases with simulated stabilization and experimental projections of actual market conditions should be completed before serious use is made of model-based management of a stabilization program. It has been my experience that repeated application is required with a model over a period of some months or years before the full response characteristics of the statistical system are well understood. In this trial or testing period it invariably happens that the performance of the model, in its applied uses, improves significantly. A start must be made, however; and it should be clearly understood, at the present time, that model use is purely experimental. All the while that systems are being used, they should be subject to continuous investigation to expand coverage and generally improve each model on its own. A priori information from market specialists should be relied on heavily to supplement, revise, and improve the formal models.

At first, commodity stocks would have to be accumulated; then buying or selling in the interests of stabilization would be carried out in much the same fashion as open market managers operate in financial markets to attain monetary stability. The same practices could be carried over to commodity markets. Gradually, we should look to the attainment of a combination of judgement from commodity specialists and objectivity from a model, interpreted through the eyes of the model builders.

It is taken for granted in the above comments that stabilization policy is desirable. Model building in commodity markets, by itself, will not be able to pass on the validity or social preference for commodity market stabilization achieved through an active policy. Economic and philosophical arguments must come to grips with the problem of desirability of stabilization policy. The econometrics of commodity markets should stay clear of that kind of influence. They should tell, if possible, what degree of stability can be realistically attained.

Econometric models seem to be the natural tool to use in a market stabilization program. They seem to be the only way to gain systematic understanding of what is going on in this area of economic analysis. They estimate the amount of noise in the system and show the range of error to be expected in making economic decisions. They should be neutral as to underlying economic preferences.

A great deal of work can be done to improve the data base—making it both more accurate and more extensive. This should also improve the error performance. Commodity specialists should add their contribution. The remaining gains will come from experience, stretching over the next few years. Whether or not the world is ready for comprehensive commodity stabilization is open to question, but the willingness of model builders to participate is probably not. They should be ready and available with the best they can put together at this particular time. The requisite econometric effort will require at least three to five years to be put on a fully workable basis if a sizable research effort is mounted. It is not therefore possible to provide comprehensive econometric support for market stabilization at this time, except on a selective basis. The gains from successful operation of stabilization programs are sufficiently great that it appears to be well worthwhile to wait until a full-scale research effort has been brought to maturity.

Part II
Theoretical Considerations of Commodity Market Stabilization

6 The Distribution of Welfare Gains from Price Stabilization: A Survey of Some Theoretical Issues

Stephen J. Turnovsky

Introduction

The desirability of price stabilization is a subject with a long history in economics. Much of the discussion has taken place in the context of agricultural commodities, where random prices, reflecting stochastic fluctuations in demand and supply, can be particularly important. The problem was first analyzed by Waugh (1944), when he established the proposition that consumers having a downward sloping demand curve and facing random prices due to stochastic fluctuations in supply are better off than if these prices were stabilized at their mean.[1] Some years later, Oi (1961) demonstrated a parallel proposition for firms. He showed that if they have an upward-sloping supply curve and face random selling prices due to stochastic shifts in demand, then they too will lose from having prices stabilized at their mean.[2]

These two approaches considered the welfare of one group only, ignoring the effects the price stabilization scheme may have on the other. This was first recognized by Massell (1969), who integrated the Waugh and Oi arguments into a single framework, within the context of a linear model, and derived a number of interesting results. First, he showed that whether price stabilization benefits one group or the other depends upon the source of the random price fluctuations. For example, while his analysis confirms the Oi result, he also shows that if the random price is due to random fluctuations in supply, then producers will in fact benefit from price stabilization. Second, when both producers and consumers are taken into account simultaneously, price stabilization will always (at least potentially) improve total welfare, even though one group may be adversely affected. Hence, overall price stabilization is desirable.

The Waugh-Oi-Massell analysis is based on (at least) two key assumptions. First, it assumes that the demand and supply functions depend upon the actual known market prices. This means that both consumers and producers are able to make their decisions with complete information available, although this information is constantly changing. Consequently, this literature can be described more appropriately as applying to a situation of price variability rather than price uncertainty, since a fundamental aspect of this latter case is the fact that some decisions must be made on the basis of imperfect information. Second, the stochastic disturbances are assumed to be *additive,* implying that the random disturbances consist of parallel shifts in the functions. As we shall show below, this assumption is directly responsible for some of the specific conclusions pertaining to the distribution of the welfare gains from stabilization.

With the uncertainty in commodity prices associated with the recent inflationary conditions, the problem of price stabilization has once again become a topical issue. The literature is growing rapidly, and it would be reasonable to say that most of these more recent contributions draw heavily on the seminal works of Waugh, Oi, and Massell, attempting to extend their analyses in various ways. The purpose of this chapter is to survey some of these more recent developments. Most of my attention is devoted to discussing the results obtained. With a few exceptions, details of proofs are not given, but are available in an expanded version of this chapter.

The chapter proceeds as follows. In the basic framework section I review the work underlying the Waugh-Oi-Massell analysis and most of the subsequent literature, while the following section reviews the basic Waugh-Oi-Massell model itself. As was already noted, one of the key assumptions underlying Massell's work (which provides the integrated treatment) is that of linear demand and supply curves and additive disturbances. While this has the advantage that the expressions measuring the welfare gains from stabilization can be calculated explicitly, linearity is nevertheless a highly restrictive assumption. Much relevant empirical work finds nonlinear relations such as log-linear functions to be superior, in which case the Massell results are inapplicable. Likewise, agricultural economists often argue that it is the slopes rather than the positions of the supply curves that are stochastic, suggesting that multiplicative disturbances may be more appropriate; see, for example, Hazell and Scandizzo (1975). The fourth section therefore considers the case where the demand and supply functions are nonlinear and the stochastic disturbances enter multiplicatively and shows how this specification leads to substantial modification of many of Massell's conclusions.

Also, as mentioned before, the basic model assumes that all decisions are made on the basis of complete information. As far as the demand side is concerned, this assumption is perfectly natural, since typically consumers need not make their decisions until they are confronted with actual market prices. For firms, however, the assumption is much less plausible. Indeed, it runs counter to virtually all recent literature on the firm under uncertainty, which emphasizes the need to make some, if not all, production decisions before the actual selling price is known.[3] This is particularly relevant with respect to agricultural commodities, where production lags may be important and producers are unable to adjust instantaneously to actual prices as they occur. Hence, in the fifth section I consider the welfare effects for both producers and consumers of stabilizing prices in the case where firms make their supply decisions on the basis of expected prices, before they learn the actual market price, and are unable to modify these decisions in the short run. This is precisely the underlying assumption of all the "cobweb" type analyses that developed from this aspect of agricultural commodity markets.[4] Two alternative expectations generating schemes are considered; the conventional "adaptive" scheme and the Muthian "rational" hypothesis.

Most of the literature relates to a single market in a closed economy. Recently, however, as a result of the worldwide nature of the current inflationary conditions, the desirability of stabilizing the prices of internationally traded goods has begun to receive increasing attention. In the sixth section, therefore, I briefly consider how the Waugh-Oi-Massell model can be extended to deal with this issue. Most of the discussion focuses on the linear-additive case, although the nonlinear-multiplicative case (the analogue to the fourth section) is also briefly mentioned.

The stabilization models are all based on "perfect" stabilization in the sense that the authorities maintain a completely stable price by buying and selling as required to exactly offset any random disturbances in private demand or supply. In practice, the lack of necessary information and the existence of adjustment costs make it impossible for the authorities to stabilize with this precision. As a consequence, they are more likely to adopt some kind of *partial* adjustment policy, the objective of which is to reduce, if not eliminate entirely, the variability in prices. This is discussed in the seventh section, where two such policies are considered. First, the authorities may allow the price to fluctuate within some band of the desired level and to intervene only when the price moves outside this band. Second, they may adopt some fixed rule, whereby, for example, their degree of intervention is proportional to the difference between the actual and the desired (long-run equilibrium) price.

In the eighth section I consider an alternative form of government intervention. Rather than entering the market directly, the stabilization authority may seek to influence the movement of prices by announcing forecasts that in turn influence the behavior of private producers. Their function in this case is purely an informational one, directed at making the market operate more efficiently.

In the ninth section some more general extensions are briefly considered. These include an extension of the basic Waugh-Oi-Massell model to a multimarket situation; a more general utility-maximizing approach to the Waugh and Oi analyses, again in a multicommodity context; and a brief introduction to the recent general equilibrium models of price uncertainty. Finally, the chapter concludes with a few general remarks.

The Basic Framework

Apart from the more general extensions discussed below, the models considered are based on a number of common underlying assumptions, which I wish to enunciate at the outset.

First, most of the existing literature is *partial equilibrium* in nature. In the present context, this term is used in two senses. The usual application of the term is to a model that focuses on a single market in which demand and supply together determine the market clearing price in that market (which is therefore endogenously determined), but that abstracts from any repercussions that market may have on the rest of the economy. However, the term is also used to refer to a multimarket situation in which the (random) prices are taken to be exogenously given; see Hanoch (1974).

Second, the typical assumption made is that price stabilization takes place by means of a self-liquidating buffer stock; that is, a buffer stock of the commodity is set up, with the stabilizing authority choosing the fixed price at which they are willing to buy and sell in such a way that at that price the long-run size of the buffer stock is expected to remain constant. In other words, at the stabilized price the authority expects the random fluctuations in demand and supply to even out, so that on the average they will neither accumulate nor decumulate stocks of the commodity. If the underlying demand and supply curves are linear, this means that the price is stabilized at its arithmetic mean. However, if the underlying relationships are nonlinear, the stabilized price at which the buffer stock is self-liquidating is *not* generally equal to the arithmetic mean; see the section on nonlinear analysis.

Third, the operation of a buffer stock obviously involves storage and administrative costs. These are typically ignored in assessing the desirability of price stabilization, although they should be taken into account.[5] Furthermore, in the case of partial stabilization schemes of the type to be discussed later, the stabilization authority will typically have a nonzero expected profit (in contrast to perfect stabilization, in which a self-liquidating buffer stock will, on the average, break even financially as well as not accumulate stock), and these too need to be taken into account as part of the benefits.[6]

Finally, in order to assess the benefits from stabilization to the different sectors of the economy—usually taken to be producers and consumers—the introduction of some welfare criteria is required. In the case of producers, this is typically taken to be expected producers' surplus or expected profit. The question of the desirability of price stabilization as far as producers are concerned can then be stated as: What are the effects of price stabilization on the expected profit of producers?

The expected profit criterion assumes that producers are risk neutral, in the sense that their underlying utility function is linear in profit. This is clearly restrictive, and authors such as Massell (1970) have also considered the effects of price stabilization on the variance of producers' profit and investigated the trade-offs between these first two moments. More generally, the benefits from stabilization under conditions of nonneutral attitudes to risk can be assessed in terms of a concave (or convex) utility function of profit; see Hanoch (1974). On the one hand, this introduces a subjective element into the evaluation, namely the coefficient of risk aversion $-U''/U'$ (where U is the utility function and the primes denote derivatives). The expected profit criterion, on the other hand, has the distinct advantage of being an entirely objective statistical measure of welfare.

Consumers' welfare is usually evaluated in terms of expected consumers' surplus. This measure of benefits, although widely used in this and other areas of applied cost-benefit analysis, has well-known limitations and has long been criticized by economists; see, for example, Samuelson (1947); and Little (1957). Recently, however, this criticism has become tempered somewhat, and the consumers' surplus measure is regaining some credibility as a useful criterion for applied work; see Samuelson (1974). For example, Willig (1976) has shown that in most cases the error committed by consumers' surplus as an approximation to a compensating variation or equivalent variation is less than 2 percent. Furthermore, contrary to what is sometimes thought, it does not necessarily imply risk neutrality for consumers (in the sense of the indirect utility function being linear in income); it is perfectly consistent with the notion of risk aversion in the sense of Arrow (1963) and Pratt (1964). In addition, as we shall show in the section on multicommodity generalizations, for realistic parameter values, the conclusions consumers' surplus yields are generally consistent with those obtained with general concave utility functions. Thus, applied with care, consumers' surplus can be a useful and operational welfare measure.

Finally, total private welfare is taken to consist of the sum of the welfare of producers and of consumers and is given by the sum of the two surplus measures.[7]

The Waugh-Oi-Massell Model

Consider a single market in which demand and supply are described by the linear relations

$$D(P_t) = A - aP_t + u_t \qquad a \geqslant 0 \tag{6.1a}$$

$$S(P_t) = B + bP_t + v_t \qquad b \geqslant 0 \tag{6.1b}$$

where D_t equals demand; S_t equals supply; P_t equals short-run equilibrium price; and A, B, a, and b, are deterministic constants. The terms u_t and v_t denote additive stochastic disturbances, which are assumed to be independently distributed over time and to have zero means and finite variances σ_u^2 and σ_v^2 respectively and to have zero covariance. This last assumption means that the random shifts in the demand and supply schedules are independent of one another.

In the absence of price stabilization, the short-run equilibrium price P_t will be

$$P_t = (u_t - v_t + A - B)/(a + b) \tag{6.2a}$$

while the equilibrium quantity traded will be

$$D(P_t) = S(P_t) = \frac{Ba + bA}{a + b} + \frac{av_t + bu_t}{a + b} \tag{6.2b}$$

Suppose now that a stabilization authority establishes a buffer stock, being willing to buy or sell the commodity at a price P_s, at which the nonstochastic components of demand and supply are equal. That is, it sets P_s where

$$E(D_t) = E(S_t) \tag{6.3}$$

so that, on the average, the market balances. In order to maintain this price, the authority must continually trade an amount

$$x_t = v_t - u_t \tag{6.4}$$

the expected value of which is zero.[8] Hence the buffer stock will be self-liquidating, in the sense that the expected size of the buffer stock will remain constant over time. Taking expected values of (6.1) and equating, yields[9]

$$P_s = (A - B)/(a + b) = E(P_t) \tag{6.5}$$

with the corresponding quantities

$$D(P_s) = \frac{Ba + bA}{a + b} + u_t \tag{6.6a}$$

$$S(P_s) = \frac{Ba + bA}{a + b} + v_t \tag{6.6b}$$

Thus comparing (6.5) with the expected value of (6.2a), it follows that in this case the self-liquidating buffer stock implies that the price is stabilized at its arithmetic mean. This result is a consequence of the linearity of the model and does not apply to the more general nonlinear model; see the section on nonlinear analysis.

Measuring producers' welfare by producers' surplus (profit), their welfare in the absence of price stabilization, when the random price P_t prevails, is

$$\pi_t = \int_{P(0)}^{P_t} S(P')dP'$$

where $P(0)$ denotes the supply price at zero output. Likewise, profit at the stabilized price P_s is given by

$$\pi_s = \int_{P(0)}^{P_s} S(P')dP'$$

so that the difference in producers' welfare in the two cases is simply

$$G_p = \pi_s - \pi_t = \int_{P_t}^{P_s} S(P')dP' \tag{6.7}$$

Substituting the linear supply function (6.1b), (6.7) integrates to

$$\begin{aligned} G_p &= \tfrac{1}{2}(P_s - P_t)[S(P_t) + S(P_s)] \\ &= -\tfrac{1}{2}\left(\frac{u_t - v_t}{a + b}\right)\left[\frac{2(Ba + bA)}{a + b} + \frac{(2a + b)v_t + bu_t}{a + b}\right] \end{aligned} \tag{6.8}$$

Similarly, measuring consumers' welfare by consumers' surplus, their difference in welfare becomes

$$G_c = \tfrac{1}{2}(P_t - P_s)[D(P_t) + D(P_s)] \tag{6.9}$$

Furthermore, assuming that total welfare can be adequately measured by the sum of producers' and consumers' surplus,

$$G = G_p + G_c = \tfrac{1}{2}(P_s - P_t)[S(P_s) - D(P_s)] \tag{6.10}$$

The expected gains from stabilization (which are usually referred to as just "gains") to producers, consumers, and the two groups together are obtained by taking expected values of (6.8), (6.9), and (6.10) respectively, yielding

$$E(G_p) = \frac{-b\sigma_u^2 + (2a + b)\sigma_v^2}{2(a + b)^2} \tag{6.11a}$$

$$E(G_c) = \frac{(2b + a)\sigma_u^2 - a\sigma_v^2}{2(a + b)^2} \tag{6.11b}$$

$$E(G) = \frac{(\sigma_u^2 + \sigma_v^2)}{2(a + b)} > 0 \tag{6.11c}$$

Equations (6.11a,b,c) immediately yield most of Massell's principal conclusions:

1. Producers lose (gain) from price stabilization if the source of price instability is random shifts in demand (supply).
2. Consumers lose (gain) from price stabilization if the source of price instability is random shifts in supply (demand).
3. Where both demand and supply are random, the gains to each group are indeterminate and depend upon the relative sizes of the variances σ_u^2 and σ_v^2, and upon the slopes of the demand and supply curves.
4. The total gains from stabilization are always positive, with the gainers in principle being able to compensate the losers.

Note also that the gains or losses are strictly proportional to the variances σ_u^2 and σ_v^2. If the demand or supply curve becomes infinitely elastic, the gains from stabilization tend to zero. Finally, these results all depend crucially on the linearity of the model and the additivity of the stochastic disturbances. One can show that with nonlinear demand and supply functions, some of these propositions cease to hold.

A Nonlinear Analysis[10]

As we have already indicated, the conclusions of the Waugh-Oi-Massell model are based on the restrictive assumptions of a linear model with additive stochastic disturbances. It can be shown that the conclusions obtained by Massell regarding the distribution of welfare gains are subject to relatively minor modifications if one assumes nonlinear demand and supply functions—as long as the stochastic disturbances are still additive.[11]

By contrast, it turns out that the distributional conclusions are highly sensitive to the form of stochastic disturbance assumed. Hence, in this section we extend Massell's analysis to the case in which the demand and supply functions are nonlinear and the stochastic disturbances are multiplicative. We are thus considering a situation in which it is the *slopes* rather than the positions of the demand and supply curves that are random. As demonstrated by Turnovsky (1976*a*), this case is, theoretically at least, as justifiable as the more familiar additive one, in the sense of being easily derivable from the underlying microeconomic considerations.

Hence, suppose now that demand and supply are specified by the functions

$$D = ud(P) \qquad d' < 0, u \geqslant 0 \tag{6.12a}$$

$$S = vs(P) \qquad s' > 0, v \geqslant 0 \tag{6.12b}$$

where D equals demand; S equals supply; P equals price; and the terms u and v denote stochastic disturbances with means $\bar{u}$ and $\bar{v}$, respectively, and having finite second moments.[12] The two random variables may be correlated; but if so, their correlation coefficient must be strictly less than unity in magnitude, thus ruling out a perfect linear relationship between them.

Because of the nonlinearity of the functions d and s, the calculation of explicit measures of benefits from stabilization becomes impractical. Instead, the analysis proceeds by investigating the convexity or concavity properties of various stochastic functions, including the various welfare measures, thereby enabling us to compare their expected values with their values in certain stabilized situations. This involves extensive use of a multivariate extension of Jensen's inequality; the details of the method are discussed at length by Turnovsky (1976*a*). Here we merely summarize the main qualitative conclusions.[13]

First it can be shown that in general $P_s \neq E(P)$, so that the stabilized price at which the buffer stock is self-liquidating is *not* the arithmetic mean price. Indeed, in general one cannot infer anything about whether $P_s \gtrless E(P)$. For example, if the functions d and s are linear in P, then $P_s \leqslant E(P)$ if the only disturbances are in supply; while if the only disturbances are in demand, this inequality is reversed.

The distribution of welfare gains from price stabilization in the present situation, where the random disturbances are multiplicative, differ in several significant respects from those of the basic model, where additive disturbances are assumed. The most important general difference is that the desirability of price stabilization for either producers or consumers *does not depend on the source of the price instability,* as it does in the additive case, but only upon the shapes of the deterministic components of the demand and supply curves. If one group benefits from having price stabilized, it will do so whether the random price arises from stochastic disturbances in demand or in supply.[14]

As in the basic model, stabilization leads to an overall welfare gain unless either demand or supply is perfectly elastic. However, the allocation of these benefits between consumers and producers is much more indeterminate than before (although as we have been stressing it does *not* depend on the source of the random price). Broadly speaking, producers gain from having either demand and/or supply disturbances stabilized if demand is elastic and supply inelastic, while they lose in the reverse situation. Similarly, consumers tend to gain if supply is elastic and demand is inelastic, and be worse off otherwise. However, we should hasten to add that these statements are generalities and certainly need not hold in particular cases. One instance where they are only partially true is where demand and supply are specified log-linearly. This example is of particular interest because it is the exact multiplicative analogue of Massell's linear-additive model. In this case, producers gain from stabilization if and only if the elasticity of demand exceeds unity (in magnitude), while consumers always gain, irrespective of the underlying elasticities. These propositions are established more formally by Turnovsky (1976*a*).

Price Expectations[15]

The models we have been discussing assume that firms make their decisions on the basis of actual selling prices. This assumption can be justified by supposing either that firms have perfectly flexible production plans—i.e., they are able to modify their original decisions at zero cost when they learn the true selling price—or that they have perfect foresight. Clearly, either of these assumptions is most restrictive in a stochastic environment.

In this section I will therefore outline a model in which supply decisions are based on expected prices. Two alternative kinds of expectations-generating mechanisms are considered. The first is the adaptive scheme. This is undoubtedly the most widely used of the autoregressive forecasting procedures, which as a class are recognized as being rather restrictive and usually nonoptimal, since they do not allow the forecaster to use all available information in forming his prediction. Accordingly, as an alternative approach, it is assumed that producers form their expectations "rationally" in the sense of Muth (1961); that is, producers are assumed to make forecasts consistent with those of the model and to use all available information efficiently. Because of the fact that these theories of expectations have been developed for only linear models, we revert to the linear model used earlier.

Adaptive Expectations

Suppose that firms make their supply decisions on the basis of the anticipated selling price. That is, (6.1b) is replaced by the equation

$$S(P_t^*) = B + bP_t^* + v_t \qquad b \geqslant 0 \tag{6.1b'}$$

where P_t^* denotes the selling price producers expect to prevail at time t.[16] The assumption that these expectations are formed adaptively is described by the equation

$$P_t^* - P_{t-1}^* = \gamma(P_{t-1} + P_{t-1}^*) \qquad 0 \leqslant \gamma \leqslant 1 \tag{6.13}$$

This equation asserts that the change in expectations equals some fraction of the previous period's forecast error, where γ describes the rate of adaptation.

Consumers are still assumed to make their decisions on the basis of actual market prices, so that demand is still described by (6.1a). However, the stochastic disturbances are now generalized to allow for first order autocorrelation in the disturbances.[17]

Because of the fact that producers supply on the basis of expected rather than actual prices, their expected gains from stabilization are given by the expression[18]

$$E(G_p) = E\left\{(P_s - P_t^*)[S(P_s) - S(P_t^*)]\right\} - E[(P_t - P_s)S(P_t^*)] \tag{6.14}$$

The gains to consumers are still given by (6.9).

It can be shown that whether or not producers facing an uncertain demand will gain or lose from having prices stabilized depends crucially on the autoregressive properties of the random disturbance, as well as on the length of lag in the formation of expectations and the relative slopes of the demand and supply schedules. Nothing conclusive can be inferred until these parameters are specified.

Turning to consumers, the Waugh proposition that consumers are hurt by having prices stabilized in the face of supply fluctuations still applies. That this result continues to hold is not really surprising, since in the present model consumers are still able to make their decisions on the basis of actual market prices, so that in this respect the consumer side of the analysis is essentially unchanged. However, it can be shown that consumers could either gain or lose from having their own demand fluctuations stabilized. Thus, despite the fact that the demand side of the market is essentially unchanged from the previous analysis, this result differs quite markedly from the corresponding response of the earlier model. The reason for the difference stems from the fact that under the adaptive-expectations hypothesis, supply becomes a function of previous prices. With demand being subject to stochastic shifts, these prices become random; so that in the absence of price stabilization, the random elements in demand induce random shifts in supply. Thus, in effect, this case creates simultaneous stochastic disturbances in demand and supply. Stabilizing for these two sources of random disturbances has offsetting effects on consumer welfare, thereby creating the resulting indeterminacy.

The preceding comments can be summarized as follows. As in the Massell model, stabilizing for supply fluctuations will deteriorate the welfare of consumers. However, stabilizing for demand fluctuations can have different welfare effects from those implied by the basic Waugh-Oi-Massell model. But again, as in that model, total welfare as measured by the sum of producers' and consumers' welfare is increased with stabilization, even though one group may be hurt.[19]

Rational Expectations

The rationality hypothesis is formally described by

$$P_t^* = {}_{t-1}\mathrm{E}_1(P_t) \tag{6.15}$$

where ${}_{t-1}\mathrm{E}_1$ denotes conditional expectations at time (t - 1). This equation asserts that the forecaster's predicted price for period *t* should equal the price predicted by the system, conditional on all the information available at time

$(t - 1)$, when the forecast is made. Thus the prediction, along with the actual realization, becomes an *endogenous* part of the model. Predicting according to (6.15) can easily be shown to minimize the variance of the forecast error and be most efficient in that sense.

Inserting (6.15) into the basic model, one can draw the following qualitative conclusions. These are essentially the same as those derived from Massell's perfect flexibility model.[20]

1. Producers lose from price stabilization if the source of price instability is random shifts in demand, provided that these random disturbances are autocorrelated (either positively or negatively). They gain from having supply fluctuations stabilized, irrespective of their autoregressive properties.
2. Consumers lose (gain) from price stabilization if the source of price instability is random shifts in supply (demand).
3. The total gains from stabilization are always positive.

If all fluctuations are independently distributed through time, these gains are independent of the slope of the supply curve, depending only on the slope of the demand curve and the variances σ_u^2 and σ_v^2. Moreover, in this case, producers will be unaffected by having demand fluctuations stabilized; all gains will accrue to consumers.

The conclusion that with rational expectations producers cannot gain from having price stabilized for demand fluctuations is an extremely important one. It means that if producers are able to forecast efficiently, they are better off being able to exploit that information. This result contrasts with that obtained under adaptive expectations, where it was shown that they would gain from stabilization unless demand fluctuations were very highly autocorrelated. Hence, whether or not the Oi proposition extends to firms that base their supply decisions on expected prices depends to a large degree on the approach by which their forecasts are generated.

Moreover, it can be shown that the total gains from stabilization that assumes rational expectations are at least as great as those obtained when the firm has perfect flexibility, so that supply is a function of current prices. The instances in which the two expressions coincide are the limiting ones, where $b \to 0$, $a \to \infty$, or the autoregressive coefficients tend to unity in magnitude. In general, one cannot deduce anything definite about the comparative gains under the two alternative sets of expectations hypotheses. For independently distributed disturbances they are equal; while if the autoregressive coefficients are negative, one can show that the gains with adaptively formed expectations exceed those under rational expectations. However, for the more usual case of positively autocorrelated disturbances, nothing conclusive can be said without further knowledge of the parameters γ and b/a.

Summary

The main results of the two expectational models we have presented may be summarized as follows:

1. Whether or not the Oi proposition (which asserts that producers lose from price stabilization if the price instability originates with fluctuations in demand) continues to hold depends crucially upon how the expectations are generated, as well as the autoregressive properties of the stochastic disturbances.
2. If expectations are formed rationally, the Oi result will continue to hold, provided the demand fluctuations are either positively or negatively autocorrelated. If they are independently distributed, producers' welfare will be unaffected by the introduction of price stabilization.
3. The Oi proposition generally will not remain true if expectations are formed adaptively, unless the stochastic demand fluctuations are highly positively autocorrelated.
4. The parallel proposition for consumers, originally established by Waugh, will continue to hold under either form of expectations.
5. Massell's result that stabilization provides a net gain to producers and consumers taken together also continues to hold in both cases. In fact, one can derive the intuitively expected result that the gains from price stability are higher when supply is based on expected prices (again in both cases) than when it depends upon actual prices (perfect information).
6. Finally, essentially all of Massell's qualitative results remain unaltered under rational expectations, although some differences, including the modification to Oi's result, emerge with adaptive forecasting.

Stabilizing for Consumption and Production

Using a framework similar to that of the section on rational expectations, but with independently distributed disturbances, Subotnik and Houck (1976) have compared the benefits from the stabilization of prices at their mean with those of alternative schemes that stabilize consumption and production at their respective means. As far as expected total gains are concerned, they show that if $a \geqslant 2b$, then the gains from supply stabilization are at least as great as those from price stabilization, which in turn exceeds those from demand stabilization. If $a < 2b$, then the relative ranking of supply and price stabilization is reversed, but both remain superior to demand stabilization.

Moreover, while Subotnik and Houck follow the previous literature and abstract from cost effects, they do give some consideration to this question by considering the variance of changes in the government stocks associated with each of the three schemes. They argue that the larger the variance in stocks, the more the government must hold in order to operate the buffer stock with a given reliability; and therefore, the more costly the scheme. They show that for each scheme, the variance of the change in government stocks is proportional to expected social gains. Therefore, the storage costs involved can be ranked in the same order as the expected gains from the different stabilization schemes; that is, the more beneficial the scheme, the higher the cost.

International Aspects of Stabilization

There has been relatively little formal analysis of the benefits from price stabilization in an international context. One of the few detailed studies is by Hueth and Schmitz (1972), who disaggregate the Massell model to two countries, one of which they identify as an exporting country, the other as the importing nation.[21]

Using the surplus measures, they investigate the welfare effects of stabilization on producers in each country, consumers in each country, each country taken separately, and the world as a whole. For expositional ease, Hueth and Schmitz focus on the benefits in the exporting country. They conclude that:

1. Domestic producers gain from the stabilization of domestic supply disturbances; they lose from the stabilization of domestic demand disturbances and from the stabilization of foreign demand or supply disturbances.
2. Consumers in the domestic country gain from the stabilization of domestic demand fluctuations; they lose from the stabilization of domestic supply fluctuations and foreign demand or supply fluctuations.
3. The domestic economy gains from the stabilization of domestic disturbances (either demand or supply) but loses from the stabilization of foreign disturbances.
4. The world as a whole, i.e., the two countries taken together, gain from stabilization.

These results are a direct disaggregation of the Massell results, and analogous conclusions can easily be established for an importing country. Indeed there is nothing particularly "international" about this model, and the conclusions can be reinterpreted as relating to two individuals (or groups) within a closed economy.

Finally, these results have been extended to the nonlinear case by Just, Lutz, Schmitz, and Turnovsky (1976). As for the closed economic model, this can lead to some reallocation of the benefits from stabilization, although aggregate benefits remain always strictly positive. Broadly speaking, convexity of the aggregate demand function tends to shift the distribution of gains from stabilization in favor of consumers in both countries and against producers. It also tends to shift them away from exporters and in favor of importers. These results are of some importance in determining how the costs of operating an international buffer stock should be allocated.

Partial Stabilization

The models considered so far have all assumed that the authorities stabilize perfectly for any random disturbance, thereby maintaining a completely stable price. In practice, to stabilize precisely in this manner would involve extremely large stock operations with prohibitively large costs. Taking these costs into account, the authorities are more likely to engage in only partial stabilization.

There are two major forms this stabilization might take. These include a price-band policy, whereby the authorities intervene only when the price deviates from its long-run equilibrium by some amount, or some kind of fixed-linear policy adjustment rule.[22]

Price-Band Policy

Reverting to the linear Waugh-Oi-Massell model, suppose that instead of stabilizing perfectly at P_s, the authority allows the price to fluctuate freely in the range

$$P_1 \leqslant P_s \leqslant P_2$$

where P_1 and P_2 are the tolerable limits to the degree of price fluctuations. That is, the price-band policy rule $P_{b,t}$, say, is

$$\begin{aligned} P_{b,t} &= P_t \qquad P_1 \leqslant P_t \leqslant P_2 \\ &= P_1 \qquad P_t < P_1 \\ &= P_2 \qquad P_t > P_2 \end{aligned} \tag{6.16}$$

Given assumptions about the probability distributions for u_t and v_t, the probability distribution for P_t given by (6.2a) and for $P_{b,t}$ given by (6.16) can be determined.

The gains from price stabilization under such a policy can also be calculated. For producers, say, they are given by

$$E(G_p) = F(P_1) \int_{P}^{P_1} S(P')dP' + [1 - F(P_2)] \int_{P_2}^{P} S(P')dP' \qquad (6.17)$$

where $F(P) \equiv Pr(P_t \leqslant P)$ is the cumulative distribution function. In order to calculate these expressions explicitly, some specific form for the probability distribution for u_t and v_t, and hence for P_t, must be assumed. More generally, the qualitative directions of these gains can be evaluated by considering the concavity or convexity of $E(G_p)$ in terms of u_t and v_t, using the methods discussed in Turnovsky (1976*a*) and underlying the discussion in the section on nonlinear analysis.

Stabilization Rules

Suppose now that the buffer stock authorities attempt to stabilize prices by means of some fixed linear policy adjustment rule. This problem raises several issues. The first, and most basic, is whether or not such a rule will in fact succeed in reducing the variability of prices and what are the restrictions on the degree of intervention for the rule to be successful in this respect. Second, because of the fact that in general such a rule provides only *partial* stabilization, the "stabilized" price (as for the price-band policy) is in fact still stochastic. As a consequence, even if the stabilization authority sets the rule such that on the average its buffer stock remains constant, it nevertheless will on average make positive or negative profits. These net revenues must also be taken into account in assessing the benefits from stabilization. If, as in the subsequent analysis, the stabilization authority is required on average to make a profit (out of which the buffer stock scheme may be financed), further restrictions on the appropriate rule may be imposed. Third, the form of intervention followed by the stabilization authority may itself introduce random disturbances into the system, and these too must be taken into account.

We consider these issues briefly within the context of the basic model. Thus, instead of stabilizing price exactly at P_s, we now assume that the stabilization authority decides to intervene in the market in accordance with the adjustment rule.[23]

$$X_t = \mu(P_{\mu,t} - \bar{P}_t^e) \qquad (6.18)$$

where μ is a constant. Interpreting X_t to be net *purchases* by the authority, $X_t > 0$ implies that the authority is buying; if $X_t < 0$, it is selling. The term $P_{\mu,t}$ is the short-run market clearing price, where, in accordance with the notational convention introduced in note 23, the subscript μ is introduced to note the fact that with instantaneous government intervention this short-run price depends upon μ (see (6.19) below) and to distinguish it from P_t as defined in (6.2). Finally, $\bar{P}_t^e$ is the authority's forecast at time t of the long-run equilibrium price $\bar{P}$. As a result of imperfections in information, this forecast is not necessarily correct, but may deviate (by time varying amounts) from the true equilibrium price $\bar{P}$.

Thus equation (6.18) asserts that the decision rule used by the stabilization authority to intervene in the market is based on the difference between the short-run market price from the authority's forecast of the long-run equilibrium price. Intuitively, one would expect $\mu < 0$, in which case the authority buys when the current market price is below the forecast equilibrium and sells when the current price is above this level. The magnitude of μ, which describes the intensity of intervention by the authority in the market, reflects the costs of adjustment, as well as the quality of the authority's information.

Assuming that the authority's forecast errors in predicting $\bar{P}$ are random yields

$$\bar{P}_t^e = \bar{P} + e_t$$

where e_t is independently distributed over time, uncorrelated with u_t and v_t, and having zero mean and finite variance σ_e^2. Taking expected values of $\bar{P}_t^e$, it follows that

$$E(\bar{P}_t^e) = \bar{P}$$

so that on average these prediction errors cancel out. Substituting for $\bar{P}_t^e$ into (6.18), the adjustment rule can be expressed as

$$X_t = \mu(P_{\mu,t} - \bar{P}) + w_t \tag{6.18$'$}$$

where $w_t = -\mu e_t$ and hence,

$$E(w_t) = 0 \qquad E(w_t^2) = \mu^2 \sigma_e^2$$

Thus the additive disturbance w_t is a consequence of the imperfect information upon which the authority's policy-adjustment rule is based. In this respect, intervention by the authority introduces independent random disturbances into the market.[24]

Hence, assuming X_t to be given by (6.18′), the short-run market clearing price with intervention by the authority $P_{\mu,t}$ is determined where

$$D_t + X_t = S_t$$

implying

$$P_{\mu,t} = \bar{P} + \frac{u_t + w_t - v_t}{a + b - \mu} \tag{6.19}$$

Thus

$$E(P_{\mu,t}) = \bar{P} \tag{6.20a}$$

and

$$\sigma^2_{P,\mu} = \frac{\sigma^2_u + \sigma^2_w + \sigma^2_v}{(a + b - \mu)^2} \tag{6.20b}$$

It therefore follows that $E(X_t) = 0$, ensuring that the buffer stock will be self-liquidating.

The first issue to be considered, namely whether the policy rule (6.18) does successfully reduce the asymptotic variance of prices, simply involves comparing (6.20b) with the corresponding asymptotic variance in the absence of intervention, namely

$$\sigma^2_P = \frac{\sigma^2_u + \sigma^2_v}{(a + b)^2}$$

This comparison yields

$$\text{sgn}\,(\sigma^2_{P,\mu} - \sigma^2_P) = \text{sgn}\left\{-(\sigma^2_u + \sigma^2_v)\mu[\mu - 2(a + b)] + (a + b)^2\sigma^2_w\right\} \tag{6.21}$$

and contains two components. First is the effect on the variances of demand and supply, σ^2_u and σ^2_v. Provided $\mu < 0$, and the authorities follow the policy of "buying cheap and selling dear," the policy rule (6.18) will reduce this component of the variance $\sigma^2_{P,\mu}$. However, this is offset by the variance σ^2_w introduced by the authority's demand function; so that overall, depending on the relative variability $(\sigma^2_u + \sigma^2_v)/\sigma^2_w$, it is possible for the introduction of a stabilization policy to *increase* the total variability of prices.

In assessing the distribution of welfare gains from such a stabilization scheme, as has been indicated, the stabilization authority itself will receive profits (or losses), and these too need to be taken into account. Thus, in addition to $E(G_p)$, $E(G_c)$, and $E(G)$, there are the benefits to the stabilization authority $E(G_g)$. Their net revenue is given by $-X_tP_{\mu,t}$; and with X_t given by (6.18′), their expected net revenue is

$$E(G_g) = E\left\{-[\mu(P_{\mu,t} - P_s) + w_t]P_{\mu,t}\right\} \tag{6.22}$$

Omitting details, the following conclusions can be drawn:

1. Provided that $\mu < 0$, producers lose (gain) from intervention if the source of price instability is random shifts in demand (supply). Producers gain from any instability induced by additive shifts in the policy rule.
2. Provided that $\mu < 0$, consumers lose (gain) from intervention if the source of price instability is random shifts in supply (demand). They gain from any instability induced by additive shifts in the policy rule.
3. The total gains to the private sector from intervention are always positive and independent of the sign of μ, or whether price is in fact stabilized.
4. Provided that $\mu < 0$, the stabilization authority gains from stabilization for demand and supply fluctuations (i.e., its expected profits are positive). It loses from the instability that its own random behavior incurs on the system.
5. Provided that $\mu < 0$, the economy will gain from stabilization for demand and supply fluctuations. However, the fluctuations induced by intervention create a net loss. Taking these into account, the total gains from intervention may indeed be negative. Note, however, that if the authority succeeds in reducing the price instability (lowering the variance of prices), it can be shown that in this instance the overall benefits will indeed be positive.

For $\mu < 0$ these results are, broadly speaking, consistent with Massell's (1969) conclusions; and indeed, letting $\mu \to -\infty$ and $\sigma_e^2 = 0$, they yield the Massell results as a limiting case. While for small $\mu > 0$ the Massell results regarding distribution will be reversed, as $\mu \to \infty$ they will once again be restored. Provided the authority intervenes in a sufficiently strong manner, it does not matter which way it operates. Either way its profits or losses will tend to zero.

This analysis has been extended to a dynamic cobweb-type market in which both the suppliers and the authority make their decisions on the basis of expected prices; see Turnovsky (1976*b*).[25] The price expectations held by producers and the stabilization authority are taken to be "partially rational" in that they are some weighted average of Muthian rational expectations and a simple autoregressive scheme. As a consequence, producers and the authority may form different forecasts, so the differential quality of the information becomes a matter of some importance. This extension is much closer in spirit to recent developments in linear stabilization theory than has characterized the previous literature in this area.[26]

Stabilization through Publicly Announced Forecasts

The extension of the analysis of linear policy rules to the situation in which both producers and the authority act on expectations has been shown by

Turnovsky (1976*b*) to be formally rather closely related to the situation in which the public authority seeks to influence the behavior of the market not by direct intervention but rather by announcing forecasts that in turn influence the behavior of private producers. The effect of such forecasts on the variance of prices was considered by Smyth (1973), who showed that the publication of rational forecasts formed by the government will indeed reduce the variance of prices. This analysis has been extended by Turnovsky to determine the allocation of the benefits from the provision of this information.

For simplicity, and without any essential loss of generality, it is assumed that these public forecasts are in fact rational, but that only a fraction δ, $0 < \delta < 1$, of producers base their decisions on them. The remainder base their supply decisions on the previous period's price.

Formally this model is described by

$$D_t = A - aP_t + u_t \tag{6.23}$$

$$S_{1,t} = \delta B + \delta b E_{t-1}(P_t) + \delta v_t \tag{6.24a}$$

$$S_{2,t} = (1 - \delta)B + (1 - \delta)bP_{t-1} + (1 - \delta)v_t \tag{6.24b}$$

where $S_{1,t}$ is the supply of producers who base their decisions on the public forecasts, while $S_{2,t}$ is the supply of producers who use the naive forecasting method. The term v_t denotes the aggregate supply disturbance that is assumed to be distributed proportionately between the two classes of producers.

In the absence of the information provided by the authority, it is assumed that all producers base their supply decisions on the previous period's price, so the asymptotic variance of the market clearing price is given by

$$\sigma^2_{P,\nu_0} = \frac{\sigma_u^2 + \sigma_v^2}{a^2(1 - \nu_0^2)} \tag{6.25}$$

where $\nu_0 = -b/a$. It is easily shown that the rational forecast provided by the authority is

$$E_{t-1}(P_t) = P_s - \frac{b(1 - \delta)}{a + b}(P_{t-1} - P_s) \tag{6.26}$$

which it will be seen depends upon the proportion of producers the authority knows will base their decisions on this information. Substituting (6.26) into (6.24a), it is shown that the asymptotic variance of price when this information is available is

$$\sigma^2_{P,\nu_1} = \frac{\sigma^2_u + \sigma^2_v}{a^2(1 - \nu_1^2)}$$

where $\nu_1 = -b(1 - \delta)/(a + b\delta) < 0$. It is easily verified that for $0 < \delta < 1$

$$\nu_0 < \nu_1 < 0 < -\nu_0$$

so that $\sigma^2_{P,\nu_1} < \sigma^2_{P,\nu_0}$, implying that the provision of rational forecasts by the public authorities does indeed lead to an increase in price stability. This finding is entirely consistent with that obtained by Smyth (1973).

In assessing the benefits of such a scheme, there are three separate groups to consider: (1) producers who follow these public forecasts, (2) producers who ignore these public forecasts, and (3) consumers. Abstracting from details, the following general conclusions can be obtained. Both sets of producers gain from the announcement of these rationally formed public forecasts, with proportionately *more* of the benefits from stabilization accruing to those producers who base their decisions on these forecasts. However, the reduction in price variability stemming from the improved information leads to a loss in consumer welfare. While this loss implies a partial redistribution of welfare from consumers in favor of producers, it is insufficient to outweigh the gains to producers; so potentially at least, aggregate welfare is increased by the announcement of these forecasts.

This alternative means of public intervention, namely through the provision of forecasts to producers, raises the question of the merit of this form of intervention relative to that of stabilization through a buffer stock scheme. Should the stabilization authority seek to stabilize prices by means of direct intervention in the market or rather should its role be to provide information? This question can be answered (within the limitations of the present framework) by comparing the benefits in the two cases. In turn it also leads naturally to the issue first raised by McKinnon (1967), who questioned the desirability of stabilizing spot prices without considering the role of private futures markets. Clearly it is important to extend the present model to investigate these kinds of issues.

Some Multicommodity Generalizations

The discussion has focused exclusively on a single commodity and the stabilization of a single price. There is much less literature dealing with stabilization within a multimarket context. But the literature is growing, and our survey would be incomplete without reference to it.

Multimarket Extension of Basic Waugh-Oi-Massell Model

The simplest multimarket discussion of stabilization is contained in Butlin (1976), who has extended the basic linear Waugh-Oi-Massell analysis to a two-commodity situation. He follows the traditional approach by basing his welfare criteria on the surplus measures and evaluates the benefits from stabilization to the various groups (producers of good 1, good 2, etc.) in terms of the variances of the underlying demand and supply curves. This analysis is a straightforward extension of our discussion of the Waugh-Oi-Massell model.

A Utility-Maximizing Approach

A recent study by Hanoch (1974) has generalized both the Waugh and the Oi analyses to a multicommodity situation. Since in each case it treats prices as exogenous—focusing on consumers and producers separately—and does not attempt to integrate them, it is still a partial-equilibrium approach. However, in one important respect it generalizes the Waugh approach; it evaluates the benefits to consumers in terms of a concave (or convex) utility function, rather than in terms of consumers' surplus. Hanoch analyzes a variety of cases, dealing with stabilization of the prices at their means, both unweighted and weighted, and under strict and expected versions of the consumers' budget constraint.[27] In some cases this leads to generalizations of the Waugh result; in others Waugh's conclusions are reversed. Similar generalizations of the Oi proposition are also derived.

In order to illustrate this approach I shall outline one proposition not considered by Hanoch, but which nevertheless is important as an extension of the discussion in previous sections. This relates to the situation in which only *one* commodity has a stochastic price and money income remains fixed, but now the consumer evaluates his welfare in terms of a general utility function. Analyzing this case enables us to determine precisely the restrictions imposed by consumers' surplus in the kind of context envisioned by Waugh and other writers.

We begin with the formal consumers' maximization problem, that is,

$$\max U(c_1, \dots, c_m) \quad \text{subject to} \quad \sum_{i=1}^{m} P_i c_i = M \tag{6.27}$$

the optimality conditions for which are

$$U_i = \lambda P_i \qquad i = 1, \dots, m$$

$$\sum_i P_i c_i = M \tag{6.28}$$

Suppose that commodity 1 has a random selling price P_1. The effect of stabilizing P_1 at its arithmetic mean $\bar{P}_1$ on the welfare of the consumer depends upon the concavity or convexity of the indirect utility function $V(P_1, \ldots, P_m, M)$ in P_1.

Using well-known properties of the indirect utility function, it can be shown that the concavity or convexity of V in P_1 is determined by

$$\operatorname{sgn}\left(\frac{\partial^2 V}{\partial P_1^2}\right) = \operatorname{sgn}\left[s_1(\eta - r) - e\right] \tag{6.29}$$

where $r = -\dfrac{\partial^2 V/\partial M^2 \cdot M}{\partial V/\partial M}$ = coefficient of relative risk aversion,

$s_1 = P_1 c_1/M$ = share of consumer's budget allocated to commodity 1,
e = own uncompensated price elasticity of demand for commodity 1,
η = income elasticity of demand for commodity 1.

It follows that the desirability of price stability decreases with the magnitudes of the price and income elasticities but increases with the coefficient of relative risk aversion. It also depends upon the share of the consumer's budget allocated to the commodity, with the direction of effect depending upon $(\eta - r)$. While it is certainly possible for $\partial^2 V/\partial P_1^2 < 0$ (in which case the consumer gains from price stabilization contrary to the Waugh proposition), empirical evidence would suggest that $\partial^2 V/\partial P_1^2 > 0$, in which case the Waugh proposition remains true. For example, taking $e = -0.2$, $\eta = 0.5$, $r = 0.8$, $s_1 = 0.3$, as typical estimates for a composite commodity such as food, we find (6.29) remains positive.

Thus the results obtained by Waugh, based on consumers' surplus, tend to be supported by this more general utility approach. For plausible parameters, one would expect consumers to lose from stabilization, especially if s_1, the share of the budget devoted to the commodity, is small. Note as a further point that this result includes the consumers' surplus measure as a special case. As observed by Turnovsky (1976*a*), consumers' surplus is justified if and only if $\partial^2 V/\partial M \partial P_1 = 0$. It can be shown this will be so if and only if $r = \eta$, in which case the criterion (6.29) reduces to

$$\operatorname{sgn}\left(\frac{\partial^2 V}{\partial P_1^2}\right) = \operatorname{sgn}(-e) > 0 \tag{6.29$'$}$$

In this case the reason that consumers lose from stabilization is due solely to the demand curve being downward sloping, precisely as it was for the original Waugh proposition.

General Equilibrium Models

In a revival of the debate on the Waugh and Oi propositions, Samuelson (1972) has reconsidered the welfare benefits from price stabilization using a simple general equilibrium model of a closed economy.[28] Using the Pareto optimality of perfect competition, he shows that stabilization at the perfectly competitive equilibrium is beneficial; destabilization away from that price is harmful, thereby refuting the Waugh and Oi results. This paper can be viewed as a generalization of the Massell (1969) analysis to a general equilibrium, although Samuelson does not relate his result to Massell's paper.

The most extensive literature on the impact of price uncertainty in a general equilibrium framework has been within the context of the simple two-factor, two-commodity model of production. While some of this deals with a closed economy in which price is assumed to be exogenously given (see Rothenberg and Smith (1971); Batra (1974)), the most natural application is to the case of the small trading economy in which the random trading price (terms of trade) are determined by world conditions; see Ruffin (1974); Turnovsky (1974*b*); Batra and Russell (1974); Anderson and Riley (1976); Feder, Just, and Schmitz (1977). Most of the emphasis of these studies has been on determining how the traditional propositions of the pure theory of international trade, such as the gains from trade, patterns of specialization, etc., are affected by the introduction of uncertainty, rather than on stabilization issues per se.

All these general equilibrium models are concerned with analyzing the uncertainty of a *relative* price ratio, and this involves the choice of a numeraire commodity. As shown by Flemming, Turnovsky, and Kemp (1977), the conventional use of the *arithmetic mean* as the "certainty price" for the comparison can make some of the results dependent upon the choice of numeraire. Since this choice is presumably an arbitrary one, this is clearly a rather unsatisfactory feature of this procedure. Flemming, Turnovsky, and Kemp go on to show how this numeraire dependence can be avoided if some other measure of central tendency is used as the certainty price. Indeed they argue that for problems involving an uncertain relative price, the *geometric mean* is the most appropriate measure to use. This issue is an important one and should be borne in mind in developing general equilibrium models of this kind.

Some Final Comments

It should be clear from this survey that the analysis of price stabilization has progressed a long way since it was first introduced by Waugh over 30 years ago.

One of the major conclusions of the literature is that although price stabilization will always, potentially at least, improve aggregate welfare, the distribution of these welfare gains between various members of society is highly sensitive to the precise specification of the model and the nature of the stochastic disturbances. This is seen most dramatically by comparing the case in which the stochastic disturbances are multiplicative with the more familiar situation in which they are additive. The *nature* of the stochastic disturbances thus becomes an important issue in assessing the distributional effects of stabilization policies. Clearly, it becomes important for the policy maker to obtain reliable information on this question; for unless he does, any stabilization policy may have undesirable effects on the group it is intended to assist.

But much work remains to be done. One of the greatest deficiencies of the existing literature is in its treatment of the costs associated with the stabilization scheme. Virtually all the work we have been discussing abstracts from this aspect, although it obviously becomes critical in any practical application. Closely related to this is the question of storage costs and the introduction of storage possibilities for the private sector. The implicit assumption made throughout the literature is that the stabilization authority is the only participant in the market able to hold stocks. In practice, of course, this is not generally so, raising the possibility of whether stabilization through private speculative activity (adding to private stocks when prices are low, consuming from private stocks when they are high) may not in fact be superior to having the stabilization undertaken by a public buffer stock authority. This question is in turn closely related to some of the informational considerations alluded to briefly in the later sections of this chapter, and these too need to be investigated more fully.

Finally, we need to progress beyond the basic partial equilibrium model upon which most of the literature is based. Stabilizing the price of one commodity will have repercussions in other markets, which in turn will have feedbacks on the first market. To consider these adequately requires the development of a complete multicommodity general equilibrium system.

Notes

1. Waugh's original contribution in 1944 generated considerable discussion about that time; see Howell (1945); Lovesy (1945); Waugh (1945). For more recent discussions, see Waugh (1966); Wegge, Sosnick, and George (1971).

2. This proposition also generated a vigorous debate; see for example Tisdell (1963); Oi (1963); Zucker (1965).

3. Building on many previous contributions, Leland (1972) and Sandmo (1971) develop quite general models in which firms are required to make *all* their production decisions before the actual selling price is known, on the basis of their price expectations. One can refer to this as the case of "total inflexi-

bility," and as such it represents the other extreme to that considered by Oi. Elsewhere (Turnovsky, 1973*b*), the intermediate case, where firms possess some flexibility, has been analyzed. In that paper, firms are assumed to make their initial production decisions on the basis of expected prices but are able to modify these decisions at some finite cost after they learn the true selling price.

4. See, for example, Muth (1961); Nerlove (1958); Pashigian (1970); Turnovsky (1968).

5. Some informal discussion of these is given in Massell (1970).

6. We also assume that the probability of the buffer stock running out over the period of stabilization is zero.

7. Given the limitations of the surplus measures, it would seem desirable to carry out the analysis in terms of the underlying utility functions. This procedure is feasible in the case where price itself is taken to be the exogenous random variable and has in fact been adopted in a series of recent papers investigating effects of price instability in a small trading country; see, for example, Anderson and Riley (1976); Ruffin (1974); Turnovsky (1974*b*). Unfortunately, this approach becomes much more difficult if, as is the case here, one wishes to go beyond prices and consider the ultimate random disturbances, such as fluctuations in tastes and technological conditions, which presumably are what the random movements in price must be reflecting.

8. It is also important to note that the net revenue of the stabilizing authorities is $(u_t - v_t)P_s$, the expected value of which is zero, implying that they can expect to break even.

9. Observe that in this case the self-liquidating buffer stock implies that price is stabilized at its mean. This result is a consequence of the linearity of the model.

10. The results in this section are based on Turnovsky (1976*a*).

11. While it is certainly possible that, given sufficient convexity or concavity of the underlying functions, for some of the Massell propositions to no longer apply, the modifications are less significant than those which result from multiplicative disturbances. In any event, this case can be easily studied using the methods outlined in this section.

12. All the results in this section generalize to the case in which

$$D = \alpha(u)d(P)$$

$$S = \beta(v)s(P)$$

13. While the convexity and concavity properties used do not appear to have been applied to multivariate stochastic problems, Jensen's inequality itself has become a standard technique for analyzing the effects of risk, where there is only a single random variable. For some recent applications, see Leland (1972); Rothschild and Stiglitz (1971); Sandmo (1971); and Turnovsky (1973*b*).

14. The *size* of the gains, however, does depend on the specific parameters of the stochastic disturbances.

15. The results given in this section are based on Turnovsky (1974*c*); see also Hazell and Scandizzo (1975); and Freebairn (1976).

16. This case is the other extreme of no short-run flexibility in production. The intermediate model described in note 3 yields a supply function of the form

$$S_t = B + bP_t^* + cP_t + v_t \qquad b \geqslant 0, c \geqslant 0$$

and this can be analyzed readily along the lines of this section.

17. This model generates a first-order stochastic difference equation for price P_t. In order to ensure that the asymptotic variance of P_t remains finite, we require that $-1 < -b\gamma/a + 1 - \gamma < 1$. This is a very weak form of stochastic stability; for an analysis of a more stringent form in the context of such "cob-web" models, see Turnovsky (1968).

18. At this point, attention should be drawn to the fact that the expression for benefits to producers in Turnovsky's (1974*c*) paper contains an error. It was based on the expression

$$E(G_p) = \tfrac{1}{2}E\left\{(P_s - P_t)[S(P_t^*) + S(P_s)]\right\}$$

instead of (6.14). This leads to some quantitative but no significant qualitative changes in the benefits to producers in the case of *adaptive* expectations. However, the results for *rational* expectations remain completely unaltered.

19. The responsiveness of these expressions for the welfare gains to parameter changes is analyzed by Turnovsky (1974*c*).

20. Strictly speaking, these statements hold except in the self-evident, limiting cases, when the corresponding expressions reduce to zero.

21. See also Bieri and Schmitz (1973).

22. See Duloy and Parish (1964) for an early discussion of such a scheme proposed by the Australian Wool Board.

23. Regarding notation, as before, P_t is used to denote the market clearing price in the absence of intervention by the stabilization authority, while $P_{\mu,t}$ is the price in the presence of intervention.

24. Where stochastic costs of adjustment are present, the term w_t can also reflect random shifts in the decision rule resulting from these disturbances.

25. A related paper by Turnovsky (1973*a*) is concerned with deriving stabilization rules directed at minimizing the asymptotic variance of prices. However, that paper does not address itself to the question of the distribution of the welfare gains from stabilization, which is the primary focus of Turnovsky (1976*b*). One result of particular interest obtained in the earlier paper is that in the presence of costs associated with government intervention (specified by a quadratic cost function), the optimal price may involve oscillations. In other

words, under these circumstances, exact stabilization may not be the optimal policy. Clearly, this kind of issue needs to be discussed in the context of more generally specified cost and benefit functions.

26. See, for example, Turnovsky (1974*a*) for a survey and application of some of these techniques.

27. Waugh (1966) and Wegge et al. (1971) also deal with the comparison in terms of *weighted* means.

28. See also the reply by Oi (1972); and Samuelson's responses (1972*b*).

References

Anderson, J.E., and J.G. Riley. "International Trade with Fluctuating Prices." *International Economic Review* 17 (1976):76-97.

Arrow, K.J. *Aspects of the Theory of Risk-Bearing.* Helsinki: Yrjö Jahnssonin säätio, 1963.

Batra, R.N. "Resource Allocation in a General Equilibrium Model of Production under Uncertainty." *Journal of Economic Theory* 8 (1974):50-63.

——, and W.R. Russell. "Gains from Trade under Uncertainty." *American Economic Review* 64 (1974):1040-1048.

Bieri, J., and A. Schmitz. "Export Instability, Monopoly Power, and Welfare." *Journal of International Economics* 3 (1973):389-396.

Burns, M.E. "A Note on the Concept and Measure of Consumer's Surplus." *American Economic Review* 63 (1973):335-344.

Butlin, M. "The Welfare Effects of Price Stabilisation: A Simple Multi-Market Extension." *Economic Record* 52 (1976).

Duloy, J.H., and R.M. Parish. "An Appraisal of a Floor-Price Scheme for Wool." New England Marketing Studies No. 1, University of New England, 1964.

Feder, G., R. Just, and A. Schmitz. "Storage with Price Uncertainty in International Trade." *International Economic Review* 18 (1977).

Flemming, J.S., S.J. Turnovsky, and M.C. Kemp. "On the Choice of Numeraire and Certainty Price in General Equilibrium Models of Price Uncertainty." *Review of Economic Studies* 44 (1977).

Freebairn, J.W. "The Value and Distribution of the Benefits of Commodity Price Outlook Information." *Economic Record* 52 (1976):199-212.

Hanoch, G. "Desirability of Price Stabilization or Destabilization." Harvard Institute of Economic Research, 1974.

Hazell, P.B.R., and P.L. Scandizzo, "Market Intervention Policies when Production is Risky." *American Journal of Agricultural Economics* 57 (1975):641-649.

Howell, L.D. "Does the Consumer Benefit from Price Instability?" *Quarterly Journal of Economics* 59 (1945):287-295.

Hueth, D., and A. Schmitz. "International Trade in Intermediate and Final Goods: Some Welfare Implications of Destabilized Prices." *Quarterly Journal of Economics* 86 (1972):351-365.

Just, R., E. Lutz, A. Schmitz, and S.J. Turnovsky, "The Distribution of Welfare Gains from Price Stabilization: An International Perspective." Department of Agricultural and Resource Economics, University of California, Berkeley, 1976.

Leland, H.E. "The Theory of the Firm Facing Uncertain Demand." *American Economic Review* 62 (1972):278-291.

Little, I.M.D. *A Critique of Welfare Economics,* London: Oxford Univ. Press, 1957.

Lovesy, G. "Further Comment." *Quarterly Journal of Economics* 59 (1945): 296-301.

Massell, B.F. "Price Stabilization and Welfare." *Quarterly Journal of Economics* 83 (1969):284-298.

——. "Some Welfare Implications of International Price Stabilization." *Journal of Political Economy* 78 (1970):404-417.

McKinnon, R.I. "Futures Markets, Buffer Stocks and Income Stability for Primary Producers." *Journal of Political Economy* 75 (1967):844-861.

Muth, J.F. "Rational Expectations and the Theory of Price Movements." *Econometrica* 29 (July 1961):315-335.

Nerlove, M. "Adaptive Expectations and Cobweb Phenomena." *Quarterly Journal of Economics* 73 (1958):227-240.

Oi, W.Y. "The Desirability of Price Instability Under Perfect Competition." *Econometrica* 29 (1961):58-64.

——. "Rejoinder." *Econometrica* 31 (1963):248.

——. "The Consumer Does Benefit from Feasible Price Stability: Comment." *Quarterly Journal of Economics* 86 (1972):494-498.

Pashigian, B.P. "Rational Expectations and the Cobweb Theory." *Journal of Political Economy* 78 (1970):338-352.

Pratt, J.W. "Risk Aversion in the Small and in the Large." *Econometrica* 32 (1964):122-136.

Rothenberg, T.J., and K.R. Smith. "The Effect of Uncertainty on Resource Allocation." *Quarterly Journal of Economics* 85 (1971):440-459.

Rothschild, M., and J.E. Stiglitz. "Increasing Risk II: Its Economic Consequences." *Journal of Economic Theory* 3 (1971):66-84.

Ruffin, R. "Comparative Advantage Under Uncertainty." *Journal of International Economics* 4 (1974):261-274.

Samuelson, P.A. *Foundations of Economic Analysis.* Cambridge, Mass.: Harvard Univ. Press, 1947.

——. "The Consumer Does Benefit from Feasible Price Stability." *Quarterly Journal of Economics* 86 (1972*a*):476-493.

——. "Rejoinder." *Quarterly Journal of Economics* 86 (1972*b*):500-503.

——. "Complementarity–An Essay on the 40th Anniversary of the Hicks-Allen Revolution in Demand Theory." *Journal of Economic Literature* 12 (1974): 1255-1289.

Sandmo, A. "On the Theory of the Competitive Firm Under Price Uncertainty." *American Economic Review* 61 (1971):65-73.

Smyth, D.J. "Effect of Public Price Forecasts on Market Price Variation: A Stochastic Cobweb Example." *American Journal of Agricultural Economics* 55 (1973):83-88.

Subotnik, A., and J.P. Houck. "Welfare Implications of Stabilizing Consumption and Production." *American Journal of Agricultural Economics* 58 (1976): 13-20.

Tisdell, C. "Uncertainty, Instability, Expected Profit." *Econometrica* 31 (1963): 243-247.

Turnovsky, S.J. "Stochastic Stability of Short-Run Market Equilibrium Under Variations in Supply." *Quarterly Journal of Economics* 82 (1968):666-681.

——. "Optimal Stabilization Policies in a Market with Lagged Adjustment in Supply." *Economic Record* 49 (1973*a*):31-49.

——. "Production Flexibility, Price Uncertainty and the Behavior of the Competitive Firm." *International Economic Review* 14 (1973*b*):395-413.

——. "The Stability Properties of Optimal Economic Policies." *American Economic Review* 64 (1974*a*):136-148.

——. "Technological and Price Uncertainty in a Ricardian Model of International Trade." *Review of Economic Studies* 41 (1974*b*):201-217.

——. "Price Expectations and the Welfare Gains from Price Stabilization." *American Journal of Agricultural Economics* 56 (1974*c*):706-716.

——. "The Distribution of Welfare Gains from Price Stabilization: The Case of Multiplicative Disturbances." *International Economic Review* 17 (1976*a*): 133-148.

——. "Stabilization Rules and the Benefits from Price Stabilization." Australian National University Working Paper, 1976*b*.

Waugh, F.V. "Does the Consumer Benefit from Price Instability?" *Quarterly Journal of Economics* 58 (1944):602-614.

——. "Reply." *Quarterly Journal of Economics* 59 (1945):301-303.

——. "Consumer Aspects of Price Instability." *Econometrica* 34 (1966):504-508.

Wegge, L.L., S.H. Sosnick, and P.S. George. "The Effect of Price Stabilization on Consumer Welfare." *Western Economic Journal* 9 (1971):289-298.

Willig, R.D. "Consumer's Surplus without Apology." *American Economic Review* 66 (1976):589-597.

Zucker, A. "On the Desirability of Price Instability." *Econometrica* 32 (1965): 437-441.

7 Buffer Stock Analysis for Agricultural Products: Theoretical Murk or Empirical Resolution?

Alexander H. Sarris and
Lance Taylor

Introduction

Until recently, the welfare evaluation of buffer stock operations for commodities seemed quite simple. In the case of agricultural products, where most unexpected fluctuation comes from the supply side, it was generally concurred that a price stabilizing buffer would help producers, harm consumers, and raise the general level of welfare on average. For a simple, though widely analyzed case, Figure 7-1 shows why.

Consider only the linear demand curve $\tilde{D}\tilde{D}'$ and assume that supply does not respond to price but randomly fluctuates between *OA* and *OC*. There are no storage costs or discounting, and a buffer stock buying at price p_1 and selling at $\tilde{p}_2$ to stabilize prices at p_s is supposed to have enough supplies on hand (from somewhere) to be able to function forever.

When the buffer buys at p_1, producers would receive a windfall gain *GDI'H* on the amount they already have for sale in the market. When stocks are sold to drive the price down from $\tilde{p}_2$ to p_s, producers would lose *HIMM'*. From the linearity of the demand curve, the benefit area exceeds the loss area and producers could be expected to favor price stabilization.

Now look at consumers. When supply is low and the stock sells, they would gain *HIMM'* from the price reduction on the amount they would be consuming at price $\tilde{p}_2$. In addition, they purchase the stocks the buffer places on the market and gain an additional "little triangle" *IJM* in benefits. The total benefit is thus *HJMM'*. When the buffer purchases, it drives prices up on a larger volume and consumers lose *GDN'JH*. This loss area exceeds the gains that accrue from price reduction, and consumers might be expected to oppose stabilization.

Finally, if welfare of consumers and producers is weighted equally, the overall gain to "society" from stabilization is just the sum of the gains of the two groups. This can be shown to be equal to *FEJM* - *EDN'J*, which is clearly positive. Hence, price stabilization can be said to increase economic welfare.

This cozy set of conclusions—which at bottom is part of the intellectual

Parts of this research were supported by NSF grant no. 7522807-PRA to the International Nutrition Planning Program, M.I.T.

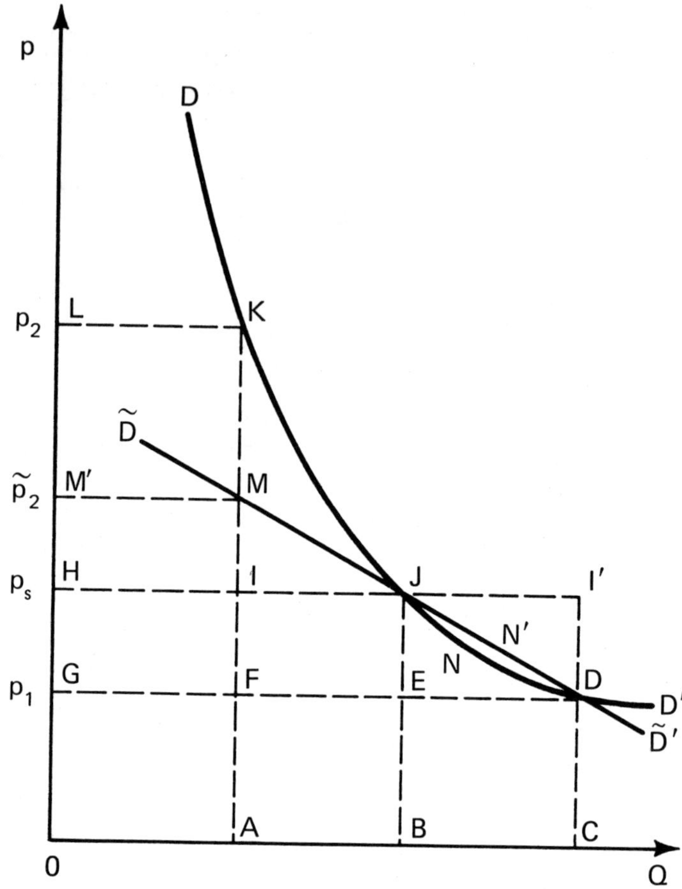

Figure 7-1. Consumers' and Producers' Surplus Calculations.

current in support of the recent spate of commodity stabilization proposals—has recently been challenged on several grounds. The objections stress the importance of certain nonlinearities in demand and the role of trade barriers and supply response in allocating gains and losses from international purchases and sales.

In this chapter, we review the theoretical reasons why it is impossible to state a priori who will benefit or be hurt by international price stabilization and illustrate the relevance of these reasons in the context of world wheat and feed-grain markets. Practical evaluation of price stabilization proposals depends inevitably on fine details of trade, which, in many cases, are just beginning to be explored.

Nonlinearity of Demand

As a factual matter, it was pointed out by Jimmye Hillman, D. Gale Johnson, and Roger Gray, as consultants for the FAO (1975), that demand in cereal markets probably becomes more *inelastic* as prices rise. In an informal way, one can claim verification of this proposition from price behavior during the 1972-1974 "food crisis."[1] Since linear demand curves become more *elastic* with rising prices, the welfare conclusions just derived for the standard case should certainly be questioned.

To see that doubt is justified, consider the nonlinear demand curve DD' in Figure 7-1.[2] Beginning with consumers, observe that they gain $HJKL$ when the buffer stock sells at the high price p_2—an area that can be significantly larger than $HJMM'$ corresponding to the linear demand curve. Their loss when the buffer buys stocks is $GDNJH$, and net surplus is

$$HJKL - GDNJH = IJK + M'MKL - FDNJI$$

It is not clear immediately whether this is positive or negative.

The net gain to producers is

$$GDI'H - HIKL = FDI'I - M'MKL$$

To shed some light on the sign of this expression, assume that the price elasticity of demand at the point (p_1, OC) is ϵ_1, while at point (p_2, OA) it is ϵ_2. Then one can show that the producer gain from stabilization can be approximated by the expression

$$AB\left(\frac{p_1}{|\epsilon_1|} - \frac{p_2}{|\epsilon_2|}\right)$$

where AB is the average size of the stock. Evidently, producers will lose from stabilization (and since total gains are positive,[3] consumers will benefit) if

$$\frac{p_1}{p_2} < \frac{|\epsilon_1|}{|\epsilon_2|} \tag{7.1}$$

In the linear case $(D = A - ap)$,

$$\frac{|\epsilon_1|}{|\epsilon_2|} = \frac{p_1}{p_2} \cdot \frac{A - ap_2}{A - ap_1} < \frac{p_1}{p_2}$$

so that condition (7.1) does not hold (and producers gain).

Notice also that since $p_1 < p_2$, it is not necessary for $|\epsilon_2| < |\epsilon_1|$ in order for producers to lose from stabilization. In fact, *an isoelastic curve will be sufficient to make producers lose* from stabilization (and, correspondingly, consumers to gain). Even if $|\epsilon_1| < |\epsilon_2|$, it is quite possible for both producers and consumers to gain from stockpiling, since total gains are positive.

This type of analysis extends in straightforward though tedious fashion to several countries engaging in international trade. For example, if demands in both an exporting and an importing country are linear and the source of fluctuation is in the exporting country's supply, then stabilization harms the importer (as it harms the consumer along demand curve $\tilde{D}\tilde{D}'$ in Figure 7-1). If, however, either the importer or the exporter has sufficiently nonlinear demand, this result can reverse. We will see later that many wheat importers could expect to benefit if the international market were stabilized. Contrariwise, feedgrain exporters would gain from stabilization.

Restricted International Markets

The results for international commerce just cited depend on assumptions of free trade between countries and compensation within them. But, in fact, world cereal trade is far from being free. *All* countries isolate their internal grain markets from the rest of the world to some extent in order to run their domestic agricultural policies more effectively.[4] In this section, we sketch out an approach to welfare evaluation of price stabilization under restricted trade and use it to upset some preconceptions about who are the gainers and losers in such circumstances.

To keep the algebra as simple as possible, assume that each country has a linear demand curve and that all fluctuations come from the side of (nonprice responsive) supply:

$$D_i(p_{it}^d) = A_i - a_i p_{it}^d \tag{7.2}$$

$$S_{it} = B_i + v_{it} \tag{7.3}$$

where p_{it}^d is the internal price in country i at time t, and v_{it} is a random variable for production fluctuations, with mean zero and variance σ_i^2. All the v_{it} are homoscedastic and independent across countries and time.[5]

Domestic excess demand becomes

$$ED_i(p_{it}^d) = c_i - a_i p_{it}^d - v_{it} \tag{7.4}$$

where $c_i = A_i - B_i$. Suppose that the excess demand exhibited by country i in international markets is not the same as (7.4), but rather

$$ED_i^I(p_t^I) = c_i^* - a_i^* p_t^I - \alpha_i v_{it} \tag{7.5}$$

where p_t^I is the international price, c_i^* and a_i^* are in general different from c_i and a_i, and α_i is the degree to which domestic fluctuations are transmitted abroad.[6] If the country is following free trade, then a production fluctuation will result in an equal shift of its excess demand curve, so $\alpha_i = 1$. If, however, it is willing to absorb all production shocks internally, then $\alpha_i = 0$. Actual countries are observed all along the spectrum of values α_i. The Soviet Union, for example, can be viewed as shifting its α_i over time from near zero to a value close to one.

Equating excess demands in (7.4) and (7.5) and solving for the domestic price, we obtain

$$p_{it}^d = \frac{c_i - c_i^*}{a_i} + \frac{a_i^*}{a_i} p_t^I - \frac{1 - \alpha_i}{a_i} v_{it} \tag{7.6}$$

This expression can be used to set the parameters of the excess demand function to model several possible restrictions. For example, an ad valorem tariff τ makes $a_i^* = (1 - \tau)a_i$, $c_i^* = c_i$, $\alpha_i = 1$; or a quota Q (when effective) makes $a_i^* = \alpha_i = 0$, $c_i^* = Q$.

Since all the international excess demand curves are linear, we can easily solve for the international price as

$$p_t^I = \frac{c^*}{a^*} - \frac{v_t}{a^*} \tag{7.7}$$

with

$$c^* = \Sigma c_i^* \qquad a^* = \Sigma a_i^* \qquad v_t = \Sigma \alpha_i v_{it}$$

Now we can analyze how international price stabilization will affect producer profits, consumer surplus, and import expenditures. If p_t^I is held at its expected value c^*/a^* by costless buffer stock operations, then country i's domestic price $\bar{p}_{it}^d$ can be found from (7.6). By using a well-known formula (exact in the linear demand curve case), the gain in consumers' surplus from stabilization can be written as

$$G_{it}^c = ½(p_{it}^d - \bar{p}_{it}^d)[D_i(p_{it}^d) + D_i(\bar{p}_{it}^d)] \tag{7.8}$$

If the domestic producer price is the same as the consumer price, then the gain in producers' surplus (profits) is

$$G^p_{it} = (\bar{p}^d_{it} - p^d_{it})S_{it} \tag{7.9}$$

Finally, the gain in country *i*'s import expenditure is

$$G^I_{it} = ED^I_i(p^I_t)p^I_t - ED^I_i(c^*/a^*)(c^*/a^*) \tag{7.10}$$

Substituting the parametric forms of the demand equations given above into (7.8) through (7.10) and taking expected values, we obtain, after some laborious algebra,

$$\bar{G}^c_i = -\tfrac{1}{2}\frac{a^*_i}{a_i a^*}\left[\frac{a^*_i}{a^*}\Sigma(\alpha_j\sigma_j)^2 + 2\alpha_i(1-\alpha_i)\sigma^2_i\right] \tag{7.11}$$

$$\bar{G}^p_i = \frac{a^*_i \alpha_i \sigma^2_i}{a_i a^*} \tag{7.12}$$

$$\bar{G}^I_i = \frac{1}{a^*}\left[(\alpha_i\sigma_i)^2 - \frac{a^*_i}{a^*}\Sigma(\alpha_j\sigma_j)^2\right] \tag{7.13}$$

Equation (7.11) contains the standard result that consumers lose from stabilization with linear demand curves and production fluctuations; (7.12) shows similarly that producers gain. Finally, (7.13) shows that a country may expect either to gain or lose foreign exchange as a result of stabilization, depending on the comparison between its contribution to fluctuations in world trade (or $[(\alpha_i\sigma_i)^2/\Sigma(\alpha_j\sigma_j)^2]$ and the relative magnitude of its net import response to price (or a^*_i/a^*). A country like the Soviet Union, which "exports" much of its own large crop variation, could expect to benefit from an international wheat buffer stock.

We can at last take up policy issues. Begin by recalling that one of the arguments recently advanced in favor of grain reserves is that international trade is not free, and thus the gains from stabilization via reserves would be larger than in the case of free trade.[7] We will see that this assertion must be interpreted *very* carefully.

Consider equation (7.12) for expected producer gains first. If trade is free in country *i*, then $\alpha_i = 1$ and $a^*_i = a_i$. If trade is restricted, then almost surely the excess demand for imports is steeper than domestic demand, or $a^*_i \leqslant a_i$. By a simple comparison, one can show that producers in country *i* gain more from stabilization under restricted than under free trade if and only if

$$\frac{a_i}{a} < \frac{\alpha_i a^*_i}{a^*} \tag{7.14}$$

where $a = \Sigma a_i$.

This condition will hold in country i if it pursues a free trade policy while some others restrict trade (so $a^* < a$). More generally, if all $\alpha_i = 1$, then the self-evident restrictions $\Sigma(a_i/a) = \Sigma(a_i^*/a^*) = 1$ imply that if some producers prefer stabilization when trade is restricted, others will not. It all depends on the steepness of country i's restricted and unrestricted excess demand curves relative to the rest of the world. As can easily be verified, even the sum of expected producer gains from stabilization over all countries under restricted trade may exceed or fall short of its value under free trade.

A similar story applies to comparisons of magnitudes of consumer losses from stabilization under free and restricted trade, as observation of (7.11) clearly indicates. The same is true of total gains, which in country i are

$$\bar{G}_i^c + \bar{G}_i^p = \frac{a_i^*}{2a_i a^*}\left[2(\alpha_i\sigma_i)^2 - \frac{a_i^*}{a^*}\Sigma(\alpha_j\sigma_j)^2\right] \tag{7.15}$$

It is clear that various values of α_i and a_i^* can completely shift around countries' desires for stabilization. A simple example will prove the point. Let country i prefer stabilization under generally free trade; i.e. let

$$½a[2\sigma_i^2 - (a_i/a)\Sigma\sigma_j^2] > 0$$

If now this country imposes a quota so that $\alpha_i = 0$, it can be seen that stabilization will hurt it. A similar line of argument applies from (7.13) to net foreign exchange gains and losses from stabilization.

Supply Response

As a final example of the a priori unpredictability of the gains from price stabilization, consider supply response under the naive expectation that last year's price in each country will also rule this year. Then the supply function (7.3) becomes

$$S_{it} = B_i + b_i p_{i,t-1}^d + v_{it} \tag{7.3'}$$

Assume that there are no trade barriers or transport costs, let $b = \Sigma b_i$ and $\lambda = (b/a) < 1$, so the world does not follow an unstable cobweb. The expected total gain from stabilization in country i is

$$\bar{G}_i^c + \bar{G}_i^p = ½a^2(2a\sigma_i^2 - k_i a_i \Sigma\sigma_j^2) \tag{7.16}$$

where $k_i = (1 + 2\lambda b_i/a_i)/(1 - \lambda^2)$. In the case of no supply response anywhere, $k_i = 1$ for all countries.

Even when there is no supply response, a country with minor fluctuations (σ_i^2 near zero) can lose from stabilization. The situation is more complicated when some or all b_i exceed zero. For example, if $b_i = 0$ for some country but there is supply response in others, then $k_i > 1$. Therefore country i might be helped by stabilization when there is no supply response in the rest of the world, but harmed otherwise. In the opposite case of $b_i > 0$ but $b_j = 0$ ($j \neq i$), then $k_i < 1$, and country i desires stabilization more when external supply response is weak.

An Applied Model

The foregoing exercises show:

1. The determination of which economic groups would gain or lose from price stabilization depends on empirical characteristics of the demand curve. In particular, the degree of nonlinearity of the curve appears to affect fundamentally the distribution of benefits. In the international trade case, importing countries may be harmed by price stabilization (under free trade) if demand curves are linear but helped if there is enough nonlinearity in the system.
2. If trade is restricted (as it certainly is for cereals), then allocation of benefits among countries depends on the detailed differences among their internal excess demand curves and the extent to which they segregate their domestic markets from the rest of the world. From the individual country point of view, the desirability of stabilization is not necessarily greater under more restricted trade (an assertion put forward by several authors recently).
3. If supply response is considered in the context of a linear free trade model, it can be shown again that contrasts among countries are important in determining whether they are helped or hurt by stabilization. An individual country may prefer stabilization if other countries' supply responses are weak, but dislike it when their responses are strong.
4. With all these complications, not all countries can expect to benefit from stabilization. Since international compensation is unlikely, potential political obstacles to international agreement on stabilization are foreseeable.

Table 7-1 demonstrates that these theoretical hesitations are of some relevance in the context of a model of price-stabilizing buffer stocks for the wheat and feedgrains markets. For each of the 19 countries or regions considered, foreign trade is modeled in a way analogous to equations (7.2), (7.3′), (7.4) and (7.5) here; i.e., worldwide excess demands for imports under restricted trade determine the international price, which, in conjunction with domestic excess demand functions, determines country internal prices, as in (7.6). Supply next year in each country is determined by an equation like (7.3′). In line with the discussion in the section on the nonlinearity of demand, both domestic and international excess demand functions are nonlinear and permit decreasing

Table 7-1
Gains and Losses from Price Stabilization for Cereals

	Wheat Market			*Feedgrain Market*		
Country(s)	*Consumers*	*Producers*	*Net Foreign Exchange*	*Consumers*	*Producers*	*Net Foreign Exchange*
U.S.A.	+	--	--	-	+	++
Canada	+	--	-	-	+	+
Australia	+	--	--	-	+	+
Argentina	++	--	++	+	-	+
E.E.C.			-	-	-	-
Japan	+	-	+	-		-
Brazil			+	+	-	-
Mexico	-	-	-			-
Egypt	-		+	-	-	-
India	+	--	+			+
Pakistan	-	-	+			+
Bangladesh			+			
U.S.S.R.			++			+
Capitalist Developed			--			+
Eastern Europe			--			+
South America			+			+
Socialist Asia			+			+
Rest of Asia			+			+
Rest of Africa			+			+

Source: Sarris, Abbott, and Taylor (1977).
Consumer and producer gains or losses marked by double signs exceed $1 billion every 20 years; similarly marked foreign exchange gains or losses exceed $250 million.

elasticities as prices rise. In practice, the internal/external market dynamics were fully modeled for only the first 11 countries in Table 7-1; for lack of data, only import equations were used for the rest.

Table 7-1 shows the effect on various measures of country welfare of a buffer stock that intervenes to maintain the international price within pre-specified bands, up to the limits of its capacity (when buying) or stocks already in hand (when selling).[8] The gains and losses are totals over a period of 20 years, averaged across 200 Monte Carlo simulation runs in which country production fluctuations (the v_{it} in (7.3′) were varied randomly in line with historical experience of the past 25 years.

Countries entering the world wheat market highly restrict their trade (except for the United States, where, in recent years, internal and external grain prices have moved together fairly closely) and, in many cases, have low internal supply response since wheat is both a subsistence and a cash crop. Demand curves also tend to be strongly nonlinear. Under these circumstances, the general impression that exporting countries (the first ones listed in the table) and producers could be expected to lose from price stabilization is scarcely surprising. Soviet trade gains stem from that country's role as an importer contributing a major share of the total variance in world production. Argentine consumer and foreign exchange gains reflect unstable cobweb dynamics in both wheat and feedgrain production, which is stabilized by the buffer stock.

In the feedgrains market, trade is less restricted; there is more supply response, and demand curves are less nonlinear. The tenor of the simulation results is much closer to traditional expectations—exporters and producers mostly gain from stabilization, while consumers and importers lose.

These results are scarcely conclusive, in part because the econometrics underlying them could be improved. And, more important, the standard errors of gains and losses from the simulations often exceed the averages summarized in Table 7-1. Nonetheless, they do serve to illustrate the importance of fairly special characteristics of the market in determining whether a specific country or economic group is likely to benefit or not from price stabilization. Until a great deal more is known about the econometrics of many important commodities, any projections of doom or salvation to come from market intervention have to be viewed askance.

Notes

1. See Sarris and Taylor (1976) for further discussion along these lines.

2. The following analysis is based on Sarris (1976); somewhat similar results were derived independently by Newbery (1976). Note also that the demand curve can be a "general equilibrium" one in the joint sense of (1) being compensated and (2) including income redistribution between producers and consumers because of price changes. Again see Sarris (1976).

3. The positive gain to "society" follows directly from Figure 7-1, where it can be seen that $FEJK > FEJM$ and $-EDNJ > -EDN'J$. We therefore have $(FEJK - EDNJ) > (FEJM - EDN'J) > 0$, or total gains in the nonlinear case exceed gains in the linear case, which were already shown to be positive.

4. The restricted nature of the grain trade is argued more fully in Sarris, Abbott, and Taylor (1977) and references cited there. The following analysis is again based on Sarris (1976).

5. Both these assumptions are in fact tolerably well observed for the major grains; see Sarris, Abbott, and Taylor (1977).

6. An excess demand curve of this form was first proposed and estimated econometrically for many countries by Abbott (1976).

7. See, for example, FAO (1975); and D.G. Johnson (1975).

8. The wheat buffer stock is assumed to stabilize prices between \$108.90 and \$180 per metric ton and to have a capacity of 15 million metric tons. The

price band for feedgrains is between \$93.10 and \$130 per metric ton, and the stock capacity is 10 million tons.

References

Abbott, P.C. 1976. *Developing Countries and International Grain Trade.* Unpublished Ph.D. dissertation, Massachusetts Institute of Technology.

FAO. 1975. "Food Reserve Policies for World Food Security: A Consultant Study on Alternative Approaches." ESC: CPS/75/2, January.

Johnson, D.G. 1975. *World Food Problems and Prospects.* Washington, D.C.: American Enterprise Institute for Public Policy Research.

Newbery, D.M.G. 1976. "Price Stabilization with Risky Production." Department of Economics, Stanford University. Mimeographed.

Sarris, A.H. 1976. *The Economics of International Grain Reserve Systems.* Unpublished Ph.D. dissertation, Massachusetts Institute of Technology.

——, P.C. Abbott, and L. Taylor. 1977. "Grain Reserves, Emergency Relief and Food Aid." Report prepared for the Overseas Development Council. Mimeographed.

——, and L. Taylor. 1976. "Cereal Stocks, Food Aid and Food Security for the Poor." *World Development* 4:967-976.

8 Commodity Instability and Market Failure: A Survey of Issues

Gordon W. Smith

Informational Efficiency in Commodity Markets

Introduction

It has long been argued that commodity markets do not generate and process information efficiently. Some observers, for example, have concluded that the late 1960s and early 1970s were periods of (avoidably) poor market forecasting by nonferrous metals producers and by those who could have counterbalanced producers' errors through carryovers of the metals.[1] The extraordinary price increases of 1972-1974, following on the heels of the large declines in the late 1960s and early 1970s, were at least partially a result of this inefficient generation and use of *longer-term* information by market participants. The *short-run* dimension is probably less important but has received more attention. Many believe, for example, that by early 1974 most commodity markets were dominated by excessive speculative fever.[2] Long-run mistakes produced short-run overshoot or overreaction, even though the best information should have indicated that such extraordinary prices were sustainable only briefly.

While skepticism about the ability of speculative markets to process information is nothing new,[3] more recent are the "efficient market" economists who maintain that this skepticism is likely to be unfounded in most markets. In part, the theory of efficient markets developed as an attempt to rationalize earlier work that supported the random-walk hypothesis for speculative prices. Although Samuelson (1965) was the first to prove rigorously that "properly anticipated prices fluctuate randomly," he was reluctant to put forward his framework as an accurate portrayal of existing markets. The intellectual leadership of this effort has probably fallen to Eugene Fama.

The author would like to thank James Dyer, J. Michael Finger, Wayne Thirsk, Thomas D. Willett, and Neil Wright for helpful comments.

Informational Efficiency

Statement of the Hypothesis. "Market efficiency requires that in setting the prices of securities at any time $t - 1$ the market correctly uses all available information."[4] Fama's 1976 elaboration of this efficient-markets hypothesis is probably the most useful for its clarity and simplicity. He assumes that at any time $t - 1$ there exists an objective, correct probability density function that maps information available at that time into the probabilities associated with security price outcomes in period t. An efficient market, in effect, forms its price expectations for period t by plugging *all available information* into this objective-density function in $t - 1$.[5] Symbolically, let F be the objective density function and Φ the set of all available information. Then

$$E(P_t) = E[F_{t-1}(\Phi_{t-1})]$$

The efficient-market hypothesis asserts that

$$F^m_{t-1} = F_{t-1} \quad \text{and} \quad \Phi^m_{t-1} = \Phi_{t-1}$$

where m refers to market-related terms. It follows that

$$E^m(P_t) = E[F_{t-1}(\Phi_{t-1})] = E(P_t)$$

Fama's informational efficiency is a particular application of Muth's rational-expectations hypothesis: "Expectations of firms (or . . . the subjective probability distributions of outcomes) tend to be distributed, for the same information set, about the predictions of the theory (or the 'objective' probability distribution of outcomes)."[6] Evidently, the terms *all available information* and *the same information set* skirt the fact that much information, including knowledge of the appropriate economic model, is not costless to market participants. *Economically* rational expectations, which take into account the benefits and costs of additional precision in the forecasts, need not correspond to the costless rational expectations of the Muth-Fama approach.[7] Given this fact, a more meaningful criterion of efficiency would thus require only that the "economically rational" expectations be fully reflected in market prices. However, such expectations need not be unbiased, so correct forecasts on average need not characterize efficient markets in this broader sense of the term. This statistical inconvenience probably explains why none of the empirical literature on commodities has employed the weaker notion of economically rational expectations.

Approaches to Testing. A completely adequate empirical test of Fama's informational efficiency would compare the "true" next period forecast with the "market expectations" entering the security pricing process.[8] This comparison is, of course, impossible, and actual tests have been much weaker. They usually sought to determine whether the behavior of prices and returns over time is consistent with informational efficiency. For this purpose, some model is required of the way the market uses its information in setting prices. Tests then become joint tests of informational efficiency and the particular model of price behavior assumed.

Most empirical work has assumed, explicitly or implicitly, that "an efficient market sets the prices of securities at $t - 1$ so that it perceives (true) expected returns to equal their equilibrium values." That is,

$$r_t \equiv P_t - P_{t-1}$$
$$E(r_t) = E(P_t) - P_{t-1}$$
$$E(r_t) = r_t^*$$

where $r \equiv$ one period returns, and $r^* \equiv$ equilibrium one period returns. "In an inefficient market, on the other hand, true expected returns and equilibrium expected returns are not necessarily equal."[9] In an efficient market, the true expected value of *excess returns* above equilibrium levels, $E(r_t) - r_t^*$, is zero for each period, and thus the sequence of expected excess returns with respect to the sequence of information follows a martingale. Now martingales have a very important characteristic in this context: the mathematical expectation of the sum of such a sequence is zero.[10] This is another way of saying that informationally efficient markets offer "fair games" in *excess* returns. Clearly this is a desirable property (and overly restrictive for economically rational expectations). To test it directly requires good models of equilibrium security (commodity) prices.[11] I know of no tests for commodity markets that have used this approach.

Empirically, the martingale property has also motivated less-powerful tests of market efficiency that employ various mechanical buy/sell rules between any given security and cash. If excess returns follow a martingale, such mechanical rules should earn no more on average than simple buy/hold rules over the same period. There have been occasional applications of this type to primary commodity markets.

Most of the empirical literature that can be related to informational efficiency has tested what is loosely called the "random walk" hypothesis(es). Following Fama's approach, "random walk" is a sequence in which the frequency distribution of returns is identical for each moment in time and independent of the sequence of information.[12] In other words, each element of any n period sequence of returns is seen as having been drawn independently, but from identical frequency distributions.[13] This, of course, is a very strong assumption. One implication—that returns (and if these are zero, the changes in prices) should be intertemporally independent[14]—has been the basis of the voluminous literature that tests for serial correlation in first (and second) differences in prices, uses spectral analysis to detect phase relations, and employs runs and other tests in attempts to discover evidence of nonindependence over time.

Empirical Results in Commodities. The volume of empirical literature testing the efficient-markets hypothesis is impressive. Stock markets, bond markets, commodity markets, foreign exchange markets, and even the consumer price index have come under scrutiny. For financial markets, very rarely have researchers been able to *reject* the hypothesis.[15] Many of the commodity studies were not explicitly in the efficient market framework, but they are relevant for the random walk and martingale versions thereof. In the early 1960s it appeared as though randomness could be rejected for many commodity markets and that simple rules could be profitable.[16] Most studies suffered from incompleteness or statistical flaws, however. More recently, the evidence has been mixed.

The Random Walk. The typical random walk test, with its assumption of stationary expected returns through time, excludes an important piece of information: that in all likelihood the assumption is *false.* Apparently, however, changes in *expected returns* are dwarfed by the random noise around them, since by far the most complete study of the random walk hypothesis in commodity markets, Labys and Granger (1970) (cited as L-G), concluded that "most series obey a random walk or near random walk."[17]

L-G hypothesized a random walk in which the series of *gross* returns is a fair game.[18] They then used spectral analysis on daily, weekly, and monthly prices for several futures contracts.[19] With the monthly data, there was a little evidence of an annual component and its harmonic. Weekly and daily data, however, almost uniformly did not permit rejection of the randomness hypothesis.[20] Of the commodities included in the Wharton Rockefeller project, copper monthly futures (London Metal Exchange, LME) were random, monthly wheat futures showed some seasonal component (evidence of "normal backwardation"?),[21] while daily coffee futures and weekly and daily wheat futures all demonstrated behavior that could not be characterized as nonrandom.[22]

Labys and Thomas (1974) update L-G for the period January 1970 through June 1974. Nine commodities in London and five in New York (including copper and coffee in both locales) were subjected to spectral analysis. *Again* the evidence did not permit rejection of the random walk, even though price instability was very violent during the years included.

Praetz (1975) reported on the efficiency of the Sydney wool futures exchange. He assumed a random walk in which the gross rate of return to holdings futures is assumed to be constant. He concludes that the

. . . correlation coefficients, runs tests and spectral analysis [of daily futures] provide only small departures from a model in which price changes are uncorrelated. Clearly, this model stands as a good first approximation to the underlying stochastic process generating price changes.[23]

While Praetz takes randomness as evidence in favor of market efficiency, L-G and Labys and Thomas (L-T) are not in that tradition and draw quite different conclusions. For L-G randomness means unpredictability, instability, and market *disequilibrium,* and they feel that their findings should (rightly) encourage commodity agreements to reduce the uncertainty.[24]

The story L-T tell about the 1972-1974 period strongly suggests informational inefficiencies.[25] Yet they find this perfectly compatible with (perhaps even reflected in) the randomness of prices. And, of course, they may be correct. The association between informational efficiency and randomness is neither necessary nor sufficient. Statistically, the random walk seems to survive more because of the magnitude of the noise component than because of its presumably erroneous (in this form, at least) fair game assumption.

Complementing L-T, I performed a runs test on the daily three-month forward copper price on the LME for the period February 16, 1973 to January 27, 1975–the big boom and bust months. Assuming randomness, the number of runs turned out to be almost exactly what one would have expected.[26] Further analysis of the same series indicated that the direction of daily price changes was completely independent of the signs of the changes in the previous two market days.[27] Time and resources did not permit similar calculations for other products.

Mechanical Rules Tests of the Martingale Property. Several authors have used mechanical buy/sell rules to test the fair game property in excess returns. None of the rules has approached the complexity of advanced chartism. Even so, they have raised doubts about the efficiency of some commodity markets.

A typical procedure runs *X* percent "filter rules" of many different bandwidths.[28] Houthakker's (1961) is the simplest. In his rule, May, September, and December futures were bought once a year on different fixed dates. The contracts were held until maturity unless they fell to a stop-loss level *X* percent below cost of acquisition, in which case they would be sold. Percentages ranging from 0 to 100 were used. In a solid majority of cases for wheat and corn, the two commodities examined, these stop-loss rules outperformed buy/hold. Houthakker is unable to assess the statistical significance of the results; even so, he concludes that his results "indicate the presence of price behavior that would not be present if price changes were random."[29]

Roger Gray (1961) also found that filter rules were profitable both in Chicago corn and wheat futures, while Stevenson and Bear (1970) rejected randomness in part because of the superiority of their 5 percent filters over buy/hold in Chicago corn and wheat.

Smidt (1965) used filter bands around moving averages of soybean futures prices ranging from 1 to 10 days prior. After subtracting trading commissions, 16 of the 20 rules tested gave positive returns. These and other filter tests led Smidt to reject randomness; but since he did not compute the comparable buy/hold returns, he did not in fact test the martingale property. Praetz (1975) ran 24 filter sizes on the Sydney wool exchange futures contracts. Less than half did better than buy/hold, a number that Praetz concluded was insufficient to reject the fair game hypothesis. However, Praetz (1976) later showed that profitability comparisons in such tests are heavily biased in favor of buy/hold if the underlying process is a random walk—the bias increasing with the proportion of time that the filter is operating in a short position. Were this bias to be taken into account, Praetz might have had trouble drawing support for market efficiency from his filter tests.

Cox (1976) examined the *spot* prices for six commodities.[30] His trading rule bought for sale one week later if current price was below a (weighted) moving average of past prices. It sold spot and replenished one week later if current price was above the moving average. These rules earned substantial profits in all six commodities when no futures markets were operating, while only two or six (potatoes and orange juice) showed profits when futures trading was active. No doubt other filter tests have been performed which the author was unable to uncover.

Conclusions. Summarizing, the evidence of informational efficiency in commodity markets is much more mixed than for the stock market. Most recently L-G, L-T, and Praetz, using spectral analysis, have been unable to reject the random walk version, while the weight of the simple filter tests appears to be *against* the *less-stringent* submartingale version. This suggests that spectral techniques may not be very powerful tools in detecting price patterns that are "not likely to be obvious or simple."[31] Indeed, it is remarkable that such simple filter rules as were tested could do so well.[32] Successful chartists employ much more sophisticated techniques. For example, autoregressive integrated moving average (ARIMA) models, as developed by Box and Jenkins (1970), should be able to outperform simple moving averages or the more traditional autoregressions in trading rules. No doubt rules incorporating ARIMA will be divulged—once their profitability has been exhausted.

In closing this section, it should be noted that even had the informational efficiency hypothesis emerged unscathed from the tests, the further premise that "all available information" or economically rational information is also *socially* optimal would have remained untested. There are reasons to believe that the information about commodities that is readily available and diffused is suboptimal: (1) international data on stocks and production are often scanty and of dubious quality; (2) the volume of serious modeling of commodities outside of American agriculture has been small until recently.

Longer-Run Informational Efficiency

Almost without exception, the tests have focused on short-term price changes—from day to day or week to week.[33] While such movements are of prime importance to traders (and most chartists), it would be relatively easy to live with an informationally unfair game that did not significantly disturb efficiency over longer periods.

Two aspects of the longer-run efficiency problem will be treated in this section: (1) what might be called the "buffer stock function" of the market and (2) investment-production decisions.

Market Buffer Stocks. Informational inefficiency, inadequate diffusion of risk, and noncompetitive market structures may all lead the private sector to carry socially suboptimal stocks of commodities, thus generating socially excessive instability. If competition can be assumed and the *private* discount rate is known, then it is possible to test for informational efficiency either through longer-term filter rules or, more directly, through calculation of privately optimal storage rules, given what might be assumed to be the best information.

If the market for storage is informationally efficient, it should be impossible to find rules that yield positive returns net of the opportunity cost of funds, some risk premium, and storage costs. In an admittedly limited test of this property, I applied the following rule for copper purchases and sales: calculate the 5-year lagged moving average of deflated LME spot prices; sell one lot at the current year's average if it exceeds the moving average by more than 15 percent; and buy one lot if current price is more than 15 percent below the moving average. The main limitation of this rule is that it permits one to buy at annual average prices, something never known in advance. With more detailed observations—say, weekly or daily—this difficulty could be corrected without (probably) any great change in the outcome. Time and resources did not permit such detailed analysis for this survey.

In any case, the results appear in Table 8-1. If we assume an 8 percent real discount rate (and basically negligible storage costs),[34] positive discounted profits were earned in the two periods in which the rule was active, 1957-1966 and 1971-1974, while the higher 10 percent discount rate incurred slight losses in the earlier period and substantial gains in the second. 8 and 10 percent discount rates are high, and allow risk premiums which themselves are larger than the average short-term interest rates charged to businesses in the United States.[35]

Obviously, no firm conclusions can be drawn from one test of this limited nature.[36] One productive line of inquiry, which to my knowledge has not been explored in the academic literature, would run similar wide-band filter rules on spot prices, perhaps using ARIMA instead of simple moving averages. If the correct opportunity costs are included, this would yield a fairly clear test of informational efficiency over the longer run.

Table 8-1
Results of ±15 Percent Rule around 5-Year Lagged Moving Average

Year	*Activity*	*Present Value of Dollar 8 Percent Real Discount Rate*	*Present Value of Dollar 10 Percent Real Discount Rate*
1957	Buy		
1958	Buy		
1959	Buy		
1964	Sell		
1965	Sell		
1966	Sell		
1957–1966		$1.131	$ .9855
1971	Buy		
1972	Buy		
1973	Sell		
1974	Sell		
		$1.252	$1.205

Source of prices: Wharton EFA.

Note: Buy one lot of copper if real LME average is at least 15 percent below 5-year lagged moving average, sell one lot if price is at least 15 percent above the lagged moving average.

With accurate models of market behavior outside of the storage sector, it may be possible to test for efficiency more directly in a manner suggested by Gustafson (1958) for agricultural products. Stockists would be assumed to know the behavior of planned supply and demand over time. Random shocks would be introduced in supply (weather, etc.) based on past yield fluctuations, and in demand via the export sector. Dynamic programming could then be used to determine for each year the optimal storage level that would maximize the total expected value of discounted (at *market* rates) consumer surplus and export revenue. This optimal stock would then be compared with actual stocks held. While this approach has been used for normative purposes,[37] that is, to determine optimal stock levels, I know of no attempt to use it to test the positive hypothesis of market efficiency. It has some promise for wheat, where, in the United States, at least, excellent data are available. The optimal storage norm is much more difficult to apply for industrial raw materials, since the primary disturbances appear as activity variables on the demand side of the market. Their probability distributions are not nearly so simple to determine as those of agricultural yields.

The Efficiency of Producer Decisions. Many commodities require long gestation periods between the decision to produce and actual output. Coffee trees, until recently, only began to yield in their fifth year. A copper mine may take five years to bring on line. The most important source of price instability–which stockists can only partially mitigate–is often miscalculation by producers of expected price or future demand.

In this context, Muth's rational expectations hypothesis is again a useful standard.[38] It asserts that economic agents use the appropriate economic model in forming their expectations. Furthermore, since it is known that the rest of the market is also rational, and therefore using the same good model, expected price will equal the equilibrium price (if the model is correct and the right information is plugged into it).[39]

None of the commodity models with which I am familiar incorporate the rational-expectations assumption. Producer expected price is some kind of average of recent past prices, either a naive projection of last period's price or some form of adaptive expectations, as in the best coffee and cocoa models. In the Wharton EFA models, stockists are also assumed to have regressive expectations around some "normal" price. If these assumptions are correct, producers and stockists are not acting on "rational expectations," since their predictions are wrong on the average, and market stability could be improved by more extensive diffusion of information or by government interference with the price mechanism in such a way as to induce irrational decision making to produce rational outcomes.

However, these models were not estimated to test rational expectations but to simulate historical experience of the principal variables accurately in a statistical sense.[40] As such, they probably do *not* constitute a fair test of the efficiency hypothesis. In some cases it may be possible to include rational expectations in new models. Then fair tests could be made against the alternative hypothesis.

It may be stretching a point to argue that Brazilian coffee producers or Ghanian cocoa producers have the faintest idea of the longer-run supply and demand models generating prices or enough information to make extended forecasts. There is certainly no denying that the rush to plant when prices are high is feverish; given the lags, it is equally obvious that lust for extraordinary profits is usually frustrated. Perhaps the long periodicity of the cycles prevents producers from learning their proper lesson!

Rational Expectations and Futures Prices. Certainly the differential between spot and futures can be interpreted as the reward to storage. Furthermore, futures prices can serve as guides to producers' decisions. It is therefore important that futures prices be set efficiently.

The pure-expectations theory holds that current futures prices are predictors of future spot prices.[41] If this is correct, one can compare predictions of spot prices derived (say) from the best quarterly models with the predictions implicit in current futures prices. A study made in 1976 showed that the Chase Econometrics Foreign Exchange Model yielded better quarterly forecasts of several exchange rates than did forward rates. Presumably the same sort of exercise could be performed with quarterly commodity models. This procedure is a bit unfair to rational expectations and informational efficiency, since it actually tests one kind of inside information (a new, costly model) against the market. Of course, if forward rates do better than the model, . . .

Another, less-demanding approach would compare predictions of future spot prices based on ARIMA (Box and Jenkins, 1970) with futures prices for delivery at the same date. If ARIMA outperformed futures prices as a predictor, there would be some evidence of informational inefficiency.

How Good Are Futures Prices as Predictors?

Futures prices act not only as guides to stockholding but also to forward pricing and production decisions. Informational efficiency per se gives no indication of how accurate futures prices are as predictors. Nor does inefficiency indicate that futures prices are poor predictors.

L-G, using cross-spectral analysis on monthly first differences of futures and cash prices for several agricultural commodities, concluded that futures prices will not be useful for predicting cash prices. Their reasoning is that if futures are to be predictors, they must lead cash prices and be coherent with them. No such leads in first differences were observed in the cross spectral. The best available information would seem to be very bad indeed.

Tomek and Gray (1970), however, show that for corn and soybeans, two of the commodities examined by L-G, there is a fairly strong relationship between April 30 futures prices—i.e., immediately before planting—and the post-harvest contract expiration price. This seems to imply that by April 30 the market has enough information to make informed guesses. However, Leuthold (1974) examined *all* contracts for corn and leads ranging from one to eight months prior to delivery. Leads above four months showed futures prices to be poor predictors. Parenthetically, it would also appear that the December price of a September future would do rather badly, since farmers' planting intentions would still be unknown.

The three sources joined together suggest that futures prices may be accurate predictors of cash prices only for near-term expirations or at times when considerable information on prospective production is already available.[42] They do poorly for longer-time horizons or during periods when production decisions can only be roughly estimated. In part this must explain why no futures contracts extend longer than 18 months and few longer than one year. In this connection, it would be useful to test the predictive capacity of other futures contracts.

Conclusions

Although the issue is not completely resolved, there does appear to be enough evidence to doubt the informational efficiency of many commodity markets. How serious are the inefficiencies? What is the order of magnitude of the economic costs they entail? At this stage these are open questions, and the absence of even tentative answers in the commodities literature is one of its bigger gaps.

Risk and Private Stockpiles

Many advocates of publicly supported buffer stocks from Keynes (1938) to Houthakker (1967) have rested their cases upon the supposed divergence between the social and private aversions to the very large risks entailed in maintaining large stocks for long periods. Private stockers are held to be overly myopic and to require excessive ex ante risk premiums. As a result, stocks are too small and price instability too large. The implied remedy is either a subsidy to storage or publicly held buffer stocks. The risk would then be spread over the entire taxpaying population. Since each citizen would bear only a miniscule share of the total risk, the social risk premium would be very low indeed. This argument is not completely correct and must be recast somewhat.[43]

Potential sources of private risk aversion include the following:

1. The fear of bankruptcy: an individual or company may face a cash-flow problem as a result of losses on inventories. This may force bankruptcy, even though over the long haul the storage activity may be profitable. In this case, risk aversion is rooted in capital market imperfections.

2. The separation of ownership from control, to the extent that it creates discretionary behavior possibilities for management, may also lead to excessive risk aversion. Large losses could threaten the control of existing management, while large gains might be unnecessary for the maintenance of the status quo. Hence, corporations may be overly timid from a social viewpoint, another market failure.

3. The costs of being wiped out in the market are surely felt to be more severe by most individuals than the gains from doubling net worth. Although the example is extreme, it is generally felt that diminishing marginal utility of income is a common attribute, and this is sufficient to generate risk aversion without market failure.

In principle, risks could be transferred and optimally pooled through "risk markets," in which shares in each individual "project" could be bought and sold by consumers.[44] Obviously, these markets do not exist to nearly the extent required for optimality, if for no other reason than the transactions and informational costs that their operation would entail. Still, we are far from the world in which *no risks* are pooled in the private sector.[45] Corporations, conglomerates, mutual funds (even in commodity futures), pension funds, insurance companies, and so on are all institutions through which risks to individuals are reduced by pooling projects and by spreading the risks of any particular project over large segments of the population.

The Keynes-Houthakker school must be arguing, in effect, that far from optimal pooling occurs in storage activities. Or, more precisely, government intervention in storage is desirable, while control of most other investment is not, because whatever imperfections result from the absence of explicit risk markets are likely to generate more costly distortions in very risky activities such as commodity storage over longer time periods.

Empirical literature on the degree of excessive risk premiums is nonexistent. It seems reasonable to believe that the truth lies somewhere between the poles of optimal pooling and no pooling at all; but where on the continuum, it is impossible to say.

Theoretical considerations suggest that private risk premiums may differ systematically between industrial raw materials and agricultural products *if optimal pooling* is assumed. Only a sketch of the argument can be presented at this point.

Assume that the variance in the returns to storage in both groups of products is the same. Furthermore, assume that the disposable income of each investor is exactly correlated with movements in national income. Now, the prices of industrial raw materials tend to follow the business cycle (and disposable income) rather closely.[46] Longer-term storage activities tend to buy and sell *countercyclically* so that paper losses are incurred when the level of economic activity (and hence disposable incomes), stock prices, yields, and so on is low. The profits are realized when economic activity is high. In other words, the correlation of realized storage profits and disposable income over time should be fairly high. Under the preceding assumptions, an individual will add storage "projects" to his portfolio only if he anticipates the receipt of some risk premium. The storage project will increase his portfolio variance, no matter how small his stake in it.

By contrast, crop failures and successes tend to be the principal source of price instability and storage profits in agricultural products. Such yield fluctuations tend to be largely uncorrelated with national income.[47] Thus price movements and storage profits should also exhibit only slight correlation with disposable incomes. Thus, under our assumptions, each investor can add a tiny portion of the project to his portfolio without increasing his risk substantially. Furthermore, the *total* risk to all individuals (the sum of money that would be needed to compensate them for the additional risk) becomes very small as the number of investors becomes very large.[48] In that case, the socially and privately optimal discount rate for the storage projects will be only slightly above the certainty rate.

I have not attempted within the framework of this survey to verify empirically the correlations that casual empiricism suggests to be invalid.[49] However, this work should be simple enough and would help greatly in judging the efficiency of private storage behavior. For example, if the preceding argument is correct, then lower discount rates should be used in the proposed filter rules (see the previous section) for storage in (say) wheat or coffee than in (say) copper.[50] Furthermore, calculation of the correlations would also permit better determination of the social rate of discount to be used in evaluating various proposals to reduce commodity instability.

Externalities and Goals Not Related to Efficiency

What factors could justify intervention in commodity markets that operate efficiently according to the criteria elaborated in the previous sections? Typically, externalities, capital market imperfections, and resource transfer goals have all been cited. Each will be considered in this section.

Externalities–Inflation

Even optimal market speculation occasionally will permit very large price rises and declines. One line of argument focuses upon the wage/price spiral that might result from upward commodity price shocks. When commodity prices rise, oligopolistic user industries take this as a sign to raise prices and their profit margins.[51] The cost of living increases as a result, and this may well provoke demands for higher wages. The government then faces a dilemma. It can accommodate these price and wage increases, which may set off something of a wage/price spiral, or it can adopt deflationary measures, which reduce real output if wages and prices are not completely flexible.[52] Commodity stockpiles designed to limit price increases in any given year to some reasonable number—say real prices 20 to 25 percent above trend—might then be justified for the quite extraordinary but still feasible constellation of events, such as occurred in 1972-1974. Private firms cannot be expected to maintain socially optimal stocks for such contingencies, since they do not capture the gains from the lower inflation rate and higher GNP.[53]

Some go farther and argue that traditional commodity agreements designed to limit price fluctuations within some band around trend might actually reduce inflation in the industrialized countries over the long haul.[54] This position rests on a supposed asymmetry in the inflationary impact of commodity price fluctuations. Commodity price increases are passed on (at least) by processing industries. When commodity prices return to lower levels, however, oligopolistic users allegedly do not reduce their prices or, more important in recent years, mitigate their price increases to reflect lower materials prices. Thus support of commodity prices when they are falling will not prevent reductions in final goods prices, which would not have occurred in any case, while maintenance of ceiling prices through buffer stock sales will indeed prevent some inflation.

Empirically, there is very little, if any, support for this supposed "ratchet effect."[55] Its rationale, particularly during periods of general inflation when oligopolies change prices more frequently, is far from clear.[56] Indeed, such ratchet behavior would imply ever-widening oligopolistic profit margins over commodity price cycles. Until some convincing evidence is set forth in its favor, the ratchet effect can hardly be considered as a significant ground for commodity agreements.

It is extremely difficult to move from the general argument for anti-inflationary stockpiles to an operational rule for individual raw materials. The social cost entailed by particular percentage increases in the *relative* price of commodities should be an increasing function of the rate of general inflation, at least over the range experienced in the United States since World War II. For example, a 20 percent rise in an 8 percent inflation rate should be more costly than an 20 percent rise in a 2 percent inflation rate. Consequently, any stockpile authority set up to reduce the inflationary externality would have to condition its actions on *general* price movements. For example, if the price level is rising by more than X percent, then restrain each commodity price below Y percent. Add to this the fact that estimation of the benefits from such actions is problematic at best, and it would appear that even a rough estimation of the "required" stocks for each commodity would be extremely difficult. Furthermore, it might be too much to expect a stockpile authority to resist dumping stocks of commodities *not* in short supply merely to reduce the rate of inflation. This could seriously prejudice private production and storage of the commodity in question.

Externalities–Information and Instability

Predictable instability need cause no resource allocation problems. Certainly, the average supply price will be higher than in a completely stable environment. But in the absence of market distortions, firms will themselves optimally adjust capacity and storage in a variation of the peakload problem.[57]

If instability is joined with uncertainty, the problem becomes more serious. Spot prices are not useful guides to future production and investment. Futures prices are of little help since they are poor predictors except in the very near term. Firms are thus forced to make their own forecasts of future demands and prices, aided perhaps by other public and private forecasting services. To the extent that firms do not follow rational expectations but rather project some weighted average of past prices,[58] price instability will generate an informational externality that will take the form of *overinvestment* and *underinvestment* in primary production. On average, production costs will be higher than they need be, and any stabilizing government intervention—say through a buffer stock—could conceivably reduce the costs of the informational externality. To be effective, the government must have better information on future prospects than is reflected in producers' expectations. Again, to assess the importance of this externality, one needs to know *how* the expectations governing investment and production are formed.

Externalities—Impact of Instability on LDCs

In the last analysis, attention has again focused on commodity instability, mainly because of the demands articulated by less-developed countries (LCDs) in various international forums. LDCs depend more upon primary commodities for their exports, and their export earnings also fluctuate substantially more than those of the industrialized world.[59] For example, at least 25 LDCs depended upon one commodity for at least 50 percent of their export earnings during 1970-1972. Thirteen more depended on two primary commodities for more than 50 percent of their export receipts in the same period.[60] The problem is particularly severe for nations depending on exports of industrial raw materials, since their price and quantity movements over time tend to reenforce each other and may in turn provoke declines in capital flows. In some cases, e.g., Chile, there can be no doubt that in the context of actual economic policy responses, export instability has played havoc with economic performance.[61]

Foreign Exchange Instability and the Second Best. The principal externality of commodity instability occurs through the foreign exchange market, as autonomous foreign exchange earnings fluctuate over the cycle. It is of little use to point out that, in a perfect market, foreign exchange speculators could iron out these fluctuations to some extent. First, speculators would probably do no better in this respect than those operating in commodity markets. Second, even if they could, the institutional market conditions required for such efficiency do not exist, if for no other reason than LDC governments will not permit them to develop. This may be totally wrongheaded on the part of LDC governments, but it is usually the reality.

Uncompensated by private or public action, fluctuations in exchange earnings may give rise to substantial adjustment costs. If aggregate demand is lowered to bring payments back into balance, excess capacity and unemployment will result. If exchange rates are allowed to clear the market freely so that payments remain in balance, the real losses from adjustment to high and then low exchange rates may be substantial.

It is to reduce the adjustment problem that governments hold foreign exchange reserves. A substantial literature devoted to the choice of *optimal* reserve holdings has developed in the last 10 years.[62] The various models differ mainly in the policy options assumed available to deal with adjustment problems. Even if optimal reserves are held by a given LDC, export instability should be accompanied by some cost and hence should reduce *potential* GNP below what it otherwise would have been. The greater the instability of foreign exchange earnings, *ceteris paribus,* the greater will be the average level of optimal foreign exchange reserves held by the Central Bank. Savings are thus diverted to a liquid form, which is almost certain to have a lower *direct* return than investment in real capital. At the very least, then, one cost of instability is the earnings foregone by holding more foreign exchange holdings. To this should be added the adjustment costs entailed even if optimal reserves are held.

With suboptimal reserves, the costs of instability will be greater, showing up as excessive compression and expansion of imports and the concomitant costs of adjustment, which may include alternating inflation and unemployment.

The foreign exchange externality arises in a second-best framework. First, LDCs may not be following optimal adjustment policies. Thus global waste could probably be reduced by damping foreign exchange fluctuations. Buffer stocks might help for countries highly dependent upon particular commodities (coffee, cocoa, and copper are three important cases). This second-best externality is not captured by private market participants.

Second, LDCs may be following optimal policies but may face imperfect capital markets. For some reason the differential between their borrowing and lending rates may be too large from a global efficiency standpoint.[63] Since instability leads governments to hold more reserves (lend to foreigners), actions that reduce instability (and hence reserves) will raise global output to some extent. Again, these gains are external to private market participants.

Finally, if LDCs hold optimal reserves and also face perfect capital markets, moves to reduce instability beyond the efficiency optimum will generate global waste but probably transfer income to LDCs, since the burden of instability is shifted from them to whomever finances the stabilization program.

Remedial distorting actions in particular commodities for the purpose of reducing the external costs of foreign exchange fluctuations can be at most only *third* best. The foreign exchange problem can be dealt with directly through the IMF's compensatory finance facilities, which have recently been expanded and liberalized,[64] while the global losses associated with overly stable markets could be avoided. If particular LDC governments should choose greater stability, they would still be free to manipulate internal buffer stocks, subsidies, and so on to achieve their goals.

Export Instability and Growth. Although there is no compelling reason why waste of the types set forth in the previous section should imply lower *average* *growth rates,* in the empirical literature the cost of export instability has most often been identified with this result. A substantial effort has been expanded to determine whether there is some correlation between various measures of export instability and the rate of economic growth.[65] Of necessity, international cross sections have been used. This practice requires that all other important factors affecting growth across countries be correctly specified if the tests are to be unbiased. Most models have not succeeded in this respect, so some skepticism about the statistical results is warranted.

Still, almost no one has turned up significant relations between export instability and growth of the sign predicted.[66] Indeed, some, including MacBean (1966) and Knudsen and Parnes (1975), even find a positive relation between the two. Instability apparently generates more investment and growth! The Knudsen and Parnes analysis provides an explanation: export instability apparently increases the average savings rates out of permanent income. The savings are converted into higher investment and growth rates; hence the paradox is explained.[67]

While ingenious, the Knudsen and Parnes analysis is inconclusive. Their measure of export instability—the sum of the ratios of squared deviations from trend to the square of the trend value—is significantly correlated across their sample with the growth rate of exports.[68] Since export growth nowhere appears explicitly as an explanatory variable for GNP growth, savings, and investment,[69] one may wonder whether it is instability or merely its correlation with export growth that produces the results they present.[70]

Probably the most warranted conclusion from this empirical literature is "that the case has certainly not been proven that export instability is a serious deterrent to growth in LDCs."[71] But this in no way invalidates the conclusions of the previous section, since the costs of instability are likely to show up in other ways than in lowered average growth rates.

Nonefficiency Goals—Transfer of Resources to LDCs

It is obvious that LDCs are more interested in receiving "fair and remunerative" prices than they are in *stable* prices. It is equally obvious that many of them do not believe that market-determined prices are sufficiently fair. The Group of 77 has heartily endorsed the formation of producer associations for all primary commodities, and one of their chief goals, of course, is to raise prices. For their part, the industrial countries, particularly the United States and West Germany, reject the notion of resource transfer through the commodity price mechanism. Whatever the true reason, the industrial nations claim that commodity markets are an *inefficient* vehicle through which to grant aid. LDCs, perhaps correctly, see this position as a ruse, a red herring, since they feel that the requisite transfer of resources will not in any case be forthcoming from normal, supposedly efficient aid channels. For them, the main issue is *distribution,* an increase in aid, not the efficient transfer of an otherwise fixed amount of resources. As a result, the two groups more often than not talk past each other.

Ironically, the only commodity agreements in which the United States has participated with a preponderance of LDC producers have both had as their primary goal increases in producer incomes through export quotas. Although our membership in the Sugar Agreements of 1937, 1953, and 1958 was primarily a "gesture of cooperation,"[72] the Kennedy administration was one of the prime movers behind the first Coffee Agreement. Special circumstances can be claimed, however. Coffee and, to a lesser extent, sugar are both LDC products. Latin America, a U.S. protectorate at the time, includes the major LDC producers and traders of both commodities.

The arguments against the use of commodity markets for resource transfer are several:

1. Only accidentally will the *distribution* of gains within the group of LDCs correspond with any rational criterion of resource transfer, e.g., need, performance, etc. Some of the prime winners from high primary commodity prices would be the richest LDCs, such as Brazil, Malaysia, Chile, Argentina, and Mexico. Clearly, if one wants to aid the poor coffee producers of Africa, higher coffee prices, which raise Colombian and Brazilian incomes, are not a particularly effective way to do it.

2. Rich countries export substantial percentages of many of the commodities included in the UNCTAD group of 18. Some of the more important examples are: copper, phosphates, iron ore, cotton, sugar, and oilseed.[73] Higher prices of these goods would lead to senseless and substantial resource transfers between non-LDCs.

3. Rich countries produce and trade substantial proportions of some commodities that are close substitutes for LDC commodities. Synthetic rubber, the substitution of aluminum for tin, synthetic fibers, and so on all come to mind.[74] This means that the demand elasticity for the LDC commodity may be high, thus defeating the resource transfer goal.

4. The burden of the resource transfer is shared according to the imports of commodities. Resource-poor countries would thus pay most of the bill. This pattern probably does not correspond to any rational criterion of ability to pay.

5. Even if the pattern of resource transfer generated through commodity prices were to be acceptable, it is sometimes claimed that it would be more efficient to raise the revenue through the general budget. Clearly, higher commodity prices–in effect equivalent to an export tax on commodities–would generate some distortion in resource allocation. But it does not follow that budgetary financing would be less distortionary.

The U.S. tax system, for example, is laden with distorting provisions. The corporate income tax, the personal income tax, and so on are clearly not neutral in their effects.[75] Whether a dollar collected through the budget is less distortionary than "artificially" higher commodity prices is an open question, and will vary from commodity to commodity. For example, if the commodity is exported and produced entirely by LDCs, if the price elasticity of demand is very low, and if there are no close substitutes, the commodity "tax" may actually be a superior means of transferring resources, again assuming that the resultant distribution between the LDCs is acceptable. Interestingly, the conditions that favor successful LDC producer cartels also tend to generate efficient resource transfers.[76]

Of the UNCTAD commodities, only two groups suggest themselves as even potentially efficient as means of resource transfer to LDCs: most importantly, coffee, tea, and cocoa; and less likely, tin, copper, and bauxite. The groupings contain the close substitutes, and LDC export shares of the groups are high. The price elasticities of the groups as a whole are probably fairly low, and many of the potential recipient countries are among the poorer nations of the world.

Conclusions

As stated in the introduction, the net outcome of this survey is ultimately inconclusive, given the current state of the literature. We have seen, for example, the key roles played by expectations, risk, and excessive risk in evaluating commodity proposals, but the empirical evidence is ambiguous. We have found one version of the inflationary externality to be plausible, but still unproven.

Perhaps it is time to change research strategies a bit, to move away somewhat from market models that assume irrationality (or rationality) to *micro studies* of expectations, investment, and speculation. If you will, these could be "industry studies" oriented toward the key issues and joining economic theory with a good institutional background. The many commodity exchanges could be so analyzed. Analytical company histories of (say) copper producers could shed considerable light upon the efficiency of investment decisions. It would also be fascinating to compare the actions of nationalized firms with those of the same units before nationalization. Micro studies of this type are difficult and very time-intensive, which probably explains why so few have been attempted. But they could form the basis of a much more precise evaluation of market failure in the important commodities.

Notes

1. James Burrows et al. (1975).
2. See, for example, Labys and Thomas (1974); Piggott and Smith (1975); Cooper and Lawrence (1975).

3. Keynes' description of stock exchange traders as seeking to anticipate "what average opinion expects average opinion to be" is perhaps the most celebrated. Keynes (1936), p. 156.

4. Fama (1976), p. 143.

5. Fama (1976).

6. Muth (1961), p. 316.

7. The term is due to Feige and Pearce (1976), although they do not actually employ the concept in an efficient markets test. Sargent (1973) calls basically the same empirical operation performed by Feige and Pearce "partly rational" expectations.

8. The meaning of *market expectations* when individual participants in fact differ in their assessments has long plagued theorists of speculative markets. For an excellent attempt to nail down more precisely the notions of market efficiency and expectations, see Rubinstein (1975).

9. Fama (1976), pp. 143-44.

10. For the properties of martingales, see H. Bauer (1972).

11. See Fama (1976), pp. 144-145; and Fama (1970), pp. 400-404.

12. Bauer (1972) deals with this type of sequence, which is a type of martingale, on pp. 352-353.

13. Although the error is of minor practical import, Fama's characterization of the random walk is overly restrictive. If spectral techniques are employed to detect the intertemporal dependence, identical *variances* of the distribution of returns over time are not required, although the mean of the distribution of returns must remain fixed. See Labys and Granger (1970), pp. 63-64.

14. This is not the case with the unrestricted martingale or submartingales model nor with the more general fair game model. For example, see Fama (1970), p. 392; Samuelson (1965), p. 44.

15. See Fama (1970).

16. For example, Houthakker (1961); Larson (1960); Smidt (1965); and Working (1960). For an excellent, brief summary of the efficient markets hypothesis in commodities since 1960, see Praetz (1975).

17. Labys and Granger (1970), p. 84.

18. That is, $E(P_t) - P_{t-1} = 0$.

19. Sixteen for monthly data, six for weekly observations, and ten for the daily price series. The number of observations varied between 186 and 260 taken from the 1950s and 1960s. L-G also worked with cash prices, but the results are irrelevant for informational efficiency unless something further is known about the costs of holding physical commodities.

20. Cocoa and cotton futures daily prices showed negative autocorrelation.

21. This has been observed by several others: Cootner (1960*a* and *b*); Gray (1961); among others.

22. One could have wished for longer series in the weekly and daily futures

prices. The former covered only August 1961-July 1965, while the latter only covered one year, 1964-1965.

23. Praetz (1975), p. 248.

24. Labys and Granger (1970), pp. 262-265.

25. Labys and Thomas (1974), pp. 21-26.

26. The number of price increases was 262; the number of declines, 228; and the number of runs was 250!

27. The conditional ex post probabilities of price increases and decreases were calculated. A Chi-square test of the difference of each of the four classes examined from the overall (nonconditional) probability showed it impossible to reject the hypothesis of independence at even the 60 percent confidence level. These tests were motivated by Niederhoffer and Osborne (1966), who found some indication of this type of dependence for the stock market.

28. Although there are many variants, in essence these rules say buy (sell) when the price rises X percent above some level, sell (buy) when it falls by X percent below some level. The procedure filters out small changes in prices that are thought to have no information content. If such rules are profitable, future price changes depend on previous changes in ways not fully reflected in current price—a violation of the (sub)martingale property.

29. Houthakker (1961), p. 168.

30. Onions, potatoes, pork bellies, hogs, cattle, and orange juice.

31. Houthakker (1961), p. 164.

32. Similar rules were also shown to be profitable in some foreign exchange markets during the float. See Logue, Sweeney, and Willett (1976).

33. Runs tests and serial correlations of daily prices with lags usually involve short time periods. Spectral analysis need not, but the time period analyzed has usually been too short to permit secure identification of longer-term correlations. The length of the filter rules tests is limited by the length of the futures contract—never longer than 18 months.

34. In LME warehouses they are on the order of 0.5 percent per year.

35. *Economic Report of the President,* 1976.

36. No other rules were tested. A 15 percent band was selected because it was obvious that with 8 and 10 percent discount rates, narrower bands were almost certain to lose money.

37. Johnson, (1976); Johnson and Sumner (1976).

38. Muth (1961).

39. This hypothesis has found some application recently in macroeconomics, particularly as regards the formation of inflationary expectations and nominal interest rates. See, for example, Sargent (1973); and Lucas (1975). I know of only one empirical application of rational expectations to commodity producer decisions, Cooley and DeCanio (1977). Using Muth's original model, they cannot reject rational expectations for U.S. cotton and wheat producers.

Since this version is empirically indistinguishable from adaptive expectations, the result hardly constitutes a strong test. On this last point, see Nelson (1975).

40. It is interesting to note that De Menil and Bhalla (1975) found that direct surveys of consumer inflationary expectations perform better in several macroeconomic wage equations than do the distributed lags on past prices assumed by the original authors of the equations. Consumers may be more rational than (some) econometricians' methods give them credit for.

41. See, for example, Working (1961), p. 161.

42. L-G's cross-spectral analysis lumps all equal-phase lags together, the probable explanation for their inability to detect the lead that becomes obvious in Leuthold, Tomek and Gray for certain points in real time.

43. Arrow and Lind (1970) show that even for public investments with no private counterparts (e.g., pure public goods) the government should use the risk-free rate only when the returns from the project are uncorrelated with past government investments and with national income.

44. A proof of this proposition for a simplified economy appears in Sandmo (1974), which is also an excellent treatment of the differences between Hirshleifer (1965, 1966) and Arrow and Lind (1970).

45. Sandmo (1974) analyzes the adverse consequences of an economy made up wholly of unincorporated businesses so that individuals have *no* possibility of diversifying their portfolios.

46. See Cooper and Lawrence (1975), for example.

47. Tree crops with long gestation periods do exhibit longer-term cyclical price movements. The shocks and lags generating the cycles need not be in any way related to the business cycle.

48. Arrow and Lind (1970) prove this proposition for public investment, the returns of which are uncorrelated with disposable income. They assume complete insurance markets in the private sector, identical preferences all around, and perfect capital markets. The government spreads the risk over the whole taxpaying population. As it does, total social cost of risk falls toward zero. The key assumption is the lack of correlation of the public project with disposable income and other public projects.

49. Brainard and Dolbear (1971) present data indicating a negative correlation of farm income with national income and its principal components. Farm income should be positively correlated with storage profits—both benefiting from high farm prices.

50. Unfortunately, the filter rules become a joint test of the excessive risk aversion *and* informational efficiency. One approach, which does not test longer-range informational efficiency, would use futures prices for the fair game tests and storage of the actual good for the excessive risk aversion test.

51. Ripley and Segal (1973), in an econometric study of pricing in 395 four-digit U.S. industries, found that higher materials costs "are not simply

passed on in higher prices but there appears to be a markup on these prices." The degree of the markup did not, however, depend on the degree of concentration in the industry.

52. See Cooper and Lawrence (1975), pp. 708-709, for a development of this line. It is unclear whether they accept or reject the hypothesis. The ECLA structuralist school first elaborated the shock-propagation-inflationary-spiral approach. It is not necessary to link the inflationary externality with still questionable hypotheses about oligopoly behavior. One could argue with some plausibility that oligopolies tend to *mitigate* the impact of materials price fluctuations, both upward and downward, through some form of long-run full-cost pricing. All that is required to develop the inflationary externality is downward wage or price instability in some sectors of the economy.

53. Care would have to be exercised, however, so that purchases for such stockpiles would not themselves have a significant inflationary impact.

54. See, for example, Jere Behrman (1977).

55. J.M. Finger and D.A. De Rosa (1977), for example, conclude that "relevant studies in the literature as well as our own tests oppose the validity of the ratchet hypothesis" (p. 16).

56. A very useful survey of hypotheses concerning the relation of oligopoly and inflation and some empirical tests appear in Lustgarten (1975).

57. For an interesting treatment of the predictable peakload problem and of the adjustments in capacity and consumption that storage permits, see Gravelle (1976).

58. In Muth's original model, the rational expectation of price turned out to be a weighted average of past prices, because only supply was subject to a disturbance or exogenous influence. Nelson (1975) showed that in the more general case, information on the structure of the economic model is also required.

59. For recent surveys of the findings on this point, see Stern (1976); and Kreinin and Finger (1976) and the works cited therein.

60. World Bank data supplied to U.S. Treasury Department.

61. See Reynolds (1963), for example.

62. See, for example, Heller (1966); Clark (1970); Kelly (1970); Flanders (1971); Frenkel (1974); Claasen (1974).

63. Substantial distortions in the allocation of capital also exist in the industrial countries. Diversion of investment from the private sector to commodity stocks may involve indirect costs even greater than the benefits accruing to LDCs.

64. For a recent analysis of these facilities, see deVries (1975).

65. MacBean (1966); Kenen and Voivados (1972); Voivados (1974); Knudsen and Parnes (1975).

66. Voivados (1974) did, but not in his two-gap model formulation.

67. Of course, higher savings may take the form of financial investments in foreign assets, e.g., foreign exchange. The relation of export instability to investment is fairly weak in their equations.

68. At the 5 percent level for the sample of 28 countries, at the 1 percent level if Paraguay is excluded, using the Spearman rank corrleation coefficient. The correlation is probably not accidental, and arises from the nature of the measure itself. If high growth rates fluctuate the same, proportionately, as low growth rates, a positive correlation between the growth rates and the Knudsen-Parnes instability index will be observed.

69. As it would, for example, in gap models.

70. Unfortunately, Chile, the worst case of export and growth instability, according to Mathieson and McKinnon (1974) pp. 325-326, is excluded from their sample.

71. Stern (1976), p. 180.

72. U.S. International Trade Commission (1975), p. 19.

73. Commodities in which LDCs accounted for 65 percent or less of world exports in 1970-1972.

74. LDCs do export almost 80 percent of the bauxite, but this material is only a small fraction of the total cost of aluminum.

75. Browning (1976), for example, estimates that the marginal cost of public funds from taxes on labor ranges from $1.09 to $1.16 per dollar of revenue.

76. The converse is not true, however, since an additional requirement for successful cartels seems to be a small number of sellers, or at least dominant sellers.

References

Arrow, K.J., and R.C. Lind. "Uncertainty and the Evaluation of Public Investment Decisions." *American Economic Review,* LX, 3 (June 1970):364-378.

Bauer, H. *Probability Theory and Elements of Measure Theory.* New York: Holt, Rinehart, and Winston, 1972.

Behrman, J.R. *International Commodity Agreements: An Evaluation of the UNCTAD Integrated Commodity Program.* Overseas Development Council, Washington, D.C., 1977.

Box, G.E.P., and G.M. Jenkins. *Time-Series Analysis, Forecasting and Control.* San Francisco: Holden Day, 1970.

Browning, E.K. "The Marginal Cost of Public Funds." *Journal of Political Economy* 84, 2 (April 1976):283-298.

Burrows, J., et al. from Charles River Associated. Interview with the author and J. Michael Finger, April 1975. Memorandum summarizing the interview available from J.M. Finger.

Claasen, E.M. "The Optimizing Approach to the Demand for International Reserves." *Weltwirtschaftliches Archiv* B. CX (1974):354-398.

Clark, P.B. "Optimum International Reserves and the Speed of Adjustment." *Journal of Political Economy* LXXVIII, 2 (March/April 1970):356-376.

Cooper, R.N., and R.Z. Lawrence. "The 1972-75 Commodity Boom." *Brookings Papers on Economic Activity,* No. 3, (1975) pp. 671-715.

Cootner, P.H. "Returns to Speculators: Telser vs. Keynes." *Journal of Political Economy* 68 (1960*a*):396-404.

——. "Rejoinder." *Journal of Political Economy* 68 (1960*b*):415-418.

Cox, C.C. "Futures Trading and Market Information." *Journal of Political Economy* 84, 6 (December 1976):1215-1238.

DeMenil, G., and S.S. Bhalla. "Direct Measurement of Popular Price Expectations." *American Economic Review* LXV, 1 (March 1975):169-180.

Fama, E. "Efficient Capital Markets: A Review of Theory and Empirical Work." *Journal of Finance* XXV, 2 (May 1970):383-417.

——. "Reply." *Journal of Finance* XXXI, 1 (March 1976):143-145.

Feige, E.L., and D.K. Pearce. "Economically Rational Expectations: Are Innovations in the Rate of Inflation Independent of Innovations in Measures of Monetary and Fiscal Policy?" *Journal of Political Economy* 84, 3 (June 1976):499-522.

Finger, J.M., and D.A. DeRosa. "Ratchet Effect of Commodity Prices on Industrial Country Inflation Rates." May 1977. Mimeographed.

Flanders, M.J. *The Demand for International Reserves.* Princeton Studies in International Finance No. 27. Princeton, N.J.: Princeton University Press, 1971.

Frenkel, J.A. "The Demand for International Reserves by Developed and Less-Developed Countries." *Economica* (February 1974):14-24.

Gravelle, H. "The Peakload Problem with Feasible Storage." *Economic Journal* 86 (June 1976):256-277.

Gray, R.W. "The Search for a Risk Premium." *Journal of Political Economy* LXIX (June 1961):250-260.

Gustafson, R.L. "Carry Levels for Grains: A Method for Determining Amounts that are Optimal Under Specified Conditions." *USDA Technical Bulletin* 1178, 1958.

Heller, H.R. "Optimal International Reserves." *The Economic Journal* LXXVI (1966).

Hirshleifer, J. "Investment Decision Under Uncertainty: Choice-Theoretic Approaches." *Quarterly Journal of Economics* LXXIX, 4 (November 1965): 509-536.

——. "Investment Decision Under Uncertainty: Application of the State-Preference Approach." *Quarterly Journal of Economics* LXXX, 2 (May 1966): 252-277.

Houthakker, H. "Systematic and Random Elements in Short-term Price Movements." *American Economic Review* LI, 2 (May 1961):164-172.

——. *Economic Policy for the Farm Sector.* Washington, D.C.: American Enterprise Institute for Public Policy Research, November 1967.

Johnson, D.G. "Increased Stability of Grain Supplies in Developing Countries." University of Chicago, Office of Agricultural Economics Research Paper No. 76:14 (April 1976). Mimeographed.

——, and D. Sumner. "An Optimization Approach to Grain Reserves for Developing Countries" (April 1976). Mimeographed.

Kelly, M.G. "The Demand for International Reserves." *The American Economic Review* LX, 4 (September 1970):655-667.

Kenen, P.B., and C.S. Voivodas. "Export Instability and Economic Growth." *Kyklos* (1972).

Keynes, J.M. *The General Theory of Employment, Interest and Money.* New York: Harcourt Brace, 1936.

——. "The Policy of Government Storage of Foodstuffs and Raw Materials." *The Economic Journal* 68 (September 1938):249-260.

Kreinin, M.E., and J.M. Finger. "A New International Economic Order." U.S. Treasury OASCA/Research Discussion Paper (1976).

Knudsen, O., and A. Parnes. *Trade Instability and Economic Development.* Lexington, Mass.: D.C. Heath, 1975.

Labys, W.C., and C. Granger. *Speculation, Hedging, and Commodity Price Forecasts.* Lexington, Mass.: Lexington Books, D.C. Heath, 1970.

——. and H.C. Thomas. "Speculation, Hedging and Commodity Price Behavior: An International Comparison." Graduate Institute of International Studies, Geneva, December 15, 1974. Mimeographed.

Larson, A. "Measurement of a Random Process in Futures Prices." *Food Research Institute Studies* I, (1960).

Leuthold, R.M. "The Price Performance on the Futures Market of a Nonstorable Commodity: Live Beef Cattle."*American Journal of Agricultural Economics* 56, 2 (May 1974):271-279.

Logue, D.E., R.J. Sweeney, and T.D. Willett. "The Speculative Behavior of Foreign Exchange Rates During the Current Float" (1976). Mimeographed.

Lucas, R.E., Jr. "An Equilibrium Model of the Business Cycle." *Journal of Political Economy* 83, 6 (December 1975):1113-1144.

Lustgarten, S. *Industrial Concentration and Inflation.* Washington, D.C.: American Enterprise Institute for Policy Research, 1975.

MacBean, A. *Export Instability and Economic Development.* Cambridge, Mass.: Harvard Univ. Press, 1966.

Mathieson, D.J., and R. I. McKinnon. "Instability in Underdeveloped Countries: the Impact of the International Economy." In P.A. David and M.W.

Reder (eds.), *Nations and Households in Economic Growth.* New York: Academic Press, 1974.

Muth, J.F. "Rational Expectations and the Theory of Price Movements." *Econometrica* 29, 3 (July 1961):315-335.

Nelson, C.R. "The Prediction Performance of the FRB-MIT-PENN Model of the U.S. Economy." *American Economic Review* LXII, 5 (December 1972): 902-917.

——. "Rational Expectations and the Predictive Efficiency of Economic Models." *Journal of Business* 48, 3 (July 1975):331-343.

Niederhoffer, U., and M.F.M. Osborne. "Market Making and Reversal on the Stock Exchange." *Journal of the American Statistical Association* LXI (December 1966):897-916.

Piggott, C., and G.W. Smith. "A New Era of Commodity Trade?" U.S. Treasury/ OASIA (April 1975). Mimeographed.

Praetz, P.D. "Testing the Efficient Markets Theory on the Sydney Wool Futures Exchange." *Australian Economic Papers* (December 1975):240-249.

——. "Rate of Return on Filter Tests." *Journal of Finance* XXXI, 1 (March 1976):71-75.

Reynolds, C.W. "Domestic Consequences of Export Instability." *American Economic Review* LIII, 2 (May 1963):65-74.

Ripley, F.C., and L. Segal. "Price Determination in 395 Manufacturing Industries." *Review of Economics and Statistics* LV, 3 (August 1973):263-271.

Rubinstein, M. "Securities Market Efficiency in an Arrow-Debreu Economy." *American Economic Review* LXV, 5 (December 1975):812-824.

Samuelson, P. "Proof That Properly Anticipated Prices Fluctuate Randomly." *Industrial Management Review* 6, (1965):41-49.

Sandmo, A. "Discount Rates for Public Investment Under Uncertainty." In J.H. Drèze (ed.), *Allocation Under Uncertainty: Equilibrium and Optimality.* London: Macmillan, 1974, pp. 192-212.

Sargent, T.J. "Rational Expectations, the Real Rate of Interest and the Natural Rate of Unemployment." *Brookings Papers on Economic Activity* 2 (1973): 429-472.

Smidt, S. "A Test of the Serial Independence of Price Changes in Soybeans Futures." *Food Research Institute Studies* 5 (1965).

Stern, R.M. "World Market Instability in Primary Commodities." *Banca Nazionale del Lavoro: Quarterly Review* 117 (June 1976):175-195.

Stevenson, R., and R. Bear. "Commodity Futures: Trends or Random Walks?" *Journal of Finance* XXV, 1 (March 1970):65-82.

Tomek, W.G., and R.W. Gray. "Temporal Relationships Among Prices on Commodity Futures Markets: Their Allocative and Stabilizing Roles." *American Journal of Agricultural Economics* 52, 4 (August 1970):372.

United States International Trade Commission. *International Commodity*

Agreements. Report to Committee on Finance of U.S. Senate. Washington, D.C.: USGPO, 1975.

Voivodas, C.S. "The Effect of Foreign Exchange Instability on Growth." *Review of Economics and Statistics* LVI, 3 (August 1974).

de Vries, J. *Compensatory Financing: A Quantitative Analysis.* World Bank Staff Working Paper No. 228. Washington, D.C.: World Bank, 1975.

Working, H. "Speculation on Hedging Markets." *Food Research Institute Studies* I (1960).

——. "New Concepts Concerning Futures Markets and Prices." *American Economic Review* LI, 2 (May 1961):160-163.

9 Is Price Stabilization Theoretically Desirable?

Edwin Burmeister

A major theoretical conclusion that emerges from both Turnovsky's comprehensive survey and the Sarris-Taylor chapter is that in principle any particular economic group either may benefit or be harmed from price-stabilizing market interventions. Policy makers should be cautioned by this result, for their actions, taken with the best of intentions for a particular group, may produce results exactly the *opposite* of those intended.

Thus, for example, Turnovsky's chapter makes clear that it is crucial for policy makers to have accurate knowledge about the way in which stochastic disturbances enter and about the price elasticities of supply and demand. Even more serious, I believe, is Turnovsky's finding that the results also hinge upon *how* expectations are generated, for I suspect that it will be difficult to distinguish empirically among alternative expectation-generating hypotheses.

Turnovsky also touches upon stabilization within a general equilibrium framework; and since this turns out to be of fundamental importance, I want to elaborate on the issue. Apparently, it is a fairly general proposition that in partial equilibrium models price stabilization in a single market produces net benefits, so that, in principle, the gainers always could compensate the losers with an overall increase in economic welfare. But this proposition is generally *false,* as I shall now illustrate with a simple example attributable to Samuelson.

Consider a model with two commodities, corn and hogs.

1. Corn can either be consumed or fed to hogs.
2. Corn harvests are subject to a probability distribution due, say, to exogenous weather conditions.
3. There is some cost associated with storing corn.
4. Consumers maximize an intertemporal welfare function given by the sum of discounted utilities in future periods.
5. Utility in each period is a concave function of corn and hog consumption.

The application of stochastic dynamic programming provides the *optimal* policy that maximizes total welfare.

Samuelson's theorem: *Prices along the optimal path oscillate,* i.e., the textbook corn-hog cycle has optimal properties! At first I found this an astonishing result; but upon reflection, it is not surprising. Intuitively, when there is an extraordinary harvest, the optimal strategy is to have the price of corn fall relative to hogs, thereby inducing increases in both corn consumption and the use of corn to feed hogs. Then, when a bad harvest comes, the relative corn-hog price increases, and consumers substitute hogs for corn. But now there also is more hog meat because hogs were fed extra low-price corn in the boom harvest years. In other words, oscillatory prices are an optimal way of handling the costly corn-storage problem.

We must, therefore, bear in mind the possibility that a dynamic market price system has certain subtle optimality properties that are not generally recognized–indeed, the name of this conference seems to pre-judge the desirability of price stability. But I'm afraid that it is a basic theoretical error to *presume* that price oscillations are detrimental–even in deterministic models without stochastic disturbances. *Price oscillations may be optimal simply because of the dynamic structure of tastes and technology.* Moreover, in both the stochastic and deterministic cases, the dynamic price equations for perfectly competitive markets are identical to the conditions *necessary* for intertemporal welfare maximization and economic efficiency.

Thus a sound theoretical case can be made for improving market competition, and one important way of doing this is to supply better public information. Turnovsky's section on announced public forecasts provides one such example, and the section on informational efficiency of Smith's chapter is directly related. The problem remains of determining the socially optimal quantities and types of information that would improve economic performance. However, provided we are obviously not near the point where the marginal cost of providing better information exceeds the marginal social benefits, better information will definitely improve economic welfare.

But one should be careful not to overstate the case against market intervention. While it is true that perfectly competitive speculation does perform the service of generating the dynamic price behavior that is necessary for optimality–provided speculators know the correct probability distributions–practical political considerations also must be recognized. Suppose, for example, that speculators know the correct probability distribution for a catastrophic event, say, a war or a famine. They will nevertheless act in a suboptimal manner because they fully realize that if that catastrophic event in fact were to occur, the previously free market would become subject to governmental regulations (e.g., quotas), and, accordingly, speculators could never realize the potential gains from arbitrage. For such reasons, as well as for more complicated reasons involving private versus social risk aversion discussed by Smith, perfectly competitive free markets may never be completely optimal. The dilemma, I fear, is that the more government interferes, the more it needs to.

I conclude, therefore, with the suggestion that the "appropriate degree" of market intervention may end up being primarily a political decision. But even with perfect planning and *complete* market intervention, *optimal* shadow prices may oscillate, as definitely illustrated by Samuelson's corn-hog cycle example.

References

Burmeister, E., and A. Rodney Dobell. "Guidance of a Developed Free-Market Economy." In *Record of the IEEE Conference on Systems Science and Cybernetics.* Philadelphia, October 1969.

——. *Mathematical Theories of Economic Growth.* New York: Macmillan, 1970.

Samuelson, P.A. "The Consumer Does Benefit From Feasible Price Stability." *The Quarterly Journal of Economics* LXXXVI, 3 (August 1972):476-493.

——. "Rejoinder." To Comments on "The Consumer Does Benefit from Feasible Price Stability." *The Quarterly Journal of Economics* LXXXVI, 3 (August 1972):500-503.

——. "Stochastic Speculative Price." *Proceedings of the National Academy of Sciences, U.S.A.* 68 (1971):335-337. Reproduced as Chapter 206 in *Collected Scientific Papers of Paul A. Samuelson,* Vol. III, edited by Robert C. Merton. Cambridge, Mass.: M.I.T. Press, 1972.

——. "Optimality of Profit-Including Prices Under Ideal Planning." *Proceedings of the National Academy of Sciences, U.S.A.* 70 (1973):2109-2111.

——. "The Periodic Turnpike Theorem." *Nonlinear Analysis* 1, 1 (1976):3-13.

Part III
Economic, Political, and Institutional Considerations in Commodity Policy

10 Political Economy of an Integrated Commodity Program

David L. McNicol

During the past few years, the less-developed countries' insistence on the creation of a set of related commodity agreements has been a major issue in North-South relations. The importance that both the less-developed countries (LDCs) and the developed countries (DCs) have attached to commodity agreements is easy to appreciate. Commodities trade is vital to most of the LDCs, and the stability of commodity supplies and commodity prices are a significant concern for the DCs.[1] Beyond this, an integrated commodity program could sharply increase the influence of the LDCs in international economic affairs.

These considerations, having been noted, will not be pursued directly in what follows. This chapter is concerned with (1) the use of political power, within an integrated commodity program, to obtain economic ends; (2) some of the political consequences of mechanisms that might be employed in such a program; and (3) possible remedies for the problems associated with commodity arrangements. These topics will be approached largely in terms of the Integrated Programme for Commodities which is currently the object of considerable international attention.

Characteristics of an Integrated Commodity Program

An *integrated commodity program* would be a set of related commodity agreements; but beyond that, the term has no specific meaning. Since an *integrated program* could be put together in many different ways, the idea is perhaps best established by describing the two leading examples.

One of these is a proposal made by John Maynard Keynes in a 1942 memorandum to the United Kingdom Treasury. Keynes was concerned with "meaningless short-period price swings" and with the business cycle. He argued that:

> the same technique of Buffer Stocks, which has to be called into being to deal with the former problem, is also capable of making a large contribution to the cure of the Trade Cycle itself.[2]

The idea that buffer stocks–i.e., organizations that buy or sell as is necessary to hold prices within established bounds—have an important role to play in dealing with the problems of unemployment and inflation has never gained much popularity. In fact, it seems a bit out of place in terms of modern macroeconomics. But the rationale that Keynes offered for his proposal is perhaps less important than the proposal itself.

Keynes suggested a series of buffer stocks, each operated by a "Commodity Control," and a General Council for Commodity Controls. The general council would review individual commodity controls before they were established to ensure that each conformed to preestablished principles; review the commodity controls' operations; and make policy recommendations to them. Finally, Keynes suggested that the buffer stocks be financed by the International Clearing Union, which was a proposed institution along the lines of what became the International Monetary Fund.

A second example, and one that is currently of much greater importance, is the Integrated Programme for Commodities (IPC) developed by the Secretariat of the United Nations Conference on Trade and Development (UNCTAD).[3] The IPC would initially be based on agreements for each of 10 "core commodities": cocoa, coffee, cotton, copper, hard fibers, jute, rubber, sugar, tea, and tin. Buffer stocks are suggested for each of these commodities,[4] but, in all but two cases—cotton and tea—the buffer stocks are coupled with supply management measures.[5]

UNCTAD documents envision a permanent use of export quotas and/or production controls in some cases. Supply management measures are then described as a way of balancing supply and demand over the long-run; for example,

> . . . it is believed that commodity arrangements should secure the maintenance of a reasonable relationship over time with the products exchanged for them in international trade. Measures to this end would therefore be based on the proposition that, where feasible, the supply of commodities should be managed to bring supply into equilibrium with demand at desired price trends.[6]

The "desired price" would clearly be above the long-run competitive price; since at the latter, the quantity that producers are willing to supply equals the quantity that buyers are willing to purchase. Most of the International Commodity Organizations (ICOs) described by UNCTAD, however, do not fall into this clear-cut case. For one commodity (copper) restrictions on supply are to be used on a strictly temporary basis in "emergency" situations.[7] In the remaining cases, UNCTAD reports leave open the question of whether restrictions on supply are to be used on a temporary or permanent basis.

The individual ICOs would be related by the Common Fund, which is conceived of as essentially a financial institution. The Common Fund's initial capital would be contributed by member nations, and additional funds would be raised by borrowing. Reports by the UNCTAD Secretariat suggest an initial contribution of $1 billion and borrowings of $2 billion, which could be followed by an additional contribution of $1 billion and additional borrowing of $2 billion, for an eventual total capital of $6 billion.[8]

This sum would be divided into two administratively separate funds, one of which would make loans to International Commodity Organizations (ICOs) to finance buffer stocks.[9] These loans are intended to be lines of credit, which the ICOs would draw on when purchases are made and then repay when the stock is sold. UNCTAD documents suggest that $5 billion be devoted to loans to ICOs for buffer stocks.[10] The Common Fund's remaining $1 billion would go into a fund that would make loans for diversification programs—research and development, market promotion, and investment projects of various sorts. These loans might be made directly to individual countries, but they would normally be made to ICOs, which would then relend the funds to their members.[11]

The Common Fund is not intended to carry on managerial functions, but there is one respect in which it would go beyond a strictly financial role. In "emergency situations," the Common Fund could, subject to certain restrictions, trade in a commodity on its own account. To do so, it would be necessary to have the approval of suppliers representing 50 percent of total supply and a qualified majority of the Common Fund's executive board.[12]

The general similarity between the IPC and Keynes' proposal is obvious, and the differences are no less real, although less apparent. Keynes recognized a distinction between restrictive schemes, designed to increase price above its long-run competitive level, and arrangements designed only to reduce price fluctuations. The former he identified with restrictions on production, and the latter, with buffer stocks. Keynes felt that the use of export controls might sometimes be "a necessary accompaniment of stabilization," but he rejected "chronic, as distinct from temporary, restriction."[13] He built into his proposal a number of safeguards to ensure that the buffer stocks' target prices would be appropriately adjusted. The IPC neither clearly honors nor entirely rejects these rules. In some cases the IPC's commodity agreements would allow the use of export quotas only in "emergency situations," but in other cases, export quotas and/or production controls would be used on a permanent basis. The documents that describe the IPC also leave open the possibility that the agreements would attempt to increase commodity price.

Operation of Commodity Agreements

It is often taken for granted that the IPC would increase the prices of the commodities included above the competitive level. While this may well be the intent, neither the IPC nor, much less so, Keynes' proposal is a straightforward set of cartel-like arrangements. Some elements of the IPC go toward price raising, some toward reducing price fluctuations, and the role of others is not immediately obvious. In addition, the management of the Common Fund and the individual ICOs involves an element of discretion. In short, the IPC presents a problem of diagnosis.

Discussions of the IPC have centered on the Common Fund. This emphasis is appropriate, but to appreciate the roles that a Common Fund might play, it is necessary first to look into the operation of the commodity agreements envisioned by the IPC.

The individual commodity agreements in the IPC, as well as in Keynes' proposal, would use buffer stocks together with controls on supply. Both buffer stocks and controls on supply are classified in discussions of commodity arrangements as stabilization measures, but they have very different properties and, for that reason, should be considered separately.

A buffer stock would begin with a fixed capital, contributed by the members of the ICO, which could be augmented by borrowing. When the market was "soft," the buffer stock would buy to support price and thereby support suppliers' revenues. In a "tight" market, the buffer stock would sell to hold price down, which would renew its capital and (implicitly) extract repayment from suppliers. These trading operations would usually be conducted in terms of floor and ceiling prices set at, say, 10 percent below and above a target price, which would be periodically revised.

For present purposes, two aspects of a buffer stock must be noted. First, a buffer stock with a fixed capital could not permanently maintain price above the long-run competitive level. In fact, a well-conducted buffer stock would filter out the "highs" and "lows" from price movements, while leaving the average level of prices over time unchanged. Second, a buffer stock would simply buy and sell and would not attempt to control the actions of other buyers and sellers.

Neither of these statements is true of supply management measures. Controls on supply are a regulatory device and can be used to maintain price above the competitive level. For these reasons, they give rise to a predictable list of problems.

The creation of an arrangement that provides for supply management requires, first, agreement among suppliers on their market shares; and it is not a foregone conclusion that such an agreement can be reached. The most difficult problems would be posed by a recent, low-cost entrant. Such a supplier would probably begin with a small share of the market but insist on a larger share and threaten to withdraw if his demands were not satisfied. The threat could be very creditable since a low-cost supplier might be able to do better outside the agreement than he could by accepting a relatively small market share within the agreement. If demand is growing, the other suppliers may be able to satisfy the demands of the low-cost producer without reducing their output. But if demand is not growing, or not growing rapidly enough, the other producers can meet the low-cost supplier's demand for an increased market share only by "moving over." If a reduction in employment is involved in this move, this would be very painful.

Second, if importing nations are included, agreement must be reached between importing and exporting nations on a price range and other aspects of the arrangement. This can be quite difficult since exporting nations have, at least up to a point, an interest in higher prices, while it is in the immediate, economic interests of importing nations to resist price increases and controls on supply.

Once an agreement is created, and controls on supply imposed, overshipping typically becomes a problem. Given that controls on supply establish a price above incremental cost, any supplier can increase his profits by overshipping so long as overshipping does not become general. However, overshipping by any one producer can lead to overshipping by others, and hence to the collapse of the agreement and lower profits for all suppliers.

The three problems that have been mentioned so far are "internal problems," in that they involve only the behavior of participants in the ICO. Entry, in contrast, is an external problem. If controls on supply are used to maintain a price above the long-run competitive equilibrium, existing producers have an incentive to expand; and, over the space of a few years, entrants will be attracted to the industry. Entrants would be admitted to the arrangement, which might permit total supply to be restricted enough to maintain price above the competitive level. However, members of the arrangement would have to "move over" to accommodate entrants, and their profits would at least be drastically reduced. The result is very likely to be the collapse of the arrangement.

The magnitude of these problems is indicated by the historical record. In the past 50 years, there have been 18 major agreements in nine commodities: bauxite (1), coffee (3), copper (2), cocoa (1), rubber (2), sugar (4), tea (1), tin (1), and wheat (2).[14] Nine of these operated before World War II, principally during the 1930s, and nine have operated since World War II.

The common feature of past major commodity agreements has been the reliance on supply management measures.[15] Only the prewar and postwar tin agreements and the International Cocoa Agreement created in 1970 provided for buffer stocks. However, the tin buffer stocks have been very small, the cocoa buffer stock has never operated, and both the cocoa agreement and the tin agreements relied primarily on export controls.

At this time, agreements are in existence for tin, cocoa, bauxite, and copper, although the copper agreement was formed without economic provisions. Tin agreements operated successfully throughout the 1930s and, in the postwar period, since 1955. The tin agreements, however, are unusual. Failure, sometimes after modest success, has been the rule for past agreements.

Six agreements ended with World War II and, while the rubber agreement

Table 10-1
The Principal Causes of Commodity Agreement Failures over the Last 50 Years for the 8 Cases with Known Causes

Cause	*Number*
Disputes among sellers over market share	1
Overshipping	1
Entry	3
Disputes between importing and exporting nations	3

might have collapsed shortly in any event, these failures cannot be attributed to economic causes. The distribution of the principal causes of failure for the eight cases for which one can be designated is given in Table 10-1. It is not entirely clear why the International Tea Agreement and the Inter-American Coffee Agreement failed.[16]

The pattern that appears in the historical record is worth recognizing as evidence in itself. In particular, entry and disputes between importing and exporting nations seem to be the major cause of the failure of past agreements. These facts, however, take on more significance in light of the economic incentives on importers and exporters and the means available to commodity agreements.

The reason why disputes over market shares have seldom led to the failure of agreements grows out of the logic of profit maximization. Suppose, for the sake of simplicity, that all producers have the same costs. In this case, it is clear that there is some total output, and a corresponding price, that maximizes the profits of suppliers as a group. If an agreement is not reached–i.e., if output is not restricted–price and total profits will be less than maximal. Consequently, simply as a matter of arithmetic, there is some distribution of market shares that would leave every producer better off than he would be in the absence of an agreement. The negotiating problem is to find such a "satisfactory" distribution of market shares. It would be virtually impossible to do so if there were a very large number of suppliers in the industry; but for most of the commodity industries, negotiation of market shares is a practical possibility.

The structure of suppliers' incentive does not provide a clear-cut rationalization of the fact that overshipping has seldom been a fatal problem. On the one hand, as was noted above, a price above incremental cost provides suppliers with an incentive for overshipping. On the other hand, the ancient insight that suppliers can increase their profit by colluding to restrict supply is valid and important. The balance of these two forces can be such that suppliers restrain themselves from overshipping. Whether a restrictive agreement would have this feature depends primarily on the degree to which supply is concentrated. In particular, if no small group of sellers retains a preponderant share of the market, significant overshipping is more likely to occur as the number of suppliers increases.

Supply of some of the commodity industries is sufficiently concentrated that controls on exports might be more or less self-policing. Furthermore, in cases where they would not be, there are means of coping with the problem.

Some past agreements have established "free zones" in which members and nonmembers can supply as much as they choose. The price in the free zone is determined by the play of the market and, presumably, would always be less than the controlled price. This creates a strong incentive for purchasers in the free zone to resell in the regulated zone, so the arrangement is viable only if the two zones are separated from one another by high transport costs, selective tariffs, or legal barriers. Furthermore, the creation of a free zone does not eliminate the producers' incentives to overship to the controlled zone; the temptation to do so is only somewhat reduced. The establishment of a free zone, then, is not a very promising way of dealing with the problem of overshipping.

The second, and potentially much more effective, mechanism is a certificate system, which transfers the problem of enforcing export quotas to importing nations. The ICO would create certificates, denominated in physical units, and allocate to each supplier the certificates required to cover his quotas. Importing nations would agree to reject shipments that were not accompanied by the appropriate certificates. A certificate system involves some administrative problems. For example, there is a question of what to do about imports to country A via country B and delays in transit. A certificate system also sets up incentives for counterfeiting and smuggling. But, since these problems are within the reach of importing nations' customs services, there is not much doubt that a certificate system could be reasonably effective.

The thrust of these comments is that neither disputes over market shares nor overshipping are critical problems. Disputes over market shares are held in check by suppliers' incentives, so no institutional means of solving such disputes as may arise is required. The incentives that work on suppliers are such that overshipping can be expected and, if left unchecked, would destroy an agreement. But overshipping is a problem for which there are solutions.

Disputes between buyers and sellers and entry are problems to which the mechanisms available to commodity agreements provide no solution. It is accordingly not surprising to find that disputes between buyers and sellers and entry account for six of the eight clear failures in the historical record.

There is no difficulty in recognizing the source of disputes between importing and exporting nations: within a restrictive arrangement their immediate economic interests are opposed. Suppliers have an interest in higher prices, while it is in importers' interest to resist restrictions of supply and higher prices. Importers do have a long-term interest in continuity of supply, but this interest is by and large served by the market and is apt to look nebulous in the face of the prospect of significant increases in price.

The difficulty of entry, and the extent to which entry is potentially a problem, differs somewhat between the metals industries and the agricultural industries. Relatively large capital costs are an impediment to entry into the metals industries. Entry into metals mining, furthermore, requires finding an ore body that can be profitably exploited. Such discoveries are made from time to time, but they are not routine occurrences. While detailed study might suggest otherwise, there is a presumption that entry into the metals industries is difficult. This does not mean, however, that entry is impossible. A significant price increase would spur efforts to find new deposits and hasten the development of deposits already known; and over the course of a decade, these forces probably would call forth a few new suppliers. Entry into the agricultural industries, in contrast, is much easier and could be expected to occur more rapidly. Some agricultural commodities require relatively specialized conditions for their cultivation; but even within these limitations, the scope for entry is substantial. In some cases, significant price increases would attract entrants within a year or two. Cocoa, coffee, rubber, and tea are exceptions to this rule. In these cases, the trees (or bushes) require several years to mature and begin yielding regular crops; so while price increases would encourage additional plantings, the effects would not be felt immediately.

Within these structural conditions, the extent to which a restrictive agreement will attract entry depends on how supply restrictions are employed. If supply is restricted only temporarily, and only in periods when demand is low relative to existing production capability, significant entry may not be attracted; although even in this case, the higher *average* price promised by the use of export controls may attract some new suppliers to the market. But an incentive for entry is definitely set up if export quotas are used on a more or less permanent basis to increase price. To say that price is above the long-run competitive equilibrium *means* that, all things considered, returns in the industry are relatively high; and potential suppliers can be expected to cash in on such a situation.

The only alternative to unimpeded entry and admitting entrants is an attempt to exclude entrants or at least to limit drastically the amount of entry. A strong certificate system, coupled perhaps with a free zone, would have a chance of succeeding. However, it is difficult to see why importing nations should agree to enforce certificate systems; and attempts to limit entry would be at the very least highly contentious. What is involved is exclusion, by an international agency, of efforts by individual nations to create and expand particular industries. Entry, like disputes between buyer and sellers, is then a problem without a clear solution.

Effect of a Central Authority on the Stability of Commodity Agreements

The financial role of the Common Fund is enough to ensure that it would be involved with any serious problems encountered by an individual ICO. Just as large creditors usually control the policy of a failing business, so would the Common Fund have a significant voice in the affairs of a troubled ICO.

Thought along this line leads to the question of the extent to which the LDCs could use the powers of a Common Fund to stabilize individual ICOs. A Common Fund could respond directly to the problems of entry and "over-supply" with loans to the ICO for acquisition of stocks and for diversification, but, if only because of limitations on funds available, such steps are unlikely to be more than palliatives. To the extent that the Common Fund could stabilize individual ICOs, the solution must lie elsewhere.

As a matter of history, disputes between importing and exporting nations were a leading cause of the failure of past agreements. More important, importing nations could enforce a certificate system, which provides a means of limiting entry. If, then, the adherence of importing nations could somehow be guaranteed, the principal causes of the failure of past agreements could be eliminated.

Where an individual ICO will almost invariably be of limited significance to the DCs, a Common Fund would bear much of the burden of the relationship between the DCs and the LDCs. The DCs, then, would be attached to a Common Fund by their broad interest in international stability, as well as a range of lesser concerns; and such an institution would not be lightly abandoned. Adherence to the Common Fund and adherence to individual ICOs are not, however, the same thing, and a Common Fund such as that described in UNCTAD reports would not exercise any direct managerial control over the individual ICOs. But a Common Fund could attack the problem of stabilizing restrictive arrangements to the extent that it could influence the outcome of bargaining with the ICO. The strength of this ability, in turn, would depend on the character of the relations between the Common Fund and the individual ICOs.

Loans for buffer stock activities as well as for diversification could, and very probably would, be conditioned on the ICOs' making provision for the use of export and/or production controls.[17] This requirement could be put as a matter of financial prudence, since the possibility of restricting supply is a way of guaranteeing the value of the stock. But, whatever the rationale, the importers' natural position in opposition to restrictions on supply would be undercut, since within the ICO it could be argued, with some cogency, that the funds required to make the arrangement effective are available only if a means for regulating supply is created.

Loans for buffer stocks would also tend to involve the Common Fund in the affairs of the ICO in another way. If an ICO fails, its stocks would, to the extent that they are financed by loans from the Common Fund, pass to the Common Fund. The failure of an agreement would then automatically involve the Common Fund in the market. Recognition of this possibility presumably would lead to a more or less direct involvement of the Common Fund in the affairs of a troubled ICO.

The strength of the Common Fund's position in such situations would be increased by power to trade on its own account in certain situations. The failure of an ICO probably would be regarded as an "emergency situation." To trade, the Common Fund would then need the approval of suppliers accounting for one half of total supply and a qualified majority of its executive board. The latter requirement might provide importers with a veto power over trading by the fund, but this is by no means certain. The prospect of direct intervention by the Common Fund if an agreement fails might then be used to put pressure on buyers to make concessions necessary to maintain the agreement.

Beyond these specific mechanisms, major issues that arise within ICOs are likely to reach the level of the Common Fund informally and there become elements in a process of log rolling. Because the commitment to establish prices that are "fair to buyers and remunerative to producers" is open-ended, the DCs would be under pressure to resolve these problems by somehow buying off one or another of the parties to the dispute.

It is possible to see in these comments the outline of a coherent approach to the problem of stabilizing ICOs. The Common Fund would mobilize and focus the economic and political power of the LDCs and, by raising the stakes on specific economic issues, bring pressure on the DCs to take the steps necessary to maintain restrictive arrangements.

Whether this solution would be effective, however, is far from clear. Apart from the power the DCs would have within the Common Fund, the weak link in the chain is the ability to make problems at the level of ICOs into major issues at the level of the Common Fund. Buffer stocks for copper, coffee, and, perhaps, tin might be so large that their failure would threaten the Common Fund; in these cases the pressures that could be brought to bear on the DCs would probably be very nearly irresistible. But the failure of an ICO in most commodities would not have this potential, and the ability of the Common Fund to stabilize the arrangement would be correspondingly limited.

Political Consequences: Evolution of the IPC

This discussion points to a basic flaw in the design of the IPC. On the one hand, it is very likely that the individual ICOs would attempt to raise prices and that the Common Fund would be deeply involved with the problems that would result from these attempts. On the other hand, the Common Fund does not have the means to deal effectively with the burdens that would be placed upon it. The IPC consequently, would tend to be unstable; i.e., it would be under pressure to evolve from its original form.

Although the way in which the IPC might develop cannot be foretold in any systematic way, it is possible to offer speculation based on the underlying problems, the structure of the IPC, and its objectives. The latter is particularly important since it is likely to set the framework within which solutions are sought.

Resolution 93(IV), adopted at UNCTAD IV, provides a reasonable indication of the expectations that the LDCs bring to the IPC. The first two objectives listed are:[18]

1. To achieve stable conditions in commodity trade, including avoidance of excessive price fluctuations, at levels which would:
   a. be remunerative and just to producers and equitable to consumers
   b. take account of world inflation and changes in the world economic and monetary situations
   c. promote equilibrium between supply and demand within expanding world commodity trade
2. To improve and sustain the real income of individual developing countries through increased export earnings, and to protect them from fluctuations in export earnings, especially from commodities.

It seems obvious from this language that reduction of price fluctuations is one objective; but beyond that, the LDCs hope to obtain through the IPC the funds necessary to speed the development of their economies.

Whether the IPC would have a significant impact on development is then a major consideration. Suppose for the sake of argument that the IPC operates smoothly. The price increases instituted by OPEC increased the oil suppliers' revenues by about $80 billion in each year, 1974, 1975, and 1976. Increases in other commodity prices do not have this potential. Rough estimates, based on the 1971 level of demand, indicate that doubling the prices of the 10 core commodities would increase annual revenues to the LDCs by about $19 billion.[19] Exporting nations would no doubt find increased revenues helpful, but they would not be sufficient to permit the massive development programs undertaken by the Middle Eastern oil producers. Furthermore, while some of the LDCs would gain from increased commodity prices, many others would lose.

This point is not worth pursuing in isolation because the supposition that the IPC would operate smoothly is grossly unrealistic. Once it was instituted, the IPC would be faced with the problems identified above. Frustration over the limited results of the IPC would appear as one major theme in a broader pattern of failures and disputes.

General dissatisfaction with the IPC as well as some specific problems, would invariably give rise to pressures for "reform" of the system, especially of the Common Fund. First, problems that apparently call for the "coordination" of various commodity agreements would appear. For example, the ICOs that maintained buffer stocks would be in competition with diversification programs for a limited amount of funds. Other circumstances that would suggest a need for coordination can also be imagined, e.g., the impact of aluminum prices on the demand for copper.

Second, the failure of individual agreements, or acute problems within ICOs, would demonstrate the inadequacy of the Common Fund. The tin buffer stock provides an example. During 1958, the International Tin Agreement was purchasing in an effort to maintain price, while at the same time the Soviet Union increased its exports of tin. This problem was solved when buyers, especially the United Kingdom, imposed quotas on tin imports from the Soviet Union.[20] Similarly, in the early 1960s, the buyers in the International Coffee Agreement, including the United States, limited imports from nonmember nations.[21] But such one-at-a-time responses are likely to be cumbersome and unsatisfactory. It is reasonable to expect, then, that the Common Fund would be under pressure to evolve toward a stronger and further reaching form.

Once the objectives and logic of the IPC are accepted, arguments such as those just sketched would have substantial appeal. In fact, there is a sense in which they are correct. The IPC, as it is described in UNCTAD documents, would not live up to expectations. Over time, the Common Fund might evolve into an organization capable of maintaining prices above the competitive level. Or, as the lessons of history are relearned, the IPC might evolve into a system of pure buffer stocks, although this seems unlikely. Finally, the Common Fund might degenerate into insignificance or collapse under the weight of accumulated disputes.

Alternative Integrated Programs

Alternative integrated programs can be generated by removing the flaws in the IPC. One possibility is to perfect the IPC as a mechanism for transferring income via higher prices, which would require strengthening the Common Fund's means of coping with the forces set up by prices above the competitive level. The other possibility is to design the ICOs so that prices are not increased above the competitive level, which would remove the underlying cause of the instability in the IPC.

This section examines organizations conceived on each of these lines. The first of these possibilities will be referred to as the *Commodity Price Authority* and the second as the *Buffer Stock Authority*.

The Commodity Price Authority

A question that emerges from the preceding discussion is whether or not the use of price increases as a means of transferring income to the LDCs is a practical possibility. If this question is approached strictly in terms of economic mechanisms, the answer is a qualified yes. The key to maintaining commodity prices above the competitive level would be certificate systems. A certificate system would directly deal with the problem of overshipping but, much more important, would provide a means of limiting entry. Given the existence of a certificate system, potential entrants would have to apply to the ICO for membership and a share of the market. It is not realistic to suppose that an international agency could entirely exclude entry, but an ICO with a strong certificate system could effectively limit the rate of entry.[22]

The problem with the IPC as a means of raising prices, however, does not lie with its economic measures but rather with the balance of political forces. In particular, the arguments of the preceding section lead to the conclusion that the Common Fund would not entirely solve the problem of gaining the adherence of importing nations to restrictive commodity agreements.

Since the principle behind the Common Fund—the focusing of the power of the LDCs and the raising of the stakes to the level of North-South relations—is cogent, the solution would seem to lie in strengthening the Common Fund. It is possible to think of a variety of ways to do so; but in terms of the problems considered here, the obvious course would be for the Common Fund to absorb the individual ICOs. An arrangement of this sort is what is taken here to be the Commodity Price Authority. There is no guarantee that a Commodity Price Authority could successfully maintain commodity prices above the competitive level. The problems of containing market forces are formidable, and the Commodity Price Authority would not have available any uniquely powerful means. It would, however, have a better chance of gaining the adherence of importing nations to restrictive arrangements and, to this extent, would have much better prospects than past commodity agreements or the IPC.

These comments simply posit the existence of a Commodity Price Authority. When political forces are considered, there is a question as to whether a Commodity Price Authority could be created·or—if it were created—would be stable.

The notion of a Commodity Price Authority as sketched here evolves (at least) three political contradictions. The first of these grows out of the fact that the DCs would be required to act against their own immediate economic interests. The theory would seem to be that the DCs are held hostage by the economic and political power of the LDCs, which, oil aside, is not so. Even within commodities trade, the balance of power runs in favor of the DCs; so the DCs would have to act voluntarily against their own interests, and domestic politics would probably preclude that.[23]

Second, it is by no means clear that a Commodity Price Authority would be to the political advantage of the DCs. The political gain usually posited is improved economic relations with the LDCs or, more generally, an organizational structure that promotes cooperative relations between the DCs and the LDCs. However, the Commodity Price Authority would be a regulatory authority, and the DCs would, through membership, be intimately involved in a variety of very painful situations. In effect, the DCs would assume the burden of policing world commodity trade; and, as the United States has learned to its sorrow, "the policeman's lot is not a happy one."

Third, the LDCs are likely to find the balance of power within a Commodity Price Authority unattractive. Under a Commodity Price Authority, many economic actions that individual LDCs might wish to undertake would be matters for negotiation and, hence, would be subject to a significant measure of control by the DCs. Furthermore, if and when the DCs took steps to maintain Commodity Price Authority, they could be expected to insist on a corresponding degree of control. But such control would probably be intolerable to the LDCs and is the opposite of one of the results sought through the IPC.[24]

These comments do not stretch to a conclusive argument that use of price increases to transfer income to the LDCs is a practicable impossibility. They do reinforce the impression left by the earlier discussion that efforts to maintain commodity prices above the competitive level would be very contentious and probably ineffective.

Buffer Stock Authority

Another alternative "integrated" program is a system of centrally financed buffer stocks. Moving in this direction from the IPC is a surgical process. The problem is not the Common Fund but, instead, the provisions of the individual ICOs, in particular, the extensive use of restrictions on supply envisioned by the IPC. To put this point in its strongest form, it is useful to assume that the Buffer Stock Authority would operate a system of buffer stocks. It would then differ from the Commodity Price Authority only in the use made of restrictions on supply.

Supply management measures are such an entrenched feature of international commodity agreements that their exclusion would be a radical step. For that reason it is useful to ask if any controls on supply could be employed while preserving the essential features of a pure buffer stock. This is a question of safeguards.

The central difficulty is that the use of supply-management measures can lead a buffer stock into price-support activities. This would occur when the target price is set too high and the resulting excess supply, instead of being allowed to force price down, is choked off with export quotas and/or production controls. The buffer stock then ceases to be a device for limiting price fluctuations and, instead, becomes a way of supporting price above the long-run competitive level.

This sequence of events might be controlled via procedural safeguards, as follows:

1. Controls on exports or production should not be triggered automatically when market price falls below the floor price.
2. Any export quotas or production controls that are imposed should automatically lapse after a relatively brief period.

These safeguards would *not* prevent restrictions on supply from being used to increase prices above the long-run equilibrium. Assuming the voting procedures typically specified in commodity agreements, they would simply give importing nations a veto over restrictions on supply.

It is conceivable that procedural safeguards would be sufficient, but they would not be very satisfactory. There would be a tendency to attempt a compromise, particularly when suppliers are faced with the prospect of making painful, long-run adjustments. Therein lies a difficulty. Importing and exporting nations can compromise on prices, but they cannot compromise away the forces set up by a price above the competitive level. It is possible to draw a conceptual line between the use of supply management measures to limit short-run declines in price and the use of restrictions on supply to increase prices above the competitive level. However, this distinction is very difficult to draw in concrete terms, and the past history of commodity agreements provides no grounds for an optimistic appraisal of the ability of commodity agreements to manage restrictions on supply.

In addition to procedural safeguards, there are substantive restrictions that could be written into an agreement on the use of supply management. These could be of an entirely arbitrary sort. For example, the agreement could specify that exports could never be restricted to less than, say, 90 percent of the base and that quotas could be in effect only, say, one year in five. Alternatively, the use of supply management could be tied to the *floor* price. Suppose that the target price is set equal to a moving average of past market prices and that the floor price is, say, 90 percent of the *target* price. If supply-management measures were used to defend the target price, it would be of no consequence that the target price is set as a moving average of market prices. This possibility can be eliminated by adopting the following rules:

1. Restrictions on supply cannot be imposed if the market price is above the floor price.
2. If the use of restrictions on supply leads to a price above the floor price, then:

a. The restrictions on supply are automatically relaxed.
b. The floor price, rather than the actual market price, is used in computing the target price.

These rules guarantee that the target price will track the market price and, via rule 1, guarantee that supply controls would, eventually, automatically lapse. Hence, if the problem is to prevent a buffer stock from turning into a price-raising mechanism, a refinement of rules 1 and 2 might be used in place of procedural safeguards.

These comments say nothing about *why* controls on supply should be used, and there is virtually no reason for using controls on supply if the purpose is simply to reduce period-to-period price fluctuations. In fact, considering both private and public costs, controls on supply are the least efficient of the available stabilization mechanisms.[25] Hence, while some combination of substantive and procedural safeguards might be adequate to ensure that a buffer stock would not be inadvertently led into price-raising activities, there seems to be no reason to face the dangers and costs involved in the use of supply management.

Concluding Comments

There is a tendency to discuss the idea of a Common Fund, or an integrated program, without regard for the differences among the types of arrangements that are included under these general headings. To some extent this is fair enough, since how commodity arrangements are designed would not effect the basic interests of importing and exporting nations and would not alter the array of political forces. However, taking these matters as given, the way in which commodity arrangements are structured does matter.

A system of pure buffer stocks related by a Common Fund would not involve any narrowly economic contradictions. The instability in such an arrangement would arise from a mismatch of economic consequences and the LDCs' expectations. While a system of pure buffer stocks could reduce price fluctuations, this would not result in a transfer of resources to the LDCs and would not have a profound impact on the rate of growth in the LDCs.

A set of commodity agreements that attempted to increase prices would, like any restrictive arrangement, be under continuous pressure from market forces. However, unlike restrictive ICOs, a Commodity Price Authority, such as that described here, contains a coherent set of means for dealing with these problems and so, like a set of pure buffer stocks, might be stable in terms of the economic forces involved. The sources of instability would, again, arise at the political level. A Commodity Price Authority might be acceptable to the LDCs, but it would be a virtually impossible arrangement for the DCs.

The IPC contains elements of both of these cases in an uncomfortable way.

In very broad terms, the flaw in the IPC lies in a mismatching of means and ends. It seems clear that the LDCs seek the IPC as a means of increasing commodity prices, but the means included in the IPC are insufficient to accomplish the task. While a weak Common Fund might survive for many years as an essentially defunct organization, the LDCs' expectations would eventually be frustrated by what would be called a failure of the DCs' "political will." This event, and the process of an IPC's disintegration would be an important source of international acrimony.

Notes

1. This is especially so for Japan and the Western European nations. Australia, Canada, and the United States are major exporters or producers of agricultural and mineral commodities.

2. Keynes (1974), p. 305.

3. The "Programme of Action on the Establishment of a New International Economic Order," adopted by the Sixth Special Session of the U.N. General Assembly, directed the UNCTAD Secretariat to develop a program along the lines of the IPC. Resolution 93(IV), adopted at the Fourth U.N. Conference on Trade and Development, called for the creation of arrangements along the lines of the IPC, and negotiations on its major component, the Common Fund, began in March 1977.

4. See UNCTAD (1975).

5. UNCTAD (1975).

6. UNCTAD (1975), p. 7.

7. UNCTAD (1975), p. 56; see also UNCTAD (1976*c*), pp. 14-15.

8. UNCTAD (1976*c*), pp. 7-8.

9. UNCTAD (1977*a*), pp. 6-7.

10. UNCTAD (1976*c*), p. 6, paragraph 21; see also UNCTAD (1976*a*), p. 15, paragraph 31.

11. UNCTAD (1976*b*), p. 5.

12. UNCTAD (1977*a*), p. 4, paragraph 12.

13. Keynes (1974), p. 299.

14. This total includes only agreements among governments or supported by governments; it excludes several minor agreements and informal arrangements under the U.N. Food and Agriculture Organization. See McNicol (1977), chap. 4, which draws primarily on Davis (1946); Rowe (1965); and Law (1975).

15. The principal exceptions are the International Wheat Agreement, which was a multilateral purchase and sales commitment, and the International Bauxite Association, whose members have individually imposed taxes on bauxite. CIPEC was formed without economic provisions, although it attempted to limit its members' exports during 1973-1974.

16. See McNicol (1977) for a more detailed discussion of the record of the agreements that enter into this distribution.

17. UNCTAD (1977*a*), p. 3, paragraphs 8 and 9.

18. Available in U.S. Congress (1976).

19. McNicol (1977), chap. 4.

20. Rowe (1965), pp. 171-172.

21. Kravis (1968), p. 306.

22. Difficulties would still arise. Suppose, for example, that country C is a relatively new, low-cost cocoa producer that has been given only a small quota. Country C might well decide to go into the chocolate business. Then, say, British chocolate producers would have to buy relatively high-cost cocoa while facing competition from low-price imports from country C. They are very likely to cry foul; and so on.

23. Suppose, for example, that an ICO in copper succeeds in substantially increasing price, and as a result, production is expanded and entry attracted. The initial response would be production controls. Now the United States is the world's largest copper producer; and if production controls were to be effective, U.S. producers would have to be included. A visible, direct, and fairly immediate consequence would be unemployment of copper workers in the United States. Could any administration explain why it supports an international organization whose actions reduce employment in the United States while increasing prices paid by U.S. consumers?

24. There is also a real possibility that an IPC would increase the LDCs' dependence on commodities. To the extent that it creates additional profits, the IPC would promote diversification. The forces tending toward an increased, or maintained, reliance on commodities lie in the pattern of restrictions that would be associated with an effective IPC. Once an IPC was in place, buyers would face a pattern of production controls, export quotas, and limitations on entry enforced, via the ICOs, by the vested interests of existing suppliers. At a minimum, many of the LDCs would find their economic options reduced.

25. See McNicol (1977), chaps. 2 and 3.

References

Davis, J.S. "Experience under Intergovernmental Commodity Agreements, 1902-1945." *Journal of Political Economy* 54 (1946):193-220.

Keynes, J.M. "The International Control of Raw Materials." *Journal of International Economics* 4 (1974):299-315.

Kravis, I. "International Commodity Agreements to Promote Aid and Efficiency: The Case of Coffee." *Canadian Journal of Economics* 1 (1968): 295-317.

Law, A.D. *International Commodity Agreements.* Lexington, Mass.: Lexington Books, D.C. Heath, 1975.

McNicol, D.L. *Commodity Agreements and Price Stabilization.* Lexington, Mass.: Lexington Books, D.C. Heath, 1978.

Rowe, J.W.F. *Primary Commodities in International Trade.* Cambridge: Cambridge Univ. Press, 1965.

United Nations Conference on Trade and Development. "Common Fund: Mode of Operations." Note by the UNCTAD Secretariat, TD/B/IPC/CF/L.5, January 15, 1977*b*.

——. "Common Fund: Decision Making and Management." Note by the UNCTAD Secretariat, TD/B/IPC/CF/L.6, January 11, 1977*a*.

——. "Common Fund: Financial Requirements." Note by the UNCTAD Secretariat, TD/B/IPC/CF/L.2, December 29, 1976*a*.

——. "Common Fund: Financing of Operations Other than Stocking. Note by the UNCTAD Secretariat, TD/B/IPC/CF/L.3, December 29, 1976*b*.

——. "Consideration of Issues Relating to the Establishment and Operation of a Common Fund." Report by the Secretary General of UNCTAD, TD/B/-IPC/CF/2, November 10, 1976*c*.

——. "Copper: The Elements of an International Stabilization Arrangement." Report by the UNCTAD Secretariat, TD/B/IPC/Copper/L.2, August 27, 1976*d*.

——. "An Integrated Programme for Commodities: Measures for Individual Commodities." Report by the UNCTAD Secretariat, TD/B/C.1/194, October 1, 1975.

United States Congress. *Report by Congressional Advisors to UNCTAD IV.* Washington, D.C.: USGPO, 1976.

11 Producers' Associations and Commodity Markets: The Case of CIPEC

Stephen A. Zorn

Introduction

Since the Organization of Petroleum Exporting Countries (OPEC) first succeeded in substantially raising the price of oil, there has been considerable governmental and academic concern over the possibility of "two, three, . . . many OPECs."[1] Some raw materials in world trade have in fact undergone sharp and sustained price increases; and in a few cases, of which bauxite is perhaps the clearest example, the price increase has been linked to the activities of an association of producing nations. In other cases—phosphate rock, for example—an individual developing country producer has exercised price leadership, and the role of the producer association, where one existed, has been less clear.[2]

The importance, actual and potential, of producer associations has been very widely acknowledged. Such groups, at government level, exist in one form or another for at least a dozen commodities—petroleum, bauxite, copper, iron ore, mercury, phosphate rock, bananas, cocoa, coffee, tea, natural rubber, and timber. For some of these commodities (and for some others, such as tin) there are producer-consumer organizations as well that undertake an active role in attempting to stabilize the market. Even the United States government, despite a long history of opposition to cartels and producer action to set the price of goods in international trade, has considered some kind of price-setting arrangement with Canada for wheat, which is one commodity in which the United States is a major exporter and a significant force on the world market.[3]

Despite this general awareness of the potential importance of producer associations, there has been relatively little analysis of how they actually affect the market, except in the case of OPEC.[4] Most discussion of the potential role of producer groups has concentrated on questions of market structure, attempting to identify those commodities in which unilateral producer action to raise the price above a "free market" equilibrium level is feasible or likely.[5] The discussion that follows attempts to provide a framework for analyzing producer associations and their role in commodities markets. The discussion focuses first on the different possible aims of producer associations and, second, on the different methods through which associations and their members may attempt to exert influence on the market, either for stabilization purposes or with the aim of pushing prices and export earnings above existing levels. These sets of possible aims and market actions are then related to the different structural characteristics of the markets for some of the commodities in which there are active producer associations. Finally, a review of the efforts of one producer association, the Intergovernmental Council of Copper Exporting Countries (CIPEC), to influence the copper market shows that an understanding of market structure is only partially sufficient to explain the success, or lack thereof, of producers in exerting any real influence over the price they receive. The internal dynamics of producer associations, including such factors as mutual trust, leadership, and good timing, as well as the response of consuming industries and importing nations' governments, are perhaps equally important.

The Aims of Producer Associations

The expressed objectives of most raw materials producer associations fall into four broad categories: (1) information, (2) defensive measures, (3) stabilization, and (4) raising the real level of prices or earnings.

Information

Most producer nations' governments have felt themselves at a disadvantage in dealing with importing countries and with the multinational corporations that are involved in raw materials production and marketing. One of the first stated aims of most producer associations is to improve members' bargaining position vis-à-vis the importers and the companies by generating greater knowledge of their industries' structures and markets. For example, one of the first major projects undertaken by OPEC was a major study of the international petroleum market by the American consulting firm Arthur D. Little.[6] One of the objectives set out in the CIPEC agreement of 1967 was "to obtain for member countries better and more complete information and appropriate advice on the production and marketing of copper."[7]

These efforts at information gathering by producer associations reflect the widespread recognition that producer countries cannot bargain effectively with multinational corporations without a thorough understanding of industry and market structure, nor can they intervene intelligently in the market. Such an understanding is significant at two different stages—first, when a government is negotiating for a larger share of revenue from company operations, or for government control of natural resource industries, and second, when a government has acquired significant ownership or control over an industry and is actively involved in arranging terms for the sale of the commodity. The collection and sharing of information among producer association members is thus seen as a necessary first step by most associations. It is also a way in which nationals of the member countries can gain experience working together and perhaps build a climate of trust in which the association can take further action.

Defense

A major reason for the formation of OPEC in 1960, and one of that organization's basic objectives in its early years, was the primarily defensive aim of preventing further cuts in the posted price of oil (on which the governments' revenues were based).[8] CIPEC's first significant policy action was also defensive—a show of solidarity in reaction to company attempts to block the sale of copper from the newly nationalized Chilean mines.[9] Defensive aims are often linked, as in the OPEC case, to stabilization goals; producer association members see coordinated action as necessary merely for the maintenance of their economic position.[10]

Stabilization

Many producer associations have expressed aims having something to do with stabilization, but it is not always clear exactly what it is that the association's members wish to stabilize. In some cases, attention has been focused directly on price stabilization, as in early statements by OPEC, and, more recently, in the attention that CIPEC has given to producer-consumer negotiations for a copper price agreement. Price stabilization has also been the primary focus of agreements covering some agricultural commodities, including coffee, cocoa, and wheat. And this is the aim of the system embodied in the International Tin Agreements.

More often, the expressed concern of producer associations is for stability of export earnings. Thus CIPEC's stated goals include the statement, " . . . to ensure a real forecast of such earnings."[11] OPEC's original aims included "study and formulation of a system to ensure the stabilization of prices."[12]

Unstable prices per se are sometimes seen as detrimental to the interests of producers, particularly in a commodity like copper, characterized by high price instability and for which there is a substitute (aluminum) with a long history of relative price stability that may influence some consumers to turn to the substitute as a matter of risk avoidance. More frequently, however, the concern of producers is that unstable prices mean unstable foreign exchange flows and consequent disruptions in development plans that rely on predictable levels of imports.[13] The effect on capacity to import depends on the nature of the commodity; for example, price variations in export grain crops tend to be linked to variations in supply, while demand is relatively steady. As a result, high prices will tend to coincide with lowered export volumes, and vice versa, leaving earnings relatively stable. (In the case of grains, the earnings flow primarily to developed countries.) In contrast, low prices for minerals tend to be associated with low demand, reflecting the business cycle in the industrial countries, while supply is relatively price-inelastic. Thus, in the absence of a buffer stock mechanism to smooth out the volume of purchases from primary producers, a downturn in metal prices will tend to coincide with a downturn in the volume of exports, thereby exaggerating the instability in export earnings. This pattern was particularly evident in the case of copper in the 1973–1975 period, when average annual prices declined by more than 50 percent and total consumption in the developed countries declined by 22 percent.[14] That actual export earnings of copper producers did not fall by as large an amount is attributable to the massive buildup of copper stocks during this period, which has continued to have a depressing effect on the market even though consumption is returning to earlier levels. In effect, the merchants, producers, and consumers who held these stocks undertook the burden that would have been borne by a formal buffer stock if one had been in operation.

Finally, producers may seek to stabilize government revenue from primary production. Where government income is largely dependent on the profitability of production units, as in the case of state-owned enterprises or where the major portion of government revenue comes from profit-based taxes instead of royalties and other fixed charges, price instability will be greatly magnified in its effect on government revenue. A drop of 50 percent in the price received by a copper producer may represent a drop of 90 or even 100 percent in profits, given the large fixed costs typical of mining projects. Few attempts have been made at the international level to stabilize government revenue from raw materials production, but a number of mineral-producing countries have acted independently, either by including minimum-payment requirements in their agreements with companies[15] or by establishing domestic stabilization schemes to even out the flow of revenue into the national budget.[16]

Increased Prices and Earnings

The final possible objective of a producer association is an increase in the real level of prices or in the real level of export earnings. This is the aim most frequently cited in comments on "the threat from the Third World."[17] And it is an aim that has been realized by OPEC, by most members of the International Bauxite Association (IBA), and by phosphate rock producers. Whether a producer association can maintain a real price increase depends on the actions of other producers, the price elasticities of supply and demand, the availability of substitutes, the reaction of importing countries, and other factors discussed below. Both OPEC and the IBA appear to have objectives that combine a large initial price increase with longer-term price stability in real terms.

Types of Producer Actions

There are three different types of actions on commodity prices that producers and producer associations can take: (1) cooperation with consumers and importers; (2) unilateral action by a single producer, acting as price leader for the group; and (3) cartel-like action by the group of producers as a whole, or other united action. These different types of actions may appear to correspond to the different goals outlined above, with producer-consumer cooperation most likely to occur when the goal is price or earnings stability, and price leadership and cartel-like action being used more when the goal is a real increase in prices above prevailing levels. In fact, there is no necessary correspondence; cartel-like actions can be, and have been, used by private-sector cartels for price stabilizing or defensive measures, as well as for seeking price increases. The choice of action by a producer association depends partly on the structure of the market for the commodity in question and also on the history of the producer association, its leadership, and the response of consumer nations' governments and of the multinational companies.[18] It should also be kept in mind that actions by producers to raise the price of their exports can be seen as merely stabilizing the purchasing power of their exports in real terms. This was certainly the case for Jamaica's price increase in bauxite, for example.[19]

Cooperation

Most of the UNCTAD Integrated Programme for Commodities involves cooperation, based on the negotiation of agreements for some or all the 18 commodities on UNCTAD's list. Preliminary discussions under UNCTAD auspices for raw materials such as copper have concentrated on analyzing possible forms of cooperation, notably the details of buffer stock action.[20]

The UNCTAD objectives are consistent with the stabilization of prices and/or export earnings. These objectives include the following:

1. To achieve stable conditions in commodity trade, including avoidance of excessive price fluctuations, at levels that would:
   a. Be remunerative and just to producers and equitable to consumers
   b. Take account of world inflation and changes in the world economic and monetary situation
   c. Promote equilibrium between supply and demand within expanding world commodity trade

2. To improve and sustain the real income of individual developing countries through increased export earnings, and to protect them from fluctuations in export earnings, especially from commodities.[21]

In this context, CIPEC has recently abandoned earlier attempts to influence the copper market through unilateral action and has focused its attention on the producer-consumer dialogue underway in Geneva.

Unilateral Action

This form of price action by individual developing country producers has had some notable recent successes. In the case of phosphate rock, for example, where Morocco accounts for more than one-third of total world exports,[22] that country took the leading role in effecting a 200 percent price increase, with Senegal, Tunisia, Algeria, and Togo, the other members of the World Institute of Phosphates, following its lead. Similarly, the increase in bauxite prices was led by Jamaica, acting through the vehicle of production levies or royalties rather than direct price setting. In this case, not even all members of the IBA followed the Jamaican lead; the largest single exporter, Australia, kept its government levies, and hence prices, well below Caribbean levels.

Unilateral action has, from the point of view of producer association members, the advantage of not requiring formal agreement. The possible success of a price leader's action can, in fact, contribute to the solidarity of an association by demonstrating the possibility of achievement. However, a price-leadership situation enhances the possibility of cheating that is present in any cartel situation. In the absence of formal price-setting procedures or allocation of markets and production quotas, it is relatively easy for one or more producers not to follow the leader and thereby to expand their market shares.[23]

Cartel-Like Actions

None of the existing raw materials producer associations has yet undertaken a full range of cartel actions, including price setting, allocation of production, and imposition of sanctions against nonconforming members. In OPEC, the burden that would hypothetically be imposed on those member nations which need maximum production (to pay for ambitious development plans), if production quotas were imposed, up to the last pricing decision on the two-tier structure, has been taken up by the willingness of Saudi Arabia to assume most of OPEC's spare capacity. The continued growth of Western, and especially U.S., oil consumption has also alleviated pressures within OPEC for a more formal system of allocating production. In the other associations—for bauxite and phosphate rock—where prices have been effectively raised, the formal mechanisms are even less well-developed than in OPEC. The IBA, for example, has taken steps to adopt a common pricing policy, but not all members adhere to that policy.[24]

Other concerted actions that producer associations could take might have a long-term impact on the market. CIPEC, for example, has informally considered a deliberate policy of exploiting its members' relatively low production costs and attempting to increase the market share of the CIPEC membership as a whole, within the framework of expected world consumption growth over a 20 to 25 year period.[25] Such an approach would require the organization to take account of internal differences between members' costs of production and to devise a system that could satisfy the high-cost producers within the group while at the same time not induce the low-cost producers to cheat. The problem of differing production costs within an association of producers is discussed in more detail below.

Market Factors

There have been numerous reviews of the factors thought to be necessary for a group of producers to exercise some effective control over a commodity market, whether for the purpose of raising prices or simply to maintain real earnings.[26] Among the more important factors typically cited are the following.

The Degree of Control Over World Exports

It would seem, a priori, that a high degree of control over production, or at least exports, is essential to effective cartel-type action or even to unilateral producer action to stabilize prices. In fact, while a certain degree of control is clearly required, there does not appear to be a direct correlation between the market share of a producer association and a history of effective price action. The data in Table 11-1 indicate developing-country market shares of some 20 primary commodities in which Third World exports account for more than half the total international trade. The market share of the six leading developing-country exporters for each commodity is given as a rough indicator of the potential control of the market by a small group of producers.

The Price Elasticity of Demand for the Commodity and Potential Substitutes

Unless price elasticity of demand is low, effective producer action to raise prices is unlikely, although action to stabilize prices may be possible. Larger

Table 11-1
Concentration of International Commodity Trade, 1972-1974 Average

Commodity	*LDC Share of World Exports (%)*	*Six Largest LDC Exporters' Share of World Exports (%)*
Abaca	96.2	95.8
Rubber	97.5	93.1
Sisal	97.9	91.4
Copra	99.1	90.9
Cocoa	98.2	83.4
Tin	84.4	82.2
Palm oil	80.3	78.8
Coconut oil	78.4	75.8
Tea	80.8	69.6
Groundnut oil	71.7	66.5
Bananas	93.1	62.3
Coffee	94.1	59.5
Bauxite	64.5	58.8
Manganese ore	59.3	58.4
Copper	58.5	56.1
Phosphate rock	61.1	56.0
Petroleum	76.5	53.0
Sugar	73.4	50.5
Groundnuts	58.3	42.4
Cotton	52.1	32.5

Source: IBRD, *Commodity Trade and Price Trends* (1976 Edition), pp. 19-20.

producer groups, embracing such potential substitutes as copper and bauxite, or tea, coffee, and cocoa, might reduce substitution possibilities but would enlarge the producer association and create problems of unwieldiness. In general, one can assume that the criterion of demand elasticity eliminates such commodities as oils and fats, hard fibers, and natural rubber. However, a mineral such as bauxite, whose value is a small percentage of the final product price, will likely have a very low price elasticity of demand over a fairly broad price range.[27]

The Price Elasticity of Supply

For most tropical crops, production can easily be shifted in a relatively short time (although new production requires approximately 5 years for the tropical beverages and as much as 10 years for copra and other coconut products). Elasticities of supply for mineral products tend to be much lower in the short term than those for agricultural products, in view of the long lead time required to put a mine into operation.[28] In view of the current excess capacity in some minerals, notably copper, one might question whether the traditional price elasticities of supply still hold. Lead times and capital requirements are much less for putting closed mines back into operation than for new projects. In addition, there are many potential copper mines that have already been evaluated and are awaiting finance.[29] Lead times for such projects may be fairly short.

Institutional Characteristics

Numerous analyses of the potential for price action by producer associations have focused on such factors as "effective institutional means of allocating production."[30] More generally, they have focused on the number of producers involved, their capacity and willingness for joint action, and their history of shared experience or shared values.[31] It is not clear how these characteristics can be measured. The successful associations, notably OPEC and IBA, have relatively large numbers of members; and in OPEC, at least, it is difficult to discern any shared value other than that of getting the maximum revenue for oil.

Country Characteristics

The usual argument is that exporting countries are better able to participate in price-setting or price-stabilizing schemes when those countries have substantial foreign exchange reserves or when the commodity in question is a small factor in the country's total export earnings.[32] Again, the examples of the successful associations do not offer unqualified support for that assertion. Table 11-2 sets out comparable reserve positions for some members of OPEC, IBA, and CIPEC at the end of 1973; it also indicates the countries' degrees of dependence on a particular commodity for export earnings. CIPEC members were somewhat more secure than IBA members with respect to reserves, but they were more dependent on copper earnings than IBA members were on their bauxite earnings. However, even the non-Arab OPEC members had relatively healthy reserve positions, but most were extremely dependent on oil. These two factors are clearly not conclusive.

Consumer Reaction

It has been argued that Western acquiescence and the ability of the multinational companies to pass price increases through to consumers were major factors in the success of OPEC's efforts to raise oil prices.[33] On the evidence thus far, it is not clear how the strength of the acquiescence or passthrough factors can be accurately measured. There has been no case in which a serious and otherwise

Table 11-2
Foreign Exchange Reserves and Commodity Dependence of OPEC, IBA, and CIPEC Members, 1973

	Reserves as Number of Months' Imports, 12/31/73	*Oil, Copper, or Bauxite as a Percent of Total Exports*
OPEC members (selected)		
Algeria	8	88.8
Ecuador	8	48.0
Indonesia	4	60.2
Iran	5	89.8
Nigeria	7	89.9
Venezuela	12	93.6
IBA members (selected)		
Guyana	1	28.4
Dominican Republic	3	3.3
Jamaica	2	21.3
Sierra Leone	5	5.0
Surinam	6	29.7
CIPEC members		
Chile	2	72.7
Peru	8	28.5
Zaire	4	67.2
Zambia	4	93.3

Sources: IMF, *International Financial Statistics,* November 1976; IBRD, *Commodity Trade and Price Trends* (1976 Edition), pp. 21-22.

feasible effort by a producer group to raise prices has in fact been met by concerted opposition from industrial-country governments. And, in the two cases in which price increases have been most significant—petroleum and bauxite—more purely economic forces have limited the potential for opposing action. In oil, the price inelasticity of demand has amply been demonstrated. In bauxite, the material's relatively low proportion of final product cost has cushioned the impact of IBA-coordinated price increases.

Management and Timing

A major factor that has been somewhat overlooked in the discussions of cartels and potential producer action is the simple competence of those involved in the producer associations—competence in judging the state of the market, in negotiating acceptable arrangements among producers who may not always have the same objectives, and in presenting producers' goals to consumers and governments. One analysis of IBA success does comment that the IBA decision to move for higher prices in 1974 showed good timing–taking advantage of the generally strong commodity demand, of the political climate favorable to a new economic order, and of the OPEC and other recent examples[34] –while producers of other commodities, including copper, iron ore, tin, and natural rubber, missed the chance to cash in on the commodity boom and force prices to a permanently higher level. This emphasis on the importance of good timing perhaps overstates the case, and tends to underplay some of the fundamental economic aspects of the markets for these raw materials. But, as the discussion of CIPEC will indicate, there is clearly some importance to good management within a producer association, whether the goal is price stability or higher prices.

This summary of factors that affect the ability of producer associations to influence the market is not exhaustive; more important, it is not possible to quantify the different factors in a way that will permit accurate prediction of the actions of any given producer association. The factors should, however, be kept in mind in reviewing the experience of CIPEC.

CIPEC and Price Stabilization

CIPEC's Goals

CIPEC has never been concerned exclusively with price issues. From the outset, the organization has been concerned with questions of control and information as much as with price. It is only within the last two to three years that member countries have acquired a significant degree of real control over their national copper industries, and especially over the sales of their copper, and have turned their attention more specifically and continuously to questions of price.

At the time CIPEC was formed in 1967, price was perhaps a secondary concern of the members. After the period of extremely low prices in the late 1950s and early 1960s, both the London Metal Exchange price and the U.S. producer price had moved sharply upward by 1966–1968. (Not all this movement, however, was translated into greater earnings for the member countries, because part of the cause of price movements was the interruption in supply in Zambia following closing of the border with Rhodesia, in Zaire following the nationalization of Union Minière properties, and in Chile as a result of strikes.) During this period of relatively high prices, most of the energy of CIPEC member countries was focused on achieving ownership and control of their respective copper industries. In 1966 ownership of all the major mines in the four member countries was held by multinational corporations; by 1971 all the members except Peru had taken over all or part of the ownership of the industry (Peru nationalized the smaller of its two copper producers, Cerro de Pasco, in 1974, but its major producer is still foreign-owned, although the output is marketed by a state agency).

CIPEC Actions, 1967–1974

As in most of the producer associations (including OPEC in its early years), the major emphasis within CIPEC in its first years of existence was on administrative organization and information gathering. The CIPEC staff in Paris were only 7 in number in 1968, and only 18 by 1970. The focus on studies and administration is also shown in CIPEC's own records; of 199 executive committee documents in the 1968–1972 period, 98 concerned administrative matters and 50 more were proposals for studies. Of 83 governing board documents during the same period, 29 were administrative and 13 were study proposals.[35]

When prices began to decline in 1970, CIPEC members were still preoccupied with questions of national control rather than with decisive market action. While there had been some discussion of a CIPEC producer price as early as 1968, and even a resolution authorizing joint action on the London Metal Exchange to halt the price slide in 1971,[36] these initiatives were never translated into definite action. Throughout 1971–1972, the organization was far more concerned with evolving a means of supporting the Chilean government in its efforts to sell copper from the recently nationalized Kennecott and Anaconda mines.

Studies within CIPEC before 1974 did, in fact, outline several possible modes of action to reduce price instability. As early as 1973 the secretariat had produced outlines of a combined pricing system that would set floor and ceiling prices but allow the actual selling price for CIPEC copper to be set on the London Metal Exchange between these limits. This proposal has since gone through several refinements within CIPEC but has never been implemented. By 1974, when CIPEC might have been in a position to establish a new pricing basis in a boom market, the necessary analysis of the industry had been completed; what was missing was the trust among members, the leadership, and the willingness to take initiatives in the pricing area. By the time CIPEC was sufficiently united to take any action at all, the boom market had collapsed and the pricing action became purely defensive.

Earlier Copper Price-Setting Efforts

CIPEC, of course, is not the first group to try to stabilize copper prices. There is a long history of such action in the industry, including some with relatively long-term success in maintaining prices at a remunerative level. The most significant earlier efforts—all before the era of state-owned mining operations—included the following.

1. *The Secretan syndicate,* a French-financed group, gained control of nearly 80 percent of world output in 1886-1888 and pushed prices up by 150 percent in less than two years, before collapsing in 1889.

2. *The American Producers' Association* responded to the low-price period of the early 1890s by cutting production by 5 percent, with, however, only a marginal effect on price.

3. *Amalgamated Copper Company,* an American selling cartel led by Standard Oil interests, succeeded temporarily in raising prices by more than 50 percent in the period around 1900 through production restrictions and buying of surpluses on the market.

4. *The Copper Export Association* used a system of export restrictions and stockpiling to regulate prices in the 1918–1923 period.

5. *Copper Exporters, Inc.,* which included U.S., U.K., and Congo producers, instituted a system of export quotas and producer prices in 1928–1929.

6. *The International Copper Cartel* began operating in 1935; members included companies producing 70 percent of world output outside the United States (and included the U.S.-owned Chilean mines). The cartel operated with intermittent success until World War II.

7. *Coordinated Production Cuts* in the early 1960s by a group including the African and Chilean mines held price fluctuations to less than 2 percent for a period of nearly 2 years.[37]

Several of these price-fixing efforts clearly had significant success in stabilizing prices, if not in lifting them to higher-than-equilibrium levels. They suggest that whatever the structural arguments against an effort by CIPEC to raise prices, there is considerable latitude for stabilization attempts.

CIPEC Actions in 1974–1977

For most raw materials producers, the most significant action of 1973 in relation to any possible producer action on prices was the OPEC initiative in raising crude oil prices. For CIPEC, however, it is at least arguable that an even more significant event was one that, on the surface, appeared to have little or nothing to do with commodity prices—namely, the coup d'état in Chile. Copper prices were rising steadily through 1973, ultimately reaching a high of £1400 per metric ton on the LME on April 1, 1974. Output in the CIPEC countries was expanding, as was the CIPEC share of total world production.[38] The market situation was at its most favorable for producer action, since the countries' foreign exchange earnings were at relatively high levels and the strong demand in industrial countries made a passthrough of raw materials costs to ultimate consumers easier than it would have been in a period of stagnating demand.

But, as a direct result of the coup in Chile, CIPEC was wholly incapable of action during this period. The regular ministerial meeting originally scheduled for Lusaka in November 1973 was not held until June 1974–by which time copper prices had already fallen rapidly away from the peak level–because the Zambian government would not deal with the Chilean junta. Eventually, in the face of the extreme difficulties for copper-producing countries caused by the 60 percent drop in prices by the end of 1974, the producers overcame this political hostility and began conducting meetings in a somewhat more peaceful tone; but the basic suspicion of other members toward Chile persists.

Discussions of the potential for cartel-like action by raw materials producers have not always resulted in agreement on the importance of shared values or outlooks among members of the group.[39] What the CIPEC example seems to indicate, however, is that, while a positive sharing of values may not be necessary for successful joint action, active hostility among members of the group will certainly make success extremely unlikely.

When the CIPEC ministers finally met in June 1974, they did not act on several well-defined suggestions from the secretariat for adoption of measures leading to more stable prices. In particular, no action was taken on the proposal to impose floor and ceiling prices or otherwise modify the extreme price fluctuations on the LME. Instead, the ministers adopted a vague proposal for direct CIPEC intervention in the market–a proposal that was never backed up with operating funds from the member countries and was never put into effect.

By late 1974 the price decline had reached extreme proportions, hastened by the action of Japanese producers (smelter-refiners whose copper was supplied in concentrate form by Canada, the Philippines, Papua New Guinea, and South American mines) in dumping excess refined copper on the LME. At this point, CIPEC did take several steps. First, it authorized an approach to the Japanese government that ultimately resulted in a Japanese agreement to keep excess supplies of refined copper off the international markets. Second, the member countries resolved to cut exports by 10 percent from the end of 1974. These cuts, in addition to being a quid pro quo for the Japanese agreement, were also the first definitive step toward common action on production that CIPEC had taken.

In April 1975, CIPEC increased the nominal level of cuts to 15 percent and applied them to production rather than exports. Actual production figures do not indicate anything like that large a decline; the mine production of the four founding CIPEC members for 1975 was only 5.8 percent below that for 1974, while non-CIPEC mine production declined by even more, 6.8 percent, in the same period.[40]

Despite several attempts by CIPEC to estimate the effect of its export and production cutbacks, it is not clear to what extent they actually stabilized the market. The analytical difficulty arises for several reasons: (1) other producers were also cutting back at the same time, especially many small, high-cost mines in North America; (2) the CIPEC cutbacks themselves were not clearly defined —it was never made clear what level of production or capacity the cuts were from; and (3) many other actors in the market assumed a de facto burden of financing stockpiles, on the exchanges, in Japan, at producers and consumers, and so on, that smoothed out to some extent the sharp fall in demand in 1974–1975.

In November 1975, CIPEC formally disavowed attempts to regulate the market unilaterally (e.g., through direct market intervention or through a producer-only buffer stock) and announced its willingness to meet with consumers to discuss a cooperative arrangement for stabilizing prices. At the same time, the organization announced a continuation of the 15 percent production cuts, but on the basis of revised figures for production capacity in each of the member countries (by this time Indonesia, Australia, and Papua New Guinea had become part of the organization). The revised capacity figures were never made public, but it was clear at the time that the basis for setting capacity was for each country to estimate its maximum feasible production for 1976, then inflate its supposed capacity by an amount large enough to allow a 15 percent cut to apply without cutting substantially into the amount of copper that would in any case have been produced. Thus the cuts that were to apply for the first half of 1976 were wholly symbolic. At the ministerial meeting of CIPEC in June 1976, the policy of production cutbacks was formally, as well as practically, abandoned.

Most recently, CIPEC has apparently proposed some limited new initiatives. At the end of the most recent session of the UNCTAD working group on copper, the CIPEC executive director outlined plans for a "CIPEC producer price" that might be implemented later in 1977 as a short-term measure. In essence, the pricing scheme would simply replace the current dependence on the LME price with either a price that was a simple average of the American producer price and the LME price or would use the LME price except when that dropped below a floor level that would in practice be the level of the U.S. producer price.

CIPEC's Organizational Difficulties

The antagonisms between CIPEC members have already been described. It is my belief that these antagonisms were a significant force in keeping CIPEC from any decisive action in late 1973 and early 1974, a period in which there was a strong possibility of successful market action aimed at stabilization. Beyond these political antagonisms, however, CIPEC also suffers from two other serious difficulties to a greater extent than other producer associations. These are, first, the differences between high and low-cost producers and, second, the general level of competence of the CIPEC staff and the degree of commitment by the member countries to strengthening that staff.

Variations in the cost of production among CIPEC member countries are fairly large. By world standards, Zambia and Zaire (and Australia, an associate member of CIPEC but not a major exporter) are high-cost producers. Their current cost of production is probably between 55 and 60 cents per pound, compared to an average LME price that has been in the 55 to 65 cent range for most of the past two years.[41] In contrast, Chile has effected significant economies in the past few years and probably has a production cost not much above 40 cents per pound. At the extreme within CIPEC, Papua New Guinea's Bougainville mine has an effective production cost (after subtracting credits for the large amount of gold produced as a byproduct) of less than 35 cents per pound.

To be sure, greater differences in production costs exist in other producer organizations. In OPEC, for example, production costs in some members are nearly 10 times those in Saudi Arabia. But a more useful way of looking at these differences may be not to focus on the magnitude of the differences in costs, but rather on the magnitude of the differences in the potential surplus that exists after costs have been taken into account. For example, in oil, a production cost of $5 a barrel leaves a potential surplus of approximately $7, while a production cost of 50 cents a barrel leaves a potential surplus of $11.50, or less than twice as much. In copper, with the LME-set price hovering at, say, 65 cents, a production cost of 60 cents leaves only a 5-cent potential surplus, compared to a 25-cent potential surplus for the 40-cent cost producer. Looked at this way, the differences within CIPEC, during a time of protracted low prices, are greater than those within other producer organizations.

While CIPEC as a whole is a lower-cost producing unit than the rest of the world, a strategy to expand the CIPEC market share by exploiting this cost advantage would create internal difficulties. Any such plan would necessarily involve some form of compensation to the high-cost producers within CIPEC, and the group appears to have neither the resources nor the inclination for such support. In the absence of any concerted policy, Chile has been pursuing its own policy of expanding production and, presumably, market share, as have other producers outside CIPEC, including Canada, the Philippines, and Yugoslavia and Poland.

CIPEC's second major difficulty lies in the quality of its staff. The majority of professional staff is supplied to the organization by the member countries; and in view of the extreme shortages of skilled professionals in those countries, especially in Zaire and Zambia, it is perhaps not surprising that those seconded to CIPEC are not highly competent. But the extent of the members' unwillingness to supply top-level staff must raise questions about their commitment to the organization.

To summarize this discussion of CIPEC's potential, while the economic structure of the copper market may not have created conditions in which a long-term movement above an "equilibrium" price could have been maintained by producer action, there has been ample scope for such action with the more limited aims of stabilizing prices and expanding the CIPEC market share. That such action was not taken is at least partially attributable to internal differences and weaknesses within CIPEC.

Summary and Conclusions

The weaknesses of CIPEC, and of other producer organizations that have been less successful in organizing their own methods of stabilizing or raising prices for raw materials, offer substantial opportunities to the governments of the industrialized nations. To take CIPEC as an example, the failure of the organization to put a price-stabilization scheme into force unilaterally, and its subsequent decision to endorse producer-consumer discussions, would seem to open the way for substantial concessions by both producers and consumers. If, for example, the U.S. government proceeds with the recently announced intention to discuss the UNCTAD Common Fund and related commodity agreements in a serious fashion, it might be possible to gain real assurances of long-term import needs in a variety of commodities at stable prices. From the point of view of planning in the industrial nations, and particularly planning by processing and manufacturing industry, such stability would be seen as a considerable advantage. The cost, perhaps, in the form of financing for a buffer stock, need not be very great, or may not even exist at all in the long term, as several recent studies of buffer stock operation have indicated.[42]

Notes

1. Bergsten, "The Threat from the Third World," *Foreign Policy* 11 (1973):102-24; and "The Threat is Real," *Foreign Policy* 14 (1974):84-90. See also Clarfield et al., *Eight Mineral Cartels* (New York; McGraw-Hill, 1975); Corbet, *Raw Materials: Beyond the Rhetoric of Commodity Power* (London: Trade Policy Research Centre, 1975); Costello, "International Cartels," *Editorial Research Reports* (1974) vol. 2, no. 18; Beloff et al., "Nonfuel Mineral Cartels," *Law and Policy in International Business* 7 (1975):863-903; Erb, "Production and Marketing Associations of Companies and Developing Countries," (Mimeo, 1976); Mikdashi, "Collusion Could Work," *Foreign Policy* 14 (1974):57-58; Rose, "Third World Commodity Power," *Fortune* 94, no. 5 (November 1976):147; U.S. Council on International Economic Policy, Special Report: *Critical Imported Materials* (Washington, D.C.: Government Printing Office, 1974).

2. For price histories of the major commodities, see IBRD, *Commodity Trade and Price Trends* (1976 Edition) (Washington, 1976); IMF, *International Financial Statistics* (November 1976):28-29; and UNCTAD, *Handbook of In-*

ternational Trade and Development Statistics 1976 (New York: United Nations, 1976), pp. 60-61.

3. "Bergland Planning Bid to Canada for Fixing of World Wheat Price," *New York Times,* February 26, 1977, p. 27. The United States and Canada account for nearly 75 percent of wheat traded internationally.

4. On OPEC, see al-Otaiba, *OPEC and the Petroleum Industry* (London: Croon Helm, 1975); and Mikdashi, *The Community of Oil-Exporting Nations* (New York: Cornell University Press, 1972). A recent attempt to analyze CIPEC is Mingst, "Cooperation or illusion: an examination of the Intergovernmental Council of Copper Exporting Countries," *International Organization* 30 (1976): 263-288.

5. Radetzki, "The Potential for Monopolistic Commodity Pricing by Developing Countries," in Helleiner, ed., *A World Divided: the Less Developed Countries in the International Economy* (Cambridge, England: Cambridge University Press, 1975), pp. 53-76; Beloff et al., "Nonfuel Mineral Cartels"; and Bergsten, "The New Era in World Commodity Markets," *Challenge* (September/October 1974): 34-42.

6. al-Otaiba, *OPEC and the Petroleum Industry,* p. 131.

7. "Agreement to Establish the Intergovernmental Council of Copper Exporting Countries," mimeo, (Paris, 1975), Article I.

8. al-Otaiba, *OPEC and the Petroleum Industry,* p. 115.

9. CIPEC, "Resolution on the Permanent Mechanism of Protection and Solidarity Against Economic and Commercial Aggression," mimeo, (Paris, 1974).

10. al-Otaiba, *OPEC and the Petroleum Industry,* p. 58.

11. CIPEC, Agreement, Article I.

12. OPEC, Resolution I.1 (1960).

13. See Erb, "Issues Affecting Trade and Investment in Nonfuel Minerals," *Case Western Reserve Journal of International Law* 8 (1976):429-451.

14. For prices, see IBRD, *Commodity Trade and Price Trends,* p. 78; for consumption, see CIPEC *Quarterly Review* (October-December 1976):62.

15. For example, Tenke-Fungurume Convention (Zaire, 1970); and Kaiser Bauxite Agreement (Jamaica, 1977).

16. A recent version of this approach is the Mineral Resources Stabilization Fund Act (1974) in Papua New Guinea. That country's taxation is heavily based on profits; the only royalty is 1¼ percent of the f.o.b. value of sales.

17. Bergsten, "The Threat from the Third World."

18. Oppenheim, "Why Oil Prices Go Up," *Foreign Policy* 25 (1976/77): 24-58.

19. Bergsten, "A New OPEC in Bauxite," *Challenge* (July/August 1976): 12-20.

20. UNCTAD Resolution 93(IV). The 18 commodites are bananas, bauxite, cocoa, coffee, copper, cotton, hard fibers, iron ore, jute, manganese, meat, phosphates, rubber, sugar, tea, timber, tin, and vegetable oils.

21. Ibid.

22. IBRD, *Commodity Trade and Price Trends,* p. 19.

23. Recent statistics on bauxite production do indicate a shift away from Caribbean producers in 1975–1976. *Metal Bulletin,* October 22, 1976, p. 22.

24. Bergsten, "A New OPEC in Bauxite," p. 17.

25. CIPEC, "Production and Investment Policy in the Copper Industry," mimeo, (Paris, 1975).

26. Brookings Institution, *Trade in Primary Commodities: Conflict or Cooperation* (Washington; Brookings Institution, 1974), p. 28; Beloff et al., "Nonfuel Mineral Cartels," pp. 867–873; Bergsten, "The Threat from the Third World," pp. 107-108; Costello, "International Cartels," pp. 849–851; Krasner, "Oil is the Exception," *Foreign Policy* 14 (1974): 68–84; Mikdashi, "Collusion Could Work," p. 60; Mingst, "Cooperation or Illusion," p. 265; Varon and Takeuchi, "Developing Countries and Nonfuel Minerals," *Foreign Affairs* 52 (1974): 497–510.

27. Earlier estimates of price elasticity of demand by Houthakker and Magee (*Review of Economics and Statistics* 51 (1969):121) include:

cocoa	-0.41
tea	-0.05 to -0.25
coffee	-0.25 to -0.44
copper	-0.10 to -0.30

Varon and Takeuchi (*Foreign Affairs* 52 (1974):506 list the following short- and long-term elasticities of demand for minerals:

tin	short	-0.55	long	-1.25
aluminum	short	-0.20	long	-2.50
copper	short	-0.20	long	-1.35

28. Radetzki, "The Potential for Monopolistic Commodity Pricing by Developing Countries," pp. 58–60.

29. See Zorn, "New Trends in Third World Mining Agreements," *Natural Resources Forum* Vol. 1 no. 3 (April 1977) pp. 239–50. Commodities Research Unit, *The Costs of Processing Primary Copper and Future Trends* (London: Commodities Research Unit, 1976) vol. III, p. 58.

30. Erb, "Production and Marketing Associations of Companies and Developing Countries," p. 9.

31. Krasner, "Oil is the Exception," p. 69.

32. See sources cited in note 25.

33. Oppenheim, "Why Oil Prices Go Up."

34. Bergsten, "A New OPEC in Bauxite," p. 14.

35. Mingst, "Cooperation or Illusion," p. 275.

36. Ibid., pp. 276–279.

37. See Clarfield et al., *Eight Mineral Cartels,* pp. 79–81; and Mingst, "Cooperation or Illusion," pp. 268–70.

38. Total mine production for the CIPEC group, including those countries that joined the organization in 1975 but were already involved in CIPEC discussions in 1974 (Australia, Indonesia, and Papua New Guinea), increased from 2421 thousand metric tons in 1972 to 2608 thousand tons in 1973 and 2828 thousand tons in 1974, rising from 43 to 46 percent of Western World mine production. CIPEC, *Quarterly Report,* (October–December 1976), p. 55.

39. Compare, for example, Krasner, "Oil is the Exception," and Bergsten, "The Threat from the Third World."

40. CIPEC, *Quarterly Report,* (October–December 1976), pp. 55–56.

41. For the most recent survey of cost-of-production data in copper, see Commodities Research Unit, *The Costs of Producing Primary Copper and Future Trends* (London, 1976).

42. See, for example, Smith, *An Economic Evaluation of International Buffer Stocks for Copper,* mimeo, (Washington, 1975).

12 A European View of Commodity Problems: Stabilization of Prices and Stabilization of Receipts

Alexandre Stakhovitch

Introduction

Basic among the factors that distinguish the European and United States attitudes toward commodity problems is the relative degree of dependence on imports of raw materials. European industrial economies must rely incomparably more heavily on imports than does the United States. In the case of minerals and metals, for example, 75 percent of European consumption comes from imports; for the United States, the comparable figure is 15 percent. A study undertaken two and one-half years ago by the Commission of the European Communities indicated that the situation was difficult, even critical, for European consumers, rather than for suppliers, in the case of 12 commodities of varying degrees of importance.

The European attitudes and policies in recent years, however, have not been governed primarily by consumer interests. On the contrary, they have been determined almost exclusively by the desire to solve, at least in part, some of the problems posed by the developing countries in the framework of the United Nations and the UNCTAD session in Nairobi. The orientation of our efforts toward solution of these problems is quite clear in the case of *stabilization of receipts* and in our approach to the question of *stabilization of prices.* Neither the European Community nor the other major industrial nations has yet formulated a complete, detailed, and coherent raw materials policy, but there is a continuing and cooperative endeavor to achieve such a course of action.

Stabilization of Prices

At present, the international negotiations in Geneva indicate more interest in stabilization of prices than in stabilization of receipts. I shall, therefore, first discuss stabilization of prices and, within that framework, the instrument of buffer stocks, with or without a Common Fund. In passing, it should be noted that there are various other means of stabilization of prices, such as diversification of production, access to markets, etc., that do not require buffer stocks and therefore are applicable to commodities for which stockpiling is not feasible.

Let us now examine the use of buffer stocks as an instrument of price stabilization. The first point to be made, and this is of extreme importance, is that the range of commodities that are amenable to price stabilization through buffer stocks is very limited indeed. In order for a buffer stock to operate successfully, the stockpiled commodities should possess certain technoeconomic characteristics. Many commodities will be automatically eliminated from the eligibility list, for example,

1. Commodities that cannot be stockpiled because of spoilage, e.g., certain fruits and vegetables
2. Commodities of great bulk but low unit price, e.g., iron ore
3. Commodities that are vertically integrated. Bauxite, alumina, and aluminum are a typical mineral complex almost entirely mined by a few integrated multinational companies that transform the raw material into the final product. Vertically integrated commodities may be susceptible to stabilization through buffer stocks, but it is not necessary, since the companies in question take care of their own stabilization. Their methods may be good or bad; in any case, they are very powerful.
4. Commodities that are not homogeneous. A buffer stock, in order to function, should, in principle, have one regulatory price.
5. Commodities for which there are close substitutes. This is typically the case for rubber, jute, and hard fibers. In all three cases, the substitutes are the products of very large petrochemical companies, which may, in addition, produce a basket of other products that are far more important. In some cases, the minor products, e.g., substitutes for jute and hard fibers, may be considered almost as byproducts; their price is, therefore, largely arbitrary. Thus, any stabilization scheme established for the natural product is subject to undercutting by the price for the synthetic substitute and may, in fact, be virtually nonfunctioning.
6. Finally, commodities that are ridden with structural problems, such as tea, for which there is a secular decrease in demand.

What commodities, then, are particularly well-suited for price stabilization through the mechanism of buffer stocks? Even if we do not take the above exclusion criteria too strictly, we are left with very few commodities. The list I shall now examine is entirely my own.[1]

1. The most favorable candidate is *copper.* It has almost none of the drawbacks I have enumerated above, except, of course, that it is competitive with aluminum and other metals, but not to an extent that might be crippling. Its production is remarkably equally shared among developing countries, developed market economy countries, and developed socialist countries. It is

easily stockable and homogeneous. The major problem is that it is very expensive, and the initial cost of a copper stockpile would be extremely high. This is one dilemma which those who will be negotiating in Geneva must resolve. If copper were cheaper, things would be much easier.

2. I would next name *tin.* There is already an agreement for tin, but its financing is not symmetrical between producers and consumers. As a result, the maximum level of the stock in terms of consumption has been of the order of five to six weeks. Lord Keynes, in a much quoted article written in 1942, established the rule of thumb that three months consumption seems to be about reasonable for the size of a buffer stock. Since then, I have not seen this proven or disproven. But it does appear that the criticisms that have been levied over the unsatisfactory functioning of the tin agreement "upwards"—that is, that the floor price has been kept, but the ceiling price has not been maintained—are largely related to the insufficient financing of the agreement and the inadequate size of the stock.

3. Third on my list would be *lead,*[2] which has one very interesting characteristic. A large part of the consumption of lead, at least in Europe, is based on recovery from scrap, such as batteries and pipes. Lead is not easily subject to cartelization, and the variations in price, therefore, are much stronger than those for its sister product zinc.

4. Another product—which I put in brackets—is *rubber.* It is subject to the difficulties involved in competition with synthetics and lack of homogeneity. At present, natural rubber comprises about one-third of the total demand for rubber. The exclusivities—that is, things that can be done only with natural or only with synthetic rubber—exist, but they are not very large.

5. Finally, I shall mention *phosphate rock.* A few developing countries, which are claimed to be the price leaders in the production of phosphate rock (the United States being a "follower"), have managed over one year to multiply this price by more than the oil price has been multiplied by OPEC, that is, fivefold as opposed to fourfold. They have created hardships for all other developing countries that desperately need fertilizers. In other respects, phosphate rock is not clearly impeded by the preceding negative characteristics.

Up to this point, the discussion has dealt exclusively with buffer stocks for the purpose of price stabilization. Some brief mention must be made of *security stocks.* Certain commodities, from the European point of view, are regarded as security risks because they are supplied by a small number of so-called insecure countries. Predominant among these commodities are chromite, platinum, and tungsten. The problem of security stocks is entirely different in kind and size from those related to buffer stocks. Quantitatively, it is much less important; security stocks of these three commodities for the entire European Community would cost something like 50 or 60 million dollars, contrasted with the hundreds of millions or even billions of dollars associated with stabilization stocks.

Let us now return to the discussion of buffer stocks. A good deal of the current negotiations is concerned with the creation and modalities of the Common Fund, which would be related to stabilization actions, mainly via buffer stocks, for a certain number of commodities. I contend that this is putting the cart before the horse. What should first be done is to determine which products are susceptible to price stabilization by buffer stocks. After this list has been determined, and I am convinced that it will be extremely short, we must study most carefully the nature of the price fluctuations in this group of, say, three to five commodities and determine how large a buffer stock for a given commodity must be in order for it to function efficiently, and how much it would cost. I feel that this has not been examined sufficiently in view of the enormous sums involved, whether $6 billion or $10 billion.

Stabilization of Export Receipts

I shall now turn to the question of stabilization of export receipts, as opposed to the stabilization of prices. STABEX is a relatively small project, but it is of particular interest because it already functions. It is incorporated in the Lomé agreement between the European Community and 46 developing countries, mainly in Africa but also in the Caribbean and Pacific areas. The population of the developing countries covered is only slightly more than 200 million, approximately the size of the population of the European Community. This means, of course, that the bulk of the population of the developing countries is excluded from the STABEX agreement. Limitation of coverage of the developing countries, however, has made it feasible for the Community to undertake a small-scale experiment. The STABEX agreement has so far been applied to 12 product groups, eleven nonmineral and one mineral. They are: groundnuts, cocoa, coffee, cotton, coconut products, palm oil and palm kernel oil, hides and skins, timber, bananas, tea, sisal, and iron ore.

The STABEX system incorporates the following characteristics:

1. The "threshold of significance," which, in principle, is 7.5 percent of the value of exports. This means that only those product groups are considered which represent more than 7.5 percent of the total value of exports of a given country.
2. The "threshold of sensitivity," which is also set at 7.5 percent. If, for any commodity that meets the criterion of the threshold of significance (i.e., that represents more than 7.5 percent of the total exports of a given country), the proceeds from exports in any given year fall below the average proceeds of the last four years by *more than* 7.5 percent, STABEX rapidly compensates the exporting country for the deficiency in proceeds. This is stabilization of receipts.

Of the 46 developing countries covered by this agreement, 36 nations have been singled out for more favorable treatment, either because they are particularly poor or because they are landlocked or island countries and presumably subject to particular transportation difficulties. For these 36 countries, both the threshold of significance and the threshold of sensitivity have been set at 2.5 percent rather than 7.5 percent.

Finally, a ceiling of about $465 million over five years, or an average of $93 million per year, has been imposed on the STABEX project. No interest is charged on the compensatory disbursements to the exporting developing countries, and reimbursement is not exacted from the 36 poorest countries.

The results of the first year of the STABEX experiment are already available. The European Community has paid out $89.5 million. The period for consideration of requests for payment by the developing countries lasts only 3 months, and payment takes place 30 days after a decision has been made, or a total of 4 months after the original request is made. This is truly a remarkable achievement, and it is made possible only through the extraordinary degree of cooperation between those who work on these problems in Brussels and those who work on the same problems in the 46 developing countries.

Of the $89.5 million toward stabilization of receipts that have been paid by the Community, about 68 percent can be attributed to decreased demand on the consumer side as a consequence of the slackening of economic growth. The remaining 32 percent stems from circumstances peculiar to the supply side, such as mine strikes or agricultural mishaps. For many products, and for many countries, these payments, small as they appear, have been of vital importance. For some small countries, the STABEX disbursements have represented between 13 and 24 percent of all foreign exchange receipts; payments have gone as high as 40 to 60 percent of the receipts for a given commodity.

A Comparison of STABEX and the IMF Compensatory Financing Scheme

A few comments should be made about STABEX vis-à-vis the IMF Compensatory Financing Scheme. The most obvious difference between the two schemes, of course, lies in the magnitude of the operations. STABEX, in its first year, paid out approximately $89 million; during the same period IMF payments amounted to $3.25 billion. There is no certainty that the IMF can continue to be so generous, but the difference in the orders of magnitude is apparent.

Second, the IMF system is not commodity-oriented. It is based on consideration of the global balance of payments, rather than on the balance of trade or the export situation of a given commodity or group of commodities.

Third, the IMF scheme involves loans that bear interest, albeit at a modest rate, and it is linked to and limited by reference to the quota system of the

IMF. Toward the close of 1975, the system was strongly liberalized. In the preceding 10 years, a total of \$1.3 billion had been lent; in the single year that followed, more than double that amount was paid out.

Fourth, the STABEX system, as described above, is deliberately discriminatory, with the poorest developing countries receiving most favored treatment. The IMF does not permit discrimination, so loans have been made to such developed countries as Iceland and Australia.

The relatively successful operation of STABEX in its initial year leads to a consideration of its extension beyond the original 46 countries, perhaps to a "World STABEX." The complexity of the problems that would arise with such a scheme cannot be underestimated.

Conclusion

The relationship between price stabilization and receipts stabilization is extremely complicated. The two systems are neither symmetrical nor alternative. They may, however, be complementary.

As I indicated earlier, price stabilization, at least through the mechanism of buffer stocks, has very limited applicability. The flexibility of receipts stabilization, which can be utilized for any commodity a priori, makes the scheme very tempting. However, price stabilization is a much more powerful tool. Theoretically, it is symmetrical in benefits to producers and consumers. Receipts stabilization is clearly a form of transfer, a form of aid that is commodity-linked. The choice between the two objectives or, conceivably, a combination of the two, depends clearly on the purposes we are pursuing and on the structure of the demand and supply of the commodities involved.

Notes

1. This list is limited to minerals and tropical agricultural products. It should be noted that two buffer stock systems already exist: tin, mentioned below, and cocoa, which does not yet function. It should be remembered also that the Community has submitted to GATT proposals for the establishment of nationally decentralized buffer stocks for temperate agricultural products.

2. Lead is not on the Manila-Nairobi list but was on the first UNCTAD list.

Part IV
Integrated Commodity Stabilization Programs

13 Commodity Trade Policy Initiatives and Issues

Constantine Michalopoulos
and
Lorenzo L. Perez

Introduction

Commodity trade issues have been and will be central to the North-South dialogue. The United States and other developed countries are engaged in a series of negotiations with the developing countries at UNCTAD over future arrangements affecting international commodity trade policy. The basis for these negotiations is UNCTAD's so-called Integrated Programme for Commodities (IPC). Under this program, consultations and negotiations for organization of the international markets of up to 18 commodities of interest to the developing countries are to occur between the fall of 1976 and the end of 1978.[1] Negotiations will also take place in late 1977 on the establishment of a Common Fund to finance buffer stocks, liberalization of existing compensatory financing facilities, and other supplementary proposals to improve commodity market conditions.

This chapter will analyze the key policy issues that arise for the United States and other developed countries from the UNCTAD integrated program proposals. It will focus on two sets of issues: those arising in the context of commodity market arrangements and those related to the establishment of the Common Fund. The next section of the chapter summarizes these issues. Subsequent sections explore the available evidence with a view to narrowing the options for action. First, commodity price movements are briefly reviewed. Then the issues of stabilization and increased commodity prices as objectives of commodity arrangements are discussed. Finally, the rationale and justifications for the Common Fund proposal are analyzed.

The authors wish to thank Gerald R. Benedick for his excellent research assistance and helpful suggestions, and Neal Riden, Jr., Keith Jay, and Danny Leipziger for useful comments on various sections of this draft. The chapter represents solely the views of the authors and is not intended as a policy statement of the Agency for International Development.

The Issues

Commodity Arrangements

The objectives of the Integrated Programme for Commodities (IPC) can be summarized as (1) the maintenance of commodity prices at levels that in real terms are equitable to consumers and remunerative to producers; (2) reduction of excessive fluctuations in commodity prices and the volume of trade; (3) assurance of access to markets for commodity exporting countries and assurance of access to suppliers of primary commodities for importing countries; (4) expansion of the processing of primary commodities and restructuring of commodity marketing and distribution systems; and (5) improved competitiveness of natural products vis-à-vis synthetics.

Underlying the first objective is a developing-country desire to organize commodity markets for the purpose of preventing the prices of their commodity exports from falling relative to prices of their manufactured goods imports. This developing-country desire is based on two contentions. The first is that demand for primary commodities is not growing fast enough to sustain economic expansion in developing countries and that, in particular, demand for primary commodities is expanding at a slower rate than demand for manufactured goods. In addition, developing countries feel that, unlike the situation in manufactures, productivity increases in commodities are passed on to consumers through lower prices. It is argued that these differences in demand and supply conditions tend to result in a long-term deterioration in developing-countries' barter terms of trade, with adverse effects on their development. The second contention is that demand for commodities is inelastic at the relevant price ranges. Thus, for any given demand level, developing-country producers will maximize total as well as per-unit rents and enhance their development prospects by offering lower rather than higher levels of supply.

The developing countries' pressure for the establishment of commodity agreements with the participation of developed countries is the consequence of a number of separate considerations: (1) there are many actual or potential developed-country producers whose participation is critical to the operation of any agreement; (2) because of conflicting interests, developing-country producers themselves are often unable to decide on how to share markets, and consumer-countries' participation might help the negotiation and implementation of the arrangements; and (3) developed consumer countries can help share some of the financial costs.

The first IPC objective gives rise to a number of issues. First is the question of facts: Has the operation of commodity markets resulted in price levels that have had detrimental effects on LDC development and what are the likely prospects for the future? Second, if, as a result of market organization, prices of primary products are increased, which countries are likely to benefit and which to lose? Developing countries as a whole expect that they will benefit because commodities are a large portion of their exports, while manufactures are a large portion of their imports, a situation that is typically reversed for most developed countries. Is this expectation correct? And which particular LDCs are to benefit?

Third, if it is correct that developed countries will on the whole be expected to lose from higher commodity prices, then the cost of their participation can be viewed as economic assistance to developing countries; if this is the case, then it is necessary to examine carefully the distribution of benefits to developing countries and the effectiveness of using commodity agreements for the attainment of the multiple political and economic objectives of economic assistance. Alternatively, costs to developed countries may be weighed against other potential benefits, such as access to supplies or stability in prices.

The second IPC objective—reduction in price and volume fluctuations—may well be shared by both developed and developing countries. But while the stability objective may be viewed as desirable for both sets of countries, a number of questions arise in its pursuit. First is the question of the feasibility of achieving more market stability through new commodity arrangements. This involves questions about the institutional structures that lend themselves to market organization and questions about the adequacy of forecasting techniques in estimating future demand and supply, and hence an appropriate range for stabilizing prices. This is especially true with respect to some tropical agricultural products, where supply changes due to weather conditions are almost impossible to predict.

Second, the objective of price stability inevitably gets mixed up with the objective of raising prices within the context of agreements in which producers and consumers with conflicting interests participate. Developing countries usually are not interested in mere price stabilization along a prevailing trend but in putting a *floor* on commodity prices or indexing prices to trends in manufacturing imports. This implies asymmetric action aimed at benefiting producers rather than consumers, and gives rise to potential conflicts of objectives between the two.

There is less disagreement over the IPC objectives involving access to markets as well as access to supplies. The issue here centers primarily on the question of discriminatory practices by the exporting or the importing country that either favor or deny access to individual suppliers or consumers. There is also little disagreement in principle about the other IPC objectives, i.e., the need to increase processing of raw materials as part of the industrialization process in developing countries or the need to improve the competitiveness of natural materials vis-à-vis synthetics.

Common Fund

In support of the objectives of the IPC, the UNCTAD Secretariat recommended the establishment of a Common Fund with a capitalization of $6 billion. These funds are to be used for the financing of buffer stocks as well as nonstocking activities such as diversification and marketing efforts. The fundamental question is whether a common funding arrangement is needed at all or whether buffer stocks should be financed separately from countries participating in individual commodity agreements.

If it is agreed that pooling of buffer stock financing in a common funding arrangement is desirable, then there are questions as to how such a funding arrangement is going to operate, what its objectives and financial needs would be, and how the financing would be obtained.

The key institutional issue concerns the role of a Common Fund in intervening in individual markets— and more generally the administration of the fund relative to the operation of the individual commodity arrangements. The relative priorities for the Common Fund in financing stocks as opposed to other activities such as marketing and processing also need to be addressed. The total amount of financing needed, in turn, depends on the overall objectives of the fund, on the number of commodity agreements where buffer stocks will be useful, and on the price objectives of the individual agreements. The requirements for individual buffer stocks depend critically on whether the objective of an agreement is to put a floor on price declines, to stabilize along a long-run trend, or to stabilize relative to movements of other prices, as, for example, prices of manufactured imports, etc. There are also various options with respect to the sources of buffer stock financing depending on the relative role of paid-in contributions and borrowings in private capital markets. A final issue is when the funding arrangement is put together, prior to the conclusion of individual agreements, simultaneously with their conclusion, or ex post.

Commodity Prices: Past Trends and Future Prospects

Trends in commodity prices and export earnings in the last 15 years vary considerably. Developing countries manufactured exports grew by 41 percent between 1960–1974 in value terms, whereas commodity exports grew by 35 percent. But individual commodity exporters' performance for the same time period ranged from –0.3 percent for India for tea to 45 percent for Malaysia for tin.

A priori one can hypothesize that prices of exhaustible raw materials will be subject to a long-run upward rather than downward trend as resources in fixed supply are progressively used up under the pressure of increasing demand from industrialization and rising population. In fact, specific commodity price forecasts are mixed.[2] Thus, it is not possible to explain the heavy pressure of developing countries for international reforms in commodity trade simply by referring to price trends.

Similarly, trends in developing countries' terms of trade do not show a long-term deterioration. Indeed, except for 1971, the barter terms of trade of nonoil exporters have been remarkably stable for over a decade. Of course, if oil exporters are included, developing countries' barter terms of trade have significantly improved.[3]

However, instability in both prices and export earnings has afflicted commodity exporters to a much greater extent than exporters of manufactures.[4] But this fact alone cannot be viewed as the reason for developing-country militancy on the issue. Indeed since early 1976, the expanded IMF Compensatory Financing Facility has helped significantly in offsetting fluctuations in developing countries' export earnings, including fluctuations that derive from commodity exports. One hypothesis is that developing countries' demands on commodities are primarily political in origin. The argument is that, spurred by the success of OPEC, developing countries have turned to commodity agreements as an alternative to obtaining increased assistance through traditional mechanisms. While the benefits of commodity arrangements are likely to be quite unevenly distributed (see below), the political leadership of developing countries, as well as UNCTAD, has nevertheless made action on commodities a symbolic issue in general North-South relations.

Stabilization

What to Stabilize and Why

Past discussion of commodity agreements has stressed the importance of stabilizing developing-country export earnings. The reason is that instability of earnings has been shown to be (admittedly after some controversy) detrimental to investment and, by inference, to growth through fluctuations in imports.[5] While the empirical evidence on this score is weak, it appears that developing countries do not accumulate international reserves in periods of rising export earnings because of the implied cost in foregone investment opportunities. When, subsequently, their export earnings drop, they are unable to maintain import levels. Frequently, their governments use rising export earnings to finance their development effort and, in the downturn, are forced to curtail investment and thus engage in costly stop/go domestic economic policies when earnings decline.

There are two approaches to stabilizing export earnings: stabilize them directly or stabilize them by reducing price and/or volume fluctuations. Earnings stabilization is being carried out at present with some success by the IMF. Its Compensatory Finance Facility extended approximately SDR 2.4 billion in 1976, with some SDR 1.6 billion going to developing countries. About one-third of the developing countries that received compensatory financing drawings were able to finance close to 100 percent of their export earnings shortfalls. However, the percentage of shortfall financed by the rest seems to have varied significantly.[6]

Price stabilization through buffer stock arrangements can also stabilize export earnings. When price instability is associated with fluctuations in demand, the effect of price stabilization on earnings stability will normally be substantial and favorable. This is due to the fact that variations in export quantities reinforce the impact that price variations have on export earnings. Purchases of a commodity by a buffer stock authority in periods of demand shortfall will prevent earnings from falling, and selling in periods of excess demand will smooth out earnings peaks.

Where price instability results from supply shifts, there is to some degree an offset between price and quantity fluctuations: as quantity increases, prices fall, and vice versa. Where market demand is particularly inelastic, price stabilization will still reduce instability in earnings; but stabilization of earnings cannot go further than the remaining fluctuations in quantities. A buffer stock that stabilizes prices completely cannot reduce instability in earnings below instability in export quantities. However, with demand elasticities low enough—the crucial elasticity values depending on the stability of the demand function—a shift to the right of the supply schedule causes a more than proportionate reduction in earnings without intervention. Under these circumstances, buffer stock intervention will still tend to reduce earnings instability.[7]

Thus for commodity markets with the main source of instability from the demand side, such as minerals and metals, stabilizing prices will tend to stabilize producers' earnings. In the case of commodities whose main source of instability comes from the supply side, e.g., agricultural commodities affected by crop failures or harvest booms, price stabilization will also lead to stabilization of earnings, provided demand is inelastic.[8]

Stability of earnings can be further enhanced by quantitative controls of production or exports. But the moment supply restrictions are relied upon for the purpose of stabilization, the possibilities of distortion in resource allocation increase significantly. In principle, a properly endowed buffer stock can stabilize commodity prices. Production controls are strictly only necessary if the aim is to raise prices.[9]

If the objective is to stabilize earnings, it is probably better to do so through a compensatory finance scheme such as that of the IMF than through market intervention. This is because the setting up of a cumbersome system of individual agreements is avoided, total export earnings fluctuations are covered, and there is less likelihood that resource misallocation will take place as a result of market intervention.

It has been argued that the IMF system is not that attractive because it extends loans rather than grants and that it is better somehow to stabilize earnings through price manipulation in the market. But if the objective is to stabilize earnings, the IMF can probably do a reasonable job. If the resulting repayments are viewed by developing countries as a burden, then the problem is not likely to be instability, but rather inadequacy of long-term resource transfers, which is a different problem entirely, needing different solutions. The real problem of the IMF facility, as far as many developing countries are concerned, is that the financing extended is not unconditional, as they would prefer it, but is extended after some scrutiny of their overall balance-of-payments situation.

Price stabilization, however, may be viewed as an end in itself both by producers and consumers. For a variety of reasons on the producers' side, stabilization of export earnings through IMF borrowing may not be passed through effectively to the rest of the economy, since there may not be adequate links between institutions whose concern is the management of export earnings at the macro level and institutional mechanisms that stabilize producers' income at the micro level. While domestic stabilization policies such as those performed by marketing boards can cope with stability of producers' incomes, their task is easier if prices at the international level are more stable. Of course, to the extent that price stabilization leads to earnings stabilization, so much the better; the task of the IMF is made easier.

Perhaps the most important beneficiaries of price stability per se may be consuming countries:

1. Price instability can be costly to consuming countries because it may promote inflationary tendencies. Inflationary tendencies can result from asymmetrical responses of firms to price increases as opposed to price decreases. Since raw material processors typically operate in oligopolistic markets characterized by price leadership, in a climate of rapidly rising raw material prices, the absence of good market information may permit them to raise prices of processed goods in excess of that justified by raw material price increases. The reverse would not tend to occur during a period of falling prices.

2. Increases in prices in particular sectors in turn often provoke restrictive action by monetary authorities. Such action would tend to dampen general business activity. Large increases in commodity prices can thus result in significant real costs to an economy via the policy response to them. However, again the response is not fully symmetrical. It is less likely that price declines, even if they were to occur in specific sectors, would evoke expansionary measures.[10]

3. Price uncertainty also creates multiple costs to consumers. First, there is a cost of obtaining cover in forward markets to reduce the uncertainty. Second, larger fluctuations tend to induce holding of higher inventories, which would also tend to increase costs of the final product. Finally, price fluctuations may themselves inhibit investment because of uncertainty. This would retard expansion of supply, which would result in higher costs of raw materials in the long run and hence would be contrary to basic consumers' objectives in the commodity area.

The existing welfare literature on price stability does not arrive at specific conclusions about its desirability as a result of the limiting assumptions used in the analysis and the large number of possible theoretical results. In fact, since most of the methodology developed so far is of the form of comparative statistics of producers' and consumers' surpluses, many of the potential benefits of price stability for producers and consumers have not been analyzed.

Massell, for example, concluded that price stabilization via buffer stocks with costless storage will yield net gains to producers and consumers taken collectively. These gains are reduced accordingly when storage costs are positive. Producers gain more than consumers and are more likely to gain with price stabilization when the stochastic supply elements display greater variance relative to stochastic demand elements and when the price elasticity of supply is less relative to the price elasticity of demand. In addition, his analysis shows that the greater the similarity between conditions affecting individual consumers and producers with the conditions facing the whole market, the greater is the probability of gains for each under a price-stabilization scheme. Also, the steeper the individual demand and supply schedules, the greater is the gain with price stabilization.[11]

In summary, there are some doubts that additional measures to stabilize developing-country export earnings are necessary. But it can still be argued that there is sufficient reason to believe that international action to stabilize commodity prices would yield benefits to producers and consumers alike and should be pursued. However, the benefits from such stabilization attempts are difficult to quantify.[12]

Feasibility of Stabilization

Even if price stabilization efforts through buffer stocks may be desirable, they may not be feasible in all commodities. Feasibility depends on four sets of factors: (1) the physical characteristics of the commodity; (2) the design of practical rules with respect to setting a price range over which stabilization is to occur; (3) the existence of certain institutions, such as commodity exchanges, which facilitate the operation of buffer stocks; and (4) the commonality of interests between participants in the agreement.[13]

Physical Characteristics. With the exception of tea and sugar, where perishability may be a problem, all other commodities in the UNCTAD core group possess characteristics that make it possible to undertake buffer stock operations for stabilization purposes. In sugar, the problem can be remedied through construction of expensive storage facilities, which would tend to add significantly to the cost of operating a buffer stock. In addition, coffee and tea present a problem because of the different grades available in international markets.

A possible solution would be to base the operations on a few well-established qualities broadly representative of the general pattern of world trade.

Institutional Factors. The existence of organized commodity exchanges where commodity transactions can take place is of considerable importance to the successful operation of a buffer stock. In the absence of an organized market, the buffer stock would have to operate through direct sales to consumers, which greatly complicates its operation. It is not clear whether the existing commodity exchanges could absorb the operations of a buffer stock in each commodity considered. This is particularly true of sisal and jute. In addition, at present there is no organized iron ore exchange, and one may probably have to be set up as part of the operations of an agreement.

Rules on Price Targets. Determining an acceptable target price range has been a problem both in theory and in practice. MacAvoy and McNicol (1976) have argued that target prices should be set so as to approximate the long-run competitive equilibrium solution and thus equate price to long-run marginal and average costs. However, if demand or supply can be manipulated in markets characterized by few buyers or sellers, this is not a practical operating rule because of the difficulties in determining what are long-run costs. For political reasons, cost of production differences among producers would have to be taken into consideration so as to allow the high-cost producers, at least in the short run, to become more competitive or move into other production lines.

A more realistic way of determining the target price is probably through a formula that predicts future price trends based on the immediate past, adjusted by expectations of future events. Moving averages or other econometric techniques could be used as general guidelines for deriving the target price. In any event, the target price and bandwidth would be subject to negotiations and subjected to frequent reviews to make the mechanism flexible.

In practice, prices have been set on the basis of bargaining between the members of the agreements. Past experience has not been very encouraging. Arrangements have frequently broken down, primarily under upward pressure on prices, or because of unforeseen changes in supply. While the technical problems in economic forecasting should not be underestimated, the key problem in setting prices, and in operating stabilization programs in general, is the divergent and often conflicting interest of participants. All technical problems involving price stabilization of commodities could perhaps be overcome, and yet no agreements would be feasible because of conflicting interests among the participants.

Price Stability versus Price Increases and Other Conflicts of Interest. Conflicts of interest abound in all commodity arrangements. The most fundamental is between developing-country producers and developed-country consumers. The former are primarily interested in using commodity arrangements to raise prices or setting a price floor but not a ceiling; the latter, only to stabilize them. There are only a few developed countries that are net exporters of unprocessed commodities and that are likely to benefit from increased prices. Developing countries as a whole may or may not benefit from increased prices in the particular group of commodities in which "stabilization" is to occur, depending on the importance of the worldwide inflationary pressures created by the price increase. Similarly, even if the group as a whole benefits, individual countries may be hurt—whether they are or not depends on whether a particular country is a net importer or exporter. Even net exporting countries do not necessarily benefit from higher commodity prices associated with commodity agreements, since some might be better off with lower price policies that would increase their market share.

For developed countries as a whole, the main policy problem is to decide whether to support the IPC, even with the expectation that higher commodity prices will ensue, in exchange for attainment of other objectives. These objectives may either be direct economic benefits, such as those derived from increased price stability or assured access to commodity supplies, or broader foreign policy objectives related to economic development of developing countries that hopefully will be assisted by the establishment of the IPC. It is unfortunately very difficult to reach a decision on the economic benefits. There is little information on the quantitative benefits to consumers from stability, and the question of access is subject to a tremendous degree of speculation as to the likelihood and feasibility of embargoes and other acts to limit access to one or more developed countries. Thus, the question arises as to whether commodity arrangements under the IPC should be supported by developed countries as a useful and effective form of economic assistance to the developing countries.

Commodity Agreements as an Aid Instrument

The basic argument against using commodity arrangements as an aid instrument is on the grounds of efficiency. If commodity prices are kept at levels higher than would have prevailed without the agreement, a transfer would occur. Except for short periods, higher prices could only be achieved through the use of supply restrictions. But supply restrictions may generate production inefficiencies, since too few resources would be allocated to the production of these commodities. The possibilities for misallocation are probably accentuated if some indexation measure relating commodity export prices to import prices is also used.

From the standpoint of the developed countries, the transfer of resources involved is equal to the reduced consumer surplus resulting from the higher prices. If they were interested in extending such assistance, they could do so through other means that do not involve these inefficiencies. But against these efficiency arguments, several points need to be raised. First, it is clear that competitive market conditions do not prevail in markets for many commodities. Thus, if monopsony imperfections exist, commodity agreements might partly offset them. While this would not necessarily result in reaching a competitive equilibrium solution, a more equitable distribution of benefits between producers and consumers may ensue. Second, of course, most other forms of aid also have imperfections and are not necessarily fully supportive of optimum resource allocation in developing countries. Third, aid through commodity arrangements has the advantage, as far as the developing countries are concerned, that it is more likely to be additional to other financing, in part because usually it would not require particular budget appropriations. In addition, it is of the highest possible quality, since it comes with no strings attached, either with respect to the use of the funds or with respect to internal developing-country policies. Developing countries in great need of additional resources might think little of the misallocation effects of commodity agreements. It should be quickly added that these very reasons make aid through commodity agreements unattractive to most developed-country donors concerned with developing-countries policy and implementation.

Another major issue in using commodity agreements as an aid instrument is equity. It has been argued that the countries that need aid the most may well end up as net losers if increased direct and indirect costs are taken into account. The actual situation is as usual quite complex. UNCTAD has shown (see Table 13-1) what is intuitively obvious: that developing countries have a much larger share in the exports of commodities under the IPC than in imports, and that

Table 13-1
World Trade in 10 Core Commodities (Average 1970-73)

Country Group Based on per Capita GNP	*Share of Commodity Exports of Total Exports*	*Share of Commodity Imports of Total Imports*
Up to $400	49.0	10.0
$401 to $1500	36.8	11.9
Above $1500	14.4	78.0
	100.0	100.0

Source: UNCTAD, TD/B/C.1/196/Add.1, October 7, 1975. The countries are grouped according to per capita gross national product, at market prices, in 1972. Exports are net of re-exports, and imports are retained imports. The source of per capita GNP data is the *World Bank Atlas, Population, Per Capita Product and Growth Rates,* Washington, 1974. The sources of trade data are FAO, *Trade Yearbook;* FAO, *Commodity Review and Outlook;* Commonwealth Secretariat, *Industrial Fibres;* and national statistics.

Totals do not sum to 100.0 because of rounding.

Table 13-2
Percentage Shares in Exports of Individual Core Commodities, 1970-1973 Average

	Commodities								
	Coffee		*Cocoa*		*Tea*		*Sugar*		*Cotton*
Income Group	*No. of Countries*	*Percent Share*	*No. of Countries*	*Percent Share*	*No. of Countries*	*Percent Share*	*No. of Countries*	*Percent Share*	*No. of Countries*
Low Income PCGNP ⩽ $500	11	28.1	11	81.6	14	96.5	4	10.9	8
Mid Income $500 ⩽ PCGNP ⩽ $1500	9	63.9	7	15.7	5	1.8	10	66.9	9
High Income PCGNP ⩾ $1500	0	0	2	1.2	1	1.6	6	12.5	3
Total	20	92.0	20	98.5	20	99.9	20	90.3	20

Source: The export share data were obtained from UNCTAD, TD/B/C.1/196, Table 3. The 1975 per capita GNP figures are from the 1976 *World Bank Atlas*.

exports are relatively evenly distributed among developing countries when they are grouped on a per capita income basis.

If we define countries with per capita income up to $400 in 1972 as low income,[14] those from $400 to $1500 as middle income, and those over $1500 as high income, we arrive at the figures in Table 13-1.

Around 50 percent of total exports of the 10 core commodities for the average period of 1970-1973 were from countries with a per capita GNP of less than $400 in 1972 (see Table 13-1). Countries with GNP per capita between $400 and $1500 accounted for another 37 percent of total exports. These two groups of countries together, i.e., all countries with less than $1500 GNP per capita, accounted for only around 22 percent of the imports of the 10 core commodities. The overall figures thus seem to indicate that the developing countries would tend to be important beneficiaries of the agreements.

Differences in the distribution of the benefits can be distinguished, however, if the aggregate data of Table 13-1 are broken down into export shares for each of the 10 core commodities (Table 13-2). Exports of three commodities, tea, jute and manufactures, and cocoa, are concentrated in countries with low income per capita (less than $500 GNP per capita in 1975). Coffee, copper, and sugar exports are concentrated in middle-income countries (between $500 and $1500 in 1975). In the case of tin, rubber, sisal, and cotton, export shares are fairly evenly distributed among countries with less than a $1500 income per capita.[15]

These figures can only be viewed as broadly indicative of benefits and costs

Commodities											
Cotton	*Jute*		*Sisal*		*Rubber*		*Copper*		*Tin*		
Percent Share	*No. of Coun- tries*	*Percent Share*	*No. of Coun- tries*	*Percent Share*	*No. of Coun- tries*	*Per- cent Share*	*No. of Coun- tries*	*Percent Share*	*No. of Coun- tries*	*Percent Share*
31.4	6	93.1	6	40.0	12	46.6	6	21.5	10	52.7
35.6	1	0.5	4	49.8	1	53.1	6	51.7	2	43.8
27.5	0	0	2	4.1	0	0	8	26.7	1	3.4
94.5	7	93.6	12	93.9	13	99.7	20	99.9	13	99.9

from action on commodities. While countries as a group might be net exporters of these commodities, individual countries may not be. Second, there is the question as to whether or not the "benefits" are supposed to derive from pure stabilization or from stabilization plus price increases.

Behrman (1976) estimated the increases of producers' real revenue as a result of the operations of a buffer stock for the period 1963–1972 for 8 of the 10 core commodities. He calculated what would be the present discounted value of increases in real revenue as a result of a successful stabilization of commodity prices around a price bandwith ±15 percent. Table 13-3 shows Behrman's estimates for the 8 core commodities according to our classification of commodities and countries.[16]

The big gainers would be rubber producers (equally distributed export shares), coffee (middle-income countries), and cocoa (low-income countries). It is interesting to note that Behrman's estimates show losses in revenue in the cases of copper and tin. It is hard to imagine that these agreements would continue in operation for a 10-year period if this happened. When Behrman simulated buffer stock operations with price increases of 2 percent every year, the estimates of Table 13-3 increased radically, by a factor of 21, and the distribution of the benefits significantly changed. For example, copper and tin producers would then have a positive gain rather than a loss, and coffee producers would account for only 25 percent of the overall gains rather than for more than half.

None of these calculations take into account the indirect costs of price

Table 13-3
Estimated Increase in Producers' Revenue under Stabilization Arrangements

Classification of Commodities	*Millions of Dollars*
Low-Income Countries:	
Tea	11.4
Jute and Manufactures	0.0
Cocoa	111.5
Middle-Income Countries:	
Coffee	266.2
Copper	-133.9
Sugar	No estimates available
Evenly Distributed Among Countries of Less than $1500	
Tin	-66
Rubber	224
Sisal	-1
Evenly Distributed Among All Producers	
Cotton	No estimates available
Overall Estimates for Eight Core Commodities	414.0

increases. General increases in commodity prices may well be transmitted back to developing countries through increased prices for their imports of manufactures. The distribution effects when these costs are taken into account are very difficult to predict, and no estimates are available.

Aid donors have preferred to focus their concessional assistance to the poorer developing countries and to the lower-income group within these countries in the recent past. On the basis of these criteria, gross benefits through commodity arrangements may be evenly distributed if the overall IPC is implemented. Even if that is the case, individual countries that import some but export more of the commodities could still lose. When indirect costs are taken into account, it is very difficult to say with certainty, with the exception of some few countries, which would benefit on a net basis and which would lose. Thus the biggest problem from an equity standpoint is the uncertainty of the distribution of benefits and costs once one goes beyond some of the more obvious beneficiaries, which are the large, established producers of particular commodities. Further, since there is no assurance that agreements can be concluded in all these IPC commodities, the probability is quite high that a commodity approach to aid will result in considerable inequities in the distribution of net benefits and costs.

Finally, it can also be argued that resource transfers through commodity agreements result in inequities within the developed consumer countries. The burden for making the transfer falls on consumers indiscriminately and could be regressive.

Common Fund Issues

The UNCTAD proposal for a Common Fund is based on the rationale that (1) advance assurance of adequate financing would accelerate the negotiation of effective commodity agreements; (2) the financial requirements of a Common Fund would be lower than those of equivalent individually financed arrangements; and (3) the management of stocking operations could concentrate on operational objectives, leaving the specialized management of sources of finance and administration of liquid funds to the Common Fund. In addition, it is claimed that the creation of a Common Fund would be a practical demonstration of the will of the international community to achieve a more equitable balance in the economic relationships between the developed and developing worlds in the commodities area.[17]

Advance Assurance of Financing

The need for a Common Fund has to be analyzed in the context of this rationale. Yet it is questionable whether a Common Fund is needed in order to guarantee the availability of financing for commodity agreements. It is easy to understand why strong proponents of commodity agreements, such as the UNCTAD Secretariat, would make this point. But their reasoning would be valid only if it could be demonstrated that lack of financing has been a major impediment to the establishment of commodity agreements. Although some agreements in the past, for example, tin, seem to have been underfinanced, the underfinancing might have been due more to the lack of agreement on the need for a buffer stock than to the lack of financing.[18] This fact highlights a major problem with the negotiation of the UNCTAD program—the negotiation of a Common Fund before negotiations of commodity objectives and operational rules of individual commodity agreements. Proponents of agreements who are completely committed to them as proper instruments of resource transfers and stabilizing prices and earnings would want to set up a pool of funds before the negotiation of individual agreements. They argue that commodity trade negotiations in the past have been plagued by procrastination tactics on the part of both consumers and producers, and that if a Common Fund is set up, thus making capital readily available, one of the major problems in the negotiations would be overcome.

Yet specific objectives and operational rules would affect the degree of support that the agreements would get from consumers and producers, as well as the amount of total financing needed for implementing the agreements. This should not be interpreted to mean that financing, for example, of a buffer stock in copper, will be easy, but rather that it is necessary first to decide the objectives and rules under which each commodity agreement would operate and then to look for the necessary financing.

Financing Requirements

A number of empirical estimates are now available that shed light on the feasibility of buffer stocks and the role they can play in commodity agreements. The UNCTAD Secretariat has released a series of financial estimates on the cost of operating buffer stocks for the 10 core commodities. The most recently released estimate is for \$4.5 billion to \$5 billion to finance stocking in the foreseeable future, assuming that agreements start operating in 1979.[19] To these figures, \$1 billion is added for activities other than stocking, such as diversification projects, research and development, and market promotion.

The UNCTAD Secretariat estimates are based on a number of assumptions. Some of the most important are (1) the Common Fund will be the sole source of financing; (2) no additional measures such as export promotion will be provided for in these agreements; (3) the price range in each agreement would be ±10 percent around a target price defined as either the 1971-1975 average in 1976 dollars or the projected 1974-1978 average in 1976 dollars; and (4) there will be no futures market activity. Other assumptions, such as the level of industrial activity in OECD countries, are also made. The estimates are quite sensitive to all these assumptions, and especially to changes in the target price or the price bandwith.

The financial estimate of \$4.5 billion to \$5 billion refers to the acquisition cost of the maximum size of stock necessary to achieve the goal of maintaining prices of each commodity within the range ±10 percent around the target price over the period 1979-1983.[20] The UNCTAD study claims that the method of calculation ensures that the required funds will exceed the indicated amount only in the unlikeliest events. For this reason, it is argued that the average amount required is rather less—in the region of \$3.3 billion. The additional \$1.2 billion to \$1.7 billion is to be used to provide a safety margin so that the price limits can be maintained by the stocking operations.

The disbursement of this \$3.3 billion will not have to occur immediately at the start of the agreements. UNCTAD calculations suggest that a Common Fund might only need to have in hand a sum up to \$2.5 billion for lending to the concerned commodity organizations at the beginning of 1979. It appears to them that it might be possible to phase the capital inflows to the Common Fund by raising one-half the total in the initial phase, of which \$1 billion would be paid-in capital, and $2 billion, loans. The remaining half could be paid in or raised later as required.

An assessment of the adequacy of the commodity models and the simulation techniques used by UNCTAD is beyond the scope of this chapter.[21] However, a series of questions can be raised about the results that are relevant for policy making:

1. How reliable are these financial estimates? The $4.5 billion to $5 billion is presented in terms of confidence intervals, but it is later argued that on the average only $3.3 billion would be needed. In this regard, it will also be desirable to explore the sensitivity of the results according to alternative specifications of the equations used to verify their robustness.

2. The financial estimates are very sensitive to the chosen target price. Price targets chosen by UNCTAD are probably on the high side by historical standards, especially for tin and cocoa. However, Behrman estimates that a more realistic figure would be around $10 billion to set up effective buffer stocks for price stabilization in the 10 core commodities except sugar and cotton. Furthermore, as noted earlier, the results are dramatically different depending on whether the objective is to stabilize prices around the trend or to raise prices.

3. There is no indication of whether there are remaining stocks at the end of the simulation period in 1983. Availability of stocks in the end period in the individual agreements is an important determinant of whether the buffer stock operations will be *self-financing* or not. If no stocks remain, the arrangement could probably not be viewed as self-financing, and the UNCTAD claim that the Common Fund would be a financially sound institution is doubtful.

4. There are very significant differences in the cost of the operation of individual buffer stocks, with copper and sugar being by far the most expensive. This leads us to believe that whatever overall figure is negotiated, if any, could prove quite inadequate if the individual commodity negotiations include provisions that deviate from the guidelines used at deriving the overall estimate. One could argue that a decision on the amount of resources available for stocking facilities before the negotiations of individual agreements would force the negotiators of these agreements to comply with the kind of guidelines used in the original overall estimate. Negotiators will probably be influenced by these guidelines, but it is doubtful that they will restrain themselves from making changes on commodity agreements of vital interest to their countries to comply with the Common Fund guidelines. In that case, there is no reason to believe that compatibility between individual agreements and Common Fund guidelines would be assured.

It is quite likely that pooling resources for individual buffer stocks could reduce overall financing requirements. To the extent that the correlation coefficient of commodity prices is not one, prices will move in different cycles and funds could be switched from one commodity market to the other. UNCTAD estimates that financing cost savings for stocks due to different price movements would amount to 25 percent. However, it remains to be seen how much flexibility there can be in actually moving funds around, since the negotiations of rules to switch funds from one commodity to the other will not be an easy matter.

Financing Sources

The current UNCTAD proposal for the setting up of a Common Fund calls initially for $1 billion paid-in capital and $2 billion in loans. The loans are supposed to be raised partly by individual governments and partly by the Common Fund itself. A debt/equity ratio of 2:1 is being considered by the UNCTAD Secretariat as a possible one for financing the Common Fund. The fund is supposed to earn an adequate net income to achieve a self-financing status.

The following comments about the Common Fund proposal would apply equally well to any fund envisioned as the basic source of commodity financing —whether the UNCTAD version or any other. First, the suggested debt/equity ratio is probably not acceptable for a new entity in international private money and capital markets. International financial institutions that have been able to borrow in the capital markets, such as the World Bank, the Interamerican Development Bank, and the Asian Development Bank, have had a 1:1 leverage ratio at AAA bond rating. Conceivably, the commodity stockpiles could provide the kind of collateral more acceptable to creditors, alowing a higher leverage ratio than the 1:1 ratio of the loan portfolio of development banks. Yet, the difficulties that international financial institutions have faced in breaking into the capital markets, despite the fact that they have been set up with unquestionable support from developed countries, should make one cautious in considering the possibility of a debt/equity ratio of 2:1. In addition, the Common Fund, unlike the development banks, has yet to establish a management record, which is also an important factor in determining security ratings.

Second, the fund's creditworthiness in capital markets will be determined in part by its expected profitability. Yet the profitability of stocking operations is hard to estimate. The basic problem is that there is bound to be a wide range of possibilities in the profitability of stocking operations making large profits or huge losses quite possible. Private investors are aware that there is bound to be high uncertainty in the profitability of stocking operations and, as a result, on the possibilities for self-financing of the Common Fund and hence are not likely to be easily persuaded to accept its offerings.[22] Thus the chances that the proposed Common Fund will be able to raise capital on its own are extremely small.

Third, UNCTAD asserts that the most important factor in determining the capacity of the Common Fund to raise capital is the readiness of the member governments to lend to the fund and to guarantee its financial commitments.[23]

The readiness of the governments to contribute to the Common Fund or guarantee its borrowings will depend, of course, on the goals of the commodity agreements that are going to use the fund resources. If developed countries were to guarantee Common Fund bonds, there would be no problem in its obtaining access to private credit. But government guarantee measures raise difficult questions of priorities for many developed countries. The United States, for example, does operate some guarantee programs that benefit developing countries' borrowings.[24] It is, however, questionable whether additional guarantees for this purpose would be given favorable consideration at the moment because of an interest in limiting the proliferation of guarantee programs that give rise to contingent liabilities outside the regular budgetary process.

In addition, a feasible scheme would have to be worked out in which commodity agreements that have a liquid position would lend to other buffer stock authorities through the Common Fund. The return the lenders receive from these loans would have to be competitive with alternative investments in money and capital markets. The profitability of the commodity agreements that are net borrowers from the fund will in this way partly determine the extent to which there is going to be pooling of funds.[25]

Management Issues

There is considerable anxiety, particularly among consuming countries, about the functions of the Common Fund, its management, and its link to operations of particular commodity agreements. The fear is that the management of the Common Fund, presumably dominated by developing countries, would exert a significant role in market operations and press for unrealistic price policies in individual commodity agreements.

One option recommended by UNCTAD is that managers of stocking operations concentrate on the stocking operations and that the Common Fund authorities manage the financial funds. However, this distinction is an artificial one. The possibilities for buffer stock operations are pretty much a function of the amount of available financing, and possibilities for tapping capital markets would depend on the kind of collateral that the stocking managers could offer.

One possible way of getting around this problem might be for the Common Fund to allocate periodically its funds among commodity agreements, with the stocking managers having to limit their operations to the level that can be financed with those funds. But setting up such an arrangement between the stocking and the Common Fund authorities would give the Common Fund authorities a lot of power in the administration of agreements. This arrangement is not likely to be practical unless one is convinced that giving the Common Fund a very strong voice in the management of the agreements will be in the best interest of all participants. This, of course, depends on one's point of view.

Since UNCTAD is viewed by developed countries as an institution promoting developing-countries interests, and these interests may be significantly different from those of developed countries, it is doubtful that such a role for the fund arrangement would be desirable or acceptable.

Buffer Stocks versus Other Commodity Objectives

Quite clearly, there are a variety of problems afflicting commodity markets that cannot be addressed by commodity agreements aimed at stabilizing or raising prices. The issue here is whether the Common Fund should be used to address these problems, and, if so, what should be the relative emphasis given to these problems compared to stocking operations.

Producers of commodities where demand is stagnant need to emphasize measures to stimulate demand, market research, and development of new uses. Demand problems in commodities such as jute can be traced in part to supply and price-instability problems relative to synthetic substitutes. Under these circumstances, the remedies should be sought more in improved supply conditions and market development than in the conclusion of international arrangements aimed at restricting supply or artificially increasing demand.

Diversification into other activities beyond those linked to particular commodities is also of obvious importance as a long-term solution to many commodity problems. Diversification is simple in principle and difficult in practice and is often synonymous with the difficult task of promoting agricultural development. In addition, the problem of expanding resource development investment in developing countries and promoting further processing may be a real one for some commodities and could also be addressed by the Common Fund.

Should the Common Fund address these issues, or can they be addressed adequately by other institutions? Would funds allocated for this purpose to the Common Fund be additional to those otherwise available? International financial institutions such as the IBRD or programs such as the UNDP can provide the type of financial and technical assistance needed by the developing countries. Since these are problems of general development, they can perhaps best be addressed by institutions that have this broad focus. Unfortunately, perhaps because of their broad focus, these institutions have not concentrated on these issues.

Additionality is difficult to prove or disprove. The main justification for setting up a new fund is to mobilize and focus attention on commodity problems, something that would not be achieved as effectively through existing institutions that have responsibility for promoting a variety of development objectives. The establishment of a properly functioning fund would also be a major political gesture to developing countries in an area in which they have expressed strong interest. Indeed, one possible alternative is that the fund have a very limited role in matters involving the operation of particular commodity agreements but become a conduit of funds for activities in support of other commodity problems.

Under such an arrangement, a Common Fund would not develop its own staff and expertise for the purpose of carrying out the specific assistance functions discussed above. Rather, it could use available expertise and technical resources of existing international institutions such as the IBRD and the various UN specialized agencies. There is no particular size for such a fund in the abstract. It could aim at contributions of $1 billion over a number of years plus whatever is negotiated for individual buffer stocks in support of individual commodity agreements. The terms of such assistance would vary depending on the financial capacity of the recipient. Provisions could also be made for periodical replenishment similar to those of IDA.

The mixture of assistance instruments and buffer stock financing could vary commodity by commodity. Resources of the fund need not be allocated in support of particular commodity agreements but be reserved to assist developing countries on commodities in which no stabilizing agreements have been concluded. Buffer stocks financing could be operated separately but integrated with different aspects of other assistance. A fund with such functions could well be set up separately or under the aegis of an existing financial institution such as the IBRD.

Conclusions

Commodity trade issues are at the center of the economic discussions between developing and developed countries. Progress in resolving some of the commodity issues will be important in setting the tone for discussion on other North-South issues. Continued confrontation, however, may sour North-South relations considerably.

The key elements in making progress should be found more in the commodity-agreements area and less in the Common Fund. From the point of view of the objective of increasing the stability of producers' earnings, it is better to achieve it directly by stabilizing export earnings. The experience of the recently liberalized facility of the IMF is encouraging in this respect. However, there are some other benefits from pure price stabilization both for producers and consumers that could form the basis for agreements in a number of commodities.

Pure price stabilization is not, however, the only pricing objective that producing countries are likely to pursue in commodity negotiations. In fact, producing countries are more interested in an improvement in their terms of trade. This objective presents consumers (mostly developed countries) with a policy decision as to what extent they are willing to use commodity agreements to transfer resources to developing countries. We have discussed how developed countries could evaluate commodity agreements in terms of their economic-assistance goals. The distribution of the direct benefits of higher commodity prices is less likely to be skewed if all commodities in UNCTAD's IPC are included. However, if only a few agreements are concluded, the benefits will undoubtedly be very skewed. Since there is no presumption that agreements should be concluded in all 10 commodities, this means that the possibility of inequitable distribution of benefits is quite serious. If one adds the potential indirect effects that could turn out to be quite important, the net impact on many countries could be negative. For these reasons and also because of the inefficiencies associated with this form of aid, we have serious doubts about the advisability of using commodity agreements to raise commodity prices.

We have not analyzed in detail the feasibility of commodity agreements for the 10 core commodities since such an analysis is beyond the scope of this chapter. In principle, it is feasible to set up buffer stocking operations in all these commodities. However, a careful cost-benefit analysis would have to be made in each case to determine whether the benefits warrant the costs of the agreements. In this respect, it should be pointed out that an optimistic prognosis for schemes that would raise prices indefinitely above equilibrium prices is bound to be proved unfounded since buffer stocks authorities would run out of funds.

We would recommend that both producing and consuming countries approach the negotiations of individual commodity agreements with an open mind about the possibilities for action. For some commodities, the possibilities for price stabilization might exist; for others, consumers might be willing to support somewhat higher prices that are not too unrealistic and could be defended over a reasonable period of time. For still other commodities, stocking operations might be so expensive or the competition from substitutes so intense that non-stocking measures might be more appropriate and international efforts should be concentrated on these kinds of measures.

In the end, choices will have to be made and agreements supported or opposed on the basis of incomplete information about the interests of participants or the effects of the agreement. The most one can say is that, if in doubt, the following additional criteria should be used by consuming countries in deciding to participate in an agreement or not: (1) whether or not more restrictive agreements resulting in higher prices might ensue if consuming countries did not participate; (2) whether or not the agreements are likely to yield benefits at a reasonable cost to commodity producers seriously harmed by commodity problems; and (3) whether or not the benefits are likely to be widely distributed within their population.

We see serious difficulties for negotiating a Common Fund before commodity agreements are negotiated. Despite what appears to be serious econometric work to estimate financing costs of stocking operations, these estimates could prove to be quite unrealistic. The plans for raising the Common Fund capital also appear to be too optimistic. The relationship of the fund to the individual agreements has not been fully specified, and it would be quite difficult to do this in general terms without the agreements in operation.

The possible gains of pooling resources of individual agreements can be better analyzed after the agreements are negotiated. If the Common Fund is envisioned as a pool of funds that would reduce the amount of financing needed to be raised as well as achieve some other economies of scale in its financial operation, then there is no real need to negotiate its organization prior to the negotiation of commodity agreements. If agreements can be negotiated over the course of the next two years, the negotiation of a Common Fund could probably be done in 1979, with the program beginning operations sometime in 1980. By negotiating commodity agreements first, more firm estimates can be made of the financing needed for stocking and other kinds of commodity activities. It will also be easier to negotiate more flexibility in the Common Fund operations. More realistic operating formulas for contribution and voting power in the fund would be negotiable if the importance of the different agreements and the major gainers and losers of the agreements are clearly identified.

This approach may not be enough to satisfy developing-country requests or to weaken the sense of confrontation that has permeated commodity discussions. The only additional possibility might be to start a small fund now whose functions would be primarily outside the scope of stabilization agreements. The need for additional efforts in this area is widely recognized. The only question is what institution should be used to address them. It makes good political sense to have it done by a new fund. However, such an approach entails considerable dangers. The main one is that such a fund may not be established without the incorporation of all the undesirable features of UNCTAD's current proposal. Prudent management practices of financial resources will be harder to establish in a new institution than in a funding arrangement under the auspices of an existing international financial institution such as the IBRD.

In the end, of course, whether or not a fund is established, and what it does will also depend on other elements in the North-South dialogue. While some of these elements are becoming more clear, it is still too early to say what is the type of bargain that can be struck.

Notes

1. International actions are envisioned for bananas, bauxite, cocoa, coffee, copper, cotton and cotton yarns, hard fibers and products, iron ore, jute and products, manganese, meat, phosphates, rubber, sugar, tea, tropical timber, tin, vegetable oils and oilseeds.

2. IBRD, *Price Prospects for Major Primary Products,* Report No. 814/76, June 1976.

3. In any event, terms of trade statistics can lead to misleading conclusions because of changes in the composition and in the quality of the products in the indices. Barter terms of trade are also not the most indicative statistics for the development impact of the price trends of traded goods, since they ignore changes in resource productivity over time. See the U.N. *Monthly Bulletin of Statistics* for terms of trade data.

4. D. Mathieson and R. McKinnon (1972); S. Naya (1973); C. Glezakos (1973); and C. Lawson (1974).

5. See Michalopoulos (1977); and Morrison and Perez (1975) for a discussion of the problems of export instability. For an opposite view, see Knudsen and Parnes (1975).

6. The export shortfalls were estimated by the IMF on a judgmental basis and negotiated with the borrowing countries. The main constraint to a 100 percent shortfall financing was the size of the country quotas. It is questionable whether a system should be devised that would fully compensate LDC exporters for the negative effects of export fluctuations, since full compensation would discourage diversification efforts.

7. See the IBRD report, *The Problem of Stabilization of Prices of Primary Products,* Chapter III, July 3, 1968, for a discussion of these conditions.

8. The simulation results in Behrman (1976) also show that price stabilization would have produced revenue stabilization for the period 1963-1972.

9. Direct intervention through production controls may be desirable in the case of commodities facing stagnant or declining demand. In such cases, their relative price would tend to decline over time thus presumably producing an incentive for factors of production to move to alternative employment. However, in many developing countries, their very underdevelopment often implies that alternative opportunities are limited and that individual producers faced with declining prices try to maximize income by producing more rather than less output, thus aggravating the problem. In this instance, government intervention to restrict supply may well be appropriate. Such action must be taken in conjunction with measures to diversify production and open up alternative employment opportunities—otherwise efforts to restrict supply alone may not be effective. But the objective in these cases is not to stabilize prices but essentially to redress a market imperfection.

10. These effects are discussed in Richard N. Cooper and Robert Z. Lawrence, "The 1972-75 Commodity Boom," *Brookings Papers on Economic Activity* 3:1975, pp 671-715.

11. See Massell (1970); and for welfare analysis of price stabilization under conditions of risk, see Turnovsky (1976, 1978); and Newbery (1976).

12. See the section on commodity agreements as instruments of aid below; and Behrman (1976).

13. Note that financing costs are not viewed here as an element affecting feasibility. They are important, nevertheless, and take the form of foregone

earnings from the resources invested in the stock. Since their size depends to a large extent on whether the objective of the buffer stock is to stabilize or raise prices, they are discussed in a later section where the overall costs and benefits of the IPC are evaluated.

14. Roughly equivalent to the IDA cutoff of \$375 in 1972, or \$500 in 1975 prices.

15. The benefits will, of course, be greater for the countries in each of the three categories that are more dependent on these commodities for their foreign exchange earnings.

16. See columns 8 and 9 of Behrman's Table V. Behrman uses 2 percent and 5 percent as two alternative discount rates. The results discussed are those with the 5 percent discount rate. The increases were estimated by comparing the revenue of producers under the stabilization schemes to that estimated by his commodity models without stabilization.

17. UNCTAD, *Consideration of Issues Relating to the Establishment and Operation of a Common Fund,* TD/B/IPC/CF/2, November 10, 1976.

18. The IMF Buffer Stock Facility has not been used extensively since its establishment. Although it might have not been used partly because its lending conditions might be too restrictive and too country-oriented, it is surprising that there seems to have been so little activity if lack of financing was a real deterrent to the formation of buffer stocks.

19. See UNCTAD, *Consideration of Issues Relating to the Establishment and Operations of a Common Fund,* TD/B/IPC/CF/L.2, December 29, 1976.

20. This estimate is given with a probability of success between 80 to 95 percent confidence. The model system is stochastic and the simulations generate a frequency distribution of stocking requirements of each commodity. See UNCTAD, Table 3.

21. Annex II of publication TD/B/IPC/CF/L.2 discusses the simulation procedures. Although it is not easy to tell from the annex, it seems that the Monte Carlo experiments carried out were based on random shocks only on the supply side. It is not clear whether random shocks were also introduced from the demand side, which might be quite crucial for some commodities, although it is claimed that changes in global demand were taken into account.

22. Note also that the fund would have to charge interest on its lending to individual agreements. The latter must be sufficiently profitable to be able to incur this cost so that the whole operation is self-financing.

23. UNCTAD, *Consideration of Issues Relating to the Establishment and Operation of a Common Fund,* TD/B/IPC/CF/2.

24. For example, the Housing Investment Guarantee.

25. If the fund is set up as a pool of funds, it is clear how this situation will arise. But even if the Common Fund is set up as a source of funds, some of the capital might still be raised through the individual commodity organizations. The question of alternative uses for these funds will still be relevant for members of

individual agreements that contribute some of their capital to the Common Fund.

References

Behrman, J. "International Commodity Agreements." Prepared as part of the Overseas Development Council New International Economic Order Research Project, October 30, 1976. Mimeographed.

Cooper, R., and R. Lawrence, "The 1972–75 Commodity Boom." Brookings Papers on Economic Activity (3:1975):671-675.

Glezakos, C. "Export Instability and Economic Growth: A Statistical Verification." *Economic Development and Cultural Change* (July 1973):670–678.

IBRD. *Price Prospects for Major Primary Products.* Report No. 814/76. June 1976.

——. *The Problem of Stabilization of Prices of Primary Products.* July 1968.

Knudsen, O., and A. Parnes. *Trade Instability and Economic Development.* Lexington, Mass.: Lexington Books, D.C. Heath, 1975.

Lawson, C. "The Decline in World Export Instability: A Reappraisal." *Oxford Bulletin of Economics and Statistics,* 1974.

MacAvoy, P.W., and D.L. McNicol. "The Benefits and Costs of Participation in International Commodity Agreements." Council of Economic Advisors, August 1976. Mimeographed.

Massell, B., "Some Welfare Implications of International Price Stabilization." *Journal of Political Economy* 78 (1970).

Mathieson, D., and R. McKinnon. "Instability in Underdeveloped Countries: The Impact of International Economy," 1972. Mimeographed.

Michalopoulos, C., "U.S. Commodity Trade Policy and the Developing Countries." A.I.D. Discussion Paper No. 37, Bureau for Program and Policy Coordination, January 1977.

Morrison, T., and L. Perez. "Export Earnings Fluctuations and Economic Development: An Analysis of Compensatory Financing Schemes." A.I.D. Discussion Paper No. 32, Bureau for Program and Policy Coordination, September 1975.

Naya, S. "Fluctuations in Export Earnings and Economic Patterns of Asian Countries." *Economic Development and Cultural Change* (July 1973): 629-641.

Newbery, D., "Price Stabilization with Risky Production." Stanford University, 1976. Mimeographed.

Turnovsky, S.J. "The Distribution of Welfare Gains from Price Stabilization: The Case of Multiplicative Disturbances." *International Economic Review* 17, 1 (February 1976).

——. "The Distribution of Welfare Gains from Price Stabilization: A Survey of Some Theoretical Issues." in *Stabilizing World Commodity Markets,* eds. F. Gerard Adams and Sonia Klein, Lexington, Mass.: Lexington Books, D.C. Heath, 1978.

United Nations. *Monthly Bulletin of Statistics.* (Various issues).

UNCTAD. "Consideration of Issues Relating to the Establishment and Operation of a Common Fund." TD/B/IPC/CF/2, November 10, 1976.

14 A Hard Look at Prospects for Commodity Agreements

*Helen B. Junz** and *Paul MacAvoy*

Introduction

The pricing of raw materials has been a concern of governments for many years, and the perception that national interests can be at stake has been confirmed by recent experience. Abrupt changes in demand and in various factors affecting supply, such as weather conditions and crop diseases can lead to large price swings, which in turn could affect supplying countries' national income and consuming countries' price behavior. At the least, these swings complicate investment decisions and tend to raise questions about the long-run supply availabilities of that commodity, even if it does not bulk large in national income.

But why should instability in commodity markets give rise to public policy problems to a greater extent than do demand and supply fluctuations in other industries? Historically, the problem of instability in commodity markets has been left to producers to solve. However, during the past couple of decades, the mutuality of concerns of consuming and producing nations has become more pronounced. Boom-bust commodity cycles detrimental to consumers and producers alike have been more pronounced or at least more publicized. At the same time, downward inflexibility of prices and wages in industrialized countries has also become more pronounced. Within this context, commodity price swings fuel inflationary tendencies in the consuming countries and these price pressures become embedded in wage structures which in turn are transmitted to the producing countries via higher import prices. Given these conditions, both producing and consuming countries have recognized the desirability of finding ways and means to bring about greater stability of commodity prices.

In recent years, however, the concern for price stabilization, at least on the part of developing countries, has broadened into increasing pressure for policy action on a much wider range of issues. Their main objective has been to increase their access to financial resources on an automatic and freely usable basis. In this respect, pressures have increased further because aid flows to developing

*The opinions expressed are those of the author and do not necessarily reflect those of the institutions with which she is associated.

countries, while continuing to rise in nominal terms, have actually fallen in real terms over the past decade. In addition, rising nationalism has sharpened the desire of the authorities in producing countries to obtain control of natural resources as a matter of obtaining economic power.

These efforts have been intensified in recent years following the supply shortages of 1973–74 and the success of the cartel action of the Organization of Oil Producing Countries (OPEC). As a consequence, political demands in recent years have concentrated on changes in international monetary arrangements that would give developing countries a greater voice in decision making, provide greater access to international financial resources on an unconditional basis, and that would establish commodity agreements to increase export earnings. In pursuing these aims less-developed countries (LDCs) have shown considerable political cohesion, in a full schedule of international conferences in various forums. Consequently, a considerable momentum has been created for positive consideration of a number of these demands, in particular, in the area of commodity agreements.

This chapter summarizes work on the analytical basis for making a case for strengthening current and adding further commodity agreements and evaluates the elements required to make such agreements effective. It appears that agreements that would serve the dual purposes of assuring increased investment flows and steadily growing export earnings to the LDCs require institutions and supply-demand conditions that do not generally exist. Even worse, a number of arrangements advocated by the LDCs themselves would not only fail to achieve their stated aims but might actually be counterproductive from their point of view. For consuming countries, such agreements to the extent that they lead to price distortions would be costly in domestic economic terms and to the extent that they did not achieve the goals of producing countries would tend to result in political losses. More positive responses that balance the interests of producing and consuming countries are needed. Above all there is a growing need, here and abroad, to cut through political rhetoric to the realistic solutions that are in the interest of consumers and producers in developed and developing countries alike.

The Sources of Initiative for Commodity Agreements

During the last five years, commodity policy has moved to the center of the work program of several international conferences, and detailed analysis and discussion of commodity issues is taking place in various international bodies. The success of OPEC in quadrupling the price of oil in 1973–74 and thereby redistributing a considerable amount of world income has increased the aspirations and expectations of other commodity producing countries regarding their own wealth positions. In addition, the unprecedented price boom for commodities in 1973–74, which had given rise to concerns regarding the longer-run adequacy of raw material supplies, gave further impetus to commodity producers to attempt to stabilize export earnings at peak levels. Subsequently, the financial requirements associated with high energy prices and the worldwide recession that followed the inflationary boom and the OPEC price decision sharpened the desire of non oil commodity producers either to emulate OPEC or at least to obtain higher export prices through commodity agreements.

The basic arguments put forward by the LDCs in favor of commodity agreements are two-fold: (1) commodity prices and export earnings fluctuate widely for reasons that are outside the control of the commodity producing countries—more directly, policies in industrialized countries create inflation and recession and the LDCs should be insulated from the effects of such policies; and (2) there has been a longer-run trend deterioration in the terms of trade of commodity-producing countries—prices of goods and services imported from industrialized countries on average have tended to rise more than have commodity prices. It is further argued that the technological advances and productivity increases in primary commodities tend to benefit the consuming countries only, while the inverse obtains for exports of industrialized countries. Given this view, a large part of the current demands of LDCs for fundamental changes in international economic arrangements centers on ways to increase their returns on the production of primary commodities and on arrangements that tie commodity prices to changes in prices for manufactured imports.

The evidence of deterioration in the terms of trade of primary producing countries, however, is not convincing. An expert group convened by the United Nations Conference on Trade and Development (UNCTAD) concluded on the basis of data running from 1900 to the early 1970s that, while fluctuations had been considerable over the period, no "clear evidence of long-term deterioration in the net barter terms of trade of developing countries" could be found. A subsequent study by the UNCTAD Secretariat based on data starting in 1953 did indicate that, indeed, there was a trend toward such deterioration. Thus, depending on the time periods chosen, and particularly depending on the starting point, widely divergent conclusions can emerge. The recent experience of considerable deterioration in the terms of trade of primary producing countries, of course, follows directly from starting the analysis with the 1973–74 cyclical high.

Perhaps more important, the increase in the price of crude oil itself has had very significant effects on the terms of trade of producing and consuming countries. In the industrial countries, increases in the price of energy directly accounted for perhaps one-third of the increase in the wholesale price index in 1974 and the indirect effects are still working their way through the various economies. The decline in the nonoil developing countries' terms of trade in 1974 and 1975 must be attributed to a very significant extent to the direct and indirect effects of the increase in the price of oil. In fact, because of the composition of trade of a number of nonoil developing countries, the effects of the oil-price increase on their trading positions have been greater than those for many other countries.

But even if clear evidence could be found regarding a trend deterioration in the terms of trade of primary producing countries, this by itself still would not furnish a basis for arguing for large commodity price increases. The terms of trade do not provide a sound basis for policy formulation, as they represent no more than the unit value of a given bundle of exports relative to that of imports at a given moment in time. Since the composition of imports of LDCs changes over time, as economic progress and rising living standards are coupled with rising demand for more sophisticated products, an apparent "deterioration" in the terms of trade may actually reflect considerable gains in well-being for these countries.

More important, it makes little sense to talk about "improvement" or "deterioration" of terms of trade on the basis of arithmetic only. If, because of substantial increases in demands at home, export prices rise, there may be a very significant recorded improvement in the terms of trade of the country in question. But, if in the process, that country's export products are priced out of the world market, the improvement in its terms of trade will lead to a considerable deterioration in its trade balance. Conversely, if export prices fall because of large productivity increases the implied deterioration in the terms of trade indicate very little, if anything, about the welfare effects of trade developments and the amount of local resources needed to obtain a certain amount of foreign resources.

Regardless of the thinness of the arguments put forward for increases in commodity prices, concern about the level of export earnings clearly is understandable, particularly in an environment where domestic financial demands in the LDCs have increased because of rising oil prices. Thus, it is not surprising that with increasing political cohesion among developing countries, commodity policy has become a central item on the LDCs' agenda in the dialogue with the industrialized consuming nations.

The LDCs appearance as a bloc dates from the first UNCTAD, held in 1964, when they formed the Group of 77, which now includes more than 110 nations. It is through this forum that the LDCs formulated and voiced their demands for a new international economic order in 1974. In a first demonstration of the effectiveness of the Group of 77's political cohesion, the United Nations General Assembly adopted a resolution in May 1974 that directed the UNCTAD Secretariat to prepare specific measures for a Program of Action on the Establishment of a New International Economic Order. From this emerged the so-called Integrated Program (IP) for commodities put forward by the Group of 77 at UNCTAD IV in 1976, the central feature of which is the establishment of buffer stocks for 18 "core" commodities spanning the main exports of primary commodity producers. The core commodities include metals (copper, tin, iron ore), materials (sisal, jute, wool), and foodstuffs (rice, wheat, sugar, beef, tea, coffee, and cocoa).

Agreements for separate commodities would be held together by a Common

Fund that would finance buffer stocks across the spectrum of commodities. The common fund would acquire physical stocks as market conditions required, with repayment made when the stock was sold off. Thus, one or the other buffer stock organization would be bolstered by financial resources from the others, thereby binding producing countries together regardless of which commodities were of principal interest to each country.

In addition, the common fund would finance activities other than buffer stocks, particularly in the area of marketing, distribution and technology. Financing is to come from producing and consuming countries, OPEC, multilateral institutions and loans raised on private capital markets. It is to be in place before the separate agreements setting up individual buffer stocks are actually concluded. In addition to setting up buffer stocks, the IP's system of commodity agreements would rely on export quotas and production controls that would determine the quantity each country sold each year. Whatever the targets or the target-achieving mechanism, the IP makes it clear that the objective would be both to reduce variation in and increase the level of commodity prices.

The Developed Nations' Response

The industrialized nations have long accepted the principle that instability of export earnings of LDCs constitutes a significant impediment to development and to the optimal use of resources. It is precisely to reduce this instability that the Compensatory Financing Facility (CFF) and Bufferstock Facilities (BF) of the International Monetary Fund (IMF) were established. When producing countries experience external financial difficulties at the same time that export earnings decline below a given trend for reasons outside the control of the exporting country, the CFF extends loans to cover the reductions in earnings.

But the industrialized countries have not accepted the notion that more can and should be done. Both developed and developing countries recognize that stable noninflationary growth worldwide is the basic prerequisite for the achievement of growth in export earnings of LDCs and that economic policies must aim to achieve the most effective use of available resources. But the developed countries argue that restrictive agreements or other artificial means for achieving higher LDC income in lieu of such macroeconomic policy measures will, of their nature, not be successful in the long run. Thus, measures such as attempts to relate the price of a particular commodity to that of some other good or bundle of goods, or to freeze the so-called terms of trade of a particular country, will tend to introduce distortions into the economy in question as well as into the world economy. If prices so determined tend to be higher than world market supply and demand relationships would produce, they will add to the inflationary impetus in both consuming and producing countries. This will occur directly through the required index price increases and indirectly through overinvestment in production facilities either for the goods in question or for substitutes whose production was uneconomic at competitive prices. If prices were to be lower than market forces would indicate, underinvestment and supply shortages would result. In either case, the eventual outcome would be detrimental to producers as well as consumers.

Indexation of commodity prices or artificial increases through restrictive agreements may well generate significant additional income for producing countries in the short-run. The inelasticity of demand for many commodities included in the IP would allow price rises to be passed on to consumers and generate considerable increases in producers' revenues, at least for some period of time. A moderate increase in the price level for wool, wheat, rice, and sugar alone could add up to about $10 billion annually to the incomes of producing countries.[1] But only a fraction of this increase would accrue to LDCs. The developed countries produce a substantial share of these commodities and would, therefore, receive substantial shares of the additional incomes. Moreover, the LDCs generally are large consumers of these products and their collective net gains would be reduced accordingly. And the poorest among them would be net losers, since they are net importers of most of these commodities.

Thus the developed countries have rejected commodity schemes that involve indexation arrangements. However, there is ambivalence in these countries' attitude towards stabilization of commodity markets. With regard to the question of what kind of commodity arrangement might be generally beneficial, views range widely. Some countries, Sweden and the Netherlands, for example, are basically willing to accept the main proposals contained in the IP. Others, recognizing that each commodity presents different production, pricing, and marketing problems, have preferred a case-by-case approach to agreements. But the developed countries have agreed that for those commodities for which buffer stocks can be negotiated, a pooling of financial resources among buffer stock organizations could yield advantages. Total funding needs normally would be less than if each commodity organization operated separately, because fluctuations among stock operations would be partially offsetting. Also, borrowing costs might be reduced and investment earnings increased because a pooling operation might allow a stretching out of maturities. Although agreements aimed at damping price fluctuations are generally thought to be desirable, most developed countries continue to oppose commodity arrangements that operate not only to decrease the instability of commodity prices but also to increase the levels of prices and thus the returns to producing countries above their long-term trends.

The Value of Pure Commodity Agreements

Agreements to set prices work some of the time, with some of those involved in purchases or sales benefiting thereby. In theory, a "pure" agreement to operate a buffer stock and thereby buy or sell against market-determined price changes can result in price stability that could benefit both buyers and sellers. Consider first the conditions that result in gains for producers. A "pure" commodity agreement could be put into effect in which buffer stocks are created by buying in low price periods and are depleted during high price periods, but where there are no attempts made to reduce the total amounts sold over the full price cycle. If demand is steady but supply changes by gradations from low to high, depending on the size of the crop or storage conditions, producers gain from low supply because price is high, but lose from high supply because price is low. Price stabilization in these circumstances increases producers' revenues over the cycle because more is received from raising prices in surplus periods than is lost from lowering prices during shortage periods.

Buyers, of course, lose by this price stabilization, since they pay relatively more for the commodity during the larger-volume periods when the agreement is holding product off the market. The higher prices then are compensated for in part by buyer gains from price reductions during stock sale periods, but only in part, because with the greater purchases occurring at higher prices the gains always fall short of the losses.

This is only one possible set of conditions, however. When demand varies while supply is fixed, buyers gain while sellers lose. In markets where both supply and demand vary substantially, either producers or consumers could gain. Suppliers may gain while buyers lose, if supply varies more; or buyers may gain while suppliers lose, if demand varies more.

The general pattern suggests that if the group that gains shares returns with the losers, both buyers and sellers could be made better off. Buyers could share net economy-wide gains with sellers by, for example, proposing pricing rules for a buffer stock that keep prices somewhat higher than for an "ever-normal granary." But such rules are extremely difficult to design and put into effect without producing unduly large long-run surpluses from which neither producers nor consumers gain. Another important reservation is that the forecast gains depend on equilibrium conditions in perfect markets and, as shown by Turnovsky, if these conditions do not hold, gains for either or both groups are not clearly delineated.

Could not as much be achieved without commodity agreements? Producers hold stocks when it is likely to be profitable to do so. With spot and futures markets for buying and selling stocks, prices are probably more stable than they would be otherwise, and overall gains are thereby obtained, although quantification of the stabilizing effect of such buying and selling is difficult and the estimations of some important past results have been controversial.[2] In any case the existence of futures markets reduces the need for commodity agreements that use a buffer stock to stabilize prices. But even where the suppliers or consumers can purchase insurance of a sort against price variations on a futures market, a buffer stock can reduce variations further and provide more insurance.[3] In addition, given the length of cyclical swings in prices in many commodities and the relatively short span of available futures contracts, futures markets may fall considerably short of eliminating the price instability that could economically be done away with. For example, there seems to be a 9-year cycle in sugar, but sugar contracts only run 18 months forward so they cannot deal with average cyclical instability. For most commodities, underlying cycles appear to be considerably longer than the forward contracts normally offered. Therefore, commodity agreements could play a positive role in further alleviating cyclical price fluctuations.[4] And a buffer stock organization that stabilized prices could be an acceptable way of bringing about the benefits attendant upon stabilization. The question remains whether the benefits to be derived from buffer stocks exceed their costs.

The Costs and Benefits of "Real-World" Buffer Stock Arrangements

The buffer stock supports prices during periods of excess supply by buying the commodity in question and limits the increase in prices during periods of tight supply by selling off the stocks purchased previously. In theory, the considerably damped series of prices should average to the long-term trend that would have occurred over the cycle. In practice, price movements resulting from buffer stock operations do not even out in that pattern. In fact, results have varied so greatly, and the documentation of these results has been so limited that no consistent pattern can be ascertained at this time.

Some indications of what might happen have been provided by computer simulations of sample markets assuming that either supply or demand varies by ±10 percent around long-run trend values for one-third of the time. Using estimates of the relevant elasticities, the simulations show that the potential gains from price stabilization for wool, wheat, rice, sugar and coffee are quite large. Since most of the year-to-year changes in these commodities occur on the supply side, the gains would mainly accrue to producers. The gains associated with buffer stocks for copper, iron ore, and tin would be smaller, and because buffer stock operations would damp the price effects of demand fluctuations, they would tend to accrue to consumers. These estimated gains from price stabilization can be compared with the annual costs of running the buffer stocks (assuming that total annual charges amount to 15 percent of the maximum capital costs of the inventory).

Calculated benefits for producers exceed costs for four commodities, cocoa, coffee, rice, and sugar.[5] Significant net benefits accrue to consumers only in the case of iron ore. The overall results imply that costs of most of the proposed buffer stocks tend to exceed or roughly equal the benefits, so that the quantitative estimates of gains do not provide a clear argument in favor of buffer stocks.

Even in cases of large benefit-cost differentials, the merits of buffer stock agreements cannot be established fully unless other conditions necessary for efficient operation of a buffer stock are present. First, operating a buffer stock is feasible only for commodities for which there are broadly based spot and futures markets. The lack of such markets rules out buffer stocks for rice, for example, at least until such time when spot and futures contracts for this product can be concluded. A second and more controversial condition pertains to the structural characteristics of the industry. Pure buffer stock agreements can only operate if there are no monopoly or oligopoly controls on production or sales. In practice, some such controls tend to be part of some commodity agreements, raising the possibility that they are to be used to restrict supply for the purpose of raising price levels. The greater the concentration among producing countries and the higher the barriers to entry for other sources of supply, the greater the chance that a buffer stock can be used restrictively.

Where restrictive agreements have been tried under oligopolistic production conditions, they have tended to be unstable. There are many problems in collusive operation of such complicated agreements. Agreements that raise prices create strong incentives for price reductions by any one producing country fearful of losing its market share. Moreover, any one supplier can increase his profits by making additional sales beyond those in his allotted share by discounting or otherwise reducing prices. If there is a large number of market participants, detection of discounting becomes difficult and, even if individual output is small, price breakdowns will occur frequently. Shipments in excess of quota by some producing countries eventually will force all prices down, in many cases below the level that would have been realized without any agreement at all. In addition, entry into an industry becomes more attractive as price is increased. And as entry occurs, market shares for producers within the agreements must fall if the higher price is to be sustained. But this reduces capacity utilization and eventually profits to, or even below, the levels existing before the agreement.

There probably would be substantial difficulties along these lines with the operations of price-increase agreements for the commodities included in the IP. However, where agreements aim only to stabilize prices around their long-term trend values, net gains may well be such as to warrant serious attempts to negotiate such agreements. Calculations show that effects of price stabilization agreements on inflation rates in consuming countries could be considerable. As a consequence, output and employment levels in both consuming and producing countries could be measurably higher than in the absence of price stabilization agreements. But past experience with commodity agreements indicates that strong short-term political incentives exist among producers to attempt to transform pure price stabilization agreements into restrictive agreements. Consequently, potential gains from price stabilization have been difficult to realize.

Lessons from the Past

For some commodities included in the IP, there is a history of efforts to stabilize markets. There have been several agreements of various sorts for tin, rubber, copper, coffee, sugar, cocoa, and wheat.

International agreements among tin producers date from the 1920s; those involving producer and consumer participation have existed only since the mid-1950s. The recurrent problem with the Tin Agreement has been that buffer stocks have been too small. In periods of high prices, the stock was insufficient to defend the target ceiling price, leading to upward movements in the buffer stock's price range. In periods of low prices, export controls were used to protect the floor price. These controls, coupled with variable export taxes in a number of producing countries, led to decreases in production and have inhibited investment. Consequently, in periods of high demand, shortages and price increases have been intensified.

The operation of agreements for the copper industry has not been successful on any accounting. Conditions in the copper market have not been favorable for operating commodity agreements; although the number of producing firms and countries in the industry has been relatively small, there has been no uniformity of interest among the producing countries; and collective control has been limited by price changes for aluminum and by cyclical changes in the demand for metals. Nevertheless, several attempts to formulate agreements have been made, the most successful taking place between 1964 and 1966. After some months of rising prices, however, price discounting began and the coordination of supplies among producers collapsed. Reforms were attempted one after another, with the most recent experience being the formation of a producers' association (CIPEC) among Chile, Peru, Zaire, and Zambia. In this latest venture, as with earlier agreements, voluntary restrictions of exports were called for but failed to obtain a significant response.

The history of the coffee agreements is a checkered one. The 1964 agreement, which followed a 10-year rise and fall price cycle, was a market-sharing agreement with export controls to be enforced by importing countries. The 1964 agreement was successful at maintaining prices at relatively stable levels, but at the cost of a short-fall in investment. Demand had a tendency to outrun supply in recent years and supply shortages were exacerbated by poor weather and interruptions of production in some major producing countries. Even so, there is no evidence that prices were ever increased above the long-run trend level consistent with an open market. The problem was that the agreement was unable to contain wide price swings. The 1976 agreement, though essentially also a market sharing/export quota arrangement, provides considerable incentive for stock holding. Thus it offers the possibility for smoother supply availabilities and less fluctuation in prices than in the past.

Mention should be made of attempts at agreements in sugar and cocoa as well. None of the postwar sugar agreements in effect from 1954, and on a restructured basis from 1968 to 1972, seems to have had a significant effect on price levels or changes, at least on the surface. The agreements might have stemmed what would otherwise have been larger price declines, but that is a speculative argument. Prices in the first year of the 1965 International Sugar Agreement fell by 4.4 percent and after the ISA was reorganized in 1968 prices fell that year by 0.5 percent. Although prices increased with the general price level in 1969-72, the ISA control provisions were suspended in 1972 when sugar prices started their most precipitous climb and terminated in 1973 after disagreement between producers and importers on appropriate price ranges. During this series of attempts to make the ISA effective, United States domestic policy had been the driving force in the sugar market. The United States sugar price was nearly always higher than the free market price. If world supplies were large and the United States imported little, free market prices dropped. If supplies were tight but the United States sought increased imports, they were usually forthcoming even if, for a short period, the free market price exceeded the United States price, since the benefits to producing nations of the United States program were simply too great for those countries to risk not fulfilling the quota. The ISA's effect on the level of sugar prices was distinctly secondary to that of the United States when it played the role of willing buyer at higher prices.

The cocoa agreement included two attempts to restrict output by producers in the 1960s. An effort in 1962 failed owing to the lack of cooperation of important Latin American producers. Subsequently, the Cocoa Producers' Alliance, consisting of Ghana, Nigeria, Brazil, Ivory Coast, Cameroon Republic, and Togo, tried to withhold part of the 1964-1965 crop. The move failed because of uneven compliance and because consumers were able to outlast the alliance by running down stocks. In 1972 an International Cocoa Agreement was negotiated, the main elements of which were a rigidly targeted price range below which export quotas would go into effect, and a stock arrangement whereby surplus stocks would be stored in the consuming countries. The agreement was not tested, however, because soon after signing, prices increased beyond the ceiling price level. The 1975 Cocoa Agreement was negotiated amidst disagreements among producers and consumers as to price targets and the need for export controls, but it has remained inoperative since it came into force.

The Economic/Political Dimension

Commodity agreements have been evaluated here in terms of their economic effects, or as revenues and costs to producers and consumers. But such economic effects were not the only consideration behind the recent push for commodity agreements. Rather, the Integrated Program was put forward to accomplish for metals, materials, and food producing countries what OPEC had gained for the oil-producing countries—both increased revenues from domestic production and increased self-respect and leverage in political dealings with Western Europe, North America, and Japan. This was to be achieved by agreements that in most cases would be assumed to include higher prices, higher incomes for producing countries, and a more important political position for UNCTAD and the producing nations in the spectrum of international organizations.

Are these the most likely economic and political results? For a short period, they indeed could be. A fully constituted IP operating along lines of a cartel with control of inventories across commodities could increase prices across member commodities so as to bring about a transfer of resources similar to that resulting from the OPEC price increase of 1973–74.[6] An increase in relative political power for the program's proponents might follow this price hike, at least for as long as the higher prices for the 18 commodities continued to hold.

For these results to be lasting, however, managers of the agreements would have to be able to control supply and limit entry into production of these commodities. But the concentration in ownership of production facilities and the internal political cohesion that governs the relations between members of OPEC would not be present among copper, tin, coffee, or cocoa producers. In fact, these conditions do not seem to be there for any of the dozen most important commodities potentially in the IP. There are too many sources of supply, too much excess capacity, and too much opportunity to enter for the present-day political cohesion to hold prices for more than two or three years. And without the ability to set higher prices the agreements could scarcely claim that they have resulted in increased political independence for member producer nations.

Where does that leave the movement for comprehensive coverage of commodities by agreements, and for common funding of agreements? Currently there is a greater chance that agreements for a dozen or more commodities might be viable than indicated by this history of failure, because there are now "extraordinary" conditions present that will make them work better. The most important of these conditions is the assistance of consuming countries in financing and enforcing agreements. If consuming countries joined and enforced commodity agreements, because of benefits they derived from a reduction in price fluctuations and from political advantages, agreements might work in certain industries. But even then, the promising candidates for effective agreements are limited, with tin, copper, bauxite, and rubber the most promising.

Recent experience within the Tin Agreement, for example, shows that even under a relatively favorable set of arrangements, the agreements tend to run into considerable difficulties. While defense of a floor price theoretically is virtually in the hands of the members of the agreements—as long as there is a willingness to cut back on supplies—this is not true for the price ceiling. Once stocks have been depleted, the ceiling price cannot be held unless supplies are elastic. Since the latter usually are inelastic, at least in the short-run, there will be considerable pressure among producers to raise the agreed price range permanently.

But under these conditions, buying countries would have to make serious efforts to control price cuts at a later stage. These efforts would likely involve not only buffer stocks, but also export controls and production limits. But such restrictions put upward pressure on domestic prices in buying countries. In the case of the United States, for example, moderate price increases for all the food products, metals, and materials included in the IP would likely add about two percentage points each to the wholesale and consumer price index. As these price increases would be seen to result from the government's participation in price-raising agreements, they would create a strong adverse political reaction.

The domestic political problems for consuming countries would be compounded, particularly in the case of agreements in metals production, which currently have the greatest chance of actually being concluded. Many consuming countries, chiefly the United States, have extensive supply capacity in copper, tin, and other metals. Whether capacity is in the form of stockpiles or reserves, it is held mainly by private corporations (except for tin). To enforce production or sales limits on them would require that buying countries control the outputs of their own domestic companies in a way that would violate antitrust prohibitions. The buying governments would have to suspend laws against cartels or combinations in restraint of trade for the copper and aluminum companies. As world prices of metals increased, and domestic wholesale and consumer price indices rose, the commitment of governments to such policies in restraint of trade in domestic markets would be put under more political pressure.

And even if the buying countries held firm in the face of consumer pressures at home, their actions would not be sufficient to hold the agreements together in the face of pressures from new entrants, and from expanded supplies of countries outside the agreement. Either way, the breakdown would occur and would eventually be blamed on the managers—in this case on the buying countries. In the long run, the political effects could well be worse than those associated with not providing the enforcing mechanism in the first place.

Thus the structure of the commodity markets, as well as past history, suggest that restrictive agreements are unlikely to be successful for more than a few years. Furthermore, as commodity agreements began to fail, they would create just the divisive issues between producing and consuming nations that participants were seeking to avoid.

What should be done? First, it is necessary to view with considerable realism what can be achieved. If developed countries enter into commodity agreements hoping that political difficulties can be defused thereby at very little real cost, they will soon be faced with both the reality of the continuing financing needs of the LDCs and commodity arrangements that may prove costly in an economic as well as political sense. If LDCs hope to obtain a large part of the transfer of resources they seek through commodity arrangements, the above analysis shows that actual revenue gains will fall far short of such expectations. All parties should recognize that stabilizing or raising prices does not necessarily imply stabilizing or raising export earnings and incomes. The temptation to take the short-run political gains in restrictive agreements without due consideration of the long-run political and economic losses of even more disruptive price swings consequent on these agreements will be great. But this temptation should be resisted by forthright rejection of any agreements containing production controls or other restrictive conditions.

The benefits that might accrue worldwide from achieving greater price stability—both through appropriate domestic policies and through agreements that avoid restrictive features—should be given greater prominence. But such agreements are not easy to negotiate. Interests of producers and consumers need to be balanced, realistic price ranges need to be agreed upon, and buffer stock sizes need to be sufficiently large to effectively defend agreed-upon price ranges. Buffer stock operations can be beneficial, but costs can run high and, for some commodities, stocking arrangements are not feasible at all. However, if negotiations on buffer agreements are approached with a sense of realism, the gains from price stabilization could be significant and the economic environment could be improved worldwide.

Finally, it must be remembered that the number of commodity agreements that actually can be concluded is relatively small and that even where they are successful, they can ease the external financial problems of the LDCs only fractionally. Thus, commitments on the part of the developed countries to commodity agreements must not be viewed as a way to achieve a transfer of resources. First, commodity agreements so concluded would likely fail in their objective. Second, the costs of failure in terms of politics and economics would be high and third, resource transfers should be effected in the light of the LDC's overall resource needs, including not only those of primary producers but also those of countries not so endowed.

Notes

1. P. MacAvoy and D.L. McNicol, *The Benefits and Costs of Participation in International Commodity Agreements,* page 67.

2. Profitable speculation is generally stabilizing, since for example, a profit

is made on material purchased now only if it is resold at a higher price. This argument is presented in Milton Friedman, *Essays in Positive Economics* (Chicago: University of Chicago Press, 1953). For counterarguments see William J. Baumol, "Speculation, Profitability, and Stability," *Review of Economics and Statistics* 39 (August 1957):263-271; and Harry G. Johnson, "Destabilizing Speculation: A General Equilibrium Approach," *Journal of Political Economy* 84 (1976).

3. See Benton F. Massell, "Some Welfare Implications for International Price Stabilization," *Journal of Political Economy* 78 (March 1970):pp. 404–417.

4. D. Gale Johnson, *The Sugar Program: Large Costs and Small Benefits,* American Enterprise Institute for Policy Research, 1974; and Helmut Weymar, *Dynamics of the World Cocoa Market,* M.I.T. Press, 1968.

5. Benefits and costs are estimated in P. MacAvoy and D.L. McNicol "Benefits and Costs of Commodity Agreements" a *Memorandum* to the Commodity Policy Coordinating Committee of August 26, 1976 and reproduced in D.L. McNicol's *Commodity Agreements and Price Stabilization* (Lexington, Mass.: Lexington Books, D.C. Heath 1978).

6. This estimate is based on multiplying the forecast commodity price increases by sales quantity and then adding the totals across all commodities. (P. MacAvoy and D.L. McNicol, *Memorandum, op cit.*)

15 An Alternative Common Fund Proposal

Richard W. Fisher and
Robert V. Roosa

UNCTAD Secretary General Gamani Corea recently visited Washington to present and discuss his organization's case for a Common Fund to finance an Integrated Programme of commodity arrangements. We were invited to attend one of the nonofficial meetings with Mr. Corea. It appeared there that since both consumers and producers have a vested interest in limiting the gyrations of commodity prices, agreement was easily reached on the need for some kind of stabilization initiative. But Mr. Corea's proposal for a Common Fund operating within the context of–and indeed "at the core of"–an integrated program, encountered resistance.

Stress was placed on the view that most of the previous attempts to establish multinational commodity agreements, regardless of how financed, have broken down. This has occurred because producing countries found that they could not hold to agreed production or stockpiling quotas, or because consuming countries found that they could not practicably hold to agreed purchasing formulas, or because of any number of other reasons related to the difficulty of maintaining a tight, cartel-like agreement among many diverse sovereign countries. It was therefore argued that until a new modus operandi for buffer stocks and other international commodity agreements is discovered, establishing a Common Fund at this stage would be a case of placing a cart before an unbridled horse.

Discouragement with past commodity agreements should not, however, encourage a retreat into the type of market that produces widely, often wildly, swinging prices for basic commodities for many producers (and indeed for many consumers). Ways surely can be found, while prices still move and supplies vary in response to underlying market forces, to avoid the whipsaw of harsh, violent swings in availabilities and prices. But to do so, somewhat less rigid conditions than those of the typical commodity agreement will have to be found for the participating countries. For binding terms as to price and production, as sought by UNCTAD through agreement among countries with divergent capacities and aims (not to mention differing commitments to private or to state-owned

Reprinted from *The Journal of Commerce* of March 21 and 22, 1977.

enterprise), are almost certain to be unattainable; or if initially attained, then unsustainable.

An Introductory Sketch of a Different Common Fund Proposal

There may, however, be a more flexible, pragmatic approach that the United States could introduce during the forthcoming UNCTAD, CIEC, and other multinational negotiations that would not only set aside a pool of potential funding but also stimulate the development of a new approach to commodity price stabilization. It would modify the procedures now being considered by the UNCTAD and other groups by setting guidelines that avoid the need for negotiated floor prices, or agreed production quotas, or commitments to hold internationally linked stockpiles. Paradoxically, such an approach may come much closer to producing a satisfactory moderation in fluctuations of price and income than the more complicated network of commodity agreements that must be reached if the current UNCTAD version of the Common Fund were to become operational.

The heart of this proposal lies in using guidelines developed by the same countries that might have been expected to enter into formal commodity agreements, but without the need such agreements would imply to reach precisely definitive conditions to which each producing (or consuming) country must adhere. That is, guidelines, once agreed, would be permissive, not mandatory, and the arrangements would function through inducements, not through reliance upon virtually unenforceable compulsion.

Moreover, instead of having to operate within the confines of an internationally integrated program that would acquire stocks of a particular commodity as production or prices reached predetermined levels and would then later sell them at other set levels, the role of the Common Fund would simply be to finance, as requested, the carrying of stocks of commodities that remain in the possession of the producing countries. And each country would in turn be free to decide whether to bring its own stocks into a national storehouse operated by its government, or instead to arrange parallel financing with its own producers, permitting them to warehouse the stocks until changed conditions made sale of the stocks attractive to them. Indeed, countries in more prosperous circumstances might simply carry (and later sell) their own stockpiles with their own domestic resources and not need to resort to the Common Fund at all.

The essential feature of the new Common Fund proposal would be reliance upon certain "trigger points," determined in terms of recent trends in the quantities or the prices of standard units of each chosen commodity in the world market. Data on the total quantity of world production and on the world price for a standard unit of each key commodity, for several past years, would be kept continually up to date. All producer and consuming countries would be invited to join conferences held by the management of the Common Fund to determine the percentage by which world production might rise above trend, or world prices fall below trend, to reach the "trigger point" at which producing countries would be free to call on the Common Fund for financing to carry a portion of their own production in a buffer stock. The percentages above or below trend might be reviewed in the light of experience, at intervals, possibly every five years; but there would not be any scope for altering the guideline percentages to meet producer or consumer pressures in particular years or seasons.

Passing over for the moment any mention of the organization or the resources of the Common Fund itself, what might actually happen under such arrangements if the proposed Common Fund were in operation? A country producing copper, for example, or sugar, or jute, or any other key commodity, would be free to call upon the fund to finance the storing of part of its production if a trigger point were passed. By agreement, the trigger set by production of copper might be evidence that world output had reached or exceeded 5 percent above the recent trend. But the trigger would not be activated if, for other reasons, copper prices were at the same time rising above their trend. The trigger related to copper prices would come at, say, 10 percent below the price trend, provided the worldwide quantity of copper production was not at the same time dropping below trend.

For example, if world copper output in 1977 should exceed the trend (or, alternatively, the average) for 1972–1976 by more than 5 percent while world copper prices were steady or declining, each copper-producing country would be eligible to go to the Common Fund to borrow an amount of funds equivalent, at current prices, to the value of all of its own production that exceeded 5 percent of its own average output for 1972–1976—provided that that "excess" production was held in earmarked stocks by private firms or a government agency within that country. Contrariwise, if there were a slump in world demand for copper and world prices began dropping while world production was steady or exceeding the recent trend, a trigger point activating Common Fund loans would be reached when the world copper price had fallen 10 percent below trend. In those circumstances, a producing country would be eligible to obtain financing from the Common Fund for a value of stocks (at the prevailing lower price) equal to, say, 10 percent of its current production.

No country would be required to stockpile; but it would have the right, whenever the trigger should be sprung, to accumulate stocks up to the amount indicated by the guidelines and to draw an equivalent amount of usable currency from the Common Fund, adjusted possibly to provide a small margin between the current value of the stocks and the amount of the loan. It would pay a rate of interest on the currency drawn from the fund and would consequently not want to continue its indebtedness if demand and prices rose to permit sale at a profit above the loan value. For a country that used the external finance from the fund as a sort of offsetting balance internally for what it may lend or pay to its own producers in local currency for the inventory being held, an internal pressure would also be at work to induce sale as markets improve.

Meanwhile, however, each country would have control over its own inventory; the Common Fund would have a claim upon it only as collateral. The fund's earnings would come from the interest payments received, or from liquidation of collateral in the improbable incidence of a default. But as an override to help cover operating costs and assure an adequate return to the suppliers of fund resources, the Common Fund might also contract to receive, say, one-fifth of any net profits received by a country on the sale of stocks that had been carried on fund loans.

There will probably be some producing countries who simply want to maintain an "ever-normal granary" on their own. They could accumulate stocks, regardless of the guidelines, and would be free to arrange their own financing, internally, or abroad, or both. They would not ordinarily need the Common Fund. But they would be expected to contribute information on their total production to the Common Fund secretariat and would take part in discussions concerning the quantitative trigger-ratio to be considered appropriate for those commodities which they produce.

There is already, of course, a very modest program of buffer stock financing in existence at the International Monetary Fund. For reasons to appear shortly below, however, there may be persuasive reasons to shift this activity instead to a Common Fund devoted exclusively to this purpose. But there is an opposite kind of situation with which the IMF is already well equipped to deal, and for which the Common Fund might have only an ancillary role, if indeed any role at all. That is the condition in which a sudden natural or man-made calamity within a country causes its production to fall sharply, thereby creating a shortfall in needed foreign earnings. The IMF Compensatory Financing Facility is intended for, and is already being heavily used to provide, bridge financing to help cover a country's balance-of-payments requirements over such periods of shortage—until a resumption of full production provides the means for repayment.

The essence of the approach suggested here is to moderate the tendency for cumulative price swings to occur whenever world conditions of supply or demand set off a change in the price of a world-traded commodity. The aim is to set the boundary conditions for access of any country to borrowing facilities in relatively simple terms, with a minimum of dependence upon solidarity of action among all the producing countries. This design of arrangements would leave room, too, for the different needs and reactions of many of the more highly developed countries that also happen to be producers of one or more of the key commodities (and in some cases, major producers of those commodities). Nor would the usefulness of these arrangements depend upon assured cooperation by a high proportion of the consumer countries for any particular commodity. Perhaps this approach would fall short of an ideal result; but it would not depend upon an unrealistic conception of the sustainability of negotiated quotas for output (or storage) on the part of all producers (or consumers) of key commodities within negotiated but fixed lower and upper limits for their prices.

The Organization and Resources of a Common Fund

The present UNCTAD approach contemplates formation of a wholly new institution, funded by the voluntary contributions of interested countries. As currently designed, one-sixth of its initial $3 billion of capital will be funded by subscriptions from the developed countries (with roughly $100 million being solicited from the United States) and one-sixth from the LDC group. The remaining two-thirds would be raised in the international capital markets. Tentative capital subscriptions have already been offered by six countries and total $156 million. There is no reason under the proposed U.S. approach to forego these contributions; indeed many more can be solicited. But a case can be made for centering the new institution midway between the IMF and the IBRD, with a heavy claim upon each of them for resources as well.

For one reason, the total sum involved may at times reach a very large figure, perhaps the equivalent of $10 billion, or even more. Requirements on such a scale may well require a claim on the resources, the competence, and indeed the credibility of the two major international financial institutions. Perhaps the best solution would be to form a new international corporation, possibly named *The Common Fund,* to which the major contribution of permanent capital would be made by the IBRD, and whose major source of borrowed funds would be the IMF. Such a Common Fund would also be empowered to accept capital subscriptions directly from any interested governments and to pay dividends on all capital, if earned. It would correspondingly be equipped and encouraged to borrow working funds (including some with no fixed-date maturity) from other governments to supplement its drawing line at the IMF and would pay interest at nominal rates.

Various formulas could be considered for determining the size and distribution of the capital. The direct IBRD subscription should probably be at least one-half billion dollars. Individual governments might be expected to make a permanent contribution of capital in amounts equal to, say, 1 percent of their net official reserves during the year that operations begin, with additional supplements welcomed. The drawing line at the IMF could probably be 15 times the capital, and countries in balance-of-payments surplus could offer demand loans to the Common Fund (with the Common Fund backstopped against withdrawals by unused IMF lines).

Questions of this kind require extensive study and negotiation, of course, but their resolution should not present a serious obstacle. Similarly, the composition of a board, and the definition of its powers, along with the role of the management and secretariat will have to be worked out in a multinational forum. A few illustrative suggestions may help to indicate the kinds of issues to be resolved.

The number of members on the board should be no larger than that of the IBRD or IMF, and preferably smaller. The boards of these organizations could each select, say, 4 directors (some of whom might be from LDCs), and other representative bodies such as UNCTAD might select, say, 7—for a total of 15. For operational convenience, a domicile in Washington alongside the IBRD and IMF might be useful; but in practice the domicile could be in any city with reasonably good communications and support facilities. The board's principal duties should be to select the management, to make final determination of the terms of all capital contributions, borrowing contracts, and loan agreements, as well as to determine which commodities should be included in the arrangements, and (on the basis of recommendations by each "commodity group advisory committee") to fix the percentages that serve as trigger points for activating the accumulation of stockpiles to be carried by Common Fund credits.

The management in turn should select and administer a staff responsible for convening advisory committees on each designated commodity, for gathering and monitoring all relevant data, for making loans, verifying collateral, collecting repayments, investing working balances, and for conducting all other operations. These are significant tasks, but none are insuperable.

Conclusion

To be sure, the foregoing proposal is but a most tentative outline for a new facility that, if it proves workable, would satisfy the Third World's justifiable demands for a new approach to commodity price stabilization (and for a new institution). At the same time it would put into meaningful form the elements of free choice, and of national diversity, that some spokesmen for the previous U.S. administration identified with "free markets," but without the implication of rigid interference with the basic determinants of supply and price which they associated with UNCTAD's Common Fund proposal.

The essential fact is that the less-developed countries that produce raw materials for the world market need more orderly market conditions, less-violent price swings, and the flexibility to develop their own economic policies within that framework. While their need is most striking, it is only in degree more impelling than the comparable need faced by most other countries—as producers and as consumers. The real challenge is to find practicable methods through the kind of positive effort among nations that can resolve difficulties rather than acquiesce in disruption.

16 International Commodity Agreements: An Evaluation of the UNCTAD Integrated Programme for Commodities

Jere R. Behrman

In the 1960s and early 1970s the developing nations became increasingly disaffected with the international economic order. They claimed that the existing order reflected a past world in which the peoples of Asia, Africa, and Latin America were in a subservient—often colonial—position, with little voice in decisions affecting their economic destiny. The rules of the game and international institutions had been established by the developed nations and operated primarily for their benefit, often within the framework of cold war bipolarism.

In reaction to this situation, some of the developing nations attempted to establish an effective international lobby for the so-called Third World. Under the leadership of Nasser, Nehru, and Tito the First Summit Conference of the Non-Aligned Countries met to this end in Belgrade in 1961. The Third World nations pressed the United Nations to create UNCTAD (United Nations Conference on Trade and Development), which held its first quadrennial meeting in Geneva in 1964. At that meeting, the Group of 77, representing the 77 developing nations in attendance, was formed as a caucus for the Third World position in United Nations and other international forums. The resolutions at UNCTAD I, as well as at UNCTAD II in 1968 in New Delhi, and at UNCTAD III in 1972 in Santiago, stressed the need for changing the international economic order through international commodity agreements, regulation of multinational corporations, generalized trading preferences, compensatory financing to offset fluctuations in export earnings, a SDR link, and other means. Some of these recommendations did lead to changes. By and large, however, the United States and many other developed nations tended to discount most of the Third World proposals as rhetoric that was not realistic and possibly not even representative of the true interests of many of the developing nations. The frustration of the developing nations at their perceived inability to affect how the international economic system shaped their economic alternatives intensified.

In late 1973 the Arab petroleum-exporting nations agreed to an oil embargo

This chapter builds on material developed in the ODC Project on the New International Economic Order under the directorship of William Cline and presented in Behrman (1977). I thank the ODC for supporting that study, William Cline for useful suggestions, and Pranee Tinakorn for excellent research assistance.

to attempt to force changes in the Middle Eastern policies of the developed nations. In December of that year they joined the other OPEC nations in doubling the price of oil, beginning a process that quadrupled the price in about a year. Since most of the other developing nations depend on imported petroleum for basic energy and on important petroleum-based products (e.g., fertilizer), they (as well as many of the developed countries) were affected quite negatively by the OPEC policies. Deficits in international payments soared, imports were curtailed, foreign debts multiplied, and development plans were suspended as a result. It seemed possible that the fragile alliance among the Third World countries would be torn asunder by the OPEC actions. The United States and some other developed nations courted the cooperation of the oil-importing developing countries in finding a way to break the OPEC cartel.

However, the alliance among the developing nations was not fragmented. Instead, President Boumedienne of Algeria took the initiative in calling the Sixth Special Session of the General Assembly of the United Nations on Raw Materials and Development in the spring of 1974. At this conference it was argued that the current economic problems of the non-OPEC developing nations arose *not* from the recent petroleum price increases but from a faulty international economic system that persistently had neglected their economic development needs in general and that had underpaid them for their commodity exports (including oil) in particular. The non-OPEC developing countries were asked to accept higher petroleum prices as the vanguard of a new international economic order that also would seek to improve substantially the terms of trade for the other primary products on which the Third World depends for the majority of its export revenues. It was a bold stroke in support of generally higher international primary prices and new commodity associations modeled after OPEC.

The OPEC strategy succeeded in gaining the support of the other Third World countries. Past UNCTAD proposals for improving the international economic opportunities of the developing nations were integrated in this spirit into a Declaration on the Establishment of a New International Economic Order and a Programme of Action (both of which, together with a number of other related documents, may be found in Erb and Kallab, 1975). These documents were adopted by acclamation, but the United States and some of the other developed nations clearly less than fully agreed. The proposals were of varying specificity, importance, and controversy. A number already had been or soon were accepted, at least in principle (e.g., progressive removal of trade barriers, liberalization of compensatory financing schemes, generalized trade preferences). Others have been much more controversial, especially the proposals for lessening the fluctuations and increasing the trend in real prices of commodity exports of the developing countries, which is at the heart of the call. Considerable confrontation grew between the developing and developed nations over these, and other, issues.

Subsequent international meetings of the developing countries emphasized the centrality of changing the functioning of international commodity markets in their call for a new international economic order. At the same time, the confrontation between the developing and the developed nations intensified. Indicative of this clash was the closing in April 1975 of the Preliminary Working Sessions for the Conference on International Economic Cooperation (CIEC) without the tripartite representatives (from the developed, nonoil developing, and oil nations) even being able to agree on a future agenda.

In September 1975 the tendency for increasing North-South conflict over international relations was reversed at least temporarily at the Seventh Special Session of the United Nations General Assembly on Development and International Economic Cooperation in substantial part because of the more cooperative attitude displayed by the United States. A General Assembly resolution instructed UNCTAD IV (to be held in Nairobi in May 1976) that "an important aim . . . should be to reach decisions on the improvement of market structures in the field of raw materials and commodities of export interest to the developing countries, including decisions with respect to an integrated programme and the applicability of elements thereof."

In February 1976 the Group of 77 (which by then included 112 developing nations) drew up the so-called Manila Declaration in preparation for UNCTAD IV. This declaration consists of 17 major economic reforms, together with what Lewis (1976) characterizes as "a threatening pledge 'to make full use of the bargaining power of the developing countries through joint and united action' to secure these aims." The centerpiece of the declaration is support for the UNCTAD-promoted proposal of an Integrated Programme for Commodities financed out of a Common Fund.

With this backing the UNCTAD (1976*a*) Secretariat prepared its final proposal for the UNCTAD IV Nairobi meetings. The proposal focused on 10 "core" commodities (cocoa, coffee, copper, sugar, cotton, jute, rubber, sisal, tea, and tin), and mentions 8 others. It proposed the creation of international commodity agreements for these commodities in order (1) to stabilize prices and (2) to ensure adequate growth in the real export revenues of the developing countries. It advocated the establishment of a $6 billion Common Fund from subscriptions by exporters and importers to assure adequate financing for these agreements. The fund also would serve as a catalyst in stimulating new commodity stockpile agreements by assuring adequate finances independent of the particular financial situation of the individual countries participating in a specific commodity agreement. The Common Fund, moreover, would pool and reduce risks and have more bargaining power in international capital markets than could a set of individual funds for the same commodities. Furthermore, it would require less financing than the aggregate of a set of individual funds because of the differences in the phasing of cycles across commodity markets.

The developed countries also approached UNCTAD IV with increased interest in international primary commodity agreements. The general increase in commodity prices in 1971–1974, and the OPEC experience in particular, had created a "scarcity mentality" and acute concern over "access to supplies"

(Eads, 1976. In the United States the Trade Act of 1974 directed the President to negotiate access to supply agreements, and the National Commission on Supplies and Shortages was instructed to report to the President and Congress on the causes of the 1973–1974 material shortages and on proposals to lessen the possibility of repetition of that experience through economic stockpiles, better information, and other means. The executive director of this Commission, George Eads (1976), reported that the discussions of the Commission with private companies "tell of a new concern on their part for stability and continuity of supply—even if it means that they must pay higher prices." Because of much greater dependence on imported raw materials, there was even greater concern about access to supplies in Europe.

Although both the developed and the developing countries expressed strong interest in international commodity agreements, there remained substantial differences. The developing countries, for example, emphasized the assurance of a "just" return to producers and indexation of commodity prices by tying them to movements in the price index of their imports. The United States, in contrast, focused more on the need for expanded resource supplies through the establishment of an International Resource Bank, assuring access to supplies, stabilization (in part through compensatory finance), and, in the words of Deputy Assistant Secretary for Economic and Business Affairs Katz (1976), "seeking an open world economy that permits market forces to operate with minimum restriction on the flow of goods, services, capital, and technology across international boundaries."

UNCTAD IV entailed a month of tense negotiation. At times, the shift from confrontation to cooperation that had occurred at the Seventh Special Session of the General Assembly the previous September, at least temporarily, was reversed. At the end, at least superficial conciliation prevailed. The conference adopted a proposal for an Integrated Programme for Commodities (IPC). This program is quite similar to the UNCTAD (1976*a*) proposal previously described. It includes a timetable that indicates very substantial activity in regard to international commodity agreements in the next two or three years.

The UNCTAD commodity program is quite important. If it is implemented, it might have widespread consequences, perhaps on the order of OPEC, for the developing and developed nations alike. And, despite past stated reservations of the United States and other countries, it well may be put into effect partially or in its entirety. The following statement of President Carter before the United Nations on March 17, 1977, for example, is far from definitive but may imply a substantially more receptive attitude toward the UNCTAD proposal than that which characterized the previous administration:

> . . . We are also examining ways to provide additional consideration for the special needs of developing countries.

The United States is willing to consider, with a positive and open attitude, the negotiation of agreements to stabilize commodity prices, including the establishment of a common funding arrangement for financing buffer stocks where they are a part of individual, negotiated agreements.

I also believe that the developing countries must acquire fuller participation in the global economic decision-making process. Some progress has been made in this regard by expanding participation of developing countries in the International Monetary Fund.

Such a possibility raises a number of important questions: What would be the gains and losses for the developing countries? Are there preferable means of attaining these aims? Is there a trade-off between additions to producers' revenue and stability of revenue? Among the developing countries, who would gain and who would lose? What order of magnitude of revenue changes might result from stabilization alone? What would be the impact of attempting to change secular price trends (or, as a special case, to index these prices)? What would be the gains and losses for the developed economies? How would they be distributed among them? Are there possibly significant gains due to the lessening of inflationary pressures if oligopolistic "ratchet" price changes are common? What would be the costs of buffer stock operations? Would the $6 billion Common Fund probably be adequate? How much would the Common Fund pool risks and reduce capital requirements?

The predominant conclusions of the analyses of the UNCTAD proposal undertaken by scholars and policy makers in the developed world is that it is inadequate on a number of grounds. Some illustrative examples of this analysis are reviewed below. However, my summary judgment is that the analysis to date is far from adequate. Most of it is a priori on the basis of simple theorizing, with no or little appeal to empirical magnitudes—even though the outcomes depend crucially on the nature of the empirical situation. Part of the limited empirical work available merely lays the groundwork for analysis of questions such as those raised above. Other studies seem misguided or wrong.

The major contribution of this chapter is the introduction of much more empirical content into the debate about the merits and shortcomings of the UNCTAD proposal. The approach is to take existing econometric models of international commodity markets for UNCTAD core commodities and to simulate the operation of the UNCTAD program over a decade. This gives estimates of possible orders of magnitude of gains, losses, cost, and financing if the UNCTAD program were instituted. The second section of this chapter elaborates on the assumptions underlying these simulations and on the results obtained thereby. As is detailed there, this empirical investigation does point to a number of problems in the UNCTAD proposal. But it also suggests more possible gains and more reasons to consider the proposal seriously than have most other previous analyses.

Previous Assessments of the UNCTAD Proposals

The predominant conclusion of previous assessments of the UNCTAD proposal by many others is negative. Examples include Johnson (1976); Kreinin and Finger (1976); McCulloch (1976); Brook and Grilli (1977); Junz and MacAvoy (1977); and Michalopoulos and Perez (1977). For the most part, these assessments are based on a priori reasoning, with no or little empirical analysis. Representative of the criticisms, together with an evaluation of them (also see Behrman, 1977), are the following.

1. *"Elementary economic analysis" (in the words of H.G. Johnson) suggests that the proposal is dubious since it mixes up two problems (i.e., shifts in supply and in demand) and fails to note the probable trade-off between levels of producers' revenues and stability of those revenues.* Johnson's (1976) argument is illustrated in Figure 16–1, in which the basic average supply and demand curves for a purely competitive international commodity market are given by solid straight lines, equally likely shifts in these curves are indicated by dashed lines, and P_0 is the average price and the price at which a buffer stock scheme would stabilize prices.

Consider first the case of instability resulting from demand shifts alone (Figure 16–1a). Without price stabilization, average producers' revenue is $(P_1 * Q_1 + P_2 * Q_2)/2$. With stabilization, it is $P_0 * Q_0$. Therefore, price stabilization in this case reduces the instability of producers' revenues, but also reduces its average level.

Consider next the case of instability resulting from supply shifts alone. In what Johnson considers to be the normal case, both supply and demand curves are elastic (Figure 16–1b). Without price stabilization, producers' average revenue is $(P_2 * Q_2 + P_3 * Q_3)/2$. With stabilization, it is $P_0 * (Q_1 + Q_4)/2$. Price stabilization increases producers' revenue, but also increases its instability.

Under his assumptions about the empirical world, is Johnson right that the UNCTAD proposal is dubious? Perhaps, but perhaps not. If demand shifts dominate and producers are risk-averse or if they perceive long-run substitution efforts by users being induced by price fluctuations, the proposal may make sense. If shifts in the supply curve dominate and the producers are not risk-averse, then the proposal may make sense.

In both cases empirical questions are raised: What are the objectives of UNCTAD? Which curve is subject to greater instability?

But the empirical questions go much further. If the curves are sufficiently inelastic and supply shifts dominate (Figure 16–1c), stabilization increases revenue and reduces revenue instability. The trade-off no longer exists. Johnson recognizes this as a conceptual possibility but does not consider it of particular real world relevance. The available estimates of such price elasticities (Table 1 in Behrman, 1977), however, suggest that it well may be the normal case for many of the markets of interest.

But that still is not the end of the story. If the supply and demand curves are nonlinear, and if the stochastic terms are multiplicative rather than additive, Johnson's "elementary economic analysis" may give the wrong answers (see Behrman, 1977; Newbery, 1976; Sarris and Taylor, 1978; and Turnovsky, 1978). There are a number of arguments and observations that suggest that these conditions may prevail. In any case, only empirical analysis, not a priori elementary theoretical examples, can give an answer.

2. *Only for commodities for which the basic source of fluctuations is from supply variation will the exporters gain from price stabilization by increased revenues. Among the important commodity exports of the developing nations only coffee and cocoa, according to Brook and Grilli (1977), are characterized by dominant supply fluctuations.* The basic theoretical underpinning of this position once again is illustrated by Figure 16–1, with the added assumption that producers are not risk-averse. Under the conditions assumed in this figure, producers' revenue increases with price stabilization if supply shifts are dominant, and vice versa. But once again, this conclusion is not necessarily correct if nonlinearities or multiplicative disturbances are allowed (see especially Turnovsky, 1978). Moreover, even in the linear-curve-additive-disturbance world, the empirical method used by Brook and Grilli (i.e., regressing quantity deviations from the trend on price deviations from the trend and interpreting a negative estimate of the coefficient of price as implying that supply shifts are dominant, and vice versa) generally does not lead to the identification of the underlying source of the fluctuations (Porter, 1970).

3. *International commodity agreements would interfere with the operation of free markets and, therefore, cause substantial losses (e.g., Katz, 1976).* This kind of assertion is not uncommon, especially among policy makers. But what are the supposed gains from free market operations? Unfortunately, they usually are not made very explicit in such statements, so we must speculate.

An extreme possibility is that free markets lead to static maximization of some social welfare function. But this is so only under a number of strong assumptions: no externalities, no risk-aversion, pure competition (i.e., no one entity can perceptibly affect market prices), and the correct (for the given social welfare function) initial distribution of the ownership of production factors. Leaving aside the problems of determining an appropriate social welfare function, the last necessary assumption is enough to raise questions in many people's minds. The current world distribution of factor ownership and thus of income is so unequal that free market operation could not lead to maximization of anything like the appropriate social welfare function in their (and my) value judgment. Efficiency concerns may be irrelevant in light of this maldistribution.

In part because of the problems in defining social welfare functions, nevertheless, economists often focus on efficiency. Under the first three assumptions above, free markets are efficient in the Paretian sense that no one can be made better off without making at least one other individual worse off. Does that

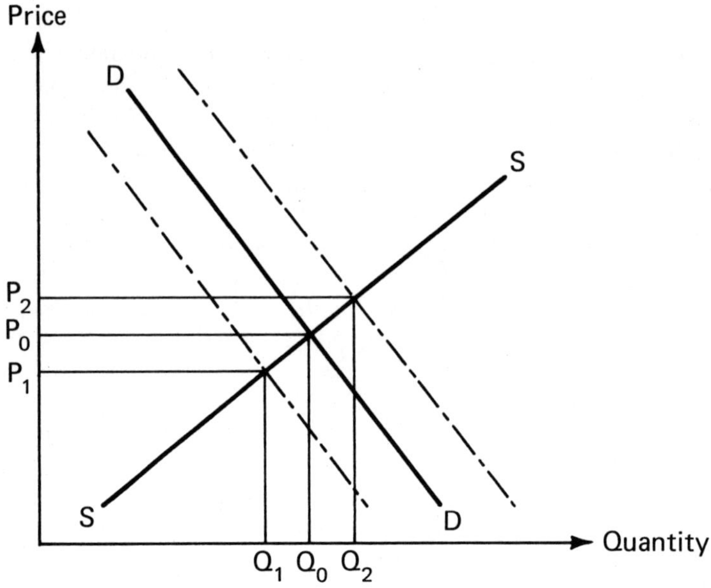
Price
D
S
P2
P0
P1
S
D
Quantity
Q1 Q0 Q2

a.

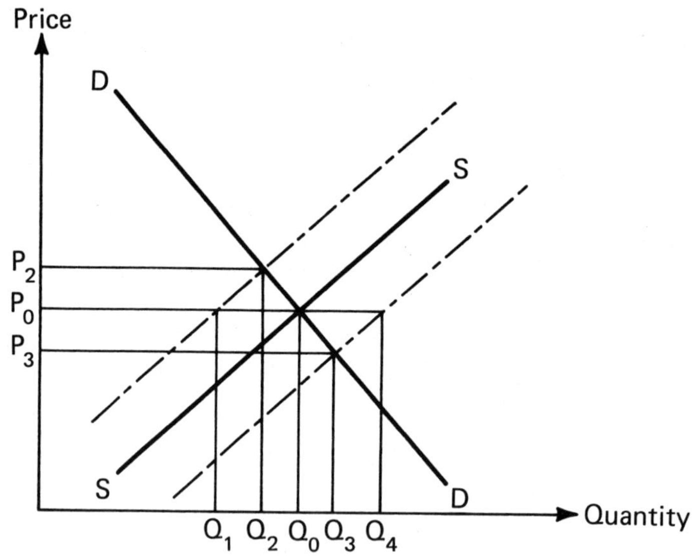
Price
D
S
P2
P0
P3
S
D
Quantity
Q1 Q2 Q0 Q3 Q4

b.

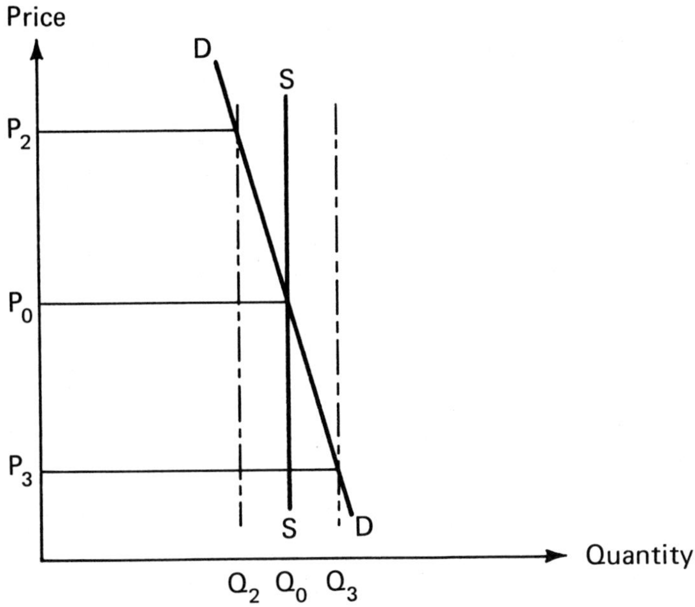

c.

Figure 16-1. Impact on Revenues of Shifts in Demand and Supply Curves with and without Price Stabilization at P_0 by a Buffer Stock. **a.** Shift in Demand Only. **b.** Shift in Supply Only (Elastic Curves). **c.** Shift in Supply Only (Inelastic Curves).

mean that international commodity agreements should be avoided because of the efficiency of free international commodity markets? The answer is no on at least three accounts. First, as is noted above, it is not clear why efficiency should be an objective if some inefficient outcomes result in higher levels of social welfare. Second, even if the first three conditions were satisfied in international commodity markets, the theory of the second best implies that they would not necessarily lead to overall efficiency unless they were satisfied everywhere else—and they obviously are not. Third, these three conditions are not satisfied in many of the relevant international commodity markets, as is illustrated, for example, by the existence of considerable market power for dealers in copper, tin, tea, and other commodities.

The last two paragraphs concentrate on static analysis. Under dynamic conditions, the conclusion remains the same: relatively free markets do seem to be relatively effective mechanisms for processing a great deal of information and for signaling about the existence of excess supplies or demands. However, the current structure of international commodity markets leads neither to welfare maximization nor to efficiency, as seems to be implied in the statements of many (see Behrman, 1977, for further consideration of these issues).

4. *Past commodity agreements and producer cartels suggest that the UNCTAD proposal would not attain the desired ends.* The survey of historical experience of international commodity agreements and producer cartels in Behrman (1977) suggests that they have not been very successful in stabilizing prices. However, a number of efforts have been successful in at least temporarily raising prices. Eckbo (1975), for example, reports that 19 of the 51 cartels for which he was able to obtain systematic data succeeded in temporarily raising prices at least 200 percent above the unit cost of production and distribution. OPEC and IBA (the International Bauxite Association, see Bergsten, 1976) are current examples for oil and bauxite, respectively. He also reports that successful efforts to raise international commodity prices substantially tended to be associated with higher concentration of production, higher concentration of foreign trade, higher price elasticities of demand,[1] higher income elasticities of demand, fewer possibilities of short-term substitution, a higher share of foreign trade controlled by members of the agreement, low cost differences among producers in the agreement, and less government involvement. The successful efforts seemed to be sustained longer where concentration of production was high, demand was price inelastic, the members' market share was high, the members had cost advantages over outsiders, and governments were not involved in operations. Successful agreements broke down most often because of competition among the members, with competition from nonmembers being the second most common cause.

Extrapolation from this experience suggests that short-run efforts to increase commodity prices might have substantial, if transitory, gains to the developing country producers that would outweigh the longer-run costs resulting from the induced expanded production from fringe producers and the induced development of new substitutes. However, the commodity markets on which UNCTAD is concentrating do not have many of the characteristics that in the past have been associated with short-run successes of producers' cartels. Therefore, even short-run market regulation may have a reasonable probability of success only if the consuming nations can be persuaded to join in the effort, as UNCTAD proposes.

But the past is not a complete guide to the future. In the late 1970s the developing producer nations may be more cohesive than in the past because of the examples of OPEC and the IBA, the growing power and latitude of movement of the Third World in an increasingly pluralistic world with some form of detente instead of cold war bipolarism,[2] and their common perceived need for a new economic order. The developed consuming nations may be more accommodating because of the same factors and the growing perception that access to primary commodity supplies and moderating inflation are important considerations for their self-interests. The result probably is a higher probability of at least short- or medium-run success for the UNCTAD-type proposal than past experience alone might suggest.

5. *The goals of the UNCTAD program can be achieved more efficiently*

through other means, such as compensatory financing for fluctuations or more direct investment. The validity of this statement depends substantially on one's perception of the goals and nature of alternatives. Stabilization of revenues, for example, might be attained better through expanded compensatory financing facilities. Increased command over resources, in principle, could be obtained more efficiently through direct transfers (but I have some doubts that they would be increased by an equivalent amount in practice). It seems unlikely that they would be increased substantially by an International Resource Bank such as the United States proposed in Nairobi, given the inelastic demands for the commodities of interest. The apparent goal of gaining more control over international transactions relevant to their major exports, finally, does not seem likely to be attained better by the alternative measures proposed by detractors of the UNCTAD program.

6. *The benefits to the developing countries from the UNCTAD program would be quite small, successful operating rules for buffer stock managers would be difficult to devise, there is not much advantage to integrating financing across commodities since fluctuations are basically in phase across commodities, and the proposed $6 billion financing is inadequate (e.g., Junz and MacAvoy, 1977; Kreinin and Finger, 1976).* This whole set of important questions is empirical in nature. The answers depend upon the underlying structural parameters or historical experience. Nevertheless, these conclusions have been presented on the basis of frightfully little empirical evidence.

This list is not exhaustive. Other examples could be discussed (e.g., regarding the distribution of benefits or the relation between fluctuations and growth). But these items suggest that much of the current debate on these very important issues is being conducted on the basis of possibly misleading analysis and almost in an empirical vacuum. The returns from obtaining better information about the underlying magnitudes indeed may be high.

Simulations of the UNCTAD Integrated Programme for Commodities

To provide insight into the questions raised in the introduction and to the largely a priori assertions made in the previous sections, I have simulated the operation of the UNCTAD Integrated Programme for Commodities for 8 of the 10 UNCTAD core commodities.[3] First the assumptions for these simulations are made explicit. Then the results are discussed.

Assumptions Underlying the Simulations

1. Simple nonlinear eight-equation (i.e., supply and demand relations for developing, developed, and centrally planned economies, a price-inventory relation,

and the ex post identity between appearance and disappearance) econometric models[4] approximate well the structures of the markets despite the operations of the buffer stock. Some more explicit implications of this assumption are as follows. Limit pricing (i.e., pricing to deter too rapid entry) and the threat of substitution in use continue to make aggregate supply and demand response relations sufficiently good approximations despite the existence of market power. National policies that altered the relation between international and domestic prices during the sample period (e.g., marketing boards, export taxes, import taxes) continue to have the same effects in the simulation period. Private inventory behavioral relations remain the same despite the existence of buffer stock arrangements. Other parameters and lags remain the same despite the reduction in price instability.

2. Nonstochastic simulations over a recent decade (1963–1972) provide useful information about likely orders of magnitude associated with the operation of buffer stock arrangements.

It might be preferable to calculate the expected values and higher moments associated with various policies by conducting Monte Carlo studies. To do so, however, would have required resources far beyond those available for this study. Since the estimated standard deviations of the disturbance terms are small relative to the standard deviations of the dependent variables in most of the estimated relations, nevertheless, the use of nonstochastic simulations should not be too misleading.

The use of the decade starting in 1963 ties the results to a particular period. However, that period is long enough to encompass a wide range of experience (e.g., substantial fluctuations in the world economy). The length of the period thus lessens the extent to which the total results are conditional on the particular choice of years, although the details of the time sequence obviously reflect that choice.

The use of a period as long as a decade also is useful because it permits covering enough years to encompass several commodity price cycles of historical duration. Smith and Schink (1975) and Smith (1975) emphasize the importance of having a sufficiently long simulation period for this very reason based on their econometric explorations of the tin and copper markets. UNCTAD (1975*b*) gives the lengths of price cycles in the 1960–1974 period for 9 of the 10 core commodities (not including tea). Across all commodities the average is 22 months, with the means for the individual commodities ranging from 13 months for sugar to 34 months for coffee. A 10-year simulation period, thus, should cover enough time for several price cycles of the duration historically experienced—although fewer for coffee than for the other commodities. It should be short enough, however, that structural changes resulting from reduced price fluctuations are not overwhelming. This is so since many of those changes relate to investment decisions with long gestations. Moreover, several years probably would be required before the stabilization was confidently viewed as sufficiently credible to induce large changes in desired investments.

3. The buffer stock managers operate with sufficient financial reserves and sufficient commodity reserves so that they can buy or sell to keep the average annual deflated commodity prices within specified bands (±15 percent) of the known secular trends for the 1950–1975 period. No export or production quotas are utilized by the commodity agreement.[5] This assumption about the operation of the buffer stock has a number of subcomponents that merit some comments.

The existence of sufficient financial reserves means that the buffer stocks can always buy to defend the price floor, which should discourage destabilizing speculation. The existence of sufficient commodity reserves to be able always to defend the price ceiling also should discourage destabilizing speculation. The reason for this assumption is to permit the simulation of the ongoing behavior of buffer stock stabilization without overemphasis on the end points of the scheme. However, for some commodities it does imply that the buffer stock must start the period with initial commodity reserves in order always to have stocks at nonnegative levels.

The presumed knowledge of the price trends tends to reduce the costs and increase the profitability of the buffer stock operation in comparison to situations in which large errors are made concerning the secular trends. In the present simulations, errors are not made because of confusion between short-run and long-run price movements.

The price target and floors and ceilings are in real terms. This choice is made because economic behavior generally is posited and empirically tested in real terms. In the absence of money illusion, moreover, long-run equilibrium prices also are in real terms, and the aim of pure price stabilization schemes is to limit fluctuations around long-run real equilibrium prices. Note that the use of price targets in real terms is not tantamount to indexing. The secular trend in the real price may be either up or down. The directions of movement reflect changes in the long-run market forces.

The prices, and all other variables in the model, are annual averages. The use of these annual averages may understate somewhat the costs of buffer stock operations. Transaction costs may be incurred during a year because the price otherwise would move above and/or below the allowable range, and yet the average price may be within the allowable range (thus indicating no transaction costs). This problem probably is most important for agricultural products with strong seasonal cycles (e.g., cocoa). For actual operation in such cases, a seasonal component might usefully be superimposed on the secular trend to avoid too many transactions that would be reversed shortly thereafter.

Finally, it should be emphasized that the simulated rules of operation for the buffer stock are quite simple and mechanical. Buffer stock managers well might have more information than is included in these simulations. More flexible rules of operation may be desirable.[6] To the extent that either of these possibilities is true, the mechanical procedure simulated in this investigation may overstate the costs of buffer stock operations.

4. The present discounted value of a buffer stock operation is the sum of three components. The first component is the present discounted value of the initial commodity stock (if any).[7] Second is the present discounted value of all activities (i.e., revenues minus expenditures) of the buffer stock during the decade. Revenues are from sales at the price ceiling (with a constant percentage discount in cases where it is necessary, such as coffee). Expenditures are from purchases at the floor price, transaction costs (a constant percentage of sales or purchases), storage costs (a constant rate for the average stocks held each year), and stock deterioration (at rates proportional to quantities). The third component is the present discounted value of the stocks still held at the end of the decade. All rates and ratios (i.e., for transaction costs, storage costs, price, quality discounts, and deterioration) are assumed to be constant in real terms at levels suggested by UNCTAD (1975*a*). The initial and final stocks are valued at the average prevailing market prices in the year before and year after the decade of buffer stock operations, respectively, which causes an upward bias in the calculation of the present discounted value. All values are discounted to the start of the period (although in 1975 prices) by using a real discount rate of 5 percent (implying a nominal rate of about 10 percent at current inflation rates).

The impact of some of the assumptions underlying the simulations is to overestimate the present discounted net value of the buffer stock programs: that private stocks do not fall due to fewer incentives for hedging and speculating, that the greater certainty does not cause shifts in the supply function or change its elasticities or shorten the supply lags within the decade, the nonstochastic nature of the simulations, the assumption that the price ceilings can be defended even though the buffer stock starts with just sufficient quantities to assure nonnegative levels during the decade of operation, that historically operative production and export restrictions on the commodities of interest are not changed, that the secular price trends are known by the buffer stock operators, that in a given year for a particular buffer stock there is not both selling and buying, that initial and final stocks are valued correctly at 1962 and 1973 prices, that storage costs would not increase with the increased volume. Other assumptions probably result in an understatement: that the greater price certainty does not result in greater private inventories and/or greater demands with shorter lags due to risk aversion, that the buffer stock managers have no better information than that described by the mechanical rules of behavior utilized in the simulations, that no additional export or production restrictions are imposed, that storage and transaction costs do not exhibit economies of scale. To a certain extent, of course, these biases are counterbalancing.[8] If one or the other dominates, however, it is my judgment that the present discounted values probably are overestimated (i.e., the costs of the buffer stocks are understated). In an attempt to offset this bias, the estimates discussed below assume a value of zero for terminal buffer stocks.

Simulation Results

These simulations lead to a number of major observations about the UNCTAD Integrated Programme for Commodities, each of which is now discussed in turn. All these comments, of course, are conditional on the preceding assumptions, which, for economy of space and clarity, are not constantly repeated.

1. *The gross revenue gains to the producing countries from the operation of this specific program are substantial.* The increase in the present discounted value of real producers' revenues exceeds 4 billion 1975 dollars for the 8 core commodities included.[9] This present discounted value is equivalent to a constant value of 536 million 1975 dollars per year over the decade. Weighting the present discounted value of real gross revenue gains for each commodity by the share of developing-country production of that commodity gives a total present discounted value of $5.4 billion to the developing countries, which is equivalent to a constant annual flow of $700 million over the decade.[10] While these numbers are not large in comparison to the numbers involved in OPEC, in my judgment they are significant in comparison to many other existing or potential sources of foreign exchange for the nonoil-producing Third World.

Part of this revenue gain reflects negative present discounted values of buffer stock operations (see point 4 below), the division of the sources of which depends on the exact details of the negotiated agreements—but at least a portion of which probably would come from the developing countries themselves. The source of the largest part, however, is increased expenditure on the sum of these commodities by consumers, who are concentrated in the developed countries. With perfect knowledge and these conditions, therefore, the motivation for the advocacy of these specific buffer stock schemes at least for the core commodities by the developing countries as a group, *ceteris paribus,* is clear. In the same situation the opposition by informed consumers is clear, unless they see the transfer of resources to commodity producers as desirable and unobtainable by other better means, or unless they see large possible gains for themselves resulting from the lessening of inflation pressures (see point 10 below). Of course, consumer interests are not always well represented in such negotiations because they are diffuse. Governments of consumers may agree to such arrangements because they think that transfers to the developing countries are desirable, but explicit direct transfers are politically unpopular among their constituents who, on the other hand, do not perceive well the nature of the transfers if they are through increased prices. To be more explicit, the International Coffee Agreement, which Fisher (1972) and Law (1975) suggest transferred $500 million to $600 million per year, may have had such a character. There was no large organized consumer opposition to the agreement, yet it is not obvious that the governments of the consuming nations could have proposed instead additional direct transfers of the magnitude involved to the coffee-producing nations without substantial political opposition.

2. *The gross revenue gains vary substantially across commodities.* For the specific programs and conditions examined, the present discounted real values of revenue gains to coffee, cocoa, and rubber total over $6 billion. The same statistic for copper and tin is about *minus* $2 billion. These differences primarily are due to differences in where the no buffer stock price path was in 1963-1972 (as a result of the underlying supply and demand forces) relative to the secular trend for the 1950-1974 quarter century. Under different conditions, or with different rules of operation, the details would change, but a large dispersion of gross gains probably would remain. Such a dispersion, especially if there were widespread perceptions of losses, would place considerable strain on any integrated program.

Another aspect of the distribution-of-gains question is related to the extent to which developing versus developed countries are producers or consumers of these commodities. For the core commodities, the developing countries dominate exports with almost three quarters of the total and over half of every commodity. They also account for roughly half of world production (although substantially less than half for sugar, cotton, and copper). The developed countries dominate imports with approximately three-quarters of the total and over half of each commodity. To the extent that international commodity agreements for these 10 core commodities affect producers or exporters, therefore, the developing countries are most affected. To the extent that they affect importers of these 10 commodities, the developed nations are most affected.

Yet another aspect of the distribution question that has received considerable attention is the nature of the distribution among the developing countries. The 10 core commodities account for over two-thirds of the export value for 8 countries (in order: Zambia, Mauritius, Uganda, Bangladesh, Rwanda, Chile, Zaire, and Sri Lanka) and over a third for another 22 developing nations (Dominican Republic, Ghana, Cameroon, Sudan, Guatemala, Bolivia, El Salvador, Haiti, Nicaragua, Togo, Ivory Coast, Egypt, Malaysia, Ethiopia, Peru, Brazil, Western Samoa, Guyana, Madagascar, Tanzania, Philippines, and Syria). Thus the distribution of effects is fairly widespread. The countries affected, moreover, generally include ones that are not among the more developed of the developing nations (although there are exceptions, such as Chile). And yet, developing countries with vast numbers of people are relatively unaffected on the export side. Non-OPEC developing countries that do not have more than a third of their export value in these 10 commodities and that have more than 20 million inhabitants include the People's Republic of China, India (with 20 percent of its exports in the core commodities), Pakistan (13 percent), Mexico (18 percent), Vietnam (although the Southern part had 56 percent in rubber in the early 1970s), Burma, Colombia (26 percent), Argentina, and Afghanistan.

The other side of the question about the distribution of effects among developing countries is related to imports and consumption. For the 10 core commodities, 12 percent of world imports are by developing countries. UNCTAD

(1975*b*) suggests that these are not particularly concentrated in the import basket of a few countries, especially not the poorer ones.

3. *Revenue does not seem to be destabilized by these programs.* As point 1 in the previous section discusses, price stabilization by buffer stock operations may (or may not) stabilize revenues. Under the assumptions of these simulations, revenue fluctuations remain the same for most commodities but are reduced for cocoa, rubber, sisal, and perhaps tea and copper. With perfect knowledge, once again, the general stabilizing effects of the agreements on prices and, in some cases, on revenues would make them desirable from the point of view of risk-averse producers and consumers.

4. *The present discounted values of the buffer stock agency operations depend critically on the evaluation of terminal stocks (and on other assumptions) but may be quite considerable in absolute value.* The present discounted value of buffer stock agency operations without including the value of terminal stocks is minus $1892 million for the core commodities. The exclusion of sugar and cotton, in addition to the biases discussed above, suggests that these estimates are probably too high (algebraically). In other words, the losses probably would be greater.

But in one respect these figures are biased downward, perhaps considerably: terminal stocks are valued at zero. If terminal stocks are valued at the post-terminal-year market price, in fact, for many of the individual commodities and for the sum of the 8 core commodities, the present discounted values are positive.

However, such a calculation is misleading since: (1) the post-terminal year's (i.e., 1973) actual prices generally were quite high (and presumably would not have been nearly as high if such programs had been in operation for 1963–1972 and had accumulated buffer stocks), and (2) stocks could not be sold in the post-terminal year without driving down the price. Under the assumption that there are no other sources of biases, for nonnegative present discounted values of buffer stock operations, the terminal stock must have been salable in the post-terminal year for at least 63 percent of the actual price prevailing in 1973 on the average for the 8 core commodities. Sales at such prices seem unlikely. When consideration is given to other biases, moreover, it appears to be almost certain that the present discounted values of buffer stock operations for most of these commodities are negative.

Does a negative value for buffer stock operations mean that they are undesirable? From the point of view of all producers combined together, the answer is no. Net gains are positive even if the losses resulting from buffer stock operations (with final stocks valued at zero) are subtracted from the gross revenues: $2248 million for the 8 core commodities.

What about a broader viewpoint? Smith (1975) argues that a necessary condition of an optimal buffer stock operation (i.e., one that maximizes the sum of consumer and producer surpluses) is that its expected present discounted value is zero. However, such a rule is not optimal if there is risk-aversion or distributional effects. Both these considerations raise the possibility that a socially optimal policy implies negative present discounted values. If that is the case, then subsidies are required to follow such a policy.

5. *The choice of price bandwidths affects substantially the order of magnitude involved.* Going from a ±15 to a ±5 percent band around the secular price increases gross present discounted producers' revenues from $4140 million to $5851 million and reduces the present discounted value of buffer stock operations from minus $1892 million to minus $4141 million for the sum of the 8 core commodities. For every individual commodity and for the aggregates, the present discounted value of buffer stock operation (ignoring terminal stocks) is reduced.

6. *The results also are somewhat sensitive to the discount rate.* Going from a 5 to a 2 percent *real* discount rate, for example, increases the present discounted real values of gross producers' revenue from $4140 million to $4856 million and of buffer stock operations from minus $1892 million to minus $2333 million for the sum of the 8 core commodities. Such differences are of some consequence. However, of much more significance than this range of discount rates are questions related to the bandwidth and the evaluation of terminal stocks.

7. *The dynamic lags suggest that there may be long periods without selling or without buying, that agreements should cover a number of years, and that the financial requirements are spread over several years.* The lag structures, especially in the production of the tree crops and of the minerals, imply fairly long supply adjustments in a number of cases. For several of these products, for example, supply increases in response to initial price rises drive down prices after six or seven years. The dynamics of the supply and demand interactions also cause long periods in which particular buffer stocks do not buy or do not sell: 7.0 and 6.0 years respectively are the average maximums across the 8 core commodities. The implications are several. First, if there is no selling for a long period of time, most of the agricultural stocks have to be rotated, which increases transaction costs and lowers the present discounted value of stock operations. Second, the possibilities of fairly long swings make it difficult to separate the cycle from secular trends and, thus, to know if inventories are too large at a particular point in time.[11] Third, likewise the judgment of the success or failure of a particular agreement is difficult to make until it has operated for a while. Fourth, for most, if not all, of these commodities, therefore, it would seem preferable if agreements were longer than the 5-year maximum suggested by the Havana Charter and followed since then. For this to be possible, the agreements probably have to incorporate a fair amount of flexibility. Fifth, for most agreements, the highest financial requirements are not at the start but only after stocks build up over several years. In the extreme case of tea, for example, no purchases are made until the ninth year. Therefore, the required funding will not be used all at once, but over a number of years.

8. *The access to financial resources of $6 billion suggested by UNCTAD is not likely to be sufficient for the core commodities.* I am assuming that the financial reserves of any buffer stock are sufficient so that its intention and ability to maintain the price floor is credible to speculators. Evaluating what this means is difficult. However, we can obtain a rough estimate for the sum of all 8 of the core commodities by asking how much would be required to purchase the maximum stocks implied by the simulations. At the average 1970–1974 prices, the answer is $5085 million, which is 75 percent greater than the UNCTAD estimate for the same 8 commodities at the same prices. And even this answer is low, for at least two additional reasons to the difficult question of what reserves are required to convince speculators of the capability to define the price floor: (1) finances are needed for transactions and storage costs, not only acquisitions; and (2) this calculation is based on the average nominal 1970–1974 price, which probably is too low because of general inflation. Changing to the average real 1970–1974 price would increase the value by 27 percent to $6473 million.

If the same proportional adjustments are made to the UNCTAD estimates for sugar and cotton, the total is about $10.4 billion. This figure ignores the gains from integration (point 9 below) but does not include backup reserves to guarantee success against downward speculation. Therefore, I concur with Kreinin and Finger (1976) that the proposed fund of $6 billion quite possibly would be inadequate.

9. *There are some substantial potential gains from integrating the financing across commodities in the sense that the total funding requirements are lower.* Table 16-1 provides illustrations for the 8 core commodities that are included. The funds released primarily by the copper and tin sales in the third through ninth years could provide some of the financing for cocoa, coffee, and sisal purchases in this period. The funds released by large coffee sales in the eighth year would cover much of the purchases of tea, rubber, cocoa, and copper in the ninth and tenth years. Of course, if there were perfect capital markets, there would not be any such gains. Also, if each participant had a complete portfolio of financing for all the buffer stock agreements for the individual core commodities, it could assure the same gains as with the Common Fund. However, capital markets are far from perfect, and individual buffer stock operations are likely to be financed only by those participating heavily in the market of interest; so individual pooling is likely to be less than complete in many cases (especially for the developing country participants who are liable to be involved in only a few or even one of the individual arrangements).

10. *Gains from the reduction of inflationary pressures, especially for consuming nations, may be substantially greater than the revenue gains to producing nations or the cost of buffer stock operations.* To this point, I have focused on the implications of the proposed buffer stock arrangements within the framework of the operations of the relevant commodity markets. Within that

Table 16–1
Value of Simulated Buffer Stock Annual Purchases and Sales in Millions of United States Dollars over Decade of Operation with ±15 Percent Band around Secular Trends in Deflated Price

	Year of Buffer Stock Operation									
Commodity	*1*	*2*	*3*	*4*	*5*	*6*	*7*	*8*	*9*	*10*
1. *Core Commodities*										
Coffee	1048	0	0	0	46	0	0	-1210	0	0
Cocoa	65	0	141	29	19	0	0	0	0	91
Tea	0	0	0	0	0	0	0	0	193	0
Rubber	0	0	0	-6	-2	0	0	1	693	627
Jute	0	0	0	0	0	0	0	0	0	0
Sisal	-2	-4	-3	-2	-1	1	5	7	7	7
Copper	95	33	-29	-92	-64	-201	-158	-43	-3	219
Tin	0	-1	-4	-8	-14	-18	-15	-8	-4	-2
Sum of 8 Core Commodities	1206	28	105	-79	-16	-218	-168	-1253	886	942
2. *Other Commodities*										
Wheat	0	0	0	203	0	0	0	-583	427	459
Rice	0	0	-2	115	-2	2	-2	2701	2	0
Wool	0	0	0	63	215	308	316	348	419	507
Bauxite	0	0	0	0	0	0	0	0	0	0
Iron Ore	0	0	0	0	0	0	0	0	0	0
Sum of 13 Commodities	1206	28	103	302	197	92	146	1213	1734	1908

framework, the simulations suggest that a fairly substantial resource transfer may occur from consumers to producers.

However, from a broader perspective it is possible that consumers would reap much larger benefits given inflation-output trade-offs. Over the quarter century ending in 1975, the 10 core commodities had average price levels substantially above the secular trends a number of times: in 27 cases there were prices from 15 to 30 percent above the trend; in 18 cases, 30 to 50 percent above; in 9 cases, 50 to 100 percent above; and in 4 cases, over 100 percent above. These commodity prices high above the trend may cause output losses because they induce restrictive anti-inflationary macro economic policies.

To explore this possibility, first consider the question: what is the magnitude of the impact of commodity price rises on inflation in the developed countries? Popkin (1974) estimates that a 14.5 percent increase in the price of nonfood and nonfuel raw materials causes a 1 percent increase in the consumer price index of the United States. The LINK model suggests that a 33 percent increase in prices of nonfuel commodity exports from the developing countries is required to increase the consumer price index of the United States by 1 percent (Waelbroeck, 1976). The latter is an underestimate of the impact of changes of international commodity prices on inflation in the Unitd States because it considers only the effect of the proportion of commodities that are produced in the developing countries. Both estimates are on the low side to the extent that there exist substantial oligopolistic industries that use commodity price rises to implement "cost-justified" increases in their own prices. However, both estimates are high for our purposes to the extent that they include more commodities than the 10 which are in the UNCTAD core group. Nevertheless, they suggest that, as a conservative ballpark range, increases of 30 to 60 percent in the prices of the core commodities would be required to cause a 1 percent rise in the United States consumer price index. In conjunction with the history of commodity price increases, such a range suggests that imposing ±15 percent bands on prices might reduce inflationary pressure at least by 0.2 to 0.4 percent for several years in a decade of operation.

Such numbers prima facie may not seem to be so large. But what do they mean in terms of real output? In order to avoid such a degree of inflation, available Phillips' curve estimates suggest that unemployment would have to be increased by about 0.03 to 0.3 percent (Perry, 1970; Wachter, 1976). Okun's (1962) law suggests that this translates into about 0.1 to 0.9 percent of real GNP. To be conservative, consider the middle of this range. It implies a gain of about $8 or $9 billion in one year for the United States economy! To continue to be conservative, assume that a gain of this magnitude is experienced only twice in a decade. The present discounted value to the United States alone still would be about $15 billion!

Such an estimate is only a ballpark figure based on rough estimates. Nevertheless it suggests the possibility that the really large gainers from international commodity stabilization programs may be the residents of the developed nations because of the amelioration of inflationary pressures. Of course, there also would be some similar, although probably smaller, benefits to the producer countries because of the reduction of world wide inflationary pressures.

11. *The financial implications of using buffer stocks to change the secular trends of deflated prices can be very large.* The second major objective of the UNCTAD IV (1976*b*) resolution is to improve the secular trend of commodity prices. Indexation of such prices (i.e., tying them to some price index, such as that for the imports of the developing countries) is not mentioned explicitly, but the UNCTAD IV discussions occurred in the context of considerable debates about the pros and cons of indexation (e.g., UNCTAD (1975*c*)). Of course, indexation is only a special case of changing the secular trend in the relevant deflated price to a value of zero.

I have also conducted a set of simulations of stockpile policies to increase the secular trend of the deflated commodity prices by 2 percent, with a ±15 percent price bandwidth. That is, instead of using the actual secular trends, 2 percent is added algebraically to each of those estimates (so the trend deflated price for coffee, for example, grows at -1.5 percent instead of -3.5 percent). As a result, the secular trends are 10.5 percent above the ones implied by the historical estimates in the fifth year and 22.1 percent above in the tenth year. This is tantamount to indexation if the growth rate in the actual trend is -2.0 percent, but less (more) than indexation if the growth rate in the actual trend is below (above) this magnitude.

A comparison of these results with those for pure price stabilization leads to a simple observation: The changes implied are enormous! For the sum of the 10 core commodities, the gross revenue gain as compared to the base simulation is $87 billion instead of $4 billion; the equivalent constant annual value is $11 billion instead of a little over a half billion; the present discounted real value of buffer stock operations, excluding final inventories (which must be valued at close to zero in this scheme, given their sizes), is minus $12 billion instead of minus $2 billion; and the maximum stocks at least double and generally increase by a factor of five or more.

The basic conclusion is obvious: to alter the secular trend of the deflated commodity prices by much for very much time implies changes and commitments of orders of magnitude that probably are economically and politically infeasible.[12] This is true whether such an effort is intentional as part of an international agreement or is accidental as a result of incorrect perceptions of the secular price trend by the buffer stock managers.

Such a result means that attempts to increase the secular trend even slightly will probably be under great strain. Considerations of the theoretical and historical factors underlying successful producer oligopolistic collusion to increase prices, moreover, suggests that in some dimensions the conditions for success with the core commodities are present (e.g., product homogeneity, frequent transactions, a common perceived interest), but in many others they are not present for all or many of the commodities (e.g., high fixed costs and scale returns, except possibly for the minerals). For none of the 10 core commodities do all the desirable conditions seem to be present.[13]

Therefore, the possibility of maintaining such price-increasing efforts even for a little while probably increases substantially if the governments of the consuming countries can be persuaded to cooperate. Such cooperation may enforce discipline and limit the expansion of fringe producers. This probably is one of the reasons that the developing countries have proposed international commodity agreements instead of producer associations.

This basic result, together with the fairly long swings previously noted, also points to the great difficulty of operating a price-stabilization agreement. Short-run fluctuations must be separated from long-run trends for such an agreement to be successful. If not, it will not add much to stabilization or it will absorb large resources (or sell everything), attempting to maintain a too high (low) secular trend. And historical experience suggests that identifying the underlying trends is indeed difficult.[14]

Conclusion

This empirical investigation leads me to a much more positive appraisal, albeit qualified, of the UNCTAD Integrated Programme for Commodities than most other analysts have made primarily on the basis of a priori reasoning. To be sure, the simulations point to significant problems: the compensation of producers who lose, the identification of the underlying secular price trends, the lack of much gain for many large developing countries, the probable greater need for access to financing than in the proposal. But the simulations also suggest that, under a plausible set of conditions, the gains to developing and developed countries alike may be substantial, with no increase in revenue fluctuations and with advantages from financial integration. It is my judgment, moreover, that such gains to the developing countries are not likely to be offset completely by reductions in other sources of foreign exchange. Therefore—despite the qualifications previously noted—it probably makes sense for the developing nations as a group to be strong advocates of the UNCTAD proposal.

Of course, the empirical analysis presented here is based on a particular set of assumptions. Further work should be undertaken to explore the sensitivity of the results to alternative assumptions, including stochastic considerations. Nevertheless, the results are provocative. And, once, again, in contrast to many previous primarily a priori analyses of the UNCTAD proposal, they suggest that the integrated program should be considered a serious effort that well might result in significant attainment of many of its stated goals.

Notes

1. This result is surprising and does not seem consistent with the claim of less short-run substitution possibilities.

2. My judgment that their political power is growing is not incontestable. Perhaps the developing nations had more political power in an important sense while they could bargain with the superpowers within the framework of the more intense cold war confrontation. In some cases, even in the earlier colonial period, producers of some commodities may have had more power relative to consumers since they were represented by the relatively strong colonial powers (which also, of course, represented the consumer interests).

3. Because of the apparent lack of robustness and stability in the experiments with the sugar and cotton models, these two commodities are excluded.

4. The models are from Adams and Behrman (1976); Agosín (1976); and Behrman (1975). The first and last of these sources discuss extensively the properties of the models.

5. Actual quotas and restrictions are used to the same extent as in the sample period, however, since the structural estimates reflect the impact of any such policies.

6. An example of a more flexible rule would be to shift the price band (or perhaps the floor or the ceiling) inversely with the size of the buffer stock. Such a procedure would increase uncertainty for the private sector and reduce price stability in comparison to a successful mixed-band scheme.

7. This initial commodity stock, as indicated above, is just of sufficient magnitude to allow the buffer stock operations always to defend the ceiling over the decade of the simulation.

8. In addition to the examples cited in this paragraph, other assumptions may be quite important. The leading example is the particular choice of exogenous world economic behavior (i.e., that experienced in 1963-1972). As compared with some other period, this assumption may bias the estimates either up or down.

9. If the UNCTAD estimates of the proportions for the purchase cost of sugar and cotton to that of the other 8 core commodities can be used as a guide, the figures for the 8 core commodities for which simulations are presented need to be multiplied by a factor of 1.5 to 1.7 to obtain estimates for all 10 core commodities.

10. For the core group, the developing countries' gain exceeds the total value because the developing countries have relatively high proportions of world production for those commodities with positive gross revenue gains.

11. This characteristic makes it difficult to know how to trigger export and production quotas. Quotas have the effect of limiting buffer stock acquisition, but have shortcomings, since they may disrupt capacity expansion (e.g., Desai (1966)), can not defend the ceiling unless they are imposed on use (which

does not seem likely) and are difficult to allocate. They also are opposed by the United States on the grounds that they artificially limit supplies (Katz (1976).

12. Perhaps this statement is overly strong. The numbers involved are only about a sixth of the value of the changes wrought by OPEC. However, we are not discussing oil here, and the required transfers are very large in comparison with historical values and with current aid and related flows. In this case, moreover, less cooperation might be expected from the industrial nations than in the price-stabilization arrangement previously discussed because of the smaller initial and eventually perverse tendency to reduce inflationary pressures.

13. Among the 10 core commodities the prospects probably are the best for a price-increasing arrangement for copper. That the developing countries only account for about 40 percent of world production of this mineral, however, implies that the developing-country producers alone could not have much probability of success. Pindyck (1976) comes to the same conclusion for copper on the basis of an optimal control model.

14. A possibly more optimistic characterization is that the identification of the long-run trend will be made easier by the magnitude of operations required if the attempt is made to move too far away from it. However, the difficult problem noted above of separating fluctuations with their long swings from changes in the trend remains.

Bibliography

Adams, F.G., and J.R. Behrman. 1976. *Econometric Models of World Agricultural Commodity Markets: Cocoa, Coffee, Tea, Wool, Cotton, Sugar, Wheat, Rice.* Cambridge: Ballinger.

Agosín, M. 1976. "Preliminary Econometric Models of Sisal, Iron Ore, Rubber, and Copper." New York: UNCTAD (draft).

Behrman, J.R. 1975. "Mini Models for Eleven International Commodity Markets." Philadelphia: Univ. of Pennsylvania (report for UNCTAD).

——. 1977. *International Commodity Agreements: An Evaluation of the UNCTAD Integrated Commodity Programme."* Washington: Overseas Development Council.

Bergsten, C.F. 1976. "A New OPEC in Bauxite." *Challenge* 19, 3 (July/August): 12-20.

Brook, E.M., and E.R. Grilli. 1977. "Commodity Price Stabilization and the Developing World." *Finance and Development* 14, 1 (March):8-11.

Cooper, R.N., and R.Z. Lawrence. 1975. "The 1972-1975 Commodity Boom." *Brookings Papers on Economic Activity,* 671-715.

Desai, M. 1966. "An Econometric Model of the World Tin Economy, 1948-1961." *Econometrica* 34:105-134.

Eads, G.C. 1976. "Address of Executive Director of National Commission on

Supplies and Shortages Before the Section of Natural Resources Law." American Bar Association Convention, Atlanta, Georgia, August 10, 1976.

Eckbo, P.L. 1975. "OPEC and the Experience of Previous International Commodity Cartels." Cambridge, Mass.: M.I.T. Energy Laboratory Working Paper Number 75–008WP.

Erb, G.F., and V. Kallab, eds. 1975. *Beyond Dependency: The Developing World Speaks Out.* Washington, D.C.: Overseas Development Council.

Fisher, B.S. 1972. *The International Coffee Agreement: A Study in Coffee Diplomacy.* New York: Praeger.

Johnson, H.G. 1976. "Commodities: Less Developed Countries' Demands and Developed Countries' Response." Paper presented at M.I.T. Workshop on Specific Proposals and Desirable DC Response to LDC Demands Regarding the New International Economic Order, May 17–20, 1976.

Junz, H., and P. MacAvoy. 1977. "A Hard Look at Prospects for Commodity Agreements." Washington, D.C. Mimeographed.

Katz, J.L. 1976. "International Commodity Policy." Statement by Deputy Assistant Secretary for Economic and Business Affairs before the House Subcommittees on International Organizations, International Policy, and International Trade and Commerce.

Kreinin, M.E., and J.M. Finger. 1976. "A New International Economic Order: A Critical Survey of its Issues." *Journal of World Trade Law* (September/October).

Law, A.D. 1975. *International Commodity Agreements: Setting, Performance, and Prospects.* Lexington, Mass.: Lexington Books, D.C. Heath.

Lewis, P. 1976. "The Have-Nots are Gaining Ground in Their Drive to Gain Concessions." *National Journal* (June 5):774–782.

McCulloch, R. 1976. "Economic Policy in the United Nations: A New International Economic Order." Cambridge, Mass.: Harvard Univ. Mimeographed.

Michalopoulos, C., and L.L. Perez. 1977. "Commodity Trade Policy Initiatives and Issues." Washington, D.C.: AID. Mimeographed.

Newbery, D.M.G. 1976. "Price Stabilization With Risky Production." Palo Alto: Stanford Univ. Mimeographed.

Okun, A.M. 1962. *Proceedings of the Business and Economics Statistics Section.* American Statistical Association.

Perry, G.L. 1970. "Changing Labor Markets and Inflation." *Brookings Papers on Economic Activity,* 411–448.

Pindyck, R.S. 1976. "Gains to Producers from the Cartelization of Exhaustible Resources." Cambridge, Mass.: M.I.T. Energy Laboratory Working Paper No. 12.

Popkin, J. 1974. "Commodity Prices and the U.S. Price Level." *Brookings Papers on Economic Activity.*

Porter, R.L. 1970. "On Placing the Blame for Primary Product Instability." *International Economic Review* 11, 1 (February):175–178.

Sarris, A.H., and L. Taylor. 1978. "Buffer Stock Analysis for Agricultural Products: Theoretical Murk or Empirical Resolution." in *Stabilizing World Commodity Markets* eds. F. Gerard Adams and Sonia Klein. Lexington, Mass.: Lexington Books, D.C. Heath and Company.

Smith, G.W. 1975. "An Economic Evaluation of International Buffer Stocks for Copper." Mimeographed.

——. 1976. "Informational Efficiency in Commodity Markets. Houston: Rice Univ. Mimeographed.

Smith G.W., and G.R. Schink. 1975. "The International Tin Agreement: A Reassessment," Houston: Rice Univ. Program of Development Studies Discussion Paper No. 69.

Turnovsky, S.J. 1978. "The Distribution of Welfare Gains from Price Stabilization: A Survey of Some Theoretical Issues." in *Stabilizing World Commodity Markets* eds. F. Gerard Adams and Sonia Klein. Lexington, Mass.: Lexington Books, D.C. Heath and Company.

UNCTAD. 1975*a*. "Progress Report on Storage Costs and Warehouse Facilities." Geneva, TD/B/C.1/187.

——. 1975*b*. "The Impact on Imports, Particularly of Developing Countries." Geneva, TD/B/C.1/169.

——. 1975*c*. "A Common Fund for the Financing of Commodity Stocks: Amounts, Terms and Prospective Source of Finances." Geneva, TD/B/C.1/184.

——. 1976*a*. "An Integrated Commodity Programme." Geneva.

——. 1976*b*. "Resolution Adopted by the Conference: Integrated Programme for Commodities." Geneva, TD/RES/93 (IV).

Wachter, M.L. 1976. "The Changing Cyclical Responsiveness of Wage Inflation." *Brookings Papers on Economic Activity,* 115-168.

Waelbroeck, J.L., ed. 1976). *The Models of Project Link.* Amsterdam: North-Holland.

Index

Index

Abe, M.A., 17
Adams, F. Gerard, 15, 16, 23, 87, 106
Africa, 40, 178, 227, 295
Agriculture:
  and agricultural products, buffer stock analysis for, 149-158
  coffee production, 35-39, 43, 168, 169, 202
  corn-hog cycle in, 189-191
  econometrics of, 105, 111
  and entry into market, 111, 168, 202
  farm income, 182n
  and futures prices, 170
  rice production, 72
  See also Climate
Agriculture, U.S. Department of (USDA), 23
  Systems Workshop Proceedings, 20
Ahn, C.Y., 17
Aid. *See* LDCs (less-developed countries)
Alaska, 22
Algeria, 220, 296
Allingham, M., 23
Amalgamated Copper Company, 227. *See also* Copper
America. *See* Latin America; United States
American Producers' Association, 227
Anaconda copper mine, 226. *See also* Copper
Anderson, J.E., 142
Argentina, 72, 158, 178, 310
ARIMA (autoregressive integrated moving average) models, 25, 166, 167, 170
  and lagged moving average, 168
Arrow, K.J., 123
Arthur D. Little, Inc., 216
Asia, 295. *See also individual countries*
Australia, 111, 211n, 220, 229, 234n, 240
  and Sydney wool futures, 164, 166
Ayres, R.U., 21

Batra, R.N., 142
Baughman, M.L., 20
Bauxite, 179, 199, 215, 222, 282
  and International Association (IBA), 211n, 218-219, 220, 221, 223, 224, 225, 304
Bawden, D., 28
Bayesian viewpoint, 26
Bear, R., 165
Behrman, Jere R., 15, 24, 87, 255, 259, 300-304 (passim)
Belgrade Summit Conference, 295
Bergsten, C.F., 304
Blakeslee, L.L., et al., 23
Boumedienne, Houari, 296
Box, G.E.P., 166, 170
Brandow, G.E., 24
Brazil, 281, 310
  as coffee producer, 38, 39, 42, 47-59 (passim), 169, 178
Brooke, E.M., 300, 301
Buffer stocks and buffer stock operations, 11, 167, 174, 255, 305-308
  analysis of, for agricultural products, 149-158
  Buffer Stock Authority (proposed), 206, 208-210
  Buffer Stock Facility and financing, 267n, 275, 290
  coffee market, 58, 59-60
  Common Fund and, 243, 246, 257, 259, 274-275, 289, 313
  costs and benefits of, 278-280
  econometrics and, 106
  and international agreements, 199, 203-204, 206, 208-210, 263, 264, 276, 271, 280. *See also* UNCTAD proposals for, *below*
  Keynes' proposal for, 195-196, 197, 198, 237
  and LDCs, 176
  loans for, 203-204
  and price stabilization, 122, 124, 127, 134, 136, 139, 143, 198, 218, 229, 235-238, 240, 248, 250, 251, 277-278, 283
  public, vs. private risk, 171-172
  rice market (simulation), 66-71, 72, 76-80, 278, 279
  simulated UNCTAD program, 305-317
  UNCTAD proposals for, 196-197, 219, 258, 259, 261, 274
  value of simulated, over decade of operation (table), 314
  See also Intervention, market
Burrows, J.C., 15, 24, 25
Butlin, M., 140
Byerlee, D., 23
Byron, R.P., 24

Cameroon Republic, 281, 310
Canada, 22, 111, 211n, 228, 230
  -U.S. wheat arrangement, 215
Carter, Jimmy, 298

Cereals and grains, 5, 97, 111, 156
futures, 164, 165
importers, 152
international agreements on, 199, 211n, 217, 280
market models for, 23
price stabilization for, gains and losses from, 157, 278
Chase Econometrics Foreign Exchange Model, 169
Chen, D.R., et al., 24
Chile, 178, 310
copper industry in, 217, 225–228 (passim), 230, 280
export instability in, 175, 184n
China, People's Republic of, 310
Christensen, L.R., 24
CIEC (Conference on International Economic Cooperation), 288, 297
CIPEC (Intergovernmental Council of Copper Exporting Countries), 111, 211n, 223
actions by, 226–229, 280
foreign exchange reserves of (table), 224
goals of, 216, 217, 220, 221, 225–226
organizational difficulties of, 229–231
Climate, 12, 27, 111, 168, 245, 248, 271
in coffee production, 38, 43, 53, 54, 280
and rice production, 64, 71, 73, 76, 78, 79
world drought simulation, 95–101
Cocoa, 202, 240n, 307, 310, 311, 313
as "core" commodity, 196
International Cocoa Agreement, 199, 280, 281
LDCs and, 179, 212n, 254, 255
price stability/instability, 100, 169, 217, 259, 278, 301
producer associations, 215, 222, 281, 282
Cocoa Producers' Alliance, 281
Coffee market:
aggregate, disaggregate models of, 40–50
agricultural aspects of, 35–39, 43, 168, 169, 202
behavior, 5, 100, 278, 301, 306, 308, 310, 313
and coffee as "core" commodity, 196. *See also* "Core" commodities
institutional and structural aspects of, 35–40
international agreements in, 111, 199, 204, 280–281. *See also* Inter-American Coffee Agreement; International Agreements
intervention in (historical and simulated), 35, 42, 50–60, 250
in LDCs vs. DCs, 59–60, 178, 179, 254, 255
producer associations, 215, 217, 222, 282. *See also* International Coffee Organization [ICO]
Cohen, K., 20
Colombia, 42, 48, 178, 310
COMLINK. *See* LINK project-system
Commission of the European Communities, 235. *See also* European Community
Commodity(ies):
characteristics (technical), 10, 236
and Commodity Price Authority (proposed), 206, 207–208
"core." *See* "Core" commodities
energy. *See* Fuel(s)
instability of, and market failure, 161–179
Integrated Programme for. *See* Integrated Programme for Commodities [IPC]
international agreements and proposals for, 52, 111, 199–200, 203–204, 271–283, 287–305. *See also* Integrated Programme for Commodities (IPC); International Agreements
modeling approaches, 11–24, 107. *See also* Market[s]
price cycles, 189–191, 306, 312
price fluctuations (table listing degree of), 10
price indexes (UN), 85, 87, 88, 92
primary, traded internationally, 4, 175
speculation, 26–27. *See also* Futures market
See also Commodity market(s); Price(s); *individual commodities*
Commodity market(s):
described, 3–7
domination of, 110
econometric approach to, 105–116
geographic distribution of major exporters, importers, 8–9
informational efficiency in, 161–171, 190, 216–217, 249
instability in, 271. *See also* Price stabilization
international (1972–1974 average, table of), 224
locations of, 6–7
and modeling methodologies, 11–28. *See also* Methodology[ies]
primary, in world model system, 83–101
producer associations and. *See* Producer associations

and simulation of buffer stock operations, 63-80, 106, 305-317
and simulation of market intervention (coffee), 35-60
See also Commodity(ies)
Common Fund, 235, 238
and assessment of UNCTAD proposal, 300-305
capitalization of, 196-197, 245-246, 258, 259, 260-261, 264-265, 291, 297, 299, 313
management and role of, 198, 203-208, 210, 211, 257, 261-263, 274-275, 288-292, 297, 299
resistance to, 287
U.S. and, 231, 243
Compensatory Financing Facility. *See* International Monetary Fund (IMF)
Consumers: DC, DEVE vs., 252, 265, 310
and oil prices, 223. *See also* Fuel[s]
price stabilization and, 127-133 (passim), 137, 141, 149, 154, 155, 158, 250, 252, 315. *See also* Price stabilization
surplus equated with welfare, 123, 125
U.S. price index, 315
Cooley, T.F., 26
Copper, 306
buffer stocks, 259, 278
CIPEC and. *See* CIPEC (Intergovernmental Council of Copper Exporting Countries)
as "core" commodity, 196. *See also* "Core" commodities
exports and export groups, 178, 179, 227, 254, 255, 310
international agreements on, 199, 280, 282
mine operation and market entry, 168, 223
model errors (table), 110
prices, 5, 95, 97, 164, 165, 218, 222, 225-231, 289
producer associations, 215, 217
revenues, 311, 313
and stockpiling (simulated and actual), 95, 218, 236-237.
See also Metals and metal markets
Copper Export Association, Copper Exporters, Inc., 227
"Core" commodities, 299, 311, 313
eighteen, 178, 232n, 243, 274
ten, 196, 205, 253, 254-255, 258, 259, 264, 297, 305, 306, 310, 315, 316, 317, 318n
Corea, Gamani, 287
Corn-hog cycle, 189-191
Cost of living index, 72. *See also* Inflation rate
Cotton, 112, 178, 196, 254. *See also* "Core" commodities
Court, R.H., 24
Cox, C.C., 166
Crom, R., 20
Cuba, 112

Data Resources, Inc., 23
Day, R.H., 17
Demand:
coffee, 39-40, 44-47
factors in and effect of, 6, 12, 87
instability in metals, 178, 248, 280
modeling, 24-25
rice, 63-65, 68, 71, 73
-supply equations, 123-127, 149-156. *See also* Supply
DEVE (developing world):
aid to, 271-272
vs. DC consumers, 252, 265, 310
and imports. *See* Import(s)
and IPC. *See* Integrated Programme for Commodities (IPC)
LINK model for, 85, 92, 100, 101
and Lomé agreement, 238-239
politics and policy of, 42, 247
stabilization of export earnings of. *See* Export(s)
UNCTAD study of, 106
See also LDCs (less-developed countries); Third World
Diversification, 262
Drèze, J.H., 26

Eads, George C., 298
Eckbo, P.L., 304
Econometrics:
and Chase Econometrics Foreign Exchange Model, 169
potentials of, for policy analysis, 105-116
Egypt, 112, 310
Epps, M.L., 14, 25
Equations, 17
coffee market modeling, 40-50
commodity market modeling, 11-15, 107
demand-supply, 123-127, 149-156
efficient-market, 162, 163
of optimal values, 113-114
price-band policy, 133-134
price expectation, 128-130
price linkage, 88-93
price stabilization, 134-139, 140-141, 155

world rice price formation, 63-65, 67-69, 71
Erb, G.F., 296
Europe:
coffee consumption in, 44, 52
Eastern Bloc, 112
and imports, 235, 237
Western, 211n
European Community, 235, 237, 238-239
grain-livestock economy model, 23
and STABEX project, 238-240
Exchange rates, 48, 72, 94, 154
and foreign exchange instability or reserves, 175-176, 223
and foreign exchange reserves of OPEC, IBA, CIPEC (table), 224
Export(s):
coal, 112
coffee, 47-59 (passim)
copper. *See* CIPEC (Intergovernmental Council of Copper Exporting Countries (CIPEC): Copper
of core commodities (tables), 253, 254-255
DEVE, 100, 246-247, 252, 310
and embargoes, 252
and exporting nations, 8-9, 178, 199, 200-206 (passim), 209, 210, 223, 252, 310
geographical distribution of exporters (table), 8-9
grain, 152, 154, 157, 215, 217-218
instability of LDCs, 175-177, 184n
OPEC and. *See* OPEC (Organization of Petroleum Exporting Countries)
prices, 219, 273, 274
prices, LINK system and, 84-85, 88, 93, 94
producer associations and, 217-218, 219, 221, 228
quotas, 47, 52-55 (passim), 58, 178, 196, 201, 202, 208-209, 211n, 212n, 318n
rice, 73
stabilization of receipts/earnings from, 238-240, 247-252, 275-276
taxes, 51, 55, 57, 280
UN price indexes, 88, 92
U.S. and, 211n, 215

Fama, Eugene, 161, 162, 163
FAO (Food and Agriculture Organization, UN), 151, 211n
Feder, G., 142
Federal Preparedness Agency, 21
Fertilizers. *See* Phosphates
Fibers, 111, 196, 222, 236, 251, 254, 262. *See also* "Core" commodities
Finger, J.M., 300, 304, 313
Fisher, B.S., 209
Fisher, J.C., 25
Flemming, J.S., 142
Foreign aid. *See* LDCs (less-developed countries)
Forrester, J.W., 20
France:
LINK model for, 84
Secretan syndicate in, 227
"Free zones," 201
French, B.C., 24
Fuel(s), 22, 88, 112, 247
consumption, 220
oil prices, 205, 215, 217, 223-224, 227, 237, 272-273, 274, 282, 296, 304
production costs, 230
See also OPEC (Organization of Petroleum Exporting Countries)
Futures markets, 4-5, 277-278
commodity speculation and, 26-27
and "random walk," 164, 165-166
rational expectations and prices in, 169-170, 174

GDP (gross domestic product), 87, 103n, 107
Geneva, international negotiations in, 220, 235, 237, 295
Ghana, 169, 281, 310
GNP (gross national product), 21, 173, 315
export instability and, 176, 177
of LDCs, 254
Government policy:
of DEVE, 47, 247
and domestic politics, 207, 283
and export quotas. *See* Export(s)
and inflation. *See* Inflation rate
and intervention in markets, 190, 306. *See also* Intervention, market
modeling, 27-28
and pricing of raw materials, 271
stockpiling, 173-174, 283, 289-290. *See also* Inventory[ies]
Grain. *See* Cereals and grains
Granger, C.W.J., 6, 25
cited as L-G, 164, 165, 166, 170
Gray, Roger W., 151, 165, 170
Great Depression, and coffee market, 51
Griffin, J.M., 16
Grilli, E.R., 300, 301
Group of 77. *See* LDCs (less-developed countries)

Guedry, L.J., 23
Gustafson, R.L., 168

Haidacher, R.C., 20
Halter, A.N., 23
Hanoch, G., 122, 140
Harris, D.P., 22
  et al., 22
Havana Charter, 312
Hazell, P.B.R., 120
Heien, D., 23
Hicks, N.L., 23
Higgins, C.I., 16
Hillman, Jimmye, 151
Hoffman, K.C., 21
Holder, S.H., Jr., et al., 21
Houck, J.P., 131
  et al., 28
Houthakker, H.S., 24, 165, 171, 172
Hudson, E.A., 22
Hueth, D., 132

IBRD (International Bank for Reconstruction and Development), 262, 263, 265, 291, 292
Iceland, 240
IDA (International Development Association), 263
IMF. *See* International Monetary Fund
Import(s):
  capacity, 217, 247
  coffee, 40, 44, 46–53 (passim), 58
  Europe and, 235, 237
  geographical distribution of importers (table), 8–9
  grain, 152
  and importing nations, 8–9, 28, 199, 200–210 (passim), 252, 281, 310
  by LDCs, DEVE, 274, 276, 310–311
  prices, LINK system and, 84, 85, 93
  quotas, 206
  U.S., 44, 235, 281
  and world trade in 10 core commodities (table), 253
Income:
  farm, 182n
  growth rate, 72
  in LDCs, 254
  transfer, to LDCs. *See* LDC (less-developed countries)
Indexation, 316
India, 246, 310
Indonesia, 229, 234n
Inflation rate:
  domestic (and cost of living index), 72
  and policies, 105, 275, 313, 315, 316
  prices and, 173–174, 249, 252, 271, 279
Information:
  and informational efficiency/inefficiency in commodity markets, 161–171, 190, 216–217, 249
  producer associations and, 216–217
Integrated Programme for Commodities (IPC), 195, 253, 256, 264, 280, 297
  and buffer stocks, 196–198, 208, 274, 275, 279
  Common Fund for. *See* Common Fund
  DCs and, 210–211, 252, 276, 283
  evolution of, 204–208, 243, 298
  objectives of, 205, 219–220, 244–245, 275, 282, 316
  simulation of, 305–317
Inter-American Coffee Agreement, 50, 52, 200
Interest rates, U.S. short-term, 167
Intergovernmental Council of Copper Exporting Countries. *See* CIPEC (Intergovernmental Council of Copper Exporting Countries)
International Agreements:
  Cocoa, 199, 281
  Coffee, 47, 50, 53, 54, 55, 58, 111, 178, 199, 206, 309
  Sugar (ISA), 281
  Tea, 200
  Tin, 206, 217, 280, 283
  Wheat, 211n, 280
  See also individual commodities
International Bauxite Association (IBA). *See* Bauxite
International Clearing Union (proposed), 196
International Coffee Organization (ICO), 48, 53, 54, 58–59
International Commodity Organizations (ICOs), 196–210 (passim), 203–204, 206, 207, 208, 210
International Copper Cartel, 227
International Monetary Fund (IMF), 176, 196, 291, 292, 299
  Buffer Stock Facility (BF) and financing, 267n, 275, 290
  Compensatory Financing Facility (CFF), 239, 247–249, 263, 275, 290
  vs. STABEX, 239–240
International Resource Bank, 298, 305
International Tin Council, 111. *See also* Tin
Intervention, market, 84–85, 94, 137–139, 172, 175, 306
  by CIPEC, 228, 229
  in coffee trade, 35, 42, 50–60, 250

by Common Fund, 204, 246
and econometric practice, 105–116
as political decision, 190–191. *See also* Government policy
and price supports, 28, 94, 111, 208
in rice trade, 66–80 (passim)
and stockpiling, 173–174. *See also* Inventory[ies]
See also Buffer stocks and buffer stock operations; Price(s); Price stabilization
Inventory(ies), 6, 10
coffee, 45–48, 50–52, 53, 66, 100
copper, 95, 218
end-of-year, in terms of month's supply (table), 11
and government stockpiling, 173–174, 283, 289–290. *See also* Intervention, market
metals, 111, 283
private stockpiling, risk and, 171–172, 190
and stockpiling simulation, 95
See also Buffer stocks and buffer stock operations
IP, IPC. *See* Integrated Programme for Commodities (IPC)
Iron ore, 112, 178, 251, 278. *See also* Metals and metal markets; Minerals
Israel, sugar import policy of, 28
Ivory Coast, 281, 310

Jamaica, 219, 220
Japan, 111, 211n, 228, 229, 282
Ministry of Agriculture and Forestry, 23
and rice market, 72, 73
Jenkins, G.M., 166, 170
Jensen's inequality, 127
Johnson, D. Gale, 151
Johnson, H.G., 300, 301
Jorgenson, D.W., 22
Judge, G.G., 17
Junz, Helen, 300, 304
Just, R.E., 24, 132, 142
Jute, 196, 236, 251, 254, 262. *See also* "Core" commodities

Kallab, V., 296
Katz, J.L., 298, 301
Kemp, M.C., 142
Kennecott copper mine, 226. *See also* Copper
Kennedy, John, and Kennedy administration, 178
Keynes, John Maynard, and Keynesian tradition, 84, 171, 172, 180n, 195–197, 198, 237
King, G.A., 23
Kite, R.C., 20
Kneese, A.V., 21
Knudsen, O., 177
Kokat, R.G., 21
Korean War, 52, 110
Kost, W.E., 23
Kraft, J. and A., 25
Kreinin, M.E., 300, 304, 313
Krueger, P.K., 21
Kuh, E., 26

Labys, Walter C., 6, 15, 24, 25, 26, 27, 164
cited as L–G, L–T, 164, 165, 166, 170
Langham, M.R., 20
Latin America, 228, 295, 310
cocoa producers in, 281
coffee and sugar production in, 37, 39–40, 42, 48, 52, 178
-U.S. cooperation (during World War II), 54
See also individual countries
Law, A.D., 309
LDCs (less-developed countries):
aid to, 111, 252–257, 261, 271–272. *See also* transfer of resources to, *below*
coffee market in, 59–60, 178, 179, 254, 255
and commodity agreements, 195, 272–274, 292, 298
commodity instability in, 175–177, 184n
and Commodity Price Authority (potential), 208, 210
and Common Fund, 203–204, 207, 211. *See also* Common Fund
GNP and income in, 254
and "Group of 77," 177, 274, 295, 297
and IPC, 205, 211, 244–245. *See also* Integrated Programme for Commodities [IPC]
as tea/cocoa producers, 111, 179, 212n, 246, 254, 255
transfer of resources to, 177–179, 207, 208, 210, 249, 252, 256–257, 264
See also DEVE (developing world); Third World
Lead, 237. *See also* Metals and metal markets
Leuthold, R.M., 170
et al., 25
Lewis, P., 297
LINK project/system, 23, 83, 84–88, 93–95, 97, 101, 106–108, 110, 315

and COMLINK, 83-85, 87, 88-99, 101
and SIMLINK, 23
Little, I.M.D., 123
Lomé agreement, 238. *See also* International Agreements
London Metal Exchange (LME), 110, 164, 165, 167, 225, 226, 227-229, 230. *See also* Metals and metal markets
Lutz, E., 132

MacAvoy, Paul W., 251, 300, 304
MacBean, A., 177
McCulloch, R., 300
McKinnon, R.I., 139
McNicol, David L., 251
Malaysia, 72, 178, 246, 310
Manila Declaration, 297
Manser, M., 24
Market(s):
commodity. *See* Commodity market(s)
efficiency. *See* Information
entry into, 111, 168, 202, 223
"expectations," 163. *See also* Price[s]
failure, instability of commodities and, 161-179
forward, 5
futures. *See* Futures markets
intervention in. *See* Intervention, market
models, 11-28, 35-60, 110, 169, 189-190. *See also* ARIMA (autoregressive integrated moving average) models; Equations; LINK project/system; Methodology(ies); Waugh, F.V.; Wharton EFA and models
spot. *See* Spot markets and prices
Martingale theory, 163, 164, 165-166
Massell, B.F., 119, 120, 122, 125-132 (passim), 137, 142, 250
and Waugh-Oi-Massell model, 119-121, 123, 126, 129, 133, 140
Matthews, J.L., 20, 24
Maunder, W.J., 27
Meadows, D.L., 17, 20
Metals and metal markets, 88, 111-112, 161, 225, 235, 251, 278
demand instability in, 178, 248, 280
and international agreements, 111, 199, 204, 206, 283
and LME. *See* London Metal Exchange (LME)
and market entry, 168, 202, 223
models, 87, 108-109
producer associations, 215, 218. *See also* CIPEC [Intergovernmental Council of Copper Exporting Countries]
scrap, 109, 110, 237
See also individual metals
Methodology(ies):
coffee market modeling, 35-60
commodity market modeling, 11-28
econometrics, 105-116
LINK system. *See* LINK project/system
price stability study, 250
rice stock operations simulation, 63-80
technological, 25
Mexico, 178, 310
Michalopoulos, Constantine, 300
Mielke, K.D., et al., 24
Mineral Resources Stabilization Fund Act (Papua New Guinea), 232n
Minerals, 218, 235, 248
demand models, 21, 22
See also Metals and metal markets; Phosphates
Model(s). *See* Market(s); Methodology(ies)
Monte Carlo experiments, 157, 267n, 306
Morocco, 220
Muth, J.F., 128
and Muthian rational expectations hypothesis, 121, 137, 162, 169, 183n

Naill, R.F., et al., 20
Nairobi, UNCTAD meetings in, 235, 297, 305
Nasser, Gamal Abdel, 295
National Commission on Supplies and Shortages, 298. *See also* Supply
Nationalism, 272
Nationalization of industry, 217, 225-226
Naylor, T.H., 14, 20
Nehru, Jawaharlal, 295
Nelson, J.P., 17
Nerlove, M., 24
Netherlands, the, 276
Newbery, D.M.G., 301
Newcomb, R.T., 25
New Delhi, UNCTAD meetings in, 295
New Mexico, 22
New Zealand, 27
Nigeria, 281

OECD (Organization for Economic Cooperation and Development) countries, 87, 95, 97, 100, 101, 258
Oi, W.Y., 119, 120, 121, 130, 131, 140, 142
and Waugh-Oi-Massell model, 119-121, 123, 126, 129, 133, 140

Oil, fuel. *See* Fuel(s)
Oils and oilseeds, 5, 24, 178, 222. *See also* "Core" commodities
Okun, A.M., 315
OPEC (Organization of Petroleum Exporting Countries), 5, 105, 106, 112, 205, 215, 225, 226, 230, 247, 275, 298, 309, 319n
  aims of, 216, 217, 218–219, 282
  foreign exchange reserves of (table), 224
  and prices, 223, 227, 237, 272–273, 282, 296, 297, 304
  production quotas of, 220–221
Oury, B., 27

Papua New Guinea, 228, 229, 230, 232n, 234n
Pareto, Vilfredo, and Paretian theory, 142, 301
Parnes, A., 177
Perez, Lorenzo L., 300
Perlman, L., 23
Perry, G.L., 315
Peru, 225–226, 280, 310
Philippines, the, 228, 230, 310
Phillips' curve, 315
Phosphates, 237
  producer associations, 215, 218, 221
  World Institute of, 220
  See also "Core" commodities
Poland, 230
Politics. *See* Government policy
Popkin, J., 315
Population growth rate, 72
Porter, R.L., 301
Portugal, inflation rate in, 72
Praetz, P.D., 164–165, 166
Pratt, J.W., 123
Prescott, E.C., 26
Price, D.H., 22
Price(s):
  -band policy equations, 133–134
  cocoa, *see* Cocoa
  coffee, 5, 35–59 (passim), 100
  commodity, in LINK system, 84–85, 88–101 (passim)
  and Commodity Price Authority (proposed), 205, 206–208
  cycles, 189–191, 306, 312
  equations. *See* Equations
  expectations, equations for, 128–130
  expectations, rational, 130–131, 169–170, 174. *See also* Muth, J.F.
  export. *See* Export(s)
  floor, 209–210, 229, 245, 252, 283, 307, 308
  fluctuations/oscillations, 5–7, 10, 12, 97, 161, 173, 189–191, 198, 205, 209, 210, 227, 249, 278. *See also* Price stabilization
  futures, as predictors, 170, 172
  government concern with, 271. *See also* Intervention, market
  increases (1971–1974), 161, 173, 272, 297
  and inflation. *See* Inflation rate informational efficiency and, 161–170. *See also* Information
  IPC and, 197–199
  linkage equations, 88–93
  models, 25
  oil. *See* Fuel(s)
  producer associations and, 215–231
  rice, 63–80 (passim)
  rubber, 202, 225
  scrap metal, 110
  spot. *See* Spot market and prices
  stabilization. *See* Price stabilization
  sugar. *See* Sugar
  supply management and, 196–202. *See also* Supply
  supports, 28, 94, 11, 208. *See also* Intervention, market
  target, 209–210, 251, 258, 259, 307
  tin, 225, 229
  UN commodity price indexes, 85, 87, 88, 92
Price stabilization:
  buffer stocks and. *See* Buffer stocks and buffer stock operations
  for cereals, gains and losses from, 157, 278
  and Common Fund (UNCTAD) proposal, 288, 300–305. *See also* Common Fund
  and conflicts of interest, 251–252
  equations, 134–139, 140–141, 155
  LDCs and concern for, 271
  producer associations and, 217–219, 225 231
  vs. receipts stabilization, 240, 248, 249. *See also* Export[s]
  welfare gains from, 119–143, 149–158, 189, 249–250, 256, 263, 316
Producer associations, 111, 215–231
  antagonisms and lack of cohesion in, 228, 229, 282, 304
  Cocoa Producers' Alliance, 281
  International Coffee Organization (ICO), 43, 53, 54, 58–59
  See also CIPEC (Intergovernmental Council of Copper Exporting Countries); OPEC (Organization of Petroleum Exporting Countries)

Pry, R.H., 25

"Random walk" hypothesis, 163, 164-166
"Ratchet effect," 174
Raulerson, R.C., 20
Resources:
  and International Resource Bank, 298 305
  transfer of. *See* LDCs (less-developed countres)
  See also Inventory(ies); Supply
Rhodesia, 225
Rice market:
  annual price formation in, 63-66
  buffer stock operations, simulations, 66-71, 72, 76-80, 278, 279
  historical simulations and results, 71-80
  U.S., systems model of, 21
RIDGE regression, 26
Riley, J.G., 142
Risk:
  and private stockpiles, 171-172, 190
  supply lag and, 24. *See also* Supply
Roop, J.M., 23
Rothenberg, T.J., 142
Rubber, 112, 215, 222, 236, 237, 313
  as "core" commodity, 196, 254
  international agreements on, 199, 280, 282
  and price, 202, 225
  revenues, 255, 310, 311
Ruffin, R., 142
Russell, W.R., 142

Samuelson, P.A., 123, 142, 161, 189, 191
Santiago, UNCTAD meetings in, 295
Sarris, Alexander H., 189, 301
Sasser, W., 20
Saudi Arabia, 220, 230
Saxton, J.C., 21
Scandizzo, P.L., 120
Schmitz, A., 28, 132, 142
SDR (Special Drawing Rights), 247, 295
Secretan syndicate (France), 227
Senegal, 220
Shink, G.R., 306
SIMLINK, 23. *See also* LINK project/system
Singer, D.A., 22
Singh, I.J., 17
Sisal, 5, 251, 254, 311. *See also* Fibers
SITC. *See* Standard International Trade Classification (SITC)
Smidt, S., 166
Smith, Gordon W., 306, 311
Smith, K.R., 142, 190
Smyth, D.J., 138, 139
South Korea, inflation rate in, 72
Soviet Union, 111, 112, 153, 154, 158, 206
Spain, inflation rate in, 72
Spot markets and prices, 4, 5, 48, 166, 167, 169, 174, 277
Stabilization:
  and STABEX scheme, 238-240
Standard International Trade Classification (SITC), 83, 84, 85, 88, 93, 95, 97, 100-101
  categories of, and commodity prices (table), 92
Standard Oil Company, 227
Stevenson, R., 165
Stocks:
  buffer. *See* Buffer stocks and buffer stock operations
  end-of-year, stockpiling. *See* Inventory(ies)
Strongman, J.E., et al., 20
Subotnik, A., 131
Sugar:
  buffer stocks, 250, 259
  as "core" commodity, 196, 306, 310, 313. *See also* "Core" commodities
  exports, 254
  international agreements on, 111, 112, 178, 199, 280, 281
  model, 28
  price instability/stability of, 5, 97, 100, 278
Summit Conference of Non-Aligned Countries, 295
Supply:
  -demand equations, 123-127, 149-156
  factors in, 6, 12, 87, 271. *See also* Climate
  lag, and risk, 24
  management/restrictions, 196-202, 207-210, 248, 252, 262, 277
  modeling, 24
  and Shortages, National Commission on, 298
  See also Buffer stocks and buffer stock operations; Inventory(ies)
Sweden, 276
Systems Workshop Proceedings (USDA), 20

Tabb, W.K., 17
Takayama, T., 17, 23
Taxes:
  on bauxite, 211n
  export, 51, 55, 57, 280

internal, 51, 55, 57
profit-based, 218
U.S. system of, 178-179
Taylor, Lance D., 24, 191, 301
Tea, 202, 236, 250, 306, 311, 312
as "core" commodity, 196. *See also* "Core" commodities
DEVE/LDCs and, 111, 179, 246, 254
International Tea Agreement, 199, 200
producer associations, 215, 222
Thailand, Bank of, 63
Thillainathan, V., 22
Third World, 221, 292, 295, 296, 304, 309
"threat from," 218, 297
See also DEVE (developing world); LDCs (less-developed countries); *individual countries*
Thomas, H., 27, 164
cited as L-T, 165, 166
Tin, 178, 179, 246, 254, 255, 306, 310
buffer stocks and stockpiles, 278, 283
as "core" commodity, 196. *See also* "Core" commodities
International Council and agreements on, 111, 199, 206, 217, 237, 257, 280, 283
prices, 225, 259
producer associations, 215, 282
See also Metals and metal markets
Tinbergen, J., 105
Tinsley, C.R., 23
Tito, Marshal Josip Broz, 295
Togo, 220, 281, 310
Tomek, W.G., 170
Torries, T.F., 22
Trade Act (U.S., 1974), 298. *See also* United States
Trade Prospects and Capital Needs of Developing Countries (UNCTAD study), 106
Tree crops, 111, 182n. *See also* Agriculture; Coffee market; Rubber; Tea
Tsurumi, H., 16
Tunisia, 220
Turnovsky, Stephen J., 126, 127, 132-142 (passim), 189, 190, 277, 301

UNCTAD (United Nations Conference on Trade and Development), 85, 92, 178, 179, 229, 247, 253, 273, 282, 308
assessments of, 300-305
and Common Fund proposal, 203, 231, 257-262, 265, 287, 288, 291-292, 300-305. *See also* Common Fund
"core" commodities listed by. *See* "Core" commodities
IPC of. *See* Integrated Programme for Commodities (IPC)
meetings of, 235, 295, 297, 305
resolutions of, 295, 296, 297
Trade Prospects and Capital Needs of Developing Countries issued by, 106
U.S. and, 298, 299
See also United Nations
UNDP (United Nations Development Program), 262
Union Minière, 225. *See also* Zaire
United Kingdom, 72, 206
Treasury, Keynes memorandum to, 195
United Nations, 235
Carter speech before, 298-299
commodity price indexes, 85, 87, 88, 92
and Common Fund, 263
FAO of, 151, 211n
General Assemblies (on Raw Materials, Development), 296, 297
See also UNCTAD (United Nations Conference on Trade and Development)
United States:
aid programs, 111, 261
and commodity agreements, 52. *See also* Commodity[ies]
consumer price index, 315
economic models of, 20, 21, 23, 84, 93, 109
as exporter, 211n, 215
grain prices (recent) in, 157
imports and import quotas, 44, 206, 235, 281
interest rates (short-term), 167
and international price-setting and trade policy, 212n, 215, 231, 243, 283, 291, 295-299 (passim), 305
-Latin American cooperation (during World War II), 54
and metals market, 110, 111, 283
oil consumption, and OPEC, 220, 296
politics of, and international agreements, 212n; Government policy; Intervention, market)
price support by, 94. *See also* Intervention market
private stock vs. public holdings, 108
resource transfer notion rejected by, 177
and rice market, 73
and sugar prices, 281
tax system, 178-179
Trade Act, 298

Vinod, H.D., 26
Vogely, W.A., 22

Wachter, M.L., 315
Waelbroeck, J.L., 315
Wallace, W., 20
Wang, K.L., 21
Waugh, F.V., 120, 121, 129, 131, 141, 142
  and Waugh-Oi-Massell model, 119-121, 123, 126, 129, 133, 140
Weather. *See* Climate
West Germany, 177
Wharton EFA and models, 23, 93, 109, 169
  and Wharton Rockefeller project, 164
Wheat Marketing Board (Canada), 111. *See also* Cereals and grains
Willig, R.D., 123
Wool, 5, 278
  and Sydney wool futures, 164, 166
World Institute of Phosphates, 220. *See also* Phosphates
World War II, coffee market during, 50, 52, 54
Wymer, C.R., 26

Yugoslavia, 72, 230

Zaire, 225, 229, 230, 280, 310
Zambia, 225, 228, 229, 230, 280, 310
Zeitner, R.H., 23
Zusman, P., 28

List of Contributors

Jere R. Behrman, University of Pennsylvania
Edwin Burmeister, University of Virginia
Olarn Chaipravat, Bank of Thailand
Richard W. Fisher, U.S. Department of the Treasury
Derek J. Ford, Wharton Econometric Forecasting Associates, Inc.
Helen B. Junz, U.S. Department of the Treasury
Lawrence R. Klein, University of Pennsylvania
Walter C. Labys, West Virginia University
Paul MacAvoy, Yale University
Constantine Michalopoulos, U.S. Agency for International Development
David L. McNicol, U.S. Department of the Treasury
Lorenzo L. Perez, U.S. Agency for International Development
Robert V. Roosa, Brown Brothers, Harriman and Company
Alexander Sarris, University of California at Berkeley
Gordon W. Smith, Rice University
Alexandre Stakhovitch, Commission of European Communities
Lance Taylor, Massachusetts Institute of Technology
Stephen J. Turnovsky, Australian National University
Stephen A. Zorn, Consultant

About the Editors

F. Gerard Adams is professor of economics and finance at the University of Pennsylvania and senior consultant and treasurer of Wharton Econometric Forecasting Associates, Inc. He has been active for many years in a broad spectrum of applied econometric studies including modeling and forecasting for the U.S. economy, international trade, energy, industries, and regional economies. His recent work has focused on modeling international commodity markets. He is coauthor (with Jere R. Behrman) of *Econometric Models of World Agricultural Commodity Markets.*

Sonia A. Klein is a senior economist on the staff of Wharton Econometric Forecasting Associates and has participated in the modeling of a broad range of nonferrous metals. She is a specialist in international economics and is WEFA coordinator of the quarterly *Newsweek International*–WEFA world economic forecast.